The Style of Connectedness

THE STYLE OF CONNECTEDNESS

Gravity's Rainbow
and Thomas Pynchon

Thomas Moore

University of Missouri Press
Columbia, 1987

Copyright © 1987 by
The Curators of the University of Missouri
University of Missouri Press, Columbia, Missouri 65211
Printed and bound in the United States of America

Library of Congress Cataloging-in-Publication Data

Moore, Thomas, 1946–
    The style of connectedness.

    Bibliography: p.
    Includes index.
    1. Pynchon, Thomas. Gravity's rainbow. I. Title.
PS3566.Y55G736   1987   813'.54   86-16093
ISBN 0-8262-0625-5 (alk. paper)

∞™ This paper meets the minimum requirements of
the American National Standard for Permanence of Paper
for Printed Library Materials, Z39.48, 1984.

See p. 312 for permissions.

To Lynn, Alexey, and
Andrew (speaking of
Connectedness; speaking
of love . . .)

Contents

1

Introduction:
Gravity's Rainbow
and Other Books

Years of increasingly mysterious silence from the mysterious Thomas Pynchon have elapsed since the publication in 1973 of *Gravity's Rainbow*: the longest, most ambitious, and most vastly intimidating of his three novels. A co-winner of a National Book Award in 1973, and honored in 1975 with the William Dean Howells Medal of the National Institute of Arts and Letters,[1] *Gravity's Rainbow* is among the most widely celebrated unread novels of the past thirty years. Favorable criticism suggested that it was one of the finest of all American novels, or even that it was the twentieth century's major novel after *Ulysses*. Such responses do not seem decent to conservative critics, who yet may expend equal vehemence on negative rulings. It is already a piece of minor folklore that *Gravity's Rainbow* was unanimously recommended by the Pulitzer Prize fiction jury for a prize in 1974 yet lost because an advisory board of journalists thought that the book was "turgid, overwritten, unreadable, obscene."[2] An obvious reminiscence is of the debate in the 1920s over *Ulysses*—a promising parallel for Pynchon's cause, since despite the doubts of a great number of early readers, *Ulysses* has come to be felt almost universally as a successful essay in "encyclopedic" fiction, to employ Edward Mendelson's useful term. This is a kind of work, says Mendelson, that contrives to be about everything human, about everything: all human history, the courses of

1. Pynchon refused the medal, "although," he wrote in a letter, "being gold," it is "probably a good hedge against inflation."

2. Peter Kihss, "Pulitzer Jurors Dismayed on Pynchon," *New York Times*, May 8, 1974, p. 38.

Author's Note: Because Pynchon uses so many ellipses in his writing, I have deleted spaces in ellipses that appear in Pynchon's text to distinguish Pynchon's use of ellipsis from my own. The normal spacing of ellipses indicates that I have omitted material from the text.

culture that culminate in itself, and great ethical, mythic, epistemological constants of human life.[3]

Although it would seem that no such work, if successful in its vast ambitions, could be described as purely either upbeat or downbeat, such unfortunately has been the tendency of much criticism of *Gravity's Rainbow*, although the novel surely fits the encyclopedic prescription. My study thereby takes incidental issue with readers and critics who have found *Gravity's Rainbow* to be essentially nihilistic, ultimately downbeat in its view of the nature of human experience. An example is Josephine Hendin, who finds the Gravity's Rainbow symbol simply to be the sign of "Death's hate, Death's grimace, the tragic mask of the heavens pulled down forever in one inviolable affirmation of depression."[4] But I would suggest that if books of this kind succeed to the point of being worth discussing at all, they can never really be caught with such fixed expressions freezing their faces: to argue over the "beat" of *The Divine Comedy, King Lear, The Brothers Karamazov,* or *Faust* is to feel ineffectual.

Of course no one now can say whether Pynchon's novel will finally be found to belong in such exalted company, but at least *Gravity's Rainbow* clearly asks to belong to high literature—the scope of its thematic ambitions, its wide erudition, the uncompromising complexity of its demands on readers, necessarily if unfortunately mean that a Pynchon industry will mesh it gently with the machinery of the academy. This study will abet the effort of academic co-option, by the novel's own stipulation one of bad faith, since I explore some of the sources that the book itself co-opts from general cultural history. There are enormous ranges of these invited guests, from mythological mother goddesses to quantum-physical theories; from early Christian apocalypticists to Shirley Temple, Groucho Marx, Margaret Dumont; from Newton and Leibniz to Plasticman and King Kong. These are not mere objects of token allusions but real presences, each exerting its own distinct sort of pressure on the historical and contemporary realities that the book contemplates. Pynchon's famed erudition does not finally have the effect, as some hostile critics have claimed, of a merely neurotic or undergraduate belaboring of vaguely hip cultural commonplaces, such that the formal critic appears as an earnest freshman and Pynchon as a graduate stu-

---

3. See Mendelson's introduction to his edited *Pynchon: A Collection of Critical Essays* (Englewood Cliffs, N.J.: Prentice-Hall, 1978), pp. 1–15.

4. Josephine Hendin, *Vulnerable People: A View of American Fiction Since 1945* (New York: Oxford University Press, 1978), p. 207.

dent, both preparing for some apocalyptic final exam. The parody is only mild, the hostile reviews having often been vehement. Rather, the novel merges its invited guests "organically," much in the manner that, in Pynchon's vision, communal/historical life merges deep psychic archetypes, Jungian dreams, symbols, metaphors of connection, in and as visible history.

Gravity's Rainbow asserts—with a creativity and synthetic power that rescues the assertion from sounding hackneyed—that at this end of a three-hundred-year Western cultural dispensation our understandings of life, our sympathies for and in it, suffer too much from the habitual reification of "either/or" contraries out of what is really a holistic cultural field. Pynchon seeks to penetrate all interfaces that seem to separate, for example, the high and low arts, the two cultures of art and science, the elect and—in various senses—the passed over, or preterite, among human beings. As I specify in detail in Chapter 2, and as the most casual reader of *Gravity's Rainbow* already knows, the book imitates the form and feel of a movie in a number of ways, with events in it continually felt to be happening on both sides of the moving film, the paranoid fabrications crossing the interface of the artist/director's imagination and penetrating our own world, where we had thought ourselves safe among real historical assemblages. Inside the movielike frames that Pynchon imposes on history, we sometimes see recognizably real events and images, sometimes imaginary and preposterous ones, sometimes surreal combinations. The typical response to this film of life's self-imagination in history is a paranoia that in turn helps to actualize more history, which, Pynchon implies, is so "made." And yet the novel comes out feeling far gentler than do most products of fashionable playings with paranoid structures. Specifically, Pynchon's work is more psychologically valid, more culturally responsible, and more compassionate than that of the writers of the Absurd tradition with whom he is often confused. He cares for political, scientific, pop-cultural, and mystical imaginations—for human imagination in its essence, which, for him, is that desire, both admirable and pitiable, to project ordering meanings onto the blank universal screen, only to lose itself in the systems created by those meanings and by the act of projection.

Pynchon sheepishly admits that his novel itself is just another synthetic, compulsive, slightly mad *mediation* of life, like the mythic, religious, artistic, social, scientific, and technological systems that it exhibits—and *Gravity's Rainbow*'s parodies remind all critics that they too should feel sheepish about what they are doing. Among Pynchon's critics, the most credibly and commendably queasy in this way has been Mendelson, who chastises Pynchon industrialists: "The book itself has already generated institutions that seem entirely innocent of any sense that the book they honor criticizes precisely the kind of honor they offer.... Collective enterprises have built themselves up around Pynchon's work ... and this book [Mendelson's edited *Pynchon: A Collection of Critical Essays*] is one of them. But I hope this book is one which is at least aware of its paradoxical dilemma in offering Pynchon an honor which he implicitly condemns."[5]

This is a way of saying that *Gravity's Rainbow*'s manner of being present in present culture is an unusually subversive one, especially in the context of the author's notorious absence from cultural view. This sense of absence percolates from outside the book to inside to bend its meanings, as "through the flowing water, the holes of the old Hohner Slothrop found are warped one by one, squares being bent like notes, a visual blues being played by the clear stream" (622).[6] One may sleuth with some success after the personal Pynchon, but the fact is that he is living, as Joyce never did to such an uncompromising degree, that species of "silence, exile and cunning" that his work consistently recommends as a valid response to the world—not, after all, sheepishly, but wolfishly, Pynchon maintains, outside as inside the moving film of his work, his own absolute "invisibility." Behind the invisibility we often sense a hauntedness that expresses itself as a quiet jeering at readers and critics—as, at Minton's jazz club in New York in the 1940s, such brilliantly inward jazzmen as Thelonious Monk, Charlie Parker, and others openly jeered from the stage at their audiences. These men are among Pynchon's heroes, as there is both internal and external evidence to indicate;[7] Rilke, for that matter, disdained to read any published commentary on his own work.

5. Mendelson, ed., *Critical Essays*, p. 9.

6. All page citations from *Gravity's Rainbow* throughout this book refer to the 1973 Viking Press edition, hardback or paperback. (These were published simultaneously and their pagination is identical.) For quotations from *The Crying of Lot 49* I use the Bantam (Lippincott) 1966 paperback; for quotations from *V.*, the Bantam (Lippincott) 1963 paperback.

7. *Gravity's Rainbow* celebrates and mourns Charlie ("Yardbird") Parker, defining him as a charismatic, death-tending victim of a Muzak culture (63); see also the sympathetic treatment of the black jazz musician in the early story "The Secret Integration" (discussed in my Chapter 5), and of *V.*'s McClintic Sphere. "External evidence": a Cornell professor who knew the undergraduate Pynchon testifies to the young man's fascination with Thelonious Monk and his music.

4

The presence, then, of *Gravity's Rainbow* in our world is a mocking activity of infiltration of, and escape from, any intellectual sheepfolds that would exclude it or cage-frames, as those of the academy, that would confine it. Highly germane to the nature of the imagination at work in the book is its vigorous life in underground cults. One seems apt to have appropriately odd experiences with these groups and their organs, as I did with "Pynchon Notes"—a collection of bibliographical data, happy notices of unearthed secrets about Pynchon's life, and occasional worshipful essays, to which, when I heard of it, I subscribed, but of which, since subscribing, I have never heard again.

Though an MLA conference on Pynchon has been held and distinguished critics have hailed him as a greatly important writer, one may also find, on the twilight interface between popular folklore and formal studies, essays like Matthew Winston's "The Quest For Pynchon," which, from its overground forum in *Twentieth Century Literature*, has shown how the tracks to the three novels' author have somehow been mysteriously covered. For example, dedicated souls in quest for Pynchon will find that even in the Cornell register for his freshman class there is a blank space where his picture should be. From here we may move, if we choose, to such theses as by no means belong exclusively anymore to undergraduate groupies, such as that "Pynchon" actually is a committee, or a computer, or Woody Allen—or that he is perhaps Professor Irwin Corey, the standup comic whose expertly manic doubletalk routine is a running parody of academic jargon and of intellectual pretentiousness generally. Sent by someone to accept *Gravity's Rainbow's* National Book Award in 1973, Corey disrupted the high-literary proceedings in a Grouchoesque way that might have belonged to a scene from the very book being honored. Such anyway are the mindless or mindful ways in which *Gravity's Rainbow* and all comments on it conspire to create the effect of the book's dynamically incomplete state of crystallization from the supersaturated solution of extranovelistic reality in which reader, critic, author, and the ongoing history of systems are immersed equally.

To speak of *Gravity's Rainbow* as asserting its identity as an "open system" (the thermodynamic metaphor is so pervasive in the book that I can no longer avoid it) is also to speak of its characteristic way of blurring distinctions between its inside fictional world and various outside worlds of historical fact. Pynchon's precise manipulations of facts from preterite folk cultures—ruptured ducks, German prison camp "75's,"

Hitler's having had only one left ball, as the song and the legend really went, and seemingly infinite numbers of others—create a mosaic so fine-grained as to achieve a compelling illusion of absolute continuity, authentic memory, though these are folkish worlds that Pynchon, being too young, could not possibly have known firsthand. A similar effect obtains in the case of historical overground facts of the kind more conventionally researched: although all novels mingle source-derived data with the products of synthesizing imagination, this one's case seems special, since we do not expect a work so full of hallucinatory surrealism to draw simultaneously on a body of many thousands of factual details, nearly all of which have a maniacal way of proving to be true, though they could have been invented without anyone's caring. Thus in the context of the fictional Franz Pökler's fictional and in many ways improbable story, the German rocket engineers who built the Peenemünde facility in the summer of 1937 really did ride, en route to their testing range on Greifswalder Oie, a ferry with turn-of-the-century furnishings and red plush seats, really did drink at an inn whose owner's name was Halliger.[8] The data typically appear in merest passing, almost microscopically (404, 405), as if he were quite indifferent about whether we trouble to verify them or not. The effect is simultaneously of pedantry and a parody of it, factual scrupulousness and irreverent offhandedness about facts: a stylistic instance of Pynchon's habit of insinuating the inclusion of all manner of phenomena in their opposites—Yin/Yang, or, as I call them, "both/and" effects[9] that point finally to the heart of his metaphysics.

And, finally, the abounding inside/outside confusions in critics' comments on Pynchon have the effect of implicating the critical context itself in the novel's themes and effects, as if *Gravity's Rainbow* has, like its own Giant Adenoid devouring whole blocks of London, "a *master plan* ... choosing only certain personalities useful to it" (15). In regard to the debate over whether Pynchon's comic-book–surrealist style, as manifested, say, in his zany character names, makes the books seem too like narcissistic, self-indulgently closed imaginative systems, consider two articles in an issue of *Critique* ("Pynchon"), both of which discuss the

8. Pynchon's source for these, as for many other details about the real German rocket program, is Walter Dornberger's *V-2* (New York: Viking Press, 1954).

9. The "both/and" effects were first denoted as such by Annette Kolodny and Daniel James Peters in "Pynchon's *The Crying of Lot 49:* The Novel as Subversive Experience," *Modern Fiction Studies* 19 (Spring 1973): 79–87.

painter Remedios Varo, the "beautiful Spanish exile" who created the triptych that Oedipa Maas sees in Mexico City (*Lot 49*, 10). One writer argues that the name is wonderfully apt for the novel's world, since it means "various answers"; the other proffers information about the Mexican painter Remedios Varo, 1913–1963, born in Spain, of whose work a retrospective was held in Mexico City in 1964.[10] The latter writer, having guessed that Pynchon might have attended this show, further speculates that he might own a Varo painting, the name of whose purchaser is suppressed in the catalogue listing of Varo's works. The next step might be to think that Varo is, as the first article seems to think, Pynchon's creation, as is, it would now appear, the second article's author.

Such are the reasons why it is a particularly exciting, valuable, and humbling exercise to try to be an explicator of Pynchon: reading his work together with that of his critics, we sense not only Pynchon's scorn for the critics but also his cheerfully paradoxical dependence on them. The book seems purposely, wryly enough built to invite and absorb an industry. Indeed, the fact that it will is part of its thematic burden. The fun, though humbling and perhaps a bit masochistic, is to learn to watch the novel refuse to hold still as either an invented or a reported system, in either case aesthetically closed. The explicator's academy-conditioned illusion of a fiction—of any imaginative system—as closed begins to break down when he finds how much apparent fantasy is true report and thus comes to suspect how much official, "framed" truth conversely may be a piece of Their "made" history. The novel has already often enough been called unreadable by critics whose real problem, Richard Poirier has observed, lies in being too literary, rather than not literary enough, to fathom the nature of the book's genius.[11] The explicator can best serve Pynchon by trying to help him locate his preterite readership outside the graduate schools, while at the same time affirming the novel's right to a presence in those schools. I conceive of myself here, in short, not so much to be writing one of those crib sheets for honors literature students that often get costumed as reader's

10. The articles in question: Mark Richard Siegel's "Creative Paranoia: Understanding the System of *Gravity's Rainbow*," and David Cowart's "Pynchon's *The Crying of Lot 49* and the Paintings of Remedios Varo," both in *Critique* 18:3 (1977). In his 1978 book-length study of Pynchon, Siegel acknowledges his earlier error about Remedios Varo but justly reiterates that, after all, the name *is* appropriate for Pynchon's novel.

11. See Poirier's early review of *Gravity's Rainbow*: "Rocket Power," *Saturday Review: The Arts* 1 (March 3, 1973): 59–64.

guides, as to be considering the question of what a putatively great book of our time might have to be like in order to be both great and fully contemporary.

Complete data for all published specimens of Pynchon studies mentioned below are in my bibliography. To date ten full-length books have been published about Pynchon by single authors: Slade (1974), Siegel (1978), Plater (1978), Cowart (1980), Mackey (1980), Stark (1980), Fowler (1980), Schaub (1981), Cooper (1983), and Hite (1983). There have been four edited collections of critical essays: Levine and Leverenz (1976), Mendelson (1978), Pearce (1981), and Clerc (1983). My study is indebted to all of these books; I do not comment very specifically here on what seem to me their various merits and demerits, since I do so as I go. All four essay collections offer various approaches to separate aspects of Pynchon. To read the books by single authors is to see Pynchon stereoscopically, with the initial moiré of off-focuses, overlaps, and interferences sharpening gradually to a clearer view that reveals more clearly the basically positive—and more complex and, I believe, interesting—reading of Pynchon that I develop in this book.

Of these ten books, only one suffers seriously from shallow thinking and clumsy writing, and one other suffers from an indefensibly reductive approach (see Chapter 6). Of the others, Slade's *Thomas Pynchon* is especially admirable for being the first, and, at that, an excellent introductory survey of the three novels and several stories; David Cowart's *Thomas Pynchon: The Art of Allusion* is remarkably sensitive to Pynchon's uses of and equivocal relations with his polyglot "sources"; and Molly Hite's *Ideas of Order in the Novels of Thomas Pynchon*, the most brilliantly written of all the books, is most brilliant too on the central subject of how Pynchon sets the grave, solemn Gravity's Rainbow symbol of obsessively closed systems against the gaiety of "open" preterite life.

Several other, more general critical works have included extensive comment on Pynchon; among these the most interesting ones written before the publication of *Gravity's Rainbow* are those of Kazin (1971), Tanner (1971), Poirier (1971), Bergonzi (1972), and Schulz (1973); of those written after *Gravity's Rainbow*, and including specific discussion of it, I would recommend Fussell (1975), McConnell (1977), Hendin (1979), and Hipkiss (1984). Of the many short articles and reviews on the three novels, the pieces by Cowart, Friedman and Puetz, Krafft, Le Vot, Levine, Lhamon, Locke, Ozier, Poirier, Sale, Solberg, Slade, Vesterman, Weisenburger, and Young seem to me the most rewarding. But interested browsers will find endearingly idiosyncratic voices to support whatever extreme views of Pynchon they may happen to hold. At one extreme, for example, Christopher Lehmann-Haupt in the *New York Times* takes *Gravity's Rainbow*, with just four others, along with him to the moon; Bruce Allen in *Library Journal* approvingly announces *Gravity's Rainbow* to be "the most demanding novel anyone has ever written" and "the most important work of fiction yet produced by any living writer." On the other hand, Ronald de Feo damns Pynchon's work as displaying chiefly a "sophomoric sensibility," and for Pearl K. Bell Pynchon "banishes" the concreteness of "ordinary existence" as he travels his "road of excess" to "hell." Perhaps most oddly, the late John Gardner takes Pynchon to task in *On Moral Fiction* for "prais[ing] the schlock of the past" while "howl[ing] against the schlock of the present," and for asserting that there is literally a "rainbow of bombs ... circling us," while this is not, Gardner stipulates, literally the case. Of the approving effusions, the two I like best are Bruce Jay Friedman's happy shout that Pynchon "is so contemporary he makes your nose bleed," and R. Z. Sheppard's observation, which borrows a figure from *Gravity's Rainbow*'s own family of metaphors for preterition, that Pynchon is "still moving, given away to the public only by his books, like one of those high-energy particles that are never seen but whose existence is inferred from the traces they leave behind."

The figure from fundamental-particle physics is particularly apt because the three novels, and especially the third, draw intimately and heavily from this most profound of the realms of the modern scientific imagination. In fact, Pynchon's unique ease with and respect for the arcana of modern physics rescues from cliché the device of finding extrascientific significances in such quantum-physical concepts as complementarity, after Neils Bohr, and uncertainty, after Werner Heisenberg (see my Chapter 5). Quantum theory posits an irremediable epistemological tension between alternate ways of "framing" fundamental reality, the tension being for us an aspect of that reality. Quite analogously, in Pynchon's world there are tensions among various "framed" mental constructs of historical, social, and natural realities, constructs that keep getting reified to become partial worlds. What we feel to be a continuous, literally unknowable ground reality is at once rescued into visibility and betrayed by any and all application to it of frame categories, the chief of which is language itself, The Word.

In his *City of Words* (1971), which contains an excellent chapter on *V.*, Tony Tanner suggests that American novelists from the beginning have typically exhibited a fundamental ambivalence about language, hence also about their own roles as purveyors of it. These writers' sense of the agency of The Word is that it presents "a quite fundamental and inescapable paradox: that to exist, a book, a vision, a system, like a person, has to have an outline—there can be no identity without contour. But contours signify arrest, they involve restraint and acceptance of limits.... Between the non-identity of pure fluidity and the fixity involved in all definitions—in words or in life—the American writer moves, and knows that he moves."[12]

My study demonstrates the large relevance of these remarks to *Gravity's Rainbow*. In Chapter 2, I explore some Pynchonian senses of "framing"; in Chapter 6, I identify Pynchon's mystical sense of the "pure fluidity" that underlies all frames. This fluidity, I suggest, is a dreamlike state that owes much to the psychological/mystical system of Jung—a major influence too little noted so far in Pynchon studies. Jung's sense of the "psychoid" acausal connectedness and indeterminacy of ground reality is such as to give rise to a "both/and" conception of that reality, some of whose implications, as also in Pynchon, are experiential and ethical. In every pulse of experience, every moment of time, both hope and despair, apocalypse and salvation, kindness and cruelty, are immanent in each other, unmanifest until such time as we choose which of the "paired opposites" to make manifest. As light is somehow both wave and particle, the plenum below, or prior to, our repressive networks of systems is conceivable as both full and void, One and Zero. Pynchon seems to share Jung's shy faith in the possibility of an ultimate One such that if you blink at the void, the void can *become*; the horrific V-ness of Pynchon's first and third novels offers the metaphysical eye, both a blank vacancy of no meaning and a continuous plenum of meaning, with all inadequate, projected *systems* of meaning melding to fill in the space. Thus the eye for the One/Zero problem beyond the world "gets tickled the way your eye does staring at a recco map until bomb craters flip inside out to become muffins risen above the tin, or ridges fold to valleys, sea and land flicker across quicksilver edges" (713)—to take one of many small, suggestive both/and images from the book.

Such images are of course ubiquitous, but it is perhaps best here to sketch a few of the transformations, sign-reversals, of the largest and grandest of them, Gravity's Rainbow itself. In Slothrop's climactic vision of it, late in his progress, the rainbow stands for earth's seamless

12. Tony Tanner, *City of Words: American Fiction 1950–1970* (New York: Harper & Row, 1971), pp. 17, 18.

organic interconnectedness and fecundity and for a mystical felicity in its knowledge: "Slothrop sees a very thick rainbow here, a stout rainbow cock driven down out of pubic clouds into Earth, green wet valleyed Earth" (626). But there later emerges an opposite-signed vision of the sky-phallus, not as colored, but as the "black-and-white bad news" (209) sign of the apocalyptic culmination of history's three hundred or so years of "fucking done on paper" (616): a "scrap of newspaper headline" with a "wire-photo of a giant white cock, dangling in the sky straight downward out of a white pubic bush" (693). The mushroom cloud of Hiroshima is a phallic, Faustian "western deity" (694), yet is also "the pale Virgin ... rising in the east" (694) whose connections snake back to the archetypal feminine great mother goddess of death and life at the pre–Indo-European root of Western religious experience. Neither is the rocket-rainbow, which bears along with it the spirit of the mechanical, bureaucratized culture that made it, simply the organic, mechanism-transcending sign that its Lawrentian cousin is in *The Rainbow*. If we ask it to prophesy, the sign gives the both/and answer of an oracle, such that to link it either with the redemptive rainbow of Lawrence or with the positive sign of God's rainbow promise to Noah never again to annihilate life is also and immediately to remember Hiroshima's "roaring and sovereign" fireburst (694), and to hear the threat implicit in Genesis, via the old slave song related by James Baldwin: "God gave Noah the rainbow sign / No more water, the fire next time!"[13] Giving up on identifying singly sufficient symbolic meanings for the rainbow, Friedman and Puetz come close to encoding the true manifold when they speak of it as "the rainbow curve of existence";[14] Mark Richard Siegel properly finds in it the announcement of all art's and all archetypes' subsumption of either/or concrete experience, such that "past, present, future, science, history and myth become associated, Plechazunga and Rocketman, Africans and Puritans, Einstein and King Kong join hands ... in an organic chain that spins faster and faster until only an elliptical rainbow blur of color is visible."[15]

13. R. W. B. Lewis has identified (pre-*Gravity's Rainbow*) these implications in the rainbow sign of *Genesis*, apropos of certain biblical and Lawrentian resonances of Pynchon's Lady V. See the chapter called "Days of Wrath and Laughter" in Lewis's *Trials of the Word* (New Haven: Yale University Press, 1965).

14. Alan J. Friedman and Manfred

Puetz, "Science as Metaphor: Thomas Pynchon and *Gravity's Rainbow*," *Contemporary Literature* 15 (Summer 1974): 345–59.

15. Mark Richard Siegel, *Pynchon: Creative Paranoia in "Gravity's Rainbow"* (Port Washington, N.Y.: Kennikat Press, 1978), p. 114.

In dreams, Jung said, charged archetypes appear that encode great complexes of polyvalent significations; the style of *Gravity's Rainbow*, in its way of manipulating symbols and interconnecting allusions, achieves a mimesis of such deep psychic processes. The reader is immersed in a kind of communal dream whose upwelling images very unstably bear discrete "meanings" for the discursive consciousness. The notion that *Gravity's Rainbow* may be read as a vast dream may be useful here, particularly in light of the well-known propensity of this century's nonnaturalistic fictions to turn objective reality inside out, to see the world generally from the inside of consciousness out. If modernist writers, particularly after Joyce, have often insisted on structuring their works on received or invented myths, making the works appear to be aggressively self-sufficient realities that are somehow superior to our common reality, Pynchon would seem to be rejecting this "totalitarian" view, as Richard Wasson has called it, of the writer's task, and to be trying instead to recapture "a world of contingency, a world in which man is free to cope spontaneously with experience."[16] *Gravity's Rainbow* does not mean to exalt private subjectivity as an aesthetic or philosophical or moral first principle; it is not a self-regarding game that takes itself as a game, or the nature of art, or creative imagination, or sovereign language, or the writer's personal genius, as essential themes. In fact, unlike the works of the master modern practitioner of this sort of "reflexive" fiction, Nabokov, Pynchon's works do not at all imply any self-celebration by their creator but rather give the impression of his complete humility vis-à-vis his material. The style of course is aggressively idiosyncratic; but I think that in Pynchon, as in James, Faulkner, and T. S. Eliot, a highly idiosyncratic style is married to a sense of the author's quiet self-effacement—the exclusion from his work's world of himself as he may appear to himself, of any claims for redemptive art, or of any personal moral or aesthetic program. Compare Pynchon in this light to such notorious self-interferers as Hemingway, Lawrence, Pound, Mailer, or, much more coolly and programmatically, Barth or Nabokov. The great dream of *Gravity's Rainbow* is a collective, communal, impersonal, Jungian one; the novel's view is "objective" in this sense, though the reality viewed is somehow in itself subjective, oneiric. The book in fact reads rather like "a dream dreamed by

16. Richard Wasson's "Notes on a New Sensibility," *Partisan Review* 36 (1969): 460-77, develops this point of contrast between early modernist writers and certain contemporaries, including Pynchon; Mendelson, in the introduction to his *Critical Essays*, makes similar points.

no one," in Borges's words in his parable of the dying Shakespeare, who, in the parable, "having been so many men," now asks God to let him be "one, and myself." But the world itself being God's dream, Shakespeare must be reminded that the artist, like God, is lost in his dream and identical with it, "Everyone and No One."

Even though I have embarked on what must be a very brief survey of Pynchon's connections with other writers, for me the question of *Gravity's Rainbow*'s strictly literary affiliations and inheritances is the least interesting of possible questions about this huge work of encyclopedic literature. As Richard Poirier has been the critic to say most distinctly, Pynchon is not primarily literary in his imaginative allegiances—not, for example, "so literary [as are Borges and Barth] to think it odd, an in joke, that literary techniques are perhaps less powerfully revealing about human nature and history than are scientific ones."[17]

For Poirier, Pynchon is chiefly interesting as a novelist of our imprisoning technological, cultural, and pop-cultural systems; but, Poirier continues, he is quite unlike such a student of the same systems as Norman Mailer, whose "limitation [is] that he hasn't shown the courage to admit, as Pynchon continually does, that there are forms of inquiry into the nature of life that are beyond the reach of the Novelist's imagination ... that the Novelist's imagination is often less inclusive or daring than the imagination of mathematics or organic chemistry."[18]

And yet Mailer makes an appropriate point of departure for a survey of Pynchon's literary resemblances, since Mailer the novelist shares with Pynchon—and both share with William Burroughs—a special, McLuhanesque interest in how our electronic/cybernetic media create the terms of experience as realized from inside the technological prisonhouse that becomes an epistemological one. All three of these writers, as opposed to McLuhan's own optimism, propose that our media painfully "mediate" us away from each other's concrete realities as much as they unite us within the terms of *their* truth. The adolescent speaker in Mailer's *Why Are We In Vietnam?*, in his role of radio disk jockey, exists for us "over the air," sharing airspace with the novelist's voice behind his, self-consciously with the magnetic force-fields of the planet itself, and most generally with the part-technological, part-extrasensory wholeness of all "mediated" communication. The Mailer of *The Armies of the Night* watches himself being filmed for television as a

17. Poirier, "Rocket Power," p. 62.　　18. Ibid., p. 63.

media event and self-consciously preens even in the fine moral heat of the Pentagon peace protest. Burroughs, for his part, often indulges in surrealistic materializations of drug-hallucinatory fantasies; and in Burroughs the mystical-tending paranoia of "control addicts," who correspond loosely to Pynchon's powerless preterites, becomes a Pynchonesque insight into the neo-Puritan equation of power with wealth with unlimited license:

> The subject must not realize that the mistreatment is a deliberate attack of the anti-human enemy on his personal identity. He must be made to feel that he *deserves* any treatment he receives because there is something (never specified) horribly wrong with him. The naked need of the control addicts must be decently covered by an arbitrary and intricate bureaucracy so that the subject cannot contact his enemy direct.... The threat of torture is useful to induce in the subject the appropriate feeling of helplessness and gratitude to the interrogator for withholding it. And torture can be employed to advantage as a penalty when the subject is far enough along with the treatment to accept punishment as deserved."[19]

As much as this recalls the totalitarian psychodynamics of Orwell's *1984*, it evokes Pynchon's preterites' paranoid/masochistic/mystical understanding of remote They's as Rilkean angels that employ submissive and powerless We's: "and what we so admire is its calm / Disdaining to destroy us" (Rilke, First Duino Elegy).

A common mistaken critical practice has been to group Pynchon with those "reflexivist" contemporary novelists whose chief concern is with what is felt to be the inherently involuted, self-referential nature of language itself. But, as I have been claiming, Pynchon's work has something much more complex and positive at its heart than the vision of a void creation in which language, thought, and myth are necessarily reflexive: the sense, in Barth, Gass, Barthelme, Hawkes, and Elkin, that, in one typical critical formulation, "All human meaning ... is established to structure the boundless world in which individuals find themselves ... all linguistic systems are fundamentally arbitrary.... Ultimately, meaning can refer only to its own linguistic system. It has only a self-referential significance."[20]

19. William Burroughs, *Naked Lunch* (New York: Grove Press, 1966), pp. 21, 24.

20. Charles Russell, "The Vault of Language: Self-Reflective Artifice in Contemporary American Fiction," *Modern Fiction Studies* 20, (Summer 1974): 351. Since deciding to quote this passage for my purposes here, I have found the same passage quoted by Thomas H. Schaub, also to help show that Pynchon should *not* be grouped among the self-referential writers for whom Russell's description is accu-

In an effective sense, *Gravity's Rainbow is* self-referential: for Pynchon all felt experience, including the experience of using language to name the world, is an epistemological funhouse in which no one, including the self-conscious novelist, can know himself to be taking reliable bearings on truth. Our lives are irremediably framed, multiply mediated, by complexly reified moirés of the projections, systems, and plots that life makes for itself. I submit, though, that Pynchon refuses to take dogmatically any void universe that would necessitate self-reference; that, rather, he offers a vastly complex series of observations of the things that life does with the ultimate fact that it can never *know,* from inside the funhouse, what it must do.

Saul Bellow has complained that "modern writers sin when they suppose that they *know,* as they conceive physics *knows* or that history *knows.*"[21] But Pynchon, far from claiming to know, troubles greatly to show that neither do science or history know: that science, for example, is neither more nor less than one among many metaphorical systems for the projection of psychic contents onto a Jungian background in which there *may* reside truths, realities that form a transcendental matrix both for the physical universe and for this very process of the psyche's self-extraverting expressions as myth, "made" history, and artistic ideas of order.

One problem with such flat critical formulations as the one quoted above is that, when the critical industry sets about to inventory, stock, and shelve this sort of contemporary fiction, the resulting generalizations imply that it all has or should have the same tone about it, the same indifference to real life, the same cooled-to-death, even amoral quality. But it is one thing to nod one's bloodless assent when William Gass utters these same general linguistic/epistemological theories, and quite another to respond with real pleasure to John Barth's or Vladimir Nabokov's happily dramatized claims for art, for imaginative play in the face of the void, as redemptively self-referential. But in Pynchon the redemptiveness comes from quite different sources than in Barth, for example. In the mirror room of Barth's own symbolic funhouse—see the title story of *Lost in the Funhouse*—"you can't see yourself go on forever, because no matter how you stand, your head gets in the way." In the same story, brilliant puns—as when the hero, thinking hard, "lost him-

rate. See Schaub, *Pynchon: The Voice of Ambiguity* (Urbana: University of Illinois Press, 1981), p. 150.

21. Saul Bellow, "Some Notes on Recent American Fiction," *The Novel Today: Contemporary Writers on Modern Fiction,* ed. Malcolm Bradbury (Manchester, Eng.: Manchester University Press, 1977), p. 69.

self in the reflection"—reinforce the point that there is nothing whatever outside our funhouses, our closed systems, even be they as beautiful, and in that sense redemptive, as the myths elaborated in *Chimera*. Pynchon seems finally to assent to the mystical intuitions of Leni Pökler and others of his characters to the effect that outside the dome entirely, there are real stars and orders of stars, subtly perhaps to validate their projected patterns on the dome. Contrast Barth's evident assent when his Ebenezer Cooke in *The Sot-Weed Factor,* having seen through to the four-dimensional chaos beyond astrology's flat pasteboard, panics, fearing that he might "fall into the stars."[22]

Pynchon's fiction is also more open than these in that his rhetoric is so often outward-reaching and mystical-tending and his dialogue generally naturalistic, while the language of many of the reflexivist writers makes a game of daring the reader to take it anywhere beyond itself. In their pearly, curved-nautilus chambers, these novels echo with dialogue like this from Elkin:

> "Hi Dick."
> " 'Lo Rick."
> "Seen Nick?"
> "Nick's chick."
> "That hick?"
> "She's sick."[23]

We find dialogue like this from the hallucinating brain of the madman and artist who is Humbert/Nabokov:

> "Mr. Potts, do we have any cots left?"...
> "...would there be a spare cot in 49, Mr. Swine?"
> "I think it went to the Swoons," said Swine.[24]

But we must discriminate, for if outside the funhouses of others' work there is nothing final, and finally nothing, outside Nabokov's there is at least, and always, Nabokov himself, supreme artist, demiurge, and superego. His work as a whole does not smell of literary chalk dust, because *he* does not.[25] *Pale Fire*, for example, written concurrently with

---

22. Peter L. Cooper makes, in rather different terms, this same distinction between the metaphysics respectively of Barth and Pynchon: see his *Signs and Symptoms: Thomas Pynchon and the Contemporary World* (Berkeley: University of California Press, 1983), p. 44.

23. Stanley Elkin, *The Dick Gibson Show* (New York: Pocket Books, 1972), p. 277.

24. Vladimir Nabokov, *Lolita* (New York: Berkley Books, 1977), p. 109.

25. There are numerous ligaments of allusion and "influence" between the work of the dauntingly illustrious émigre Professor of European Literature and that of the much younger man who once took a course from him at Cornell. A song about the nymphet-fancying of Mucho Maas in

the scholarly translation/annotation of Pushkin, whose manner it parodies, explicitly shows Nabokov's contempt for reflexive solipsism at its most insanely literary. Barth, for his part, has called for a kind of ideal postmodernist fiction that will neglect neither "the heart" nor "the head." He has praised *Pale Fire* for striking this balance and has added that in his own works the heart is meant to be felt as coming in first, with the head a very close second.[26] Yet my own feeling about reflexive fiction (including Barth's) is that it is addressed primarily to that kind of "head" whose impulse will be to bring to bear on the understanding of literature some conscious *theory* of literature, a product probably of a theory or two of linguistics, mythography, metaphysics.

By contrast, the sensibility, or at least one large component of it, to which Pynchon's work seems addressed is designated in *Gravity's Rainbow* at one point as the "sensitive head"—whose difference from Barth's intellectualized "head" is suggested by the drug-denotations of Pynchon's phrase, by its evocations of dreaming, preterite subcultural and countercultural life. It is not at all to belittle Pynchon to say that his vision is in part a vast elaboration of many of the characteristic insights, moods, and mores of that neo-Romantic movement of the American sixties that we have commonly called the counterculture. The "amateur" head (as I call it in Chapter 5) that belongs to *Gravity's Rainbow's* familiar spirit has briefly thought of blowing up the library but has instead gone "scuffling" (a favorite word in the novel) among its stacks, in vague search of the erudition that the head knows it prizes but that it also radically distrusts. In Chapter 5, I consider the large subject of

Lot 49 designates him a "Humbert Humbert chap"; Max Schulz has suggested that one of *V.*'s minor characters is a parody of the same Humbert (see *Black Humor Fiction of the Sixties*, p. 80); *Lolita's* considerable use of movie lore anticipates Pynchon. In *Bend Sinister*, an interest in the "inside" feel of repressive political systems, and, in *Ada*, Nabokov's attack on the metaphysical premise of linear time, are remotely, at least, Pynchonesque. It is even possible that the wonderful descriptions of a poor man's Weimar Berlin in *The Gift*, Nabokov's last and best Russian novel, have had their effects on Pynchon's conception of Franz Pökler's Weimar "Street."

26. These remarks of Barth's were deliv-

ered at the June 1979 meeting of the Deutsche Gesellschaft für Amerikastudien at Tübingen University. He has expanded the same remarks in his "The Literature of Replenishment," *Atlantic*, June 1980, an essay meant to update his widely influential earlier essay on postmodernist fiction, "The Literature of Exhaustion."

At Tübingen, Barth professed his immense respect for, even sometimes awe of, Pynchon, though with the qualifications that "awe is not love" and that he and Pynchon are "doing entirely different things." Neither William Gass nor John Hawkes, also present, volunteered any comments on Pynchon.

Pynchon's inheritances from nineteenth-century Romanticism, insofar as we call Romantic the paradox by which the ordering of facts into systems, instincts into ideas, life into art, is both a betrayal of final reality and the only imaginable means of making reality visible to consciousness. Pynchon is far from adopting the antiintellectual or antihistorical attitudes of the popular wing of the countercultural movement, whose members did not think to call themselves neo-Romantics, since to learn to do so would have meant to use the library as fact rather than blow it up as symbol. But Pynchon clearly feels tender toward his hedonistic preterites, although their nihilism is not his own, and although he disapproves of their defensive wish to deny history and moral responsibility by reveling in mindless pleasures. And, further, Seaman Bodine's, Slothrop's, the later Roger Mexico's neo-Romantic wish to affirm life by subverting systems is also, in the main literary succession, the wish of the Beat movement of the fifties, for which Pynchon has recently confessed much old fondness.[27] Thus Mailer's comments in *The White Negro* on the "Be Thyself" ethic of 1950s Hip sugggest the underlying affirmativeness of Pynchon's preterite world: "The nihilism of Hip proposes as its final tendency that every social restraint and category be removed, and the affirmation implicit in the proposal is that man would then prove to be more creative than murderous and so would not destroy himself…. It requires a primitive passion about human nature to believe that individual acts of violence are always to be preferred to the collective violence of the State; it takes literal faith in the creative possibilities of the human being to envisage acts of violence as the catharsis which prepares growth."

Although Seaman Bodine, and probably Pynchon, would not put them so solemnly, these are some of the better feelings of the outlook

27. The confession comes in the introduction to *Slow Learner* (Boston: Little, Brown & Co., 1984)—a collection of all but one of Pynchon's earlier published short stories, and the first book he has published since *Gravity's Rainbow*.

The introduction is reticent but good-humored, nostalgic, self-critical; the forty-eight-year-old Pynchon asks of the much younger self who wrote the short stories, "how comfortable would I feel about lending him money, or for that matter even stepping down the street to have a beer and talk over old times?" Pynchon condemns what are in my view the "right" flaws in the sto-

ries, e.g., the strained dialogue in all of them, the over-self-conscious literary allusiveness in most of them, the priority of an abstract intellectual concept over character in "Entropy." Oddly, though, especially in view of the frankness about the stories' weaknesses, Pynchon does not include in the collection, or even mention in the introduction, his "Mortality and Mercy in Vienna," first published in Cornell's *Epoch* in 1959. Another omission, disquietingly, is any hint of any new novel-in-progress. Nevertheless, my optimistic guess is that the publication of this collection is partly intended to prepare the ground for such a new novel, soon to come.

that produced, in the countercultural era and during the auras on either side of it, not only a great number of mediocre books but also a few very good ones. Pynchon has written kind reviews of the novels of Tom Robbins and of the one novel that his close friend Richard Fariña wrote before Fariña's death at age twenty-nine. And yet it is finally Pynchon's erudite range, his sense of responsibility to the real histories of facts and systems, that sets him far apart from Vonnegut's bestselling stance against science and its evil effects, or Donleavy's cheerful enshrinement of moral anarchy, or Brautigan's watermelon-sugar-spun escapism, or Ken Kesey's or Hunter Thompson's not altogether playful advocacies of hallucinogens as ends in themselves. We may, somewhat priggishly here, use the term *stature* to suggest the difference between these writers and Pynchon: it is the difference between a complacent huddle of colorfully decorated shacks somewhere in the San Joaquin Valley and a vast, Guadiesque cathedral to be imagined towering all out of scale above them.

One may rather sentimentally wonder, however, whether Fariña, to whom *Gravity's Rainbow* is dedicated, would have gone on in something like Pynchon's direction—since, for one thing, many Fariña passages sound so eerily like early Pynchon: "Venus, just passing the zenith, was mistaken for a large star by Harry and wished upon silently. A *sonata da chiesa* proclaimed itself from the single outdoor speaker, and momentarily the *ribiendo* regained its musical advantage. Standing there silently, with the knowledge that the unknowing pulses in the street below could be retained or dissolved by a magician's gesture, Kristin and Harry had an interlocking epiphany, a simultaneous sense of magic and motion about to be entered upon, if one could but find the key."[28] In *Long Time Coming and a Long Time Gone* Fariña mentions his enthusiasm for Plasticman, *Gravity's Rainbow*'s favorite comicbook hero; David Cowart has guessed that the brief appearance of Lewis Carroll's White Rabbit in *Gravity's Rainbow* may be a glance in the direction of Fariña's benign ghost, since Fariña once read this part for a record of *Alice in Wonderland*.[29] Cowart suggests also, still more intriguingly, that the character Heffalump in Fariña's *Been Down So Long It Looks Like Up To Me* is modeled distantly on Thomas Pynchon. If so, *Gravity's Rainbow*, with

28. From "Harry and the Celluloid Passion," in the Fariña miscellany *Long Time Coming and a Long Time Gone* (New York: Random House, 1969), pp. 23, 24.

29. For this and further suggestions about Fariña's presence in *Gravity's Rainbow*, see Cowart's *Thomas Pynchon: The Art of Illusion* (Carbondale: Southern Illinois University Press), pp. 113, 114.

its dedication to the dead Fariña, may even be seen as a reply to the little quatrain of farewell uttered by Fariña's autobiographical protagonist when Heffalump is gunned down near the end of the novel. The idea of *Gravity's Rainbow* as the 760-page answer to the little salute would appeal, certainly, to Pynchon: a fond completion of a sub rosa exchange "beyond the Zero."

*   *   *

In interesting, incidental ways, in the foreground, Pynchon has points of convergence with miscellaneous other contemporary and late modernist writers. Esoteric cultists of the personal Pynchon should not neglect to notice that, in the author's reclusiveness, his tendencies to mysticism, and his helpless affection for children, especially girl children, there are affinities with J. D. Salinger. A few of Pynchon's semi-parodic performances of a poetic prose that implicates eroticism in surrealism, especially in his early work, link him with the Lawrence Durrell of the Alexandria novels and *The Black Book*, with Henry Miller (an early Pynchon story, "Entropy," bears a headnote quoted from *Tropic of Cancer*), and with Djuna Barnes. Like Pynchon, Samuel Beckett metaphorizes the modern consciousness as a form of psychosis, although the difference between inward-spiraling catatonia and system-erecting paranoia is perforce a large one. And to the extent that *Gravity's Rainbow* may be understood as an antihistorical novel whose absurd excess of plottedness parodies the over-easy, complacent *données* of meaning and purpose implicit in straight "historical" novels, it belongs to an important post-1945 genre including Günter Grass's *The Tin Drum* and *Dog Years*, Thomas Berger's *Little Big Man*, Barth's *The Sot-Weed Factor* and *Giles Goat-Boy*, and Heller's *Catch-22*.

Another would-be encyclopedic contemporary novelist, William Gaddis, would seem to beg comparison with Pynchon, if only because his two huge novels have attracted a cult following of sorts, though one much more uniformly academic and high-minded than Pynchon's. *The Recognitions*, which employs a body of learning hardly less massive but at once deeper and narrower than that of *Gravity's Rainbow*, is not so much a creatively open, hauntedly ambivalent exploration of the history of systems as it is a jeremiad against the debasement of systems by and in contemporary culture. While Gaddis's humor is usually funny enough, though it is always splenetic, *The Recognitions* lacks Pynchon's delight in the varied, zany, countercultural aspects of popular culture. It also lacks Pynchon's scientific and occult interests, his brilliant colloquial style (though Gaddis is a better and thoroughly damning mimic of spoken colloquial voices), and Pynchon's warmth. This last may be said also of Gaddis's second novel, *JR* (published after *Gravity's Rainbow*), a book that shows powerfully how present popular culture in America can debase precise thought, aesthetic perception, and moral acuity. Both of these novels are, it would seem by design, at once deadly dull and relentlessly harrowing to read. They also require far more cult dedication and dutifulness than Pynchon's to finish reading. Gaddis's greatness, if posterity comes to believe in it, will always be guarded by Trespass At Your Own Risk signs; in his gray gardens, cheerless and as strung-out as overwrought nerves, there is nothing like Pynchon's lush, prophetic perspectives on anything outside, other than our quotidian hysterias.

Of all living writers, perhaps the nearest to Pynchon imaginatively is Jorge Luis Borges, the master fantasist, in his gracefully, lazily luminous parable-stories of a dream metaphysics in which familiar Cartesian parameters of mind and matter, fantasy and history, dreamer and dreamed, float free of any fixed axes. Almost any selection of Borges's stories reveals his affinity with Pynchon by way of his interest in labyrinth-building inside, and as effecting realities outside, the mind. "The Babylon Lottery" imagines, with some debts to Kafka, the same patterns of paranoid ideation that Pynchon's characters find available to them as they try to understand the worldly systems that branch above their heads and visible histories. "The Garden of Forking Paths" creates a fantastic and secret labyrinth of metaphysical convolutions of time below history's flat surface, explaining thereby a small uncertainty in the "facts" given by a historical reference work; the uncertainty's nearly invisible passage underground is much like one of those subtly camouflaged entryways out of mundane life and into the Tristero System, or Fantasy, or Conspiracy, that Oedipa Maas finds lurking everywhere in downtown San Francisco. Perhaps the most interesting Borges story in a Pynchonian light is "Tlön, Uqbar, Orbis Tertius," whose mission is to play with fantastic extrapolations of philosophical idealism: with ideas that make worlds. What begins as a collective fantasy of a self-contained world, an intellectual lark of scholars in a secret society, becomes a world that takes over "the" world, precisely in fulfillment of the extreme idealism that the scholars have posited for their world to believe in. In a suggestive parallel, the British desk-warriors' joint fantasy in *Gravity's Rainbow* of black rocket troops, Operation Black Wing, seems in fact to call up the Schwarzkommando. That Borges's inventions of such a kind have helped stimulate congruent areas of Pynchon's imagination, and that Pynchon, again, feels most ambivalent in turn about those areas, is made explicit enough after all in *Gravity's Rainbow*. The Argentine anarchist Squalidozzi complains to Slothrop: "We are obsessed with building labyrinths, where before there was open plain and sky. To draw ever more complex patterns on the blank sheet. We cannot abide that *openness:* it is terror to us. Look at Borges" (264).

Of the great modernist writers of the first half of this century, Rainer Maria Rilke is the weightiest presence by far in *Gravity's Rainbow*—so weighty that I defer discussion of Pynchon's Rilkean elements to later bits, pieces, and paragraphs along the way of this study. T. S. Eliot was a major influence in Pynchon's early work—see, for example, the plethora of allusions and quotations in the 1959 story "Mortality and Mercy in Vienna"—but *Gravity's Rainbow*'s Eliotisms, although more artfully integrated and apt, are fewer and seem essentially token and honorary. Of the major modernists, it is probably Joyce whose degree of connection with Pynchon stands most in danger of overstatement. Although *Gravity's Rainbow* accepts the Joycean demand that would-be great, important books be committed to the practice of an omnibus informal erudition, a great deal of sophisticated stylistic experimentation, and an extremely large thematic purview, these are profoundly different kinds of encyclopedists. Perhaps their chief similarity is in how their big novels, built to be inherently subversive, lay traps in advance for their Industries, as Sara M. Solberg has shown in an excellent essay.[30]

It is, on the other hand, of central thematic significance that the Deutsch Südwest Afrika sections of both *V.* and *Gravity's Rainbow* parodically paraphrase the early Conrad of *Lord Jim* and *Heart of Darkness*.[31] Here Pynchon's post-colonialist and post-Freudian vantage and more active sense of humor enable him cheerfully to play with Conrad's solemn, guilt-haunted equation between European imperializing and an

30. See Sara M. Solberg, "On Comparing Apples and Oranges: James Joyce and Thomas Pynchon," *Comparative Literature Studies* 26 (March 1979): 33–40.

31. An anecdote, by the way, from a Cornell professor who knew Pynchon there. The class was assigned to read a modest selection of Conrad stories, and for the next several weeks Pynchon, who had not read Conrad at all before this, failed to appear, not only in the class, but also among his circle of friends. When he reappeared he said, and indeed could prove, that during this time he had read *all* of Conrad.

evil plunge out of rational "civilized" consciousness: "It's like going to that Darkest Africa to study the natives there, and finding their quaint superstitions taking you over" (281). The parody is, in turn, part of Pynchon's program of adapting from Conrad—and from Thomas Mann in *Death in Venice* and many stories, and from D. H. Lawrence in *Women in Love*—the game of opposing a symbolic North (intellect, abstraction, Faustian will, the mechanization of life) and South (instinct, body minus mind, creative fecundity, sexuality): see, in *V.,* the imputation to North Europeans of a neurotic "southsickness" that brings them first to Italy, finally to the scene of their "dark, unconscious" brutalities in German Südwest. *Gravity's Rainbow* offers this version: "Colonies are the outhouses of the European soul, where a fellow can let his pants down and relax, enjoy the smell of his own shit. Where he can fall on his slender prey roaring ... and guzzle her blood with open joy. Eh? ... Out and down in the colonies, life can be indulged, life and sensuality in all its forms, with no harm done to the Metropolis, nothing to soil those cathedrals, white marble statues, noble thoughts.... No word ever gets back" (317).

The "Metropolis" derives in part from the deathly white "sepulchral city," colonial Brussels, which employs Marlow in *Heart of Darkness*—the Conrad image as sinister as Pynchon's paranoid vision of Their headquarters from which Slothrop is "employed": "His erection hums ... like an instrument installed, wired by Them into his body as a colonial outpost ... another office representing Their white metropolis far away" (285).

Further, in Pynchon's Metropolis/cathedral imagery, at a level far below parody, is the uncertainty implied everywhere in his work about whether the counterentropic energy of self-elaboration characteristic of organic life, as of European man's elaborated works, leads essentially to a hopeful progress out of entropic decline and fall or to a kind of double-agent's alliance with deathliness, a Freudian death instinct. One aspect of Pynchon's equivocated affirmativeness is to be found also in Rilke: it is the insight that life and death must necessarily be affirmed together, in "parallel, not series" (159).

Pynchon may in fact be most essentially, in *V.*'s phrase, "the century's child," in being as haunted as he is by this apparent identity-in-opposition between the urban, "white" machine principle and some vaguely redemptive sense of organic "blackness." The modernists at their hearts, much more strongly than the three generations or so preceding them, felt this tug of the underground: despite modernism's anti-

Romantic bias, its stylistic rigor, its interest in urban/cosmopolitan life and in formal erudition, the writers of this time absorbed from Jung, from quantum and relativistic physics, from Sir James Frazer, from the nineteenth-century vitalists, "process philosophers," and Romantics that mystical strain that took the sense of connectedness far below strictly cultural or linguistic denotations, "under the net," as Pynchon says (720), of the systems that only parody connectedness, and down into a germinal matrix. This whole current of feeling is discussed best by Hugh Kenner in *The Pound Era*, chiefly apropos of the organicism that came to Pound via Chinese metaphysics (cf., for Pynchon, the Taoist elements discussed in my Chapter 6), Transcendentalism, and disparate other strands in the erudite net: "Transcendentalism was aware of its own affinities with the Far East; and Transcendentalism's other affinities are with Whitehead and Frazer and the Gestaltists and field physicists, and the synergism of Buckminster Fuller: with the coherent effort of 150 years to rectify Newton's machine by exploring the hierarchic interdependencies in nature and in history and in myth and in mind, detecting wholes greater than the sums of parts, organisms not systems, growth not accretion, process and change and resemblance and continuity."[32]

Hence, for example, Pound's late Rock Drill Cantos—the drill, splitting rock, is the living tree's root, assimilable to the Chinese ideograph that means axis, unity, center—and hence Pound's celebration, in *The Spirit of Romance*, of "our kinship to the vital universe, to the tree and the living rock ... the universe of fluid force, and below us the germinal universe of wood alive, of stone alive."

The surprisingly Lawrentian sound of Pound's passage leads me to state my feeling that of all the novelists of this century it is D. H. Lawrence whom Pynchon most closely resembles in essential vision. The Lawrence who constantly inveighs, in the name of the life-force and redemptive irrationality, against the West's mechanical-mindedness, inveighs, like Pynchon, against the consequences of Descartes' Second Rule for the Direction of Mind: "Only those objects should engage our attention, to the sure and indubitable knowledge of which our mental powers seem to be adequate" (*Gravity's Rainbow*'s reply: "just cause you can't see it doesn't mean it's not there!" [677]). Lawrence and Pynchon both like to sound in sourly ironic tones the words "mental," "will,"

32. Hugh Kenner, *The Pound Era* (Berkeley: University of California Press, 1971), p. 231.

"system": witness, from *Women in Love,* the description of how the "snow-white" magnate Gerald Crich "found his eternal and his infinite in the pure machine-principle of perfect co-ordination into one pure, complex, infinitely repeated motion.... He had his life-work now, to extend over the earth a great and perfect System in which the will of man ran smooth and unthwarted, timeless, a Godhead in process."

The character resembles Pynchon's Dr. Pointsman in, among other things, believing that he can force the science that he misconceives as strictly mechanical-deterministic to yield that perfectability of control ("infinitely repeated motion") that genuine science, as a matter of fact, in its Second Law of Thermodynamics and in quantum physics, prohibits. In a world reified out of such people's faith in control, a private "rebirth to somewhere," as Lawrence puts it, is possible only, and perhaps only temporarily, for those who have learned to escape Their mechanical separation of selves, by integrating, in love, their essential otherness with selflessness, like mutually orbiting stars—the figure from *Women in Love* that describes the relationship of Ursula and Birkin, and that will do nicely also for *Gravity's Rainbow's* Roger and Jessica before they are separated by Pointsman. In Lawrence, too, earlier and more mystical belief systems than Christianity are wistfully conceived as possibly healthy alternatives: *The Plumed Surpent,* in its Aztec context, uses the same vastly ancient archetypal mythology of Earth Serpent and Sky Bird that Pynchon employs in *Gravity's Rainbow.* And, most generally, both writers' styles seem to set up mysterious forcefields, such that inert "things" suspiciously squirm with a vivid, secret life; secret underground worlds tangential to "this" one seem created in which, as Lawrence puts it in *Apocalypse,* "Everything [is] *theos* ... whatever *struck* you was god."

This stylistic quality is what E. M. Forster has in mind when he includes Lawrence among those rare novelists who write "prophetic" fiction. Here is a snag, though, for Lawrence is alienating just in proportion to his preaching conscious "ideas." The trouble is that when he reaches for words to express ideas about the reductive effects *of* words on prophetic realities much further back, the resulting jargon, bad enough in nonfiction works like "Psychoanalysis and the Unconscious," quoted below, can be terrible in novels—precisely because, as the jargon has it, "The motivizing of the passional sphere from the ideal is the final peril of human consciousness. It is the death of all spontaneous, creative life, and the substitution of the mechanical principle."

As "novelist of ideas," then, Pynchon is superior to Lawrence in that he never takes himself with the preacher's seriousness and can acknowledge words' paradoxical trap by making the trap felt both as the characters' predicament—witness Tchitcherine in Central Asia—and as his own. But Lawrence, on the other hand, is vastly Pynchon's superior in characterization—in drawing people in believably realistic depth, such that prophetic content shows through the psychologized narrative. If we are to read either of these prophets appreciatively, we need to feel that they have made virtues of their respective weaknesses, turning them, as artistic strategies, toward prophetic ends. In Pynchon, the comicbook surrealism and thinness of characterization, in Lawrence, the humorless preaching of weak intellectual theses, both make for effects that function as "veils" through which we look to see, meaningfully refracted, the prophetic life below.

Somewhat the same generalizations could be made as well for Dostoevsky, another of Forster's exemplary novelist-prophets. Certainly Dostoevsky's fiction is freer of overtly preached ideas than is Lawrence's, but for our purposes here, such things as his Russian and Christian Orthodox jingoism and his blanket hatred of science are best understood as the conscious traces of Dostoevsky's membership in that community of spirit, of which Lawrence and Pynchon are heirs, that guarded the small, fierce flame of late nineteenth-century distrust and fear of materialism, Western technology, and predatory capitalism. Dostoevsky, like Pynchon, felt that from these issued moral anarchy: thus such repulsively "rational" characters as Luzhin in *Crime and Punishment* and the westernized nihilists in *The Devils*; thus also that great hymn to antirationalistic perversity that is *Notes From Underground*. Dostoevsky is one of Pynchon's direct predecessors also in that he made extensive and brilliant use of the dream life to render that "underground" continuity in which, like Pynchon, he felt that all men share in some way. Discard the frame of Orthodox religiosity, and Dostoevsky's insistence on the moral unity of all men—as in *The Brothers Karamazov*, where, finally, "all are responsible for all"—echoes Pynchon's prophetic discoveries of Oneness in the moral, psychic, and material orders of Creation.

Further back in the nineteenth century, we can discover some major bequests to Pynchon from German Romantic literature, and quite importantly, from Goethe's *Faust* (see my Chapter 5). In nineteenth-century America there is Hawthorne, whose neo-Puritan conscience, compulsively worrying about the lasting effects in American life of the imagination of seventeenth-century Calvinism, shares something large with the conscience of the living novelist who is descended from the Massachusetts Bay "Pyncheons." (Hawthorne's use of the name for his Puritan family in *The House of the Seven Gables* elicited, Matthew Winston has found, some angrily literal-minded letters from the leading representatives of the Pyncheon family, and Hawthorne had to calm the distinguished gentlemen down as best he could.)

In Edgar Allan Poe we can find, at the very end of his lone novel, *The Narrative of Arthur Gordon Pym*, a great shrouded form, "of the perfect whiteness of snow," that rises ahead of the sea voyagers as they suddenly break into a region of surrealistic imagination surrounding the South Pole. The figure is quite possibly an ancestor of the one that rises, "too immediate for any eye to register," onto the "white and silent screen" on the last page of *Gravity's Rainbow*.[33] Poe's colossal figure of whiteness has been proposed, inevitably, as an inspiration for Melville's; and very obviously the White Whale, in its symbolization of both/and ultimacies, is recapitulated (with differences; see Chapter 5) in Pynchon's V-2. Melville, yet a third of Forster's prophets, has in common with Pynchon a general preference, strongest in *Moby Dick*, for starkly symbolic action and characterization, for long self-indulgences in pure rhetoric, and for a general extreme of melodramatic effect to which is sacrificed most "realism," except for the minutiae of whaling facts in the foreground. Forster finds this pendatic precision on *Moby Dick's* surface essential to Melville's prophetic effect, as analogously Pynchon's foreground scrupulousness in matters of fact may be essential to his.

In fact, Pynchon's way of embedding symbolic or surrealistic elements in a thick texture of historical and social reportage may be seen as connecting him with a conception of fiction far older than the nineteenth century—*Gravity's Rainbow* reaching around to find its lineage in the symbolic picaresque of Candide, Gulliver, Lazarillo de Tormes, Pantagruel. Why not, while we are at it, the *Satyricon* of Petronius? The game of literary connection at this point begins to feel a bit arbitrary. Why not, while we are at it, suggest that *Gravity's Rainbow* may be concerned with parodying the Henry James situation of American-innocent-in-corrupt-Europe, Slothrop a Lambert Strether as imagined by Marvel Comics?

Clearly it is time now to proceed with the real work at hand, which, as

33. David Cowart also has made this connection: see his *Thomas Pynchon,* pp. 100, 101.

I have said, does not chiefly consist of poking about in literature but rather of making available to the reader the appropriate Pynchonian understandings of motlies of cultural figures, ideas, events, icons, and modes of metaphor where they lurk in *Gravity's Rainbow*. A sketch-list of the main ones must include seventeenth-century Puritanism; nineteenth-century scientific, especially thermodynamic, theory; twentieth-century quantum physics; the cyberneticism of Norbert Wiener and media theories of Marshall McLuhan; Pavlovian behaviorism; the Germans' development of the V-2 rocket, and some physical and mathematical techniques apposite to that development; some main lines of the political, cultural, and intellectual history of modern Germany; international business cartels of the twentieth century; vitalist philosophical systems, particularly those of Bergson, William James, and A. N. Whitehead; the Romantic tradition; several mythologies, especially the Greek and Teutonic; modes of the occult and of mysticism, including the Tarot, the Kabbala, astrology, and Freemasonry; the sociological theories and observations of Max Weber; the poetry of Rilke; several of the central ideas of Freud and a great many of Jung's; the popular culture, especially the movie culture, of the German 1920s and the American 1930s and 1940s; comicbook heroes; the drug culture; American politics right up to the date of the book's publication. Most generally, the reader of *Gravity's Rainbow* must learn to see the quasi-magical, part-hallucinatory web of interconnections, variously familiar, obscure, farfetched and hitherto unthought-of, among all these images, signs, and omens; he must learn many specific translations, some reductive parodies of others, of the narrator's assertion that *"everything is connected*, everything in the Creation" (703). In other words, I am proceeding on the conviction not only that Pynchon's work fully earns it intellectual pretensions, but also that it remains movingly humane, since its author, as agonized mediator of this bewildering field of cultural information, is so excruciatingly sensitive to each human image and gesture that passes through the field. He is possessed of a shy, pained tenderness for human vulnerability, frailty, need—for whatever chances for love and connection still hide between the impersonal frames, in the vast designs of things.

To work on anything so peculiar as a book about a book for any such long time as I have worked on this one is inevitably to invite self-doubts. But in this exploration of *Gravity's Rainbow*, and tangentially of Pynchon's other works, I hope at least to convert the reader to what has been on the whole my reassuringly stable conviction of the greatness that makes the novel deserve such treatment. To everyone who has helped me, or even simply borne with me, in this absurdly protracted attempt to measure Pynchon's stature at something like full height—and most particularly to my amazingly patient wife Lynn, to whom this book is dedicated—I here proffer a Thanks as weakly inadequate-sounding as it is sincere.

2

Gravity's Rainbow
as the Incredible
Moving Film

Framing

The 1973 Viking edition of the novel features an odd design element:
between each two adjacent blocks of narrative is a row of seven precise
little squares, these suggesting movie frames, and the rows in turn suggesting sprocketed separations between successive frames of the novel/
film.[1] Although the little squares are rumored to have been a Viking
editor's inspiration, not Pynchon's, the fact of their thematic pertinence
remains: the manifold frame-images of the novel—comicbook panels,
harmonica holes, train or bus windows, hotel rooms on the stages of
long, preterite journeys—reinforce this first little underground message that in this book we may not expect the smooth continuities of
traditional fiction, with lifelike plots pretending to have been somehow
there all along. Rather, we are confronted with a frank succession of
narrative quanta that are to be integrated by us imaginatively as we
read. The writer's creativity actualizes what Richard Poirier was the first
to call the "creative paranoia" of the reader.[2] We assume no simple
mimesis of story but knowingly share an illusion of plot. The reader or
critic who feels the book's challenges as the early Puritans felt their com-
pulsions of Calling will feel a duty to abstract the idea of framing: we

1. For convenience, and to be cute
about it, we might agree to call the four
major subtitled divisions of the novel
"reels," noting further that the several
separately titled fragments of frames at the
end of the last reel, "The Counterforce,"
may be meant to suggest the catching and
blurring of an old film, much spliced at its
ends, as it jerks its way through the projector. David Cowart in fact has proposed

that the word *catch*, as it punctuates the
narration of Gottfried's final Ascent on the
next-to-last page, is meant to imply just
such a catching and jerking before the film's
final break after the last word of the book.

2. Richard Poirier, "Rocket Power," *Saturday Review: The Arts* 1 (March 3, 1973):
59–64. This is in my opinion the best of all
the early reviews of *Gravity's Rainbow*.

want to know what Pynchon means by this central epistemological symbol, which is everywhere in the book, a secret sign flashed like a Masonic handshake. Accordingly, in this section I discuss Pynchon's uses of movies as technological and cultural inheritances and then follow the widenings of the circles of reference to the framing operation as, in general, it affects and effects reality.

Clearly, what the movie audience sees on the screen is not the unmediated motion of life but rather "the rapid flashing of successive stills to counterfeit movement" (407), a sort of mechanical imitation or parody of the world's raw continuity. The operation of movie technology creates a reflex arc, which we may think of as parabolic, like Gravity's Rainbow. The director directs, edits, splices, arranges his scenes to yield the completed film; run past the projector and beamed onto the screen, the sequence creates the illusion of continuity for what Pynchon calls "the nation of starers" (429)—that is, for the culture that has collectively created the technique and whose members suspend disbelief in the technique's intervention between them and "life." The discreteness of adjacent frames is precisely as real, or as illusory, as the separateness of souls in the staring theater at the origin and end point of the reflex arc, who, "condemned to separate rows, aisles, exits, homegoings" (663), do not feel their true continuity, their connectedness, out here in the dark.

For any novel that so aspires to be filmic, the first corollary of what is said about film-frames must necessarily be linguistic: the Word, as evoked in many connections by Pynchon, is also understood as a way of ordering chaos by subdividing it, naming the void. "Names by themselves may be empty, but the *act of naming...*" says Blicero (366), borrowing from a Rilkean passage about the poetic Word, ceremonially bestowing on Enzian the name by which his existence is actualized for the novel's reader as for Blicero himself. Originally nameless voids are apparently more easily stepped into if framed in a verbal image. The escaped lunatic from the White Visitation, standing on Dover Cliff, hears the Lord of the Sea: " 'Dear me, and what's his name?' 'What would be a good name?' 'Bert.' 'Bert is fine,' he says, and steps back into the void" (73). Pirate Prentice asks Katje Borgesius where she will go now that she is back in England; after some discussion, " ' "The White visitation" is fine,' she said, and stepped into the void" (106).

The novel itself, like all novels, gestures similarly; for the novelist, Henry James explained, his figure differing only incidentally from Pynchon's, "relations stop nowhere, and the exquisite problem of the artist is eternally but to draw, by a geometry of his own, the circle within which they shall happily *appear* to do so."[3] In *V.*, Pynchon invents a great number of characters, events, and supposed causal contingencies; by the assembly of these between the book's covers (the outer frame or circle) he implies a set of conventional causal relationships, in mimesis of history understood as a train of linkages along a world-line. But at the same time the arrangement of discrete events seems just random enough to suggest Trick Number One about apparently coherent plots: they may not be there at all, except as crypto-paranoiac fantasy by novelist or reader. Trick Number Two, of course, is that they may be, after all. The scrambled time sequences of Lady V.'s appearances and the obvious weirdness of Stencil's paranoid quest suggest that V.'s historical manifestations are not connected, even that there may not be such a continuous persona as V. at all. Yet most of the time, for us as for Stencil, the pattern seems real, and the fiction holds. Like Slothrop, we would on the whole "rather have that *reason*" (434); we need that *plot*. Mechanical printing, which mediates novels that activate plots, is for Marshall McLuhan the technological archetype of diverse post-Renaissance framing techniques, just as, by McLuhan's account, "The … Gutenberg fact of uniform, continuous and indefinitely repeatable bits inspired … the related concept of the infinitesimal calculus, by which it became possible to translate any kind of tricky space into the straight, the flat, the uniform, and the 'rational.'"[4]

So, Pynchon implies, the sense of the self itself is perhaps created from nothing more than sequences of framed perceptions. As Joseph Slade explains, "Implicit in the construction of Pynchon's characters is the idea that the self is really an endless fluctuation of sensibility, rather like a film sprocketing through a projector. At any given moment the focus or frame changes. The self is thus not so much thought as lived; its existence is predicated on shifting multiple states of consciousness."[5]

One of Pynchon's major sources in other connections, the mythographer Mircea Eliade, has suggested that the kind of time we pass in watching a film is really a wedge of Great Time in an ancient mythological sense—a permanent and timeless time in which ordinary

3. Henry James, preface to *Roderick Hudson* (New York: Harper & Bros., 1960), p. 8. Coincidentally once again, Thomas H. Schaub has also used this quotation; see Schaub, *Pynchon: The Voice of Ambiguity* (Urbana: University of Illinois Press, 1981), p. 112.

4. Marshall McLuhan, *Understanding Media* (New York: McGraw-Hill Co., 1964), p. 116.

5. Joseph Slade, *Thomas Pynchon* (New York: Warner Paperback Library, 1974), p. 152.

duration, ordinary mortality, and self disappear, and the gods are with us.[6] By this lofty view of the meaning of being a "fan," we can recognize that the films of the 1930s and 1940s brought excruciatingly near, and yet separated, the respectively sacred and profane realities of Gable and Dillinger (516), Shirley Temple and Mrs. Krodobbly (741), the Ice Palaces and the daily breadlines. "Thomas Pynchon is out to commit penetration," says W. T. Lhamon;[7] he means that Pynchon wants to show the permeable nature of these interfaces of art and fantasy and technology with our lives, and yet how they keep us from mutual connection, and yet how they deliver all our lives' terms. He wants to bend the novel's life to our own, like water bent through the holes of Slothrop's harmonica.

Framing in *Gravity's Rainbow*, then, generally connotes the imaginative or cognitive energy, analysis, the will to order and systematize, which both divides and unites, separates and links subject and object, inside and outside. Self conceives and projects a patterned reality (in Pynchon, grids, labyrinths, systems, structures, assemblies), such that the pattern is imagined to have preexisted and can be introjected, coming back to the self as observation, intuition, revelation, in a reflex arc. Artists frame works of art and critics frame analyses of them; scientists frame laws of nature in created mathematical languages, like the calculus; historians frame trending truths, moralists imperatives, religious mystics and ecstatic paranoids orders of angels. Litters of instances tumble out from the common culture and into *Gravity's Rainbow*, a gambol of erudition to watch with a smile. The framed dogma of Pavlov's neural mechanical behaviorism asserts that the cerebral cortex is a mosaic of framelike patches of discrete conditioned behaviors; it is in the name of the dogma that Pointsman "frames" Slothrop, in both abstract and colloquial senses. In calculus, framing is differentiation, the process by which a point, or a line segment approaching a point as limit, is isolated in order to compute instantaneous conditions there. The concept of the quantum of action, of an ultimate discontinuity in reality's texture, is crucial in modern physics, and any metaphysical, ethical, or political system can tyrannize humans by framing them in value categories. Finally, in the Jungian theory of archetypes, primordial symbols, residing in deep collective levels where shapes and mean-

6. Mircea Eliade, *Myths, Dreams, and Mysteries*, trans. Philip Mairet (London: Fontana Library of Theology and Philosophy, 1968), p. 34.

7. W. T. Lhamon, Jr., "The Most Irresponsible Bastard," *New Republic* 168 (April 14, 1973): 624–31.

ings are one and undifferentiated, may rise to be projected as images, radiant frames, into our dreams and technologies and religions; society is in this sense for Pynchon a Jungian film, a collective fantasy or collective dream.

In a sequence beginning on page 381, Slothrop/Rocketman raids the Potsdam Conference to retrieve the hashish that Seaman Bodine has left at the site. For this mission into the heart of Their rational power, he assumes the comicbook charismatic identity of Rocketman, in emulation of two of his heroes, Plasticman and Sundial, who are flexible and can escape all frames simply by bending and flowing around them. The frames they escape are not only those of the nefarious plots of villains inside the comicbook panels but sometimes also the panels themselves, the very structures by which they are actualized. Like Slothrop, they are subversives with a death wish; but the death wish, a wish to relinquish the self in surrounding reality, is also a resource for dangerous missions, hence a life wish. It means they can hide, and so Slothrop can be

> invisible. It becomes easier to believe in the longer he can keep going. Sometime back on Midsummer Eve, between midnight and one, fern seed fell in his shoes. He is the invisible youth, the armored changeling. Providence's little pal. *Their* preoccupation is with forms of danger the War has taught them.... It's a set of threats he doesn't belong to. They are still back in geographical space, drawing deadlines and authorizing personnel, and the only beings who can violate their space are safely caught and paralyzed in comic books. They think. They don't know about Rocketman here. (379)

Slothrop stands to Their order as life does to film, or as real heroism stands to the safely rationalized comicbook fantasies that They peddle to children. From his embeddedness in the night, in history's underground, Slothrop can see Mickey Rooney on the terrace of the Potsdam White House, but Mickey Rooney, "wherever he may go, will repress the fact that he ever saw Slothrop.... So they stay absolutely still, victory's night blowing by around them, and the great in the yellow electric room scheming on oblivious" (382).

Rooney's framing against the electric windows of power is a clever directorial effect: the pet celebrity is framed in Their order as ever in Their celluloid. He saw no such thing as a Rocketman at the Potsdam Conference; you can ask him today. "Invisible" Slothrop, meanwhile, is lost in effect to any transmittable history. When Tchitcherine's men catch him and inject the sodium pentathol, his fading foreshadows the slow dissolve he will do in the novel: "He's away, on the Wheel, clutching in terror to the dwindling white point of himself" (383). Obscurely tangential to the historical moment like some *n*th dimension in physics, he might have been "there," but there is no way to sense his presence except in the very form given, a novelist's fantasy that is, as is the official version of Potsdam, a framed form.

Pynchon further implies that movies are a kind of dream-framing of archetypes within a culture when he equates the collective movie interface with the private interface between waking life and the art-fantasies of our dreams, especially when these include Hollywood dreams. The opening passage of Reel Four, like that of Reel One, is the inside of a dream that so gradually opens to waking that we are hardly aware of the change, "where we are" in the funhouse:

> Bette Davis and Margaret Dumont are in the curly-Cuvillies drawing room of somebody's palatial home. From outside the window, at some point, comes the sound of a kazoo, playing a tune of astounding tastelessness, probably "Who Dat Man?" from *A Day at the Races* (in more ways than one). It is one of Groucho Marx's vulgar friends. The sound is low, buzzing, and guttural. Bette Davis freezes, tosses her head, flicks her cigarette. "What," she inquires, "is *that*?" Margaret Dumont smiles, throws out her chest, looks down her nose. "Well it *sounds*," she replies, "like a *kazoo*." For all Slothrop knows, it *was* a kazoo. (619)

Slothrop's dream has borrowed a voice from that Marching Kazoo Contraband that buzzes, low and guttural, all through Pynchon's novel. On the other side of sleep's interface, the sound is that of a small plane that Pirate Prentice is flying into the Zone, into the vast invisible designs of history and novel. One-way traffic across a frame: such is Slothrop's dream, and such also is the scene that he dreams. Groucho sees in, but Margaret Dumont doesn't see out. Davis's pompous "What"—an echo of Richard Nixon's on the previous page—is exactly in the spirit of the humorless Establishmentarians, under Margaret Dumont, who dauntlessly repressed the Brothers' subversions so that Groucho enjoyed a perilous safety. Like Rocketman, he was "invisible." We share also an allusion and joke with Pynchon: *A Day at the Races* is about horse racing, and when the Brothers sing "Who Dat Man?" they are being danced and cakewalked around by a mass of lovable Hollywood Darkies—hence "races in more ways than one." There are hundreds of pieces of movie trivia like this in *Gravity's Rainbow,* each one a test and a mockery of our framing skills. We shouldn't play too obsessively, but we should enjoy random discoveries. For example, when Bloody

Chiclitz says, "For DeMille, young fur-henchmen can't be rowing" (559), it is both the Great War expression "forty million Frenchmen can't be wrong" and, probably, an allusion to the Marx Brothers film *Monkey Business,* in which Groucho taunts the ponderous gangster Alky Briggs, "You're wise, eh? What's the capital of North Dakota?...Who is chairman of Chase Manhattan Bank?...How many Frenchmen can't be wrong?" In his apt incarnation as Chiclitz, Briggs finally gets around to answering the question.

Pynchon's parodies of movie genres include a good deal of romance-adventure-spy-melodrama, as in *V.,* and as also in Sax Rohmer's Fu Manchu fiction, useful in *Gravity's Rainbow* as an evocation of 1940s-style Manichaean-paranoid visions of Caucasian virtue and Mongoloid vice. There are also westerns (see Major Marvy in his giant white Stetson [312] riding a diesel car, chasing Slothrop in the Mittelwerke), and horror flicks (the Giant Adenoid: "Yes, it's horrible ... like a stupendous *nose* sucking in snot ... wait, now it's ... beginning to ... oh, *no...*" [15]). But the films of most consistent use to Pynchon are the movie musicals of the 1930s and 1940s, self-consciously choreographed for wide-screen effects in vulgarly precise style: "Then comes a chorus for ukuleles and kazoos and so on while everyone dances, black neckerchiefs whipping about like the mustaches of epileptic victims, delicate snoods unloosening to allow stray locks of hair to escape from their tight rolls, skirt-hems raised to expose flashing knees and slips.... on the final chorus the boys circle clockwise, girls anticlockwise, the ensemble opening out into a rose-pattern" (594).

Might these spectacles have been felt, in 1973, as remote enough, in the grainy black-and-white of the late-late show, to insinuate mild paranoias? How can anything so singleminded and simpleminded not really have other purposes in its soul? And, Pynchon insists, such displays belong as surely to the novel's characters' sense of reality as does World War II, and the frames moreover are permeable. When Franz Pökler meets Slothrop for the first time, the former turns out to be "some kind of fanatical movie hound all right—'On D-Day,' he confesses, 'when I heard General Eisenhower on the radio announcing the invasion of Normandy, I thought it was really Clark Gable, have you noticed? the voices are *identical'*" (577). And Slothrop isn't surprised. Nor do characters show surprise, nor do we expect them to, when lyrics intrude or chorus lines appear to comment on the action. We feel only that pained bemusement as when on the late show a plodding streetful of Great Russian paupers suddenly breaks, on an invisible downbeat, into synchronized song, stretched smiles, choreography.

Pynchon's descriptive style sometimes imitates the roaming and panning effects of the movies.[8] As the dolly moves in, the frames jump nervously, self-sufficiently, over any images that might resonate: "Soft, faded berets against the slate clouds. Mark II Sten set on automatic, mustache mouthwide covering enormous upper lips, humorless" (20). Katje Borgesius's first appearance is framed by a sentence that we see moving in on her on page 92, and on page 133 moving away, restless, perfectionist, sensitive as the camera: "In silence, hidden from her, the camera follows as she moves deliberately nowhere longlegged about the room, an adolescent wideness and hunching to her shoulders, her hair not bluntly Dutch at all, but secured in a modish upsweep with an old, tarnished silver crown" (92).

We are free to think of the camera that *is* the sentence as Pynchon's own, filming *Gravity's Rainbow*, but the camera *in* it is filming a concentric reality: the cameraman follows Katje on Pointsman's orders, the better to keep Slothrop under surveillance when he will have rescued her from the octopus whom the film will condition—and so on, into plot.

It is Pynchon's point that from and through such technologized nestings of realities there emerge archetypes: dreaming, resonant shapes to be flung out and seen at the peak of their arc on the screen, then regathered by the culture of starers, having peaked for a moment, in common view, into mundane time, as a rocket, before Earth takes it back, peaks into the black floor of space. In the Grouchoesque epigraph to Reel Two, producer Merian C. Cooper promises Fay Wray, "You will have the tallest, darkest leading man in Hollywood" (178). Subsequently we see not only images direct from *King Kong* but also several earnest "interpretive" endeavors, since, as Pynchon implies, these always accompany genuine archetypes in activation:

> "Yeah well," as film critic Mitchell Prettyplace puts it in his definitive 18-volume study of *King Kong*, "you know, he *did* love her, folks." Proceeding from this thesis, it appears that Prettyplace has left nothing out, every shot including out-takes raked through for every last bit of symbolism, exhaustive biographies of everyone

8. I am pointing out here a few of Pynchon's movie-mimetic devices not mentioned in Scott Simmon's much fuller list of such devices in his "Beyond the Theater of War: *Gravity's Rainbow* as Film," in *Critical Essays on Thomas Pynchon*, ed. Richard Pearce (Boston: G. K. Hall & Co., 1981).

connected with the film, extras, grips, lab people ... even inter-
views with King Kong Kultists, who to be eligible for membership
must have seen the movie at least 100 times and be prepared to pass
an 8-hour entrance exam.... And so, too, the legend of the black
scapeape we cast down like Lucifer from the tallest erection in the
world has come, in the fullness of time, to generate its own children, running around inside Germany even now—(275)

Thirteen pages later, confirming Prettyplace on the force of the archetype, Major Marvy regrets that "V-E day just about everyplace you had
a rocket, you had you a nigger."[9] And not only do the last lines of the
passage point us to what Treacle of PSI Section correctly identifies as a
"Jungian frame of mind" (276), but the Prettyplace satire meanwhile
directs itself both to fans—short for *fanatics*—and cult-followers of particular artists and art, and finally to all systematic criticism of art,
including literary scholarship, even the scholarship that *Gravity's Rainbow* is built to absorb. When we follow Pynchon's trail of erudite bread
crumbs back into the stacks, we are literature's Puritans, framing the
framing Word, actualizing a joke that's on us.

The movie archetype manifested chiefly by Greta Erdmann's
daughter Bianca and Franz Pökler's daughter Ilse is a precious one to
Pynchon and of much use in the novel: that of the vulnerable, tender-
tough kid whose cuteness is both a rigid frame and a creative survival
tactic. She is proposed in the novel as everyone's favorite perverse fantasy, clearly fated to some exploitation or prostitution or other, so that
for the nation of starers she is secretly a sex *object*. Even those who can
melt with pity for her, feeling wonder and love, feel also a lust that is a
perverse parody of the tenderness and is inseparable from it. Shirley
Temple in movies, Nabokov's Lolita in literature, Orphan Annie in comics, and the cutesy stage baby of Hollywood myth all help express her
outside the novel. Inside she is everywhere, victim of every power plot,
caught in every guillotine frame. Bianca's life is a running stage-baby
role forced on her by Greta and Thanatz: she follows up a perverse parody of Shirley Temple's "The Good Ship Lollipop" number with camp/
vamp affectations for Slothrop: "Oh, she's gone out of her mind, she
just accused me of having an affair with Thanatz. *Mad*ness, of course

9. The symbolic equation here, of
course, is of the black Hereros to Kong
(organic nature and primitive sexuality),
and of the white, phallic rocket to the
Empire State Building (the sterility and/or

sexual perversion of a deathwishing
culture). Pynchon himself uses these symbols quite seriously in parts of *Gravity's
Rainbow* but here parodies their standardized applications to *King Kong*.

38

we're good *friends*" (468). She is twelve, Thanatz is her stepfather, and we must be able to catch her lovely sexy integrity here, the shy humanity that is now in peril worse than any Orphan Annie has known but that is still not quite wholly caught in the frame. Even all through "The Good Ship Lollipop" her eyes remain "mocking, dark, her own" (466). And as, in the hold of the Bad Ship *Anubis*, she is about to die, "Bianca is closest, this last possible moment below decks here behind the ravening jackal, closest to you who came in blinding color, slouched alone in your seat, never threatened along any rookwise row or diagonal all night" (472).

We—"you"—who have just sexually "come" with Bianca have had fantasies masturbatorily dependent on Shirley's image up on the screen, and this is a loneliness we share unknowingly, "strangers at the films" (663); coming secretly, separately, in the "blinding color" of the projector's beam overhead, each of "you" may believe for a moment in an Eliadean magic that breaks down the interface of official film-fantasy, delivering you up to Shirley—as if paranoiacally, or just wistfully, to half-believe that all the time "she favors you, most of all" (472).

Ilse Pökler on her side is framed by the Reich concentration camps, by Blicero's scheming, by the plot (which also involves, far beyond her knowledge, a third child-sacrifice, Gottfried). She may see her father just two weeks out of the year—cruelly framed appearances that, Pökler thinks, may not even be connected. They may be using a different "Ilse" on him each time, as adjacent movie frames do not have to represent the same scene. "These techniques had been extended past images on film, to human lives" (407); the line prepares one of the book's most beautiful passages, telling all what it must mean for Pökler as well as for Ilse to be a movie child:

> So it has gone for the six years since. A daughter a year, each one
> about a year older, each time taking up nearly from scratch. The
> only continuity has been her name, and Zwölfkinder, and Pökler's
> love—love something like a persistence of vision, for They have
> used it to create for him the moving image of a daughter, flashing
> him only these summertime frames of her, leaving it to him to build
> the illusion of a single child ... what would the time scale matter, a
> 24th of a second or a year (no more, the engineer thought, than in a
> wind-tunnel, or an oscillograph whose turning drum you could
> speed or slow at will)? (422)[10]

10. The technical aspects of this passage are, as usual in Pynchon, quite correct and carefully understated. "Persistence of vision" is the name that the

The wind tunnel Pökler is thinking of was a real one, used at the Peenemünde rocket facility for testing rocket models at simulated supersonic speeds; thus it points to another "movie child" of Pökler's, also framed in a film: the V-2 itself. Its "life" while in flight is measured by the projective techniques of calculus, delta-t's trailing out on the curve, as the human child's life comes in summertime frames. It takes Pökler most of the book to reach imaginatively up over his head, to the level on which Blicero's designs are also Pynchon's shining Designs, to discover this symmetry, the awful incest of inanimate with animate, Apparat with girl child.

The rocket's apposite film is also historically real: a 1929 piece by Fritz Lang called *Die Frau im Mond*. It was popular in Weimar Germany, though a modern audience would laugh at its technical clumsiness and scientific naïveté; modern computerized science fiction accustoms us to more righteously "realistic" sorts of effects. But Lang's movie, the first film ever made about rocketry and space travel, was a pure Expressionist dream. The young rocket engineers of the real-historical Verein für Raumschiffahrt—Wernher von Braun among them—saw it, as does Pynchon's fictional engineer, who knows von Braun: "[Franz and Leni] saw *Die Frau im Mond*. Franz was amused, condescending.... He knew some of the people who'd worked on the special effects. Leni saw a dream of flight. One of many possible. Real flight and dreams of flight go together" (159).

And because they go together, the first A4 rocket successfully fired from Peenemünde, on October 3, 1942—in a crucial test demonstration that won the applause and assured the support of some high Nazi authorities—had the emblem of a woman sitting in a crescent moon painted on its shaft: "Die Frau im Mond." It is interesting that this "Frau" is not, though it easily could have been, specifically mentioned in *Gravity's Rainbow*. To find it we have to go back to the stacks,[11] to official history, and the "real world" that we ourselves share with Wernher von Braun, though not with Franz Pökler, except from the

precinematic nineteenth century gave to the phenomenon of the mind's momentary after-imaging of what the eye has just seen, the imaginative "filling in" of a space between frames of perception. The makers of movies early discovered that a film speed of 24 frames per second past the projector beam was ideal for accommodating persistence of vision, hence Pökler's "24th of a second."

11. One can see a picture of the 1942 "Frau" in the photo portfolio section of Ernst Klee and Otto Mark's *The Birth of the Missile*, trans. T. Schoeters (London: George G. Harrap & Co., Ltd., 1965).

other side of *Gravity's Rainbow*'s moving film. The collective dream of the Weimar movie, of the Peenemünde program, ancient fantasies of space flight, the history assuredly "made" by the "master fantasists" (410) in Nazi Berlin, the technology that records all these in movie frames, and a human daughter—all meet on the interface, on the cortex of Pökler. This sort of connectedness is what Leni is trying to tell him about, but "Mickey Rooney will repress Rocketman."

Irving Howe, interested, like Pynchon, in the psychology and epistemology of mass culture, observes that "daily experience and mass culture are so interlaced that it would be futile to seek causal relationships between them. Does Gregory Peck model himself after the American Lover or does the American Lover model himself after Gregory Peck?"[12] But Howe tries un-Pynchonlike to locate a crucial difference between the dreams of mass man as manifested in movies and the much sharper set of stresses that work through a piece of high art: "Mass Culture elicits the most conservative response from the audience. So long as the audience feels that it must continue to live as it does, it has little desire to see its passivity and deep-seated boredom upset; it wants to be titillated and amused, but not disturbed.... Joyce makes it hard for us, but he offers us the tempting possibility of reaching his heights of sensibility. But mass culture is safe, for its end is already present in its beginning."[13]

Now Pynchon himself assumes that masscult inclines toward "safety"—hence its political uses—but he probably would not like Howe's implication that low and high art differ fundamentally in the ways in which they create consciousness. Howe ends his paragraph, it is impossible to say how deliberately, with a paraphrase of T. S. Eliot, and this might be taken to indicate that he is as compliant an "audience image"[14] for Joyce and Eliot as is the average consumer for Cecil B. deMille. Movies for Pynchon are a test case, a metaphor, for a general

12. Irving Howe, "Notes on Mass Culture," in *Mass Culture*, ed. Bernard Rosenberg and David Manning White (Toronto: Free Press, Collier-Macmillan, 1957), p. 498.

13. Ibid., p. 499.

14. "Audience image" is the key term in Herbert Gans's argument that every movie is a symbolic expression of its director's concept of the audience for it: giving the "audience image" what it is thought to want, the movie actualizes the image, as simultaneously the behavior of the audience shapes future movies. See Gans, "The Creator-Audience Relationship in the Mass Media: An Analysis of Movie-Making," in *Mass Culture*, ed. Rosenberg and White.

process by which any art, technology, or other mediating assembly creates its audience, creates its creators, and implants these in itself. The result is that in a time of endlessly labyrinthine assemblies, like the present, what results is a total culture from which to be absent is to be preterite, but from which no preterite can be wholly absent without great effort.

I must strongly emphasize that Pynchon's feeling for the flicks is always respectful and frequently full of delight; the point should be obvious unto fatuity that the novel does not just "satirize" movies, comic books, mass culture generally—nor does it amount to any populist argument for the superior ethical strength of majority tastes. But among the interfaces that Pynchon would dissolve is the one that separates sympathies for the differently affirmative energies of the high and pop arts, and the related one that is too often felt to exist between "our" culture and the underground or subcultures to which ours, Pynchon implies, is about as sensitive as the world of the cops and dicks to the Tramp in the movies of Chaplin. Yet there is also the fact that movies make an excellent metaphor for the workings of historical and political paranoia. This observation in its more fashionable forms is literal, not metaphorical; it is, in itself, an exercise in paranoia as media theory. In an essay Dwight McDonald opts shamelessly for a belief in a plot by the elect of moviedom, the servants of rational power, to keep consumers brainwashed via the movies;[15] C. Wright Mills plays with the same suspicions in *The Power Elite*; Siegfried Kracauer has had ideas on the ways in which certain Weimar films were conscious efforts to prepare the German masses for Nazism. But the paranoid situation in *Gravity's Rainbow* is much more complex than these theories of conscious, causal intent would have it, since, in Poirier's words, Pynchon "is locating the kinds of human consciousness that have been implanted *in* the instruments of technology and contemporary methods of analysis; not content with recording the historical effects of these, he is anxious to find our history *in* them."[16]

Put it more evilly: the ancient metaphor of world-as-theater or world-as-dream, which drives so many of Shakespeare's plays, becomes in Pynchon a metaphor of world-as-film. Rilke's Fourth Duino Elegy would add world-as-puppet-stage, where invisible angels ("they")

15. Dwight McDonald, "A Theory of Mass Culture," in *Mass Culture*, ed. Rosenberg and White.

16. Poirier, "Rocket Power," p. 63.

manipulate the puppetlike feelings of the persona: "Then in the sketch-work of the moment painfully a backgound is prepared as contrast, to help us see; for they are very clear with us. We do not know the contour of our feeling, but only what informs it from the outside. Who has not sat before the curtain of his heart, frightened?"[17]

To the powerless paranoiac, visible history may seem to be a film that is as phony and yet as cryptically revelatory as any of Gerhardt von Göll's. World War II is a mere diversionary set:

> "They said it was a stroke," Säure sez.... A band of doctors in white masks that cover everything but the eyes, bleak and grown-up eyes, move in step down the passage toward where Roosevelt is lying. They carry shiny black kits. Metal rings inside the black leather, rings as if to speak, help-let-me-out-of-here.... Whoever it was, posing in the black cape at Yalta with the other leaders, con-veyed beautifully the sense of Death's wings, rich, soft and black as the winter cape, prepared a nation of starers for the passing of Roosevelt, a being They had assembled, a being They would dis-mantle. (374)

At Yalta, three Figures of Power on cane chairs before white columns, as if to suggest demigods on heaven's porches; the omen in the black cape, the need for casual "aides" to fill out the frame—official history stands little aesthetic chance against this exalted paranoid's vision, which after all has, like Enzian's similar visions, "a stern, an intense beauty, [it is] a symphony of the North" (327). The effect is frightening because we can never be sure that it is confined merely to individual characters' pathologies; we swim through the paranoid medium, past fantastic reefs, finding that nowhere is there any airlit surface, any clear interface beyond which we can retreat to the fatherly company of some omniscient narrator who will tell us, don't worry, it's safe out here.

Thus we may worry about the narrator we do have: Is it "his" para-noia we are hearing? And may we transfer some of the worry to the mysterious Pynchon himself? Wayne Booth, in *The Rhetoric of Fiction*, acutely discusses unreliable narrators, showing the great delicacy of relations that may obtain among the ambiguously distinct mental worlds of characters, narrator, personal author, and "implied author" (that is, who the author becomes in the book, his persona as uniquely implied by the book). In James's *The Turn of the Screw* and Joyce's *A Por-trait of the Artist as a Young Man*, especially, Booth locates the slight irre-

17. Rainer Maria Rilke, Fourth Duino Elegy, lines 14–19. I use the translation of Stephen Garmey and Jay Wilson (New York: Harper Colophon Books, 1972).

ducible mystery that results when one or more of these personages are wild cards. When any or all of them may be flaming paranoiacs, however, the situation is surely past sorting out; on a strictly literary level, a subtle parody is necessarily involved. What is parodied is the unreliable narrator convention itself, in its usual use as a means to render the flux of subjectivity: in extreme form, that novelistic reflexiveness in which an unpleasantly leering novelist disappears, as a professor I know likes to put it, up his own asshole.

An utter destabilization results also when we play at taking the novel as a kind of "documentary" film of history, with the narrator as the putatively authoritative newsreel voice. How "past" is the year 1945 for the narrator, and is there any reason (no reason at all, of course) why *our* time should not be also, for him, the past? The world of the 1980s, or of whenever it is that we read the book, may in fact be a distant, qualitatively different past, if the narrator's own world is taken to be that of the Raketen-Stadt: "It's a giant factory-state here, a City of the Future, full of extrapolated 1930's swoop-facaded and balconied skyscrapers, lean chrome caryatids with bobbed hairdos, classy airships of all descriptions drifting in the boom and hush of the city abysses.... It is the Raketen-Stadt" (674).

That this description owes something to comic books, something to the City of Pain in Rilke's Tenth Elegy, something perhaps to the New Jerusalem of *Revelation,* and a great deal to certain shots in the Fritz Lang film *Metropolis,* need not deter us. The Stadt is being fit inside some frames we happen to know, and it hints at what our future will be in part because these and other frames will have actualized that future. But we may be skeptical of the narrator's claim to represent historical truth if, for one thing, Those who control his world have an interest in framing the past as this very strange movie we are watching. In that case the narrator's state of mind, a smashing movie effect in any case, is a trick, a pose—or it could even be a real paranoid psychosis, a mental health problem at large in his culture: the Raketen-Stadt as Thomas Gwenhidwy's "City Paranoiac" (172). At any rate, the documentary film proposes a fiction, a plot, for the past; in doing so it necessarily confronts the problems described by Erich Auerbach in *Mimesis,* as he discusses the difficulty of separating "historical" from "legendary" materials in the Homeric epics:

> How difficult it is to represent historical themes in general, and
> how unfit they are for legend; the historical comprises a great
> number of contradictory motives in each individual, a hesitation

and ambiguous groping on the part of groups; only seldom (as in the last war) does a more or less plain situation, comparatively simple to describe, arise, and even such a situation is subject to division below the surface, is indeed almost constantly in danger of losing its simplicity; and the motives of all the interested parties are so complex that the slogans of propaganda can be composed only through the crudest simplifications—with the result that friend or foe alike can often employ the same ones. [Pynchon: "Money be damned, the very life of (insert name of nation) is at stake"— 521]. To write history is so difficult that most historians are forced to make concessions to the technique of legend.[18]

Gravity's Rainbow, then, for its narrator, may be history or legend. To choose legend is to assume that the whole of the book comes from the Raketen-Stadt-Zeit; the rationalized Slothrop legend is part of the frame, in that case, although Slothrop is as remote and fabulous for the Stadt as Plasticman and Sundial had been for him:

> "We were never that concerned with Slothrop *qua* Slothrop," a spokesman for the Counterforce admitted recently in an interview with *The Wall Street Journal*.
>
> INTERVIEWER: You mean, then, that he was more of a rallying-point.
>
> SPOKESMAN: No, not even that. Opinion even at the start was divided. It was one of our fatal weaknesses [I'm sure you want to hear about fatal weaknesses]. (738; brackets Pynchon's)

Who is the "real," i.e., historical, Slothrop? Perhaps some unimaginable complexity was there all along and is not being transmitted: is the narrator on Mickey Rooney's side of the film? It is not clear whether he knows, or thinks he knows, or pretends to know, or thinks he pretends.

Or we may choose to believe in none of this. The Stadt may only be a fantasy, based more or less on movies and comics, idly indulged in by a more or less straight-talking narrator whose time is our time.

"Which do you want it to be?" (131).

Framing and Integration

The "process philosopher" Alfred North Whitehead believed that in apprehending time and space we falsely impose on them a "separative," differentiable character, but that in fact no subunit of space can be extracted without loss of the "prehensive unity" of the whole, pre-

18. Erich Auerbach, *Mimesis* (Princeton, N.J.: Princeton University Press, 1968), p. 20.

hension being defined as "uncognitive apprehension"; an "instant" of time is a fiction, because each time duration mirrors in itself all temporal duration, all time.[19] A footnote in William James's *Varieties of Religious Experience* describes a similar ontological plenum in particularly Pynchonesque terms:

> If I should throw down a thousand beans at random on a table, I could doubtless, by eliminating a sufficient number of them, leave the rest in almost any geometrical pattern you might propose to me, and you might then say that the pattern was the thing prefigured beforehand, and that the other beans were mere irrelevance and packing material. Our dealings with Nature are just like this. She is a vast *plenum* in which our attention draws capricious lines in innumerable directions. We count and name whatever lies upon the special lines we trace.... Yet all the while between and around them lies an infinite anonymous chaos of objects that no one ever thought of together, of relations that never yet attracted our attention.[20]

For Pynchon, reality may be just such a continuous plenum, which might be in some sense insouled. Overfull, charged with meaning, it might, in certain "relations that never yet attracted our attention," spill over into something like sentience (as of James's beans subversively chattering to each other, in Munchkin voices, just too high to be heard). That the world subsists, as Whitehead finally maintains, in a sort of pan-psychic connectedness Pynchon's novel takes not as fact (it is by

19. See Alfred North Whitehead, *Science and the Modern World* (New York: Macmillan Co., 1923), p. 102. It is largely in the chapters called "The Eighteenth Century" and "The Romantic Reaction" that this system is sketched out.

20. William James, *Varieties of Religious Experience* (New York: Modern Library, 1936), footnote on p. 429. At this point James is showing the arbitrariness of the argument-from-design proof for God—indeed showing how irrelevant all strictly intellectual "proofs" are to the real nature of religious imagination, faith, and life. Anything can be made the starting point of an argument from design; in any microcosm we may see any macrocosm we choose to see (as Robert Frost knows in his terrifying poem "Design"). For James, as for the Voltaire of *Candide*, the Lisbon earthquake of 1759 is an exemplary case: "The truth is that any state of things whatever that can be named is logically susceptible of teleological interpretation. The ruins of the earthquake at Lisbon, for example: the whole of past history had to be planned exactly as it was to bring about in the fullness of time just this particular arrangement of debris of masonry, furniture, and once living bodies. No other train of causes would have been sufficient."

Pynchon may quite possibly have this passage in mind when he has Enzian paranoiacally imagine that the ruins of the Jamf Ölfabriken Werke are a prearranged shape of destruction (520). Enzian's fantasy depends on a notion of conspiracy based on causal efficacy, since straight causality is Their creed. But this paranoid reasoning backwards from outward-and-visible-sign to conspiratorial first cause is subject, of course, to James's criticism: teleological inferences cannot pretend to be descriptions of *necessary* processes.

definition a "framed" intellectual construct), but as the One alternative for belief, or for faith. Pynchon is not in fact so endlessly reductive, tonally, as to be "sterile ... loveless ... perverse"—as critics claim who want to fit him into some absurdist Cool School where he can be kept under easy surveillance. There is indeed a "faith" encoded by the terms *connectedness* and *integration*; its caricature is paranoia and other forms of projective systematizing, successive stills to counterfeit motion, but the original motion and ground-connectedness, tidal and deep, may go on, be real, all the time. I explore its nature in much greater detail in Chapter 6, but I will begin the exploration here.

On a hillside in Germany down which I am walking, I see a traffic sign indicating a dead-end street, "Ende," tilting slightly over a church-yard wall in the direction of a small group of graves. I have a choice among ways to feel about this wry little "comment" discovered; they are basic epistemological choices, much the same ones open to Oedipa Maas at the end of *The Crying of Lot 49*, as she tries to explain the "evidence" for the Tristero System's existence. The apparent bubble of sentience bounded by sign and gravestones may be located entirely in my subjectivity, my sense of language and frame of accidental attention, and the Tristero may be wholly Oedipa's fantasy. Or I may be paranoid and believe that someone, some Purpose, has arranged these materials for me with "intent to communicate" (*Lot 49*, 13), that my epiphany has been *caused*. There may be a plot to make Oedipa think there is a Tristero, or she may be imagining some such plot. The remaining alternative is to assume "that it was all true" (*Lot 49*, 134). The little dialogue may in fact be going on, in some way independent of anyone's noticing it or framing of it; all of reality may be continuously "filled in" with meaning. Tristero may be real and may really offer a humane alternative to the technocratic condition. James's beans are Fungus Pygmies, sentient pinballs from the planet Katspiel, sentient rocks running at frames per century, Byron the Bulb. There may be, if only we look, "a Face in ev'ry mountainside / And a soul in ev'ry stone" (760).

Gravity's Rainbow is always suggesting the third alternative by pointing urgently under, around, past all plots and appearances of them, to take us "out, and through, and down under the net ... [to] all the presences we are not supposed to be seeing—wind gods, hilltop gods, sunset gods—that we train ourselves away from to keep from looking further even though enough of us do, leave Their electric voices behind in the twilight" (720). By the precarious state of its syntax the passage connotes the presence of such Titanic forces as thrust impatiently up

from under the nets of plots to erase our habitually "framed" perceptions. Secretly there lurk faces, not only in mountainsides, but also in all
sorts of urban "wan and preterite places," such as the entrance to Säure
Bummer's Berlin tenement: "above the mouth two squared eyes,
organdy whites, irises pitch black, stare [Slothrop] down.... It laughs as
it has for years without stopping, a blubbery and percussive laugh, like
heavy china rolling or bumping under the water in the sink. A brainless
giggle, just big old geometric me, nothin' t'be nervous about, c'mon in"
(436–37).

A related secret, the "grand joke on all the visitors to Baedeker's
world" in *V.*, is that the "natives" in preterite places, such as non-Cauca-
sian countries, really *are*, under their instrumental functions, genuine
human beings—and, if people are not just things, why necessarily must
things, why must even government buildings, be things? "The permanent residents are actually humans in disguise. This secret is as well
kept as the others: that statues talk (though the vocal Memnon of
Thebes, certain sunrises, has been indiscreet), that some government
buildings go mad and mosques make love" (*V.*, 66).[21]

If They insist on trying to deanimate us and the world, then why, in
opposing Them, stop short at any claims for life? There need be no
secrets: if Being is everywhere, its cry is that of the newly preterite
Thanatz: "When mortal faces go by, sure, self-consistent and never
seeing me, are they real? Are they souls, really? or only attractive sculp-
ture, the sunlit faces of clouds?" (672). Across the mirror-interface, the
question inverts: are *they* real, are They alive? The "grand joke" is the
question: where *is* the life?

It is because they are such false arbitrations of an essentially holistic
field that Pynchonian frames seem terrible jailors; each framing image
in *Gravity's Rainbow* has connotations of capture, imprisonment, bondage. The open door of Osbie Feel's oven is called a frame for Katje's face
looking in (93); she recalls the wartime "Kinderofen" that, in Blicero's
perverse fantasy, had framed her and Gottfried as Gretel and Hansel.
What is framed for Blicero in the prisms of the instruments at the rocket
sites has "taken over what used to be memory's random walk, its inno-

21. The "vocal Memnon of Thebes" in
the sunrise is a most Pynchonesque
image, which any reader ought to be
happy assuming originates in *V.* But in
truth, the book's interface has here been
crossed: "Egyptian Thebes is known for a
colossal black statue—a seated stone

figure—which utters a sound like the
breaking of a lyre-string every day at sunrise. All Greek-speaking people call it
Memnon." Suetonius' and Pausanias'
authorities are cited in Robert Graves, *The
Greek Myths* 2 (London: Penguin Books,
1955), p. 316.

cent image-gathering" (101). A photographer in a Berlin crowd threatens to catch Franz Pökler in a "stray frame" (158); the train station waiting room in London, where soldiers shuffle into and out of the war, is a "white frame" (51). Slothrop remembers with pity "the faces of children out the train windows" (626); the narrator shows us "the row of faces in the bus, drowned-man green, insomniac, tobacco-starved, scared" (693); even the roll of toilet paper that Pointsman picks out of the channel, with PROPERTY OF H. M. GOVERNMENT stenciled on each paper "frame," shows official power, official vigilance (92). And a more extended example: When the anarchist Squalidozzi meets Blodgett Waxwing and other fugitives in a harmonica factory someplace in Bavaria, large framing images infiltrate from outside to show his ongoing entrapment, anyway, in Their control. The windows along the factory's walls ripple with light as a Bob Steele movie is shown: "film-light flickered blue across empty windows as if it were breath trying to produce a note" (385)—rather as the clear stream in the Harz will play a "visual blues" on Slothrop's recovered harmonica (622). As these movielight frames flicker over their heads, the men who sit in silent rows remain unaware that they are held in a Great Film being projected from some other order of being: alternatively, from the zonal plot-structure now reforming outside, all around them, or from Pynchon's film, *Gravity's Rainbow,* arresting these our actors as stills.

Late in his progress, Slothrop runs into a similar narrative warp-zone in Cuxhaven where frame images hover very near, coalescing about his head, their signatures obscurely felt as "zonal shapes he will allow to enter but won't interpret, not any more. Just as well, probably. The most persistent of these ... are the stairstep gables that front so many of these ancient North German buildings.... They hold shape, they endure, like monuments to Analysis" (567).

"Analysis" here denotes the congruent techniques of calculus and movie projection:

> Three hundred years ago mathematicians were learning to break the cannonball's rise and fall into stairsteps of range and height, Δx and Δy, allowing them to grow smaller and smaller.... This analytic legacy has been handed down intact—it brought the technicians at Peenemünde to peer at the Askania films of Rocket flights, frame by frame, Δx by Δy, flightless themselves ... film and calculus, both pornographies of flight. Reminders of impotence and abstraction. (567)

And the children playing the game of Himmel und Hölle on the stairstep frames of the buildings move—like the rocket itself—"from heaven to hell by increments" (567).[22]

As the scene continues, Slothrop becomes Plechazunga, acquires his pig suit, and plays happily with the children, but soon the MP's arrive to break up the black-market dealings; a young girl takes Slothrop home with her and hides him. She has snapshots of her father, a printer ("it touches Slothrop's own Puritan hopes for the Word, the Word made printer's ink") who is or was an anti-Nazi refugee on the run. All the girl and her mother have of him now are the snap-shot frames: "The delta-x's and delta-y's of his drifter's spirit ... how he was changing inside the knife-fall of the shutter, what he might have been hearing in the water, flowing like himself forever, in lost silence, behind him, already behind him" (572).

Again, the flow of water—in the harmonica, of living breath—between frames foretells the stream where Slothrop finally will lose his framed self—"Like that Rilke prophesied" at the end of *Sonnets to Orpheus*: "And though Earthliness forget you, / To the stilled Earth say: I flow. / To the rushing water speak: I am" (622). Now Slothrop and the girl lie still in bed, hearing the loudspeakers outside proclaiming curfew:

> "What's the best way out of town?" She knows a hundred. His
> heart, his fingertips, hurt with shame. "I'll show you."
> "You don't have to."
> "I want to."

She is a child, she explains, and so knows how to hide: she is invisible. She shows him an old city gate "with stairsteps to nowhere on top" (573), and he leaves: "Docile girl, good night. What does he have for her but a last snapshot of a trudging pig in motley, merging with the stars and woodpiles, something to put beside that childhood still of her father? He impersonates flight though his heart isn't in it and yet he's lost all knowledge of staying ... Good night, it's curfew, get back inside your room ... good night" (573).

Although a bit of high literature (*Hamlet* and *The Waste Land* in those final good-nights) may lurk here, Roger Sale has designated this scene

---

22. The mythographer Mircea Eliade tells us that in the "symbolism of Ascension" common to many mystical systems, both primitive and developed, the mystic, shaman, or demigod achieves freedom, transcendence of earth's limitations, by a quantized ascent through (frequently) seven distinct steps, stages, or "levels": "heaven by increments." Eliade, *Myths, Dreams, and Mysteries*, p. 113. See further my Chapter 6 on the "Myth of the Center."

as one of Pynchon's rare moments of "touching earth"[23]—meaning, I believe, for once forgetting his peculiar historico-scientific obsessions and literary self-consciousness and showing us, simply, what it is to be alive, vulnerable, available for compassion. In fact, the obsessions are not forgotten—frame imagery is everywhere in the scene, the rocket and its legacy of "analysis" therefore lurks everywhere too—nor is this passage, tonally, an especially rare moment, nor is its tenderness independent, let alone corrective, of large "abstract" themes. The "abstract" and the "human" dimensions of meaning in *Gravity's Rainbow* do not take separate vacations; the tough-mindedness as well as the tenderness of the book are in their congruency. Compassion aches as it does for Pynchon because it is always in some measure impersonal; it must be defined as an eddy against the awesomely general currents in which the powerless are trapped, including *this* or *that* passing, once-glimpsed, excruciatingly specific face.

When Squalidozzi remarks of his Argentine countrymen that "We are obsessed with building labyrinths where before there was open plain and sky," he and Pynchon are taking the gradual fencing-in and -off of the Argentine pampas as a metaphor for the effective psychology and metaphysics of Western man. The subdivision of Rilkean "openness"[24] is the conquistadoring of self over other, a framing of primeval oneness felt as threat, as evil, the world outside not only open to conquest but deserving of it. The doctrine of providential history in which the English Puritans framed their American "errand" is attached, of course, to the movie-borne myth of (elect) cowboys and (preterite) Indians, the country having been seen at first as a demesne of Satan, the savage place foreordained to be won (as good guys always win) by the

23. Roger Sale, "American Fiction in 1973," *Massachusetts Review* 14 (Autumn 1973): 841–46. Another very perceptive critic who tries, however, to separate head and heart in Pynchon—admiring the former, missing the latter—is Richard Locke in the *New York Times Book Review,* March 11, 1973.

24. "Openness" as a Pynchonian code word derives from Rilke's Eighth Duino Elegy, where our framed, adult, judgmental selves, inward-looking, are hardened against "the Open," but animals know and children might know a "Free outgoing":
    With all their eyes all creatures gaze
    into

the Open. Only our eyes, as though
    turned in,
on every side of it are set about
    like traps to circumvent its free
    outgoing.
What is *without* we know from the
    face
of animals alone, for even the
    youngest child
we turn around and force to see the
    past
as form and not that openness that
lies so deep within the face of
    animals. (lines 1–9)

Puritan Saints, the elect of the blessed theocracy. Original Puritanism sometimes liked to conceive of the American openness as the setting in which certain prophecies of *Revelation* were to be fulfilled. According to St. John of Patmos via the Calvinist vision, the Reformation would culminate in European chaos, while the elect would escape to America, the "ends of the earth," there to found a city on a hill, the secular new Jerusalem that would at once complete and impel forward the prophecies implicit in Ararat, Zion, Calvary—prefiguring, with these, the Heavenly City.[25] This was a plot for history, to be projected onto the New World's blank screen: the city would shine forth over a darkening world, as the fourth and last corner of earth heard the trumpets of doom and the credits rolled by.

The Raketen-Stadt, if we like, is available as a parodic fulfillment of these original, crack-brained, paranoid-apocalyptic visions of the American destiny. The city that the Calvinists' system, in its rational evolution, built at last is the "white metropolis," a perverse-bureaucratic New Jerusalem whose secret charter is not in the scheme of the predestinarian God but in Max Weber's *The Protestant Ethic and the Spirit of Capitalism*. William Slothrop's coreligionists came to the New World in hopes of actualizing the fantasy of an apocalypse that would find God's elect prepared for their apotheosis. Now, with apocalypse in human hands, "their enterprise," Roger Mexico knows, "goes on" (628).

Integration

The style of connectedness, or of integration, as felt throughout *Gravity's Rainbow* is a continuous crackle of meaning-sparks leaping between charged points: in Poirier's term, a "performing" style,[26] self-consciously an exercise in caricature of that coherency of effect with which any good prose overlays the "pure informationless state of signal zero" (404)—or, alternatively, overlays the mystic's One, the world-space already continuously filled in with meaning. Pynchon, admitting and displaying this texture of the imagination's attempts to unite itself with what it imagines—whether with One or Zero, since either would absorb the crackling in silence—lets his prose suggest the grainedness of the

25. See Sacvan Bercovitch's introduction to his edited volume, *The American Puritan Imagination* (Cambridge: At the University Press, 1974).

26. Poirier's *The Performing Self* (New York: Oxford University Press, 1971) is largely devoted to discussing modern literature and art as a self-conscious, self-parodic "performance" by the artist; on pp. 23–26 he considers, in these terms, Pynchon specifically.

films, bureaucracies, paranoias through which the characters move, while suggesting that all the time, as a ground context, there lies some mysteriously continuous "flow":

> Still Slothrop keeps his map up daily, boobishly conscientious. At its best, it does celebrate a flow, a passing from which—among the sudden demolitions from the sky, mysterious orders arriving out of the dark laborings of night that for himself are only idle—he can save for a moment here or there, the days again growing colder, frost in the morning, the feeling of Jennifer's breasts inside cold sweater's wool held to warm a bit in the coal-smoke hallways he'll never know the daytime despondency of ... cup of Bovril a fraction down from boiling searing his bare knee as Irene, naked as he is in a block of glass sunlight, holds up precious nylons one by one to find a pair that hasn't laddered, each struck flashing by the light from the winter trellis outside ... nasal hep American-girl voices singing out of the grooves of some disc up through the thorn needle of Alison's mother's radiogram ... snuggling for warmth, blackout curtains over all the windows, no light but the coal of their last cigarette, an English firefly, bobbing at her whim in cursive writing that trails a bit behind, words he can't read. (23)

Held just "for a moment," barely glimpsed, in this smoky prose, reticulate winter trellises, brittle light-blocks, nylons' fabric, laddered stockings suggest grid-traceries on life's surface, whereby lives are parceled and given names. But these reticulations seem too somehow to be tending toward a final submergence in a continuous life beneath, smooth and softly breathing as the breast under the sweater. Slothrop as a discrete persona is far less salient than the sense of his life as a "flow, a passing" of imagistic perceptions; the girls' names flicker auroralike, interchangeable; progressive verbs with *-ing* endings prevail; ellipses blur normal full-stop interfaces. Cigarette light may be flashing cryptic informational quanta out to all manner of paranoid terminals, but Slothrop can't read the words, can only see the "cursive," continuous trailing. Outside, the weather apparently flows toward homogeneity, maximum entropy, as in the early story "Entropy"; inside, heat energies level entropically across the interface of cup with bare knee, and between snuggling bodies. Blackout curtains erase the frames of the windows, blurring as if to merge inside and outside, Slothrop and Pointsman, love and war. The convection currents here on the surface, then, tug gently but unmistakably downward, toward that underground life that is the domain, for example, of Sundial, who, "flashing in, flashing out again, comes from 'across the wind,' by which readers understood 'across some flow, more or less sheet and vertical: a wall in constant motion'—over there was a different world, where Sundial took care of business they would never understand" (473).

It is this same "wall" that suddenly ripples toward us when Géza Rózsavölgyi (Their stooge, rigidly an Abteilung man) is backed by Roger Mexico into a corner in a stark white office building, and comic-book colors surrealistically well to engulf him:

> The walls—they don't appear to be ... well, *solid*, actually. They flow: a coarse, a viscous passage, rippling like a standing piece of silk or nylon, the color watery gray but now and then with surprise islands in the flow: saffron spindles, palm-green ovals, magenta firths running comblike into the jagged comicbook-orange chunks of island as the wounded fighter-plane circles, flaps to just above a stall, wheels up as the *blue* (suddenly, such a violent blue!) rushes in just before impact throttle closed *uhhnnhh*! oh shit the *reef*, we're going to smash up on the—oh. Oh, there's no reef? We'-we're *safe*? We are! Mangoes, I see mangoes (634).

The rippling and blurring, even as it engulfs Rózsavölgyi, engulfs the narrative matrix: not even a comma marks the interface with "as the wounded fighter-plane circles." There are, further, internal subversions of the comicbook colors themselves, fifth-column imagery from Their white world: "watery gray" is the color of Imipolex, and the silk or nylon wall alludes to the curtains of Imipolex with which Blicero surrounded Greta Erdmann in the petrochemical plant. Pynchon, riding these flows and cross-currents, crash-landing but coming up safe, has obvious fun going "too far," like Groucho, meaning it, daring us to object. He may have had a difficult time with editors begging him to cut, trim, frame.

The same sort of flamboyance informs Pynchon's descriptive metaphors: acts of connection that are, like Donne's famous conceits, strange enough to announce themselves as worked-up, artificial, but also nearly always brilliantly right—"Dogs, spooked and shivering, run behind walls whose tops are broken like fever charts" (434); "The half-moon shines among hazy clouds, its dark half the color of aged meat" (104). Humblest manifestations of the same connecting principles are, of course, puns: Grouchoesque leers are built into Cecil B. deMille and the Forty Million Frenchmen; the law firm of Salitieri, Poore, Nash, de Brutus and Short; the I Ching devotees who have hexagrams tattooed on each toe and can't stand still ("Can you guess why? Because they

54

always have I Ching feet!" [746]). And there may be seen inside the simplest word, once we have learned Pynchon's code-lexicon, a flux of differentiations and connections going on constantly, like the mysterious seethings inside an atomic nucleus: I've been *framed*, making a *synthesis, plotting, projecting*, even, indeed, waiting for a *connection*:

> In the shadows, black and white holding in a panda-pattern across his face ... waits the connection Slothrop has travelled all this way to see....
>
> Slothrop: Where is he? Why didn't he show? Who are you?
>
> Voice: The Kid got busted. And you know me, Slothrop. Remember? I'm Never.
>
> Slothrop (peering): *You*? Never? (A pause). *Did* the Kenosha Kid?
> (71)

Pynchon also has "travelled all this way" to score something: to this permutation of "you never did the Kenosha Kid," it seems, the last ten manic pages about the trip down the toilet have been directed, as in some terrible shaggy dog joke; the scene connects to the strains of kazoos, and takes its tail in its mouth.

And "connection" is also, as above, drug talk, and "underground life" is also drug life. Like metaphors, dreams, and art, drugs actualize connections that in themselves are truths, realities; Laszlo Jamf, himself an all-purpose nexus for plot connections, calls his favorite hallucinogenic invention Oneirine, after *oneiros*, dream. One of Jamf's former corporate employers within the I. G. Farben cartel is "a spinoff from Sandoz (where, as every schoolboy knows, the legendary Dr. Hofmann made his important discovery)" (250)—the discovery being that of LSD, the schoolchildren in question being, in arch-anachronism, the counterculturites of the American 1960s. Pynchon's stoned internal monologues are always good-humoredly faithful to the experience: for example, Slothrop in ruined Berlin, after smoking a couple of joints with Säure, sees King Kong, "or some creature closely allied, squatting down, evidently just, taking a shit," but "on closer inspection, the crouching monster turns out to be the Reichstag building" (368). And this is the building—if we want a subtle, *sub rosa* connection—that Hitler burned down in order to purge some undesirable "blackness" (Communists, Social Democrats) from the new Nazi order, as King Kong the black scapeape was purged by the culture of whiteness.

There is, too, the matter of literary connectedness—usually, in

Pynchon, taking the form of subtle stylistic parodies. Brigadier Pudding's half-senile consciousness strokes Great War memories:

> [Pointsman's] father was M. O. in Thunder Prodd's regiment, caught a bit of shrapnel in the thigh at Polygon Wood, lay silent for seven hours before they, without a word before, in that mud, that terrible smell, in, yes Polygon Wood ... or was that—who *was* that gingerhaired chap who slept with his hat on? ahhh, come back. Now Polygon Wood ... but it's fluttering away. Fallen trees, dead, smooth gray, swirlinggrainoftreeslikefrozensmoke ... no use, no bleeding use, it's gone, another gone, another, oh dear. (76)

"Swirlinggrainoftreeslikefrozensmoke"—brilliant as description, credible as remembered image, self-conscious as stylistic gimmick—recalls the word-blends of Joyce; Prufrockian melancholia under an etherized sky; Great War soldiers' journals, ironic and deathwishing.[27] It is the Modernist style, an interior riverrun that paradoxically must be rendered by a high artist's craft, framed in an elaborate stylistic technology.[28]

No technology, Pynchon implies throughout the novel, can possibly help but stylize, parody, or cartoon the truths it mediates; culture's wide screens mock our putative unity with experience. As *V.*'s Victorians turned to their Baedekers for authorized realities, we may consult Disney or Lowell Thomas or the professional tour guide if we care to imagine, say, sailing the postwar summer Baltic on a black market boat:

> *We come now in sight of mythical Rügen off our starboard bow...Our captain, Frau Gnahb, heads into the Greifswalder Bodden, to comb the long firths for her quarry. After an hour* (comical bassoon solos over close-ups of the old recreant guzzling some horrible fermented potato-mash lobotomy out of a jerrycan, wiping her mouth on her sleeve, belching) *of fruitless search, our modern-day pirates head out to sea again, and up the eastern coast of the island.* (527–28)

Life magazine can bring you Rocketman: "A SNAFU FOR ROCKETMAN, reads the caption—'Barely off the ground, the Zone's newest celebrity

---

27. See Paul Fussell, *The Great War and Modern Memory* (New York: Oxford University Press, 1975), for an account of some of these journals—especially Chapter 5, "Oh What a Literary War."

28. From McLuhan's *Understanding Media:* "In modern literature there is probably no more celebrated technique than that of stream of consciousness or interior monologue. This technique is really managed by the transfer of film technique to the printed page, where in a deep sense it really originated; for as we have seen the Gutenberg technology of movable type is quite indispensable to any industrial or film process.... film and the stream of consciousness alike seemed to provide a deeply desired release from the mechanical world of increasing standardization and uniformity" (p. 295).

"fucks up" ' " (377)—or a TV quiz show can afford, the MC says, mystery insights (691); you may see the Zone from behind the window-framed safety of a packaged bus tour (413).

Parody connections may even be nested inside each other, as, at some moments of Slothrop's Progress—itself a parody of, among other things, a Bunyanesque Pilgrim's—the Progress is subjected to pop-cultural parodies from within. Blodgett Waxwing gives Slothrop a zoot suit to aid his escape from the Casino Hermann Goering: " 'I know a lot. Not everything, but a few things you don't. Listen Slothrop—you'll be needing a friend, and sooner than you think. Don't come here to the villa—it may be too hot by then—but if you can make it as far as Nice—' he hands over a business card, embossed with a chess knight" (248). Pure James Bond, Humphrey Bogart—and yet, read in context, the passage is apt to strike the reader as refreshingly straight, since for the previous two pages or so he has been hearing this innermost parodic frequency:

> The story here tonight is a typical WW II intrigue, just another evening at Raoul's place, involving a future opium shipment's being used by Tamara as security against a loan from Italo, who in turn owes Waxwing for a Sherman tank his friend Theophile is trying to smuggle into Palestine but must raise a few thousand pounds ... and so has put up the tank as collateral to borrow from Tamara, who is using part of her loan from Italo to pay him.... Waxwing ... is now being pressured by Raoul for the money because Italo, deciding the tank belongs to Tamara now, showed up last night and took it away to an Undisclosed Location as payment on his loan, thus causing Raoul to panic. Something like that. (247)

But low comedy can sometimes intensify, rather than cancel, background paranoid frequencies. During a chase scene in the rocketworks under the mountain at Nordhausen, Marvy's Mothers sing limericks to the man who gets hard-ons for rockets:

> There once was a thing called a V-2
> To pilot which you did not need to—
> You just pushed a button
> And it would leave nuttin'
> But stiffs and big holes and debris, too. (305)

And suddenly something arches broodingly over the scene, over the slapstick conventions, the cartoon characters who don't quite yet feel the Presence: "Slothrop does not know that they are singing to him, and neither do they." The limericks get grosser:

> There was a young fellow named Slattery
> Who was fond of the course-gyro battery.

> With that 50-volt shock
> What was left of his cock
> Was all slimy and sloppy and spattery. (311)

And as Marvy bears down, wearing his giant white Stetson and waving two .45 automatics, a chill scientific abstraction intrudes:

> There was a young fellow named Pope
> Who plugged into an *oscilloscope*.
> The cyclical trace
> Of their carnal embrace
> Had a damn nearly infinite slope. (311)

And now, when someone shoots off a flare, all color and motion fade, and the Angel casually bends:

> Whiteness without heat, and blind inertia: Slothrop feels a terrible
> *familiarity* here, a center he has been skirting, avoiding as long as he
> can remember—never has he been so close as now to the true
> momentum of his time: faces and facts that have crowded his
> indenture to the Rocket, camouflage and distraction fall away for the
> white moment, the vain and blind tugging at his sleeves *it's impor-*
> *tant ... please ... look at us ...* but it's already too late, it's only wind,
> only g-loads, and the blood of his eyes has begun to touch the
> whiteness back to ivory, to brushings of gold and a network of
> edges to the broken rock ... and the hand that lifted him away sets
> him back in the Mittelwerke— (312)

This lifting upward is an ecstatic and terrible mystic's dissolve, in a deathly symmetry with life's undergound trip, as into the Mittlewerke, toward black earthliness. In White Visitation, the pigments of things— "brushings of gold" to connect later with the whorled hair, "fine German gold," on Gottfried's naked back as he huddles inside the white rocket—are bleached by "Nothing's hand" (24), the same hand that lifts Slothrop away from comicbook colors and into the memory of his obscure childhood fear of the Northern Lights: "What Lights were these? What ghosts in command? And suppose, in the next moment, all of it, the complete night, *were* to go out of control and curtains part to show us a winter no one has guessed at" (29). White Visitations have the fierce indeterminacy of rocket hits themselves, blasting and freezing the action: Roger and Jessica may play cute tickle games, but when a rocket falls nearby, "Death has come in the pantry door: stands watching them, iron and patient, with a look that says *try to tickle me*" (60).

It is the constant possibility of this white styptic touch that makes men's movements, however low-comic, always resemble the dazed, puppetlike "leaping" that Rilke imagines for the pensive acrobats in Picasso's *Saltimbanques,* the painting that inspires the Fifth Duino Elegy:

> But tell me who these *are,* these traveling men
> even more fugitive than we ourselves,
> compelled from birth, oh for *whose, whose* sake
> wrung by some never-satiate will?
> But it wrings them, bends them, flails, devours them,
> hurls and catches them; as from oiled
> and polished air they fall again
> upon the threadbare carpet their
> eternal leaping has worn thin. Carpet
> lost in space, and laid on
> like a plaster where the sky above the outskirts
> had scraped the earth. (lines 1–12)

In Pynchon the futile "leaping" takes place against a sky that might always unfurl as a scroll, revealing angelic orders. The apocalypse-paranoia that visits characters huddled under that sky is congruent with our awareness, from outside, of the book's design, designedness, of the artistic eschatology that structures it. Outside the novel, as inside—in our own noncommittally roiling skies, in our history, paranoias, bureaucracies, daily news—we find Dillinger, Gable, Groucho, I. G. Farben, Malcolm X, Richard Nixon, Jive Ass Mother Fuckers (black California slang: JAMF); a topological twist, and outside is inside, sky's scroll is book's page or film's screen.

Sky-paranoia may sometimes be gentle, a mere comic Slothropian matter of seeing animal crackers in cloud racks:

> the jaws and teeth of some Creature, some Presence so large that nobody else can see it—there! that's the monster I was telling you about. —That's no monster, stupid, that's *clouds!* —No, can't you *see?* it's his *feet*— (241)

But because they mark interfaces with other orders, the book's ubiquitous skyscapes are always felt *brightly,* omenlike, whether or not the Presences in them quite assume visible shape:

> an enormous sky all sea-clouds in full march, tall and plum, behind her (106)

> out at the horizon, out near the burnished edge of the world, who are these visitors standing … these robed figures—perhaps, at this distance, hundreds of miles tall—their faces serene, unattached, like the Buddha's, bending over the sea…. What have the watchmen of the world's edge come tonight to look for? (214–15)

the Eis-Heiligen—St. Pancratius, St. Servatius, die kalte Sophie ...
they hover in clouds above the vineyards, holy beings of ice, ready
with a breath, an intention, to ruin the year with frost and cold ...
there's no telling how the ice-saints feel—coarse laughter, pagan
annoyance, who understands these rear guard who preserve winter
against the revolutionaries of May? (281)

Sometimes, you know those fine Boston Sundays, when the sky
over the Hill is *broken* into clouds, the way white bread appears
through a crust you hold at your thumbs and split apart ... You
know, don't you? Golden clouds? (682)

To point to the power and urgency of this kind of imagining is the best
answer to critics who accuse Pynchon of coldness or of frivolousness; in
George Levine's words, "Only a writer who cares can see with
Pynchon's intensity and range, can remember with such vividness, can
juxtapose so recklessly and creatively."[29] And although Pynchon's language constantly thrusts forward mad images of annihilation, still
everywhere in it is earthliness, sensitivity to the palpable *things, Dinge,*
that Rilke's language also caresses. Details are rescued from preterition,
from being merely "passed over" as waste—picked from the roadside
like "Kleenex wadded to brain shapes hiding preterite snot, preterite
tears" (626). This reverent rescue work on the real is done, not only in
the three novels, but also, where we might least expect it, in the 1966
essay on the Watts riot that is Pynchon's only published nonfiction:

Everything [in Watts] seems so out in the open, all of it real, no
plastic faces, no transistors, no hidden Muzak, or Disneyfied land-
scaping, or smiling little chicks to show you around. Not in
Raceriotland. Only a few historical landmarks, like the police sub-
station, one command post for the white forces last August,
pigeons now thick and cooing up on its red-tiled roof. Or, on down
the street, vacant lots, still looking charred around the edges, wink-
ing with emptied Tokay, port and sherry pints, some of the bottles
peeking out of paper bags, others busted.[30]

Empty One Joseph Ombindi tries to explain to Enzian the virtues of
suicide, but the lyric that filters in from offstage, "Sold on Suicide,"
wholly subverts the argument that it pretends to support. The song has
such a good time imagining and listing things that, to "renounce the
world," the suicide must renounce; such a good time that Ombindi's
easy nihilism looks absurd, unreal. By Murphy's Law, there will always

29. George Levine, "V-2," *Partisan
Review* 40 (Fall 1973): 517–29.

30. Thomas Pynchon, "A Journey Into

the Mind of Watts," *New York Times Magazine,* June 12, 1966.

be something *more* to name and renounce, and so "the 'suicide' of the title might have to be postponed indefinitely!" (320). It is the *naming* that counts, though naming also be framing. Of Rilke's most apposite passage, the one from which Blicero takes a name to bestow on Enzian, Pynchon quotes the German on page 101; I give Garmey and Wilson's translation:

> For the wanderer brings down from the mountainside
> not a handful of earth to the valley, all
>   indescribable,
> but the word he had gained there, pure, the yellow
> and blue gentian [Enzian]. Are we perhaps here
>   only to say: house,
> bridge, brook, gate, jug, olive tree, window,—
> at best: pillar, tower ... but to *say* them, understand
>   me,
> *so* to say them as the things within themselves never
> thought to be. (Ninth Duino Elegy, lines 27–34)

Several lines later Rilke speaks of the urgency of this duty, manifestly the poet's, of naming; *he* must rescue the secret life to which twentieth century mechanocracy, "without image," is blind:

> *Here* is the time for what can be *told*, here its home.
> Speak and confess. More than ever
> do the things we live with fall away, and
> what displaces them is an act without image.
> An act under crusts it will rip as soon
> as its strength outgrows them and seeks new limits.
> Between the hammer strokes
> our heart endures, as does
> the tongue between the teeth, which still
> is able to praise. (Ninth Elegy, lines 41–50)

Such runs Rilke's sanction—the deepest sense in which his vision "influences" Pynchon's—for the style of connectedness, the style also of "anything that might come up by surprise, by Murphy's Law, where the salvation could be" (471). By this style's insistence we must stop to notice, say, "the purple and orange creatures" that snow crystals make when they settle on eyelashes (58); when a baby, no one's in particular, somewhere in Säure's tenement, learns to say "Sonnenschein," the small act of naming is noted (686). In a "cold fieldmouse church" in England is a scratch Christmas choir and a black face, which the reader will never see again, from Jamaica, and Jamaica, suddenly, is real as a rocket, this moment, a face and a voice, signifying its permanent being:

A Jamaican corporal, taken from his warm island to this—from singing his childhood along the rum-smoky saloons of High Holborn
Street where the sailors throw mammoth red firecrackers, quarter
of a stick of dynamite man, over the swinging doors and run across
the street giggling, or come walking out with high-skirted girls,
girls of the island, Chinese and French girls ... lemon peels crushed
in the gutters of the streets scented the early mornings where he
used to sing, O have you seen my darlin' Lola, with a shape like a
bottle of Coca-Cola, sailors running up and down in the brown
shadows of alleys, flapping at neckerchief and pants-leg, and the
girls whispering together and laughing. (128–29)

There are similar effects in Shakespeare: marginal, brief clairvoyances
that, in their grace, are sharings. No formal irony about reality and the
imagination is quite enough to explain why Edgar *sees*, down to the
minute stick-figure precision of the samphire-gatherer, such a scene as
he says he sees from where he kneels with his blind father on what they
play as Dover Cliff. No strict *need* exists for the songs or for Falstaff to
throw away such a line as "we have heard the chimes at midnight, Master Shallow." Reason not the need: this is part of what Shakespeare and
Pynchon both mean by a word that recurs, variously and mysteriously,
in both: the word *kind, kindness*.

For Alfred North Whitehead, all entities in the universe, from stones
to God, have forms of consciousness and feel all other entities; all of
reality moves, through the flux of beings responsive at depth to their
whole surroundings, toward a teleological goal of maximum realization
of value, or, approximately, love. Life and being, all blending frames,
tend to effacement through transformation—as for Rilke's Orpheus—

> He who pours himself out as a spring is perceived
>   by Perceiving,
> that conducts him enraptured through all the
>   cheerful creation,
> which often ends at the start and begins at the
>   end.
>
> Every happy space is a child or grandchild of
>   Leaving,
> in which they wander astounded. And Daphne, since
>   transformation,
> feeling herself laurel, wills that you change to
>   a wind.[31]

31. Rilke's *Sonnets to Orpheus*, trans.
C. F. MacIntyre (Berkeley: University of
California Press, 1960). The quoted lines
are from Part II, Sonnet 12, p. 79.

3

Character Moires
in *Gravity's Rainbow*

Cartoons and Ghosts

In this chapter I discuss the most prominent characters of *Gravity's Rainbow* and try to elucidate Pynchon's architectonic arrangements of them inside metaphors of labyrinth, hierarchy, and moire. That the subject already evokes such abstract terms signifies that I must face, too, the most common general complaint about Pynchon's characterization: that in his books it is precisely such imperatives of abstract and abstracting design and theme that prevent the characters from seeming really characterized and even the books as wholes from seeming humane. The writer's obsessive concern with theme, the complaint runs, in effect prevents the characters from pulling away toward any appearances of self-sufficiency. Characters cannot be imagined *personally*, and the novels are therefore merely authorial self-indulgences, mind games; they are "imperialistic," "mandarin."[1]

The case, as Pynchon certainly knows, is arguable; to incur its complaints is a risk he takes, to deserve them a mortal risk inside the risk. Some of its representative questions about character and motivation might be: Why would a force of black rocket troops live that underground life, in constant danger and hardship, solely in order to build a

1. The term *imperialistic* is used generally to imply the novelist's exultantly self-conscious "imperial" conquest of his thematic materials. See Roger Sale, "American Fiction 1973," *Massachusetts Review* 14 (Autumn 1973): 841–46.

A good definition of *mandarin* as stylistic or genre description is found in Peter Prescott, "Mandarin's Apprentice," a *Newsweek* review (June 7, 1976) of Don DeLillo's *Ratner's Star*. The novel is much indebted to Pynchon, who is in fact the

"mandarin" of Prescott's title. "Among serious writers of American fiction mandarin is the most admired style. The reader is confronted with cleverness, skittering symbols, pockets of amiable pendantry, a language so musical that he can almost sing the paragraphs. Plots have been jettisoned for a theme-and-variations effect, a story that extends but does not progress. Characters have been dumped with the result that all the voices in the story echo but one voice—the author's."

rocket whose meaning is solely defined, so it seems, by the author's extrinsic symbolism? Why would anyone have spent the whole of World War II scheming to launch an ultimate rocket, with no practical meaning or use in terms of that war or of anything else, in order to propel a symbolic boy-icon toward the North Pole? In what way could a man be conditioned in infancy by an aphrodisiac plastic, and how could the rocket hits during the 1944 London blitz have come exactly where the erections somehow related to the conditioning somehow occurred? Where, inside these surreal convolutions of symbols, is there any room for credible, careworthy humans?

We might at first say, platitudinously, that Pynchon wants to define history as a reified paranoia, to show that we are all victims of more lushly improbable, but quite real, plots than we know; Slothrop's paranoia, recall, is mostly a real sensitivity to real combinations against him. At any rate, the red-herring answer seems to account for some of the novel's most striking effects, by way of explicating its real undercutting of over-easy myths of the possibility of free volition under contemporary conditions, and even of the ontologically prior "self" itself. But the trouble is that, to critics worried about its characters' cartoonishness, these observations will not make the novel seem any more compassionate or less quirky. To take more or less literally the paranoid metaphor for history is to restrict the book to paranoiacs only, setting it up for a kill by the mimetic fallacy: novels that merely imitate unpleasant worldviews are merely unpleasant novels.

Even if we can avoid the fallacy, moreover, we do have to agree that Pynchon's characters, if not exactly "flat" in E. M. Forster's famous sense, are at least sketchy, curiously vague: there is probably as much of Tyrone Slothrop on the printed page as there is of Leopold Bloom, but I don't know what Slothrop looks like. The author's personal reclusiveness could be felt, too, as further complicating the problem. Perhaps, the fantasy goes, he doesn't make "real" characters because he can't; maybe, despite his novels' constant advice to us about the need for human connection, Pynchon himself can't connect sympathetically with the human world. And if, being inhuman, he dehumanizes his characters, thus implicating his novel's whole personality and sense of purpose in the perversions it is "about,"[2] we are back in the cul-de-sac

2. For this kind of reading of Pynchon see Jeremy Larner, "The New Schlemihl," *Partisan Review* 30 (Summer 1963): 273–76, and David Thorburn, "A Dissent on Pynchon," *Commentary* 56 (September 1973): 68–70.

of mimesis: Pynchon and/or his narrator stand condemned as typical products of the very culture the book reveals, which is their and our own. The argument is absurd if meant to *excuse* a book felt as inhuman and, if we still prize the book, leaves us wondering uncomfortably on what moral grounds outside thematic hungers it stands, if we do ask that books be morally freestanding, not grossly at odds with responsible human feelings.

I will try to show that the rescue of *Gravity's Rainbow*'s humaneness quite centrally involves seeing its imaginative system as an "open" one, the metaphor from thermodynamics proposing that a work of art might in effect subvert itself by breaking the closed illusion of framing form and "opening out" to destabilize the outside, in the subversively entropic manner of radiant coals minutely changing the temperature of a room. In seeming to relinquish the sharp outlines that, in traditionally "closed" fiction, signify the created beings' removal from our own world of real ones, Pynchon's characters begin to resemble archetypal images, or subnuclear particles, whose life is in some sense everywhere; they are free energy-quanta to be exchanged with the world. As such they would seem to remind us, too, that novels are ideally unsafe, that is, are not mere passive Cartesian objects for safe critical subjects to dissect and "work on"; that our feelings about a book must merge in, and help reveal, our feelings about the common culture and our relationships to and in it, our sense of responsibility for it. Thus Enzian, name-framed by Blicero, Rilke, and Pynchon, is assimilable to King Kong, to the Nibelungen of Germanic epic, to the Christ-Messiah, to the "mindbody" of Earth in Lyle Bland's and F. A. von Kekule's dreams. Lady V. is fictional Victoria Wren, Vera Meroving, Rat Veronica, and others, while she is also the Venus, Virgin, and subsidiary icons, including V-2, of history. If we are not always aware of these resonances, of their promiscuous energies in the books' undergrounds or in our own, that "doesn't mean [they're] not there!" (677).

The novels' own vectors of sympathy "inside" for their characters are usually sharply pointed, in fact achingly tender, yet also complexly ambivalent: "And the cold street seemed all at once to've bloomed into singing. [Benny Profane] wanted to take the girl by the fingers, lead her to someplace out of the wind, anyplace warm, pivot her back on those poor ballbearing heels and show her his name was Sfacim after all. It was a desire he got, off and on, to be cruel and feel at the same time sorrow so big it filled him, leaked out his eyes and the holes in his shoes to make one big pool of human sorrow on the street, which had every-thing spilled on it from beer to blood, but very little compassion" (V., 128).

Schlemihls, even, feel "sorrow," if only "off and on"—and V. regrets the "off and on," too; it doesn't, as some critics have claimed, endorse the flip tone as authoritative in any absolute way.[3] In "ballbearing heels," in the sexual violence that is apparently imminent, there is Pro-fane's and perhaps, if you wish, the author's perverse attraction to the inanimate, a sadomasochist relish for sex-objectification. But "poor" in front of the ballbearing heels signals, as "poor," "dear," "kind" so often do in these novels, an anguish so unapologetically pure, despite its camouflage as mere sentimentality, that it is, rightly heard, beautifully moving. Profane wants less to rape the girl than to smash through the frames that enclose and define her—remember that the novel itself is such a frame—and thus to effect her rescue. And *Gravity's Rainbow* emphasizes the further, complicating awareness that even where rescue from entrapping systems may be possible, freedom's "option for the self"[4] may be worse than entrapment, since it means a paradox-ical self-relinquishment: Slothrop's fate of dying into earthliness, "invisible."

In the open system of *Gravity's Rainbow,* these ambivalent judgments and sympathies are as likely to attach themselves to real historical peo-ple outside the book as to characters inside it. In the sense of Laszlo Jamf's "who sent [F. A. von Kekule] the Dream [of the Great Serpent]?" (413), who sent into actual history the punning name of Livingstone, Freemason and African pioneer, so that Pynchon's narrator might shiver "living stone? oh yes" (587)—and so that masonic chronicler A. E. Waite might intone: "The growth of our years in masonry is a growth in the sense of life. The evidences are about us continually, pro-vided only—as a condition on the part of us each—we carry within us a certain gift of life which corresponds to life about us. It is in this manner that we become and remain living stones built up into a House of Life."[5] "Gift of life," a phrase attaching in *Gravity's Rainbow* to William

3. For this view see Bernard Bergonzi, *The Situation of the Novel* (Middlesex, Eng.: Pelican Books, 1972). In Chapter 4, "Amer-ica: The Incredible Reality," Bergonzi admires Pynchon's first two novels but claims that Pynchon there regards "the mechanization of humanity ... as a subject for cool, amused contemplation" (p. 118).

4. See Joseph W. Slade, "Escaping Rationalization: Options for the Self in *Gravity's Rainbow*," *Critique* 18 (1977): 27–38.

5. A. E. Waite, *A New Encyclopedia of Freemasonry,* 2 vols. (New York: Weather-vane Books, 1970) 1: 460.

Slothrop and his preterite pigs (555), points thus to that mysterious ground of being where even stones may be living, of which the reticulate masonic structure, in history and novel, is a flashing-still parody and betrayal: Freemason Livingstone, we are to recall, helped make the African Open available to European encroachment and rationalization, Hereroland to von Trotha's troops.

Among *Gravity's Rainbow*'s numerous other ghost figures at home on either side of the fictional interface, a few seem worthy of a glance here. In a sodium-pentathol-dream passage haunted by John F. Kennedy's memory—Slothrop recalls the Harvard classmate, we and the narrator the murdered president—Slothrop chases his harmonica down the toilet as he rings changes on "You never did the Kenosha Kid," the Kenosha Kid being, as Richard Poirier was first to recognize, Orson Welles.[6] In the country under the toilet there appears one "Crutchfield or Crouchfield, the westwardman" (67) and his "little [homosexual] pard" Whappo (68). Someone nearby is playing "Red River Valley" on a harmonica (Slothrop's lost one?), and I would suppose that Crutchfield and Whappo are ghost-overlays on John Wayne as Dunson and Montgomery Clift as the boy Matthew Garth in the classic John Hawkes western *Red River.* Wayne the old cattle driver, conquering prince of "this vast alkali plain" (68), adopts the boy Clift and carries on with him throughout the film a love-hate relationship in which one easily may read homosexual currents; Clift's homosexuality in real life is another clue. But Mark Richard Siegel plausibly sees in this episode an allusion to Conrad Aiken's poem "The Kid," about the half-mythical westwarding New Englander William Blackstone.[7] I suspect other overlays, including Jungian ones, as well.

We must wonder too about one Steve Edelman, compiler of the *Tales of the Schwarzkommando,* "Kabbalist spokesman" in the Raketen-Stadt, evidently a preterite champion; *edel* means valuable, precious, generous. As "a Hollywood businessman," he is suspected of subversion by "Richard M. Zhlubb, night manager of the Orpheus Theater" (754): "It is alleged that Edelman, in an unauthorized state of mind, attempted to

6. The first to make this identification in print was Richard Poirier in "Rocket Power," *Saturday Review: The Arts* 1 (March 3, 1973): 59–64.

7. See Mark Richard Siegel, *Pynchon: Creative Paranoia in "Gravity's Rainbow"* (Port Washington, N.Y.: Kennikat Press, 1978), pp. 48, 49. It might also be worth noting that Blackstone is mentioned in Hawthorne's *The Scarlet Letter,* perhaps the greatest American novel on the theme of Puritanism and its American legacy. Pynchon elsewhere unmistakably links the Hollywood Cowboy, whose archetype is John Wayne, with that ongoing legacy.

play a chord progression on the Department of Justice list" (755). Daniel Ellsberg? A Watergate figure (wasn't *Gravity's Rainbow* too early for Watergate?)?[8] Zhlubb's identity at least is perfectly clear: "fiftyish and jowled, with a permanent five o'clock shadow ... and a habit of throwing his arms up into an inverted 'peace sign'" (755). Elsewhere Pynchon plants a reference to Richard Nixon's own Whittier, California, from whence come the "Anglo vigilantes" who beat up preterite Ricky Gutiérrez (249); Nixon in person opens "The Counterforce" by saying "What?" In "this old theater" of America where we have "always been at the movies" (760), Zhlubb/Nixon is night manager—"Lord of the Night he is checking your tickets" (413), an earlier fantasy runs, though this time they are only bus tickets.

Zhlubb believes in closed systems: driving on the California freeways, he seals his limousine against the noise of Edelman-sponsored harmonica-playing freaks, whom he wants to lock up in a safe place near Disneyland. Inside the car he plays tapes from his vast library: "CHEERING (AFFECTIONATE), CHEERING (AROUSED), HOSTILE MOB in an assortment of 22 languages, YESES, NOES, NEGRO SUPPORTERS, WOMEN SUPPORTERS, ATHLETIC—oh, come now—" (756). When the limousine passes a funeral convoy—John F. Kennedy's?—Zhlubb sniffles, " 'He was one of the best. I couldn't go myself, but I did send a high-level assistant. Who'll ever replace him, I wonder,' punching a sly button under the dash. The laughter this time is sparse male *oh*-hoho's with an edge of cigar smoke and aged bourbon. Sparse but loud. Phrases like 'Dick, you character!' and 'Listen to *him*,' can also be made out" (756). An adenoidal condition makes Zhlubb talk funny; "friends and detractors alike," the narrator casually notes, "think of him as 'the Adenoid'" (754). And here thousands of eager readers go flipping back to the other end of the novel to make the connection: the Giant Adenoid rampaging through London in the fantasy that Pirate Prentice pirates from Lord Blatherard Osmo, a minor British desk diplomat occupied with the Novi Pazar question in Balkan politics before the Great War.[9] Though we feel

8. One critic has already suggested that Pynchon invented Watergate and named its characters: "Haldeman (dead-heap man), Ehrlichmann (nobleman), Kalmbach (quiet stream—still waters run deep, you know) ... And who else would have provided a secretary named Harmony, a group called the 'Plumbers,' with its star Egil Krogh (Eagle Crow) and its comically bewigged spy named Hunt. Pynchon

planted the sense of conspiracy and the actual discontinuities, irrationalities, incoherences, as well as the passionate faith of the doomed young subordinates." George Levine, "V-2," *Partisan Review* 40 (Fall 1973): 517–29.

9. As we might expect, the Sanjak of Novi Pazar (or Novibazar) is a real place and

the joke in the connection's "capricious line of attention," like William James's little beans, we also see a furtherance of the motif of closed versus open perceptual systems. "Osmo" becomes an ironic "osmosis," the seeping of matter or information across interfaces; Pirate absorbs Lord Osmo's fantasy, but the Adenoid by contrast is locked up in itself, besieged by a hostile Outside whose forces bring "*hods* full of the white substance [cocaine], in relays, up the ladders to smear on the throbbing gland creature, and into the germ toxins bubbling nastily inside its crypts, with no visible effects at all (though who knows how that *Adenoid* felt, eh?)" (16).

Here, yes, is Nixon at a Watergate press conference, hard-pressed, paranoid—"Alone in his tar circle, his chalk terror" (756), and Zhlubb, in turn, reaching for the knob of his car radio, trying for once to listen to the outside world—but, as the novel's first page has long ago prophesied, "It is too late" (3); the sirens announce "the last delta-t" of the rocket (760), as inside the Orpheus Theater the lamenting starers hold hands.

In the following pages I discuss the characters who, in the more usual sense of the term, Pynchon *has* invented; working from the top of their hierarchy downward, I examine along the way the manner of their arrangements there—in the paranoid labyrinth or "moire."

Them

"You're a novice paranoid, Roger.... Of course a well-developed They-system is necessary—but it's only half the story. For every They there ought to be a We. In our case there is. Creative paranoia means developing at least as thorough a We-system as a They-system—

"... I mean what They and Their hired psychiatrists call 'delusional systems.' Needless to say, 'delusions' are always officially defined. We don't have to worry about questions of real or unreal. They only talk out of expediency. It's the *system* that matters. How the data arrange themselves inside it ... delusions about ourselves, which I'm calling a We-system...."

"Delusions about ourselves?"

really played a small role in the development of Europe's pre-1914 Balkan neurosis. Of ambiguous ownership, the Sanjak buffered Montenegro and Serbia; Austro-Hungarian troops intermittently garrisoned its mountainous strip. After the Great War it was absorbed in Yugoslavia, but one can still see the town of Novi Pazar on a map.

"Not real ones."

"But officially defined."

"Out of expediency, yes."

"Well, you're playing Their game, then."

"Don't let it bother you. You'll find you can operate quite well. Seeing as we haven't won yet, it isn't really much of a problem." (638)

The passage paraphrases a formulation by the (hired?) psychiatrist R. D. Laing, in which "The We is a form of unification of a plurality composed by those who share the common experience of its ubiquitous invention among them."[10] Further,

> Each person [in a We-system] is expected to be controlled, and to control the others, by the reciprocal effect that each has on the other. To be affected by the others' actions or feelings is "natural" ... This reciprocal transpersonal cause-effect is a self-actualizing presumption....
>
> From outside, a group of Them may come into view ... it is still a type of unification imposed on a multiplicity, but this time those who invent the unification expressly do not themselves compose it ... The Them comes into view as a sort of social mirage. The Reds, the Whites, the Blacks, the Jews. In the human scene, such mirages can be self-actualizing. The invention of Them creates Us, and We may need to invent Them to reinvent Ourselves.[11]

Pynchon's people, of course, generally operate by these rules. They project what is what, who is who, as paranoid symbolizations of their particular transient states of mind, perils, predicaments. Their They-systems may overlap and interfere, forming complex "moires"—and any private system or any part of any moire may actually represent some plotted reality as known perhaps to the angels. These principles of "creative paranoia" should be intuitively familiar to any experienced reader of Pynchon.

That the forces of secular power, of business cartels and of government, provide the first and easiest of They-metaphors, is underlined by the narrator's occasional sly references to real postwar American paranoias: "so well have They busted the sod prairies of his brain, tilled and

10. R. D. Laing, *The Politics of Experience* (New York: Pantheon Books, 1967), pp. 60, 61.

11. Ibid.

sown there, and subsidized him not to grow anything of his own" (210). And on the opening page, in Pirate's dream, is a fantasy of elect VIP's who shepherd and differentiate Us: "Only the nearer faces are visible at all, and that only as half-silvered images in a view finder, green-stained VIP faces remembered behind bulletproof windows speeding through the city" (3).

Through the early frames the fantasy swells:

> Jessica notes a coal-black Packard up a side street, filled with dark-suited civilians. Their white collars rigid in the shadows.
>
> "Who're they?"
>
> He shrugs: "they" is good enough. "Not a friendly lot." (40)

And much later, in Zürich, Slothrop notices

> a black Rolls parked, motor idling, its glass tinted and afternoon so dark he can't see inside. Nice car. First one he's seen in a while, should be no more than a curiosity, except for
>
> Proverbs for Paranoids, 4: *You* hide, they seek. (262)

Is Slothrop, were Roger and Jessica, really under surveillance? Pointsman later regrets that "military intelligence" lost sight of Slothrop in Zürich, but, since Pointsman also is paranoid, his information is quite unreliable. Could Slothrop, projecting a They-system, somehow have "called up" the black Rolls and his own surveillance, as somehow he "calls up" rocket hits? A later passage (270 ff.) suggests that some at least of his sexual conquests in London were fantasies—yet the rockets still fell where his map showed stars. No less than the reader, the narrator looks desperately for any objective confirmation of They-systems but is never quite able to sort the "evidence" convincingly.

Thus when the narrator directs his glance as far up the hierarchy, toward Them, as ever in *Gravity's Rainbow,* the view is very suspiciously lurid, fantastic, unreal (615–16). British MP Sir Marcus Scammony is an absurdly effeminate high angel of secular power who calls himself Angelique: "Even in the chastisement room ... the foreplay is a game about who has the real power, who's had it all along ... the humiliations of pretty 'Angelique' are calibrated against their degree of fantasy" (616). So, it seems, is this fantasy of the narrator's calibrated on predictable paranoid symbolism. Sir Marcus reads *British Plastics,* refers to blacks as "target groups," and generates the inclusive symbolic mode in which power-mystique, perverse sex, and the white Inanimate are one: "Yes. Clive Mossmoon feels himself rising, as from a bog of trivial frustrations, political fears, money problems: delivered onto the sober shore of the Operation, where all is firm underfoot, where the self is a petty indulgent animal that once cried in its mired darkness. But here there is no whining, here inside the Operation. There is no lower self.... Each of us has his place, and the tenants come and go, but the places remain" (616).

The last sentence recapitulates Max Weber's description of power-slots as stably arrayed in the ideal bureaucracy—"Once established and having fulfilled its task, an office tends to continue in existence and be held by another incumbent."[12] Lower-ranking operatives like Clive Mossmoon may then cast languid, masochists' glances up the hierarchical levels, as paranoiacs or mystics may yearn to surrender themselves quasi-sexually to angelic orders—thus Rilke's First Duino Elegy, read most darkly: "Who, if I cried, would hear me from the order of Angels? And even if one suddenly held me to his heart: I would dissolve there from his stronger presence. For beauty is only the beginning of a terror we can just barely endure, and what we so admire is its calm disdaining to destroy us."[13]

If Angelique is marked as probably a superfluous fantasy of the narrator's, Laszlo Jamf and Lyle Bland comprehend on the other hand most of the book's major plot-nerves. Close to the angels as they are, both seem in some way apocryphal: Jamf is never seen directly, but only reconstructed, largely by Slothrop, and remembered, largely by Pökler; Bland appears only in one of the narrator's surreal fantasy-frames and, dimly, in Slothrop's childhood memory of an "Uncle Lyle" who used to visit the Slothrops' home. Slowly Slothrop discovers, or comes to imagine, or comes to accept planted "evidence" to the effect that these two men have conspired to frame his whole life from infancy. Jamf of Darmstadt came to Harvard on an academic grant, sometime late in the 1920s, where, on the model of the Watson-Rayner experiments in which an "Infant Albert" had been conditioned to feel reflex terror of all furry things (84), he conditioned Infant Tyrone to respond to a certain mysterious smell by getting an erection. The smell was— Slothrop comes to think, "though according to these papers it would have been too early for it" (286)—that of Imipolex G, an "erectile" poly-

12. Max Weber in *Wirtschaft und Gesellschaft*; quoted in *From Max Weber: Essays in Sociology,* trans. and ed. H. H. Gerth and C. Wright Mills (New York: Oxford University Press, 1958), p. 197.

13. Rainer Maria Rilke, *The Duino Elegies,* trans. Stephen Garmey and Jay Wilson (New York: Harper Colophon Books, 1972), First Duino Elegy, lines 1–7.

mer which Jamf developed, according to the accessible reports, *after* switching his field from behavioral psychology to organic chemistry: the initial (apparent) reversal of cause and effect in Slothrop's history. Broderick Slothrop agreed to let the I. G. Farben cartel of Germany pay for Tyrone's future education at Harvard and signed a contract committing the Slothrop Paper Company to manufacture the Notgeld banknotes of the calamitous German inflation of the early 1920s. Linkages for these various deals ran through Massachusetts businessman Lyle Bland, who had "arrangements" with German financier Hugo Stinnes, who, in historical fact, was widely suspected of having deliberately set off the German inflation by flooding the economy with Notgeld in order to get Germany out of paying its Versailles reparations. During the inflation, Laszlo Jamf sat on the board of directors of the Swiss Grössli Chemical Corporation, a firm soon to be incorporated into the Farben cartel (284). The Farben cartel in turn had linkages with German General Electric and, therefore, with American GE "under Swope, whose ideas on matters of 'control' ran close to those of Walter Rathenau, of German GE" (581), and later German foreign minister. In short, Slothrop is enabled to discover that he has been "sold to IG Farben like a side of beef" (286) and has been under surveillance since the original Jamf experiment. His facility for predicting rocket strikes is somehow bound as a strand in a web of international corporate plotting to which World War II itself may be only incidental.

Slothrop wistfully watches his comicbook heroes flow out of and past their confining frames, but Laszlo Jamf is the novel's own real, hard-ass Plasticman. In their usual connotation in *Gravity's Rainbow*, plastics mean "synthesis and control"; the intricate reticulations of synthetically structured molecules, like the most labyrinthine paranoid plots, like the flow charts of the Farben cartel's bureaucracy, reify a will-to-structure that yields the Jamfian mystique, "Plasticity's virtuous triad of Strength, Stability, and Whiteness ... how often these were taken for Nazi graffiti" (250). Franz Pökler remembers the aging Jamf's lectures on "National Socialist chemistry," which contemned the soft, organic carbon bond, where electrons are merely shared, and exalted the ionic, the inorganic, by whose strategy "electrons are not shared, but *captured. Seized!* and held! polarized plus and minus, these atoms, no ambiguities" (577)—restating the binary determinism of Pointsman's behaviorism, silicon-nitrogen bonding giving sign of the SiN that is actualized by both points of view. The gray plastic sheets that billow around Greta Erdmann in the petrochemical plant and that "flared like the northern lights" (487) thus bond with the flaring aurorae, "ghosts of the North" (29), that spooked Slothrop's childhood. Blicero in drag wears a false cunt made in part of Mipolam, "the new polyvinyl chloride" (95)—studded with stainless steel blades so that Katje may imitate cunnilingus and then trail blood-kisses down Gottfried's back. Plastics—inanimation, whiteness, sexual perversion—are for polarizing, excluding middles, tracing out lines of control and deathly libido to wire Us back to the Angels: "Slothrop's erection hums from a certain distance, like an instrument installed, wired by Them into his body as a colonial outpost here in our raw and clamorous world, another office representing Their white metropolis far away" (285).

The hardon-that-points-to-the-sky alludes, further, to the character who is, among other symbolic functions, a sort of higher, more abstract power of Slothrop: as the latter gets straightforward hardons for rockets, Captain Blicero sees V-2 as a symbolic-phallic means to penetrate absolute Being, angelic orders. The real name, as *V.* tells us, is Weissmann (an already symbolic enough "white man"), but he assumes the SS code name "Blicero" for, presumably, its irresistible etymologies of bleaching, blankness—even of Bleicheröde, a real Harz town near the white rocket's home at *Nord*hausen. Blicero obviously thus caricatures the German and northern style of mystic obsessiveness and, as a Nazi, we might say, caricatures the caricature. He "embraces" the "Reich's flame" (98) in the moth's manner and reads Rilke's Sonnet 12 of Part II of *Orpheus*, "Want the Change ... O be inspired by the Flame!" as the call, simply, of voluptuous death. He finds it exciting that the rockets often go out of control after launch, falling back on the men, "making them as much target as launch site" (86), destroyers and destroyed. Enzian, who knows him best, "even in Südwest ... had seen *that*: a love for the last explosion—the lifting and the scream that peaks past fear.... Surely he'd have found something splendid enough to match his thirst" (324). Wagner, for one, as Hitler also knew, is splendid enough: Blicero's last long speech to Gottfried (722 ff.) is one of those "ungodly coloraturas" (465) that Thanatz remembers; Pökler notices that Blicero's eyeglasses are "like Wagnerian shields" (416). Inside a more intimate myth, a *Märchen*, Blicero plays a drag witch to Gottfried's and Katje's Hansel and Gretel. The familiar *Volk*-frame provides shelter against an outside that "none of them can bear—the War, the absolute rule of chance, their own pitiable contingency here, in its midst" (96). Blicero voluptuously knows the destiny of the witch: to fall "out of the winter, inside the Oven's warmth, darkness, steel shelter, the door behind him in a narrowing rectangle of kitchen-light gonging shut forever. The rest is foreplay" (99). A Nazi irony: surely Dora's ovens, Buchenwald's, helped frame the feeling, obscenely candy-house sweet with the help of the *Märchen,* that the destroyers were playing at a sort of deathly sadomasochistic incest with the destroyed.

Blicero's paranoia is of the megalomaniacal kind described by Freud as based in homosexual libido combined with an ambivalence about the father image. The alienated libido withdraws its normal connectedness, or its love, from the world and implodes into itself; all people outside become irrelevant, mechanical, "cursory contraptions," as the self tries to establish new "cathexes," this time with some metaphysical power-image by which the self is both exalted and threatened. Freud's 1911 paper,[14] surely an influence on Pynchon's conception of Blicero, diagnosed the case of Herr Dr. jur. Daniel Paul Schreber, once Senatspräsident in Dresden, from a memoir written by Schreber when his delusional system was still intact. In the mature psychosis, Schreber believed that God planned to change him gradually into a woman and then to impregnate him with a race of superbeings who would redeem mankind. (It is impossible here not to think of Pynchon's description of the mushroom cloud of Hiroshima as "a giant white cock, dangling in the sky straight downward out of a white pubic bush" [693].) Schreber's body, he believed, was threaded by a network of "nerves of voluptuousness," "as women have"; he was "God's wife." The pleasure of merging with God in sex, with God playing the male part, is very much like the bliss enjoyed by the dying—since at death a man's nerves merge with God's and with those of higher "soul-complexes." God is two beings who sometimes contend with each other: a lower God who favors the dark races and a higher God who favors Aryans. The language of God is an archaic form of German. God's image sometimes merged with that of Schreber's physician, Flechsig, who continually sought to persecute (castrate or homosexually assault) Schreber; Freud of course explained both Flechsig and God as sublimations of Schreber's affectionate but severely punitive father. God did not really understand living men (being used to dead ones: Schreber's father had been a physician) and sometimes tried to kill or castrate exceptional men; God often tried also to prevent Schreber from defecating, sending someone to the bathroom to prevent it, then derisively asking Schreber,

14. Sigmund Freud, "Psychoanalytic Notes Upon an Autobiographical Account of a Case of Paranoia (Dementia Paranoides)," in Freud, *Three Case Histories* (1911; reprint ed., New York: Collier Books, 1963).

"Why can't you shit?" A successful shit, when it came, was "spiritually voluptuous." Finally, in the all-pervasive, shimmering "nerves" of God, sometimes sun rays, sometimes divine spermatozoa, which for Schreber animated the natural world, Freud saw not merely a degenerative symptom of the disease but a symbolization of the self's unconscious attempts to heal itself. Projecting these cathexes, Schreber tried to reestablish connectedness, for "the paranoiac builds [the world] up again, not more splendid, it is true, but at least so that he can once more live in it. He builds it up by the work of his delusions … the man has recaptured a relation, and often a very intense one, to the people and things in the world, although the relation may be a hostile one now, where formerly it was sympathetic."[15]

And years later, still more generally, in *Totem and Taboo*:

> There is an intellectual function in us which demands unity, connection and intelligibility from any material, whether of perception or thought, that comes within its grasp; and if, as a result of special circumstances, it is unable to establish a true connection, it does not hesitate to fabricate a false one. Systems constructed in this way are known to us not only from dreams, but also from phobias, from obsessive thinking and from delusions. The construction of systems is seen most strikingly in delusional disorders (in paranoia), where it dominates the symptomatic picture.[16]

I cannot agree with Siegel and others who want to take Captain Blicero largely positively, as an inspired mystic and charismatic prophet who seeks to transcend a dull, rationalized world. He does fit this mold in a sense, but his charisma is all negation of life, as is made explicit in, for one thing, its expression as homosexual lust: "Death in its ingenuity has contrived to make the father and son beautiful to each other as life has made male and female" (723). The madness into which Greta and Thanatz remember him falling at the end may be a Freudian withdrawal and implosion—"his eyes rolled clear up into his head" (465)—which presages his final building of a sexual cathexis, through Gottfried and the V-2, with death. At the final ascent, his "I want to break out—to leave this cycle of infection and death" (724) can be taken to point to a positive kind of "transcendence," as Siegel takes it, only if we interpret the "cycle" in question as Their rationalized, death-serving order. But if, instead, the cycle is that greater one to which *Gravity's*

15. Ibid., p. 174.

16. Sigmund Freud, *Totem and Taboo*, trans. James Strachey (New York: W. W. Norton & Co., 1950), p. 95.

Rainbow constantly directs its awe—the ring-continuity of the organic creation—then Blicero's vicarious ascent is an active denial of life and of life's soul-force, which is gravity, to which the final ascent is "betrayed" (758) when the rocket starts falling from its parabola's peak. Blicero's imagination is wholly of sky, hardly at all connected to the book's earthly life; whatever rises simply to escape and negate gravity will be thrown back to that Earth that, as Rilke affirmed, is the matrix both of life *and* death. At book's end Blicero may well have simply become—as the 175's, homosexual prison-camp inmates, believe—an earthly refugee, on the loose somewhere, his evil unconquered, like Iago or like any escaped Nazi killer: "He's out there ... alive and on the run" (667).

Dr. Ned Pointsman, unlike Blicero, is seen in consistently sharp focus, most particularly in the first reel, where long passages describe his personal manner, eccentricities, fantasies, dreams, even rare impulses to kindness: "Here is someone he wants, truly, with all his mean heart, to see preserved ... though he's been too shy, or proud, ever to've smiled at Gwenhidwy without some kind of speech to cancel out the smile" (171). With his talent for bureaucracy, he smoothly plays They for many others: Slothrop, Pirate Prentice, Roger and Jessica, Katje, and spectacularly for Brigadier Pudding. Jessica feels "a bleakness whenever she meets him. Scientist-neutrality" (58), but at least Pointsman "knows in a general way what it is; he's creepy. He's even aware, usually, of the times when he's *being* creepy" (141). In one visible bonding, when Sir Marcus Scammony holds him "in disgrace" (615), Pointsman even becomes one of Us. In the hierarchy's reaches above him, in other words, there is visible space, and he can act complexly, sometimes in part sympathetically.

For this positivist, paranoia is simply the necessary conclusion from one's empirical observations. He cannot accept chance. When five friends are killed in ways that look dialectically patterned—jeep accident, bomb, artillery, V-1, V-2—he feels that the deaths must reveal some plot, however "transmarginal": "mummy's curse, you idiot" (139). The supersonic V-2 spooks him, as indeed it must have spooked many in 1944, with its mirage of cause and effect reversal: one heard the final explosion before one heard the incoming scream. The phenomenon seems to Pointsman somehow a solemn allusion to the Slothropian hardons' "predicting" rocket strikes. Even though Jamf had conditioned Slothrop with something that, Pointsman presumes, is now part of the rocket, still the "response" precedes the "stimulus" by as much sometimes as several days. If the sacred principle of strict causal determinism is to be held inviolate, Pointsman's only recourse is to believe that in some way the stimulus was already "here"—that the universe is, quite as Slothrop's Puritan ancestors thought, a subtle tissue of predestination: "But if it's in the air, right here, right now, then the rockets follow from it, 100% of the time. No exceptions. When we find it, we'll have shown again the stone determinacy of everything, of every soul. You can see how important a discovery like that would be" (86). In such a willed belief Pointsman is, he says, "not grandiose ... [but] modest, methodical" (89). And yet in his favorite fantasy he is a sort of schlemihl-hero Theseus penetrating causality's labyrinth, "Once, only once," with no Ariadne or thread to lead him back out. As he masturbates to the fantasy, reaching the "central chamber," the Minotaur turning its face, the hero "begins to expand, an uncontainable light, as the walls of the chamber turn a blood glow, orange, then white and begin to slip, to flow like wax, what there is of the labyrinth collapsing in rings outward, hero and horror, engineer and Ariadne consumed, molten inside the light of himself, the mad exploding of himself" (143).

But self-pityingly he thinks, They don't authorize private orgasmic apocalypses of this kind; "The intermediaries have come long since between himself and his final beast. They would deny him even the little perversity of being in love with his death" (143). Pointsman settles instead for the worldly fantasy of winning the Nobel Prize—although, given the hopeless outdatedness of his scientism, there is no hope for this "rational" kind of transcendence, either. He can elicit pity as, near the end, he moves toward old age and a thoroughly commonplace death, his sterile philosophy guaranteeing that "his mineral corridors do not shine" (753).

As Pynchon had pointed out earlier (see *Lot 49*, 76), the British railroad term *pointsman* denotes the man who throws the switch at some critical junction to change the configurations of tracks. Causal-deterministic history metaphorically plotted as railroad grid, then, is subject to the powerful local control of "faceless" pointsmen who cause binary dividings of routes:

> Skippy, you little fool, you are off on another of your senseless and retrograde journeys. Come back, here, to the points. Here is where the paths divided. See the man back there. He is wearing a white hood. His shoes are brown. He has a nice smile, but nobody sees it. Nobody sees it because his face is always in the dark. But he is a nice man. He is the pointsman. He is called that because he throws

the lever that changes the points. And we go to Happyville, instead of [Rilke's Tenth Elegy's] Pain City. (644)

The paranoia here is the narrator's own; it is the fear that They have designated just such unknowing employees—for example, in an earlier fantasy, "personnel like Liebig" (411)—to pull critical switches to route history along Their preferred paths. And it is the half-conscious belief of Pointsman himself that Ivan Petrovitch Pavlov was just such an employee; after his behaviorist hero, Pointsman would like to confirm the routing of science, philosophy, history onto the path of control by verifying the principle of control that is deterministic physics and metaphysics: "You can see how important a discovery like that would be."

Pynchon lets us hear the Russian master's own voice when, on page 89, Pointsman closely paraphrases the Open Letter to Pierre Janet, which in Pavlov's original sounds like this: "A truly mechanical interpretation is still the goal of natural-science research: the study of reality as a whole, including ourselves, is advancing very slowly toward this goal.... Modern natural science as a whole is but a series of many *stages of approximation* to this mechanical interpretation, stages linked throughout by the supreme principle of causality or determinism, according to which there is no action without cause."[17]

Just as Pointsman reports, Pavlov thought of the cerebral cortex as a "mosaic" or "switchboard" of discrete points, each open to the imposition of a reflex; his explanation of paranoia, as given in the Janet letter and its companion essay,[18] also cited by Pointsman, is paraphrased in *Gravity's Rainbow*, page 90. According to the theory, a point of a lab animal's cortex, if overstimulated or contradictorily stimulated by the researcher, may become "pathologically inert" and damp by "negative induction" all points around it. The result is a transnormal psychological state, such as the "ultraparadoxical," in which positive stimuli evoke negative responses. Pavlov understood paranoid psychosis as just such a "confusion of ideas of the opposite"; as Pavlov paraphrases Pierre Janet, with whose symptomatic description, at least, he agrees, paranoiacs "want to be independent, but they are adamant in believing that

17. I. P. Pavlov, "Feelings of Possession (*Les Sentiments d'Emprise*) and the Ultra-paradoxical Phase (Open Letter to Prof. Pierre Janet)," in Pavlov, *Psychopathology and Psychiatry* (Moscow: Foreign Languages Publishing House, 195[?]), p. 308.

18. I. P. Pavlov, "Attempt at a Phys-

iological Interpretation of Compulsive Neurosis and Paranoia," *Psychopathology and Psychiatry*, pp. 309–24. See also Lecture 13 in Pavlov, *Conditioned Reflexes*, G. V. Anrep, trans. & ed. (New York: Oxford University Press, 1927).

other people regard them as slaves who are obliged to execute orders. They want to be respected, but it seems to them that they are being insulted. They want to have their own secrets, but it appears to them that their secrets are constantly being disclosed."[19]

This recalls the Freudian postulation of projection/introjection/mirror reversal of homosexual libido in paranoia, from unconscious *I love him* to perceived *he hates me*. But Janet, foreshadowing modern revisionist psychiatrists like R. D. Laing, defended these epistemologies of the mad, since in truth, he believed, "these contrasts are not so easily distinguishable…. *To tell* and *to be told* form a single whole and the one is not easily distinguished from the other…. *The act of insulting and the act of being insulted* are united by the general concept of insult."[20] Pavlov of course took issue with such holistic speculations, and Pointsman smugly concurs: "Pierre Janet—sometimes the man talked like an Oriental mystic. He had no real grasp of the opposites. 'The act of injuring and the act of being injured are joined in the behavior of the whole injury.' Speaker and spoken-of, master and slave … The last refuge of the incorrigibly lazy, Mexico, is just this sort of yang-yin rubbish" (88). But on the bleak Channel beach, in Pointsman's "aural hallucination" at the end of Reel Two, " 'Yang and Yin,' whispers the Voice, 'Yang and Yin …' " (278).

The cruelty into which Pointsman can fall is thus shown to be a consequence of his rigidly rationalistic assumptions, his inability to feel Yang and Yin becoming an inability to feel others' pain: "Hands that could as well torture people as dogs and never feel their pain" (58), thinks Jessica. Pavlov distinguished types of nervous constitutions among his dogs, observing that some, of the "strong" type, were especially resistant to ultraparadoxical conditioning—inducement of madness—but, once conditioned, were especially subject to "chronic pathological inertness"—continuation in madness. "Of course," Pavlov added, "by intensifying the pathogenic procedures it was possible, in the long run, to overcome, break down also the balanced strong type, especially if some organic trauma, for example, castration, was added beforehand."[21] This passage, where it waits for us outside the novel,

19. Pavlov, "Feelings of Possession," pp. 303, 304.

20. Ibid., pp. 304, 305. Pointsman and Pynchon in *Gravity's Rainbow* use another translation of this passage, that of Dr. Horsley Gantt, as acknowledged on p. 88.

21. Pavlov, "Physiological Interpreta-

tion," p. 316. Pavlov's prose gives every tonal sign that, like Pointsman, he lacked the ability to think of his dogs nonclinically. E.g.: "Such [nervous and vivacious] animals, when they get acquainted with men, which they do very quickly and easily, often become annoying

clarifies Pointsman's hints, inside, of his plans for Slothrop: "a strong imperturbable. It won't be easy to send him into any of the three phases. We may finally have to starve, terrorize, I don't know ... it needn't come to that" (90). Much later in the book, Spontoon, one of the agents sent to castrate the man in the pig suit, says admiringly of Pointsman, "Let's hope he never turns to a life of crime, eh?" (609). But he already has. The terror of this castration scene, under the moon's "perfect ice" on the beach, achieves the truly ultraparadoxical effect of winning our pity for, of all people, Major Marvy:

> "Hey, hey, hey. Not me, I'm a *major*." He should be more emphatic about this, more convincing. Maybe it's the 'sucking pig mask in the way. Only he can hear his voice, now given back entirely to himself, flatter, metallic ... they can't hear him. "Major Duane Marvy." They don't believe him, don't believe his name. Not even *his name*. (608)

The magical act of naming is undone, mirror-reversed: after this point Marvy disappears from the book, while Slothrop, the real target, is at this moment making love (610)—his apt reply to an attempted castration, but the knowledge of it inaccessible to him, in the plot's "perfect ice."

Major Marvy, Bloody Chiclitz, Géza Rózsavölgyi, Jeremy Beaver, Hilary Bounce, Teddy Bloat, I. G. Verbindungsmann Wimpe—these are among the book's minor demons, unknowing legmen in service of Them. Marvy is of course a cartoon of a *Volk*-fascist American-style, his tendencies loud and pure:

> OH ... thur's
> Nazis in the woodwork,
> Fascists in the walls,
> Little Japs with bucktooth grins
> A-gonna grab yew bah th' balls.
> Whin this war is over,
> How Happy Ah will be,
> Gearin' up fer thim Rooskies
> And Go-round Number Three. (314)

He is an education for Slothrop in the American sound and sense of

---

by their continuous demonstrativeness" (*Conditioned Reflexes*, Lecture 12). This lecture may be the source of the incident of Pointsman's trying to adopt a dog "of his own, outside the lab," because somebody tells him that to do so would make him "more human, warmer" (52). But Glou-

cestershire, the springer spaniel, turns out to be a failure: "It could open doors to the rain and the spring insects, but not close them ... knock over garbage, vomit on the floor, but not clean it up—how could *anyone* live with such a creature?" (52).

closed-system certainties and brutalities, as are also the voices of the MP's in the hallways of the Zürich hotel:

> American voices, country voices, high-pitched and without mercy.... For possibly the first time he is hearing America as it must sound to a non-American. Later he will recall that what surprised him most was the fanaticism, the reliance not just on flat force but on the *rightness* of what they planned to do. (256)

But Marvy, unlike these MP's, is dimly conscious of his function as minor field agent for "General Electric ... Dillon, Reed ... Standard Awl ..." (565). And, alike in Their and Pynchon's designs, he is expendable: as he couples with the prostitute Manuela in Putzi's pool, the ice is invisibly closing, and Muffage and Spontoon are sharpening Pointsman's knives (cf. Chiclitz's dim-witted prophecy long ago, "instead of fucker thou become fuckee" [559]). The plot, with no further use for Marvy, slices him out very literally "bah th' balls."

Much more highly placed in the hierarchy is V-Mann Wimpe the organic chemist, employee of I. G. Farben, colleague of Jamf, and prophet of Jamf's Oneirine. His Kartellized version of the general obsession with structure, design, and dividedness is revealed as he raptly explains to Tchitcherine the molecular structures of artificial opium alkaloids:

> German dope in amazing profusion ... "Here is Eucodal—a codeine with two hydrogens, a hydroxyl, a hydrochloride"—gesturing in the air around his basic fist—"hanging off different parts of the molecule." Among these patent medicines, trappings and detailing were half the game—"As the French do with their dresses, nicht wahr? a ribbon here, a pretty buckle there, to help sell a sparer design." (345)

The "design" that the cartel seeks, Wimpe says, is that of a miracle drug that will kill pain without causing addiction, since private addictions, private demands, are by their nature incalculable: "A rational economy cannot depend on psychological quirks. We could not *plan*" (349). The immense openness of the carbon atom's bonding potential, the capacity of the life-chains for variety, must be rationalized. Wimpe—to whom I return later—is a sort of minor Jamf whom we hardly know, himself a critical bonding point or switchpoint for the plot, helping to connect Tchitcherine with Germany and I. G. Farben, with Enzian, the rocket, and all the rest of "Pynchon's Paranoid History."[22]

22. This phrase is the title of an article by Scott Sanders in *Twentieth Century* *Literature* 21 (1975): 177–92.

Them and Us

The next class of characters, the largest, is that composed of people trapped, knowingly or not, somewhere in the "middle"—lost in the moire between Them and Us. Its most sympathetic members are the founders of the Counterforce: ex-employees of Them who, now contrite, are trying to return to life. Although the chief of these are Katje Borgesius and Pirate Prentice, the heroically ineffectual, schlemihl-like Counterforce spirit is perhaps caught best by the voice of Sir Stephen Dodson-Truck, who, redemptively incompetent through his brief career of spying on Slothrop, confesses drunkenly to the latter: "I'm the perfect man for [observing you and Katje in sex]. Perfect. I can't even masturbate half the time ... no nasty jissom getting all over their reports, you know. Wouldn't want that. Just a neuter, just a recording eye ... They're so cruel.... They aren't even sadists ... There's just *no passion at all*" (216).

Thus passionless, They have turned, for example, Pirate Prentice's talent for penetrating the fantasies of others to the uses of "terrible paper gaming" (14). One paranoid night at the movies, his guilt surfacing, Pirate "identifies" with one Lucifer Amp, a scrofulous exhibitionist in a newsreel. Amp, says the documentary voice, loiters in front of a ruined East End hotel—quite possibly the one in Pirate's dream of the Evacuation on the novel's first page—and is an ex-employee, a fallen Lucifer, of the Special Operations Executive. Or at least a supposed ex-employee: SOE man Pirate hears or fantasizes a voice from the row of seats behind him, in paranoid explication—"You hear? 'Used to work.' That's rich, that is. No one has ever left the Firm alive" (543). Pirate, determined to do just that, rushes out of the theater. Further, this straightforward, officer-caste "Chapel" man's decision to rebel against Them may owe something to his old, clumsily hopeless love for Scorpia Mossmoon, wife of ICI executive Clive.

The history of Katje Borgesius is much more complex. Her initial employment is for conventional wartime espionage: she transmits German rocket data to England and works with the Dutch underground and with SOE. She contacts Pirate, after her escape from Blicero, at a windmill interestingly called "The Angel" (106). Her next orders, indirectly from Pointsman, are to join Slothrop at the Casino Hermann Goering (the knowledge of Octopus Grigori's role as intermediary is kept from her), there to brief Slothrop for his rocket-quest. The scene of her appearance out of the sea as love-bait for Slothrop subtly begins a pattern of suggestion by which Pynchon makes her an aspect of that force of Venus, V-ness, which, as the same motif moves through *V.*, drafts the great Botticelli painting as icon:

> Well ... she must have come out of the sea. At this distance ... she is only a dim figure ... her bare legs long and straight, a short hood of bright blond hair keeping her face in shadow.... She only continues to stand, the breeze pushing at her sleeves. (186)

> Katje's skin is whiter than the white garment she rises from. *Born again* ... out the window he can almost see the spot where the devilfish crawled in from the rocks. (196)

Later, she may be said to play Venus to Slothrop's Tannhäuser and Greta Erdmann's "helpless Lisaura" (393)—holding Slothrop in thrall at the Casino as V-2 holds him briefly under the mountain at Nordhausen.

Katje's multiple framing inside this and several other extrinsic allusions constitutes Pynchon's own design-metaphor for the fact of her growing bondage to, and external definition by, Them. As she and Slothrop stand by a roulette table in the Himmler Spielsaal at the casino, he feels her "European darkness" (208), sees the "futureless look" (209) in her eyes "behind blonde lashes full of acid green," above "one of those thin-lipped European mouths" (187). The suggestion is of Marlene Dietrich, perhaps particularly in the 1931 film *Dishonored*, in which Dietrich, playing a Mata Hari-like Austrian spy, had a vamping scene at the gaming tables with a man she would later betray. In Blicero's "little state," Katje plays Gretel, more active, resourceful, and firmly committed against the witch than Gottfried's passive Hansel. "Borgesius" surely alludes to Lucretia Borgia, perhaps also to Jorge Luis Borges, maker of labyrinths, proclaimed admirer of spy thrillers. But inside all these frames, from the very beginning, Katje is restless, with a guilty, nervous impatience that is her integrity, her clarity, and to which style refers by always describing, *seeing* Katje so clearly. Her characteristic "tough, young isolate's shrug and stride" (107) is her way of expressing resistance to framing. Blicero has schooled her in "European darkness"—for example, in the understanding of "the great airless arc [of the rocket's parabola] as a clear allusion to certain secret lusts that drive the planet and herself, and Those who use her—over its peak and down, plunging, burning, toward a terminal orgasm" (223). But her instinct below the schooling is always to quit Their game. And yet her moral commitment, that of the Counterforce, against Them, means that at the end, although she is what Enzian calls "set free" (661), she wants to go back "in," find Slothrop and make it all up to him, ask "How can They be stopped?" (662). Thus, like the majority of Pynchon's people but with more conscious agony and ambivalence than any others of them, she is lost in the world-moires; though she gravitates toward freedom, selflessness, invisibility, her strong self pulls her back into guilt, commitment, framing.

To the extent that such commitment is masochistic, it points us to the large metaphorical role of perverse, and especially sadomasochistic, sexuality in evoking the feel of living these "middle" lives. The both/and indeterminacy of the sadomasochist metaphor for connection is suggested by, for one thing, Pirate's talent for penetrating others' fantasies—metaphorical rape or communion? And the indeterminacy is perhaps best of all displayed in the surreal frame beginning on page 537, where Katje and Pirate find themselves in what seems to be a kind of hell or limbo for Their discarded employees. The frame's first line, "Who would have thought so many would be here?" (537), conjures *The Waste Land's* "I had not thought death had undone so many," and, via one of Eliot's slyly self-parodic scholarly footnotes, Canto III of Dante's *Inferno*, where the souls of those who in life had served different masters opportunistically now race endlessly after a banner fleeing before them in hell's vestibule. In Pirate's redaction, the endless chase has become a labyrinthine taffy-pull, the souls winding taffy ropes from room to room, getting perpetually entangled in each others' sticky guilts. In the surrounding set, all is glassy and brittle, refracting—"Everyone here seems to be *at least* a double agent" (543)—with the mirrors facing also inward: "I can't even trust myself? can I" (543). "Heresies" are vaguely mentioned but never defined; there are spectral committees meeting behind closed doors, and a "devil's advocate" discourses on Their intentions—we can't tell how meaningfully or reliably, since we don't know who defines devil. This splintered, urbanized hell, where mirrors fragment the self's image, is a symbolization of the kind of guilt one buys in working for Them: "[Pirate] turns his face upward, and looks up through all the faintly superimposed levels above ... all the clanging enterprise and bustle of all those levels, extending further than Pirate or Katje can see for the moment, he lifts his long, his guilty, his permanently enslaved face to the illusion of sky, to the reality of pressure and weight from overhead" (548).

The multiply mirrored guilt-fetishism recalls the sexual fetishism of V. in Paris, watching her lover Melanie pose between mirrors. V. wants to engulf the other, romantically, but sees also that the other is her, V.'s, mirror self; as facing mirrors fragment and disperse the image, Melanie becomes an "impersonation" of V. and of V.'s secret, which is death, inanimation. But here the indeterminacy enters: the breaking or transcending of the self's frames might always point either to death, or subversively, simultaneously, to unities, reassemblies, of life. The heterogeneous sexual fantasy that "passes" for Pirate and Katje in limbo is as equivocal as everything else there, since, again, we cannot identify its creator(s) or sponsor(s). A caption coyly debunks the fantasy as "horny Anonymous's ... megalomaniac master plan of sexual love with every individual one of the People in the *World* ... a rough definition of 'loving the People'" (547). The spectacle is a porn parody, proposing sex and love as mechanical rape-penetration: Their notion of human connectedness as a perverse power game. We think here of Angelique and of Wimpe's distrust of "private demands." But, as Thanatz suggests in making his case for Counterforce sadomasochism, out of the They-metaphor might unfold, at any time, a subversive We-metaphor: "Why will the Structure allow every other kind of sexual behavior but *that* one? Because submission and dominance are resources it needs for its very survival. They cannot be wasted in private sex. In *any* kind of sex. It needs our submission so that it may remain in power. It needs our lusts after dominance so that it can co-opt us into its own power game. There is no joy in it, only power. I tell you, if S and M could be established universally, at the family level, the State would wither away" (737).

This speech in turn is undercut by the fact that Thanatz is using it as a come-on to Ludwig, to seduce him into being an *object* of sex. Conversely, the sexual fantasy in limbo is followed, subverted, by a sudden upwelling of tender rhetoric, as if mirrors have shattered: "And they do dance: though Pirate never could before, very well ... they feel quite in touch with all the others as they move, and if they are never to be at full ease, still it's not parade rest any longer ... so they dissolve now, into the race and swarm of this dancing Preterition, and their faces, the dear, comical faces they have put on for this ball, fade, as innocence fades, grimly flirtatious, and striving to be kind" (548).

In that Pirate and Katje are at least conscious of their confusions, ambivalences, about matters of dominance and submission, they contrast very favorably with characters who either surrender completely, with straightforward masochism, to manipulation (Greta Erdmann), or foolishly think they can detach themselves from structures and attain the safe side of the angels (Gerhardt von Göll), or indulge befuddledly in variations and combinations of these responses (Brigadier Pudding). In moments of "grace" Slothrop tries to ride the "network of all plots" (603), hoping that transferring onto and off different lines "may yet carry him to freedom" (603). But Greta, Der Springer, and Pudding have no such resourcefulness, perhaps because they can somehow "see" the grand moire itself, whose image indeed dominates these characters' stories more than any others': "What happens when paranoid meets paranoid? A crossing of solipsisms. Clearly. The two patterns create a third: a moire, a new world of flowing shadows, interferences" (395).

When this comment intrudes, Greta and Slothrop are meeting in the old Neubabelsberg movie studios, on the set of an old film of Gerhardt von Göll's. In the lighting scheme, Greta explains, "The light came from above and below at the same time, so that everyone had two shadows: Cain's and Abel's, Gerhardt told us. It was at the height of his symbolist period" (394).

Here again we touch Pynchon's brilliant experimentation with movie mimeses—as well as his interest in the lurid, pretentious, humorless films of the German Expressionist period. As Slothrop and Greta stand on the set of *Alpdrücken*, a movie in which Greta starred, she reminisces about her time with von Göll. By the end of Pynchon's frame she is strapped to *Alpdrücken*'s torture rack as of old; Slothrop has reluctantly beaten her and is now having sex with her. In her orgasm she screams her daughter Bianca's name—and a cool ellipsis on Pynchon's page detaches us and leads us across the row of frame-squares and, on the other side, to Franz Pökler in sex with Leni, recalling the torture rack scene in *Alpdrücken*, planting the seed of Ilse, as Thanatz, Schlepzig, or someone had planted the seed of Bianca during the filming. Across film's interfaces are mixed, lasciviously, Bianca and Ilse, von Göll and Pökler, sadist director and masochist starer, the Manichaean/paranoid world of Expressionist films and the similarly textured one of the Weimar Berlin streets. As Pynchon puts it:

> [Ilse] was conceived because her father saw a movie called
> *Alpdrücken* one night and got a hardon. Pökler in his horny staring
> had missed the Director's clever Gnostic symbolism in the lighting
> scheme of the two shadows, Cain's and Abel's. But Ilse, some Ilse,
> has persisted beyond her cinema mother, beyond film's end, and so
> have the shadows of shadows. In the Zone, all will be moving under
> the Old Dispensation, inside the Cainists' light and space: not out
> of any precious Göllerei, but because the Double Light was always
> there, outside all film, and that shucking and jiving moviemaker

> was the only one around at the time who happened to notice it and
> use it, although in deep ignorance, then and now, of what he was
> showing the nation of starers. (429)

"Deep ignorance" is indeed a good general tag for Gerhardt von Göll, "once an intimate and still the equal of Lang, Pabst, Lubitsch" (112), whose interest in light-shadow plays survives his later change of professions. After the war he becomes obsessed with the parapolitical; perhaps, like the Schwarzkommando he claims to have actualized, the "paracinematic" black-market grid. By a cognate metaphor, when von Göll first meets Slothrop, "The mackerel sky has begun to look less like a moire, and more like a chessboard" (494), for von Göll is now, he has decided, Der Springer, the chess knight who leaps above, "transcends," the board's patterns: "Elite and preterite, we move through a cosmic design of darkness and light, and in all humility, I am one of the very few who can comprehend it *in toto*" (495). In fact, though, he cannot escape the moire in which elect and preterite "define each other" (495), any more than, in mad King Ludwig's Herrenchiemsee palace, he could resist "those *long corridors* … von Göll, long after running out of film, still dollying with a boobish smile on his face down the golden vistas" (394). As Der Springer, he tries to come on as The Man, fully in control— "about 50, bleak and neutral-colored eyes" (494)—careful to wear *white* suits, like a self-made angel, as he manipulates the preterite *black* market. He appears briefly in Pirate's limbo, which might suggest a return to some sort of grace; but when last seen he is lost, appropriately, inside one of his own movies and is now a sodium amytal freak, in memory of the occasion when he had been rendered ludicrously incompetent by this drug while Slothrop and Närrisch labored to save him from Tchitcherine's men: "Närrisch, we're risking our ass for *this slob*?" (514). He is not, finally, the directorial figure of power behind the cameras, above the board, that he thinks he is, but rather a loser—a pawn, not a knight—self-conning in his white suits.

Greta Erdmann, the former porn star, is aware of but masochistically reconciled to her volitionlessness, her former roles having taught her sex-object immobility: "I never seemed to *move*. Not even my face … it could have been the same frame, over and over" (394). The frame that begins "It was always easy for men to come and tell her who to be" (482) paraphrases Greta's account of her life to Slothrop and is subdivided, "the same frame over and over," in that the dominant image in all of the short features is that of a deeply buried blackness, black flowing mud. In the preapocalyptic summer of 1939, Greta had murdered several Jewish children and thrown them into the black radioactive mud of a Prussian spa that Pynchon cutely names Bad Karma. She thinks that the children, nourished to adulthood by so much earthliness, may now return, riding up on the organic cycle, which is also a Bad Karmic wheel, to take vengeance on her. Her paranoid guilt inverts *Gravity's Rainbow*'s more usual symbolism of black and white: for her, the black Earth means not life but death, i.e., an organic vitality that turns death, what should have been her own safe death, perversely back into life. Her stage name, Erdmann, was meant by the Nazis who imposed it on her to connote the usual phony *Volk*-mysticisms of blood, soil, race; the name's Earth-trace is thus ironically a sign of her co-option by white Nazi orders. Her masochism, as amid the plastics in the petrochemical plant, reaches toward whiteness, toward the annihilation of self, in contrast to Katje's (662), which is Earth-directed, away from Blicero's whiteness. And somewhere offstage, right about now, after so many of these facile inversions, we might listen for *V.*'s McClintic Sphere softly singing:

> Flop, flip, once I was hip,
> Flip, flop, now you're on top,
> Set-REset, why are we BEset
> With crazy and cool in the same molecule. (*V.*, 273)

Subjected to Pynchon's black/white shadowplays, the reader's sense of symbolic significances, customarily solemn enough, "gets tickled"— again—"the way your eye does staring at a recco map until bomb craters flip inside out to become muffins risen above the tin, or ridges fold to valleys, sea and land flicker across quicksilver edges" (713). It is our constant, perverse will to try to dissociate wholeness into binaries, then to try to read their moires for "signs," tealeaf-wise, or as Säure Bummer reads prophecies in the wrinkles of joints.

Greta Erdmann's husband Miklos Thanatz is a minor character, but the subtle and subtly cheering way in which he flips across a "quicksilver edge" from election to preterition deserves a glance here. His name suggests death, *Thanatos,* and he is enthusiastically one of the self-styled elect on "the white *Anubis* [going] on to salvation" (667), as these decadents foolishly believe. His "return" to life begins when he suddenly slips on a spilled pot of stew on deck and goes over the side: a random, banana-peel subversion, although in introducing it the narrator wearily gestures, humoring us, "You will want cause and effect. All right" (663). Having descended thus from white deathly heights into preterite, underground life, the "Angel Thanatz" (673) can brief the underground Schwarzkommando on the firing of Rocket 00000, which he had witnessed: it is his unexpected kindness, committed for and in that flowing blackness that Greta had feared, the continuous life he has joined—"Swimming and drowning, mired and afoot, poor passengers at sundown who've lost their way.... Men overboard and our common debris" (667).

In *V.* Herbert Stencil interprets external moires in political terms, as balance-of-power metaphors, as the senior Stencil had done, and as do such texts as *Things That Can Happen in European Politics,* the senilely ambitious writing project that Brigadier Pudding begins between wars but cannot finish, since of course Things do keep Happening, "changing out from under him. Oh, dodgy, very dodgy" (77). Pudding wanders back into active duty for the Second War, but since here, he finds, "death [is] no enemy, but a collaborator" (616), he can only try ineffectually to keep personal balance through feeble bureaucratizing, mild senile comedy; his interest in "surprise" foods may even be a bleary survival of some former faith in the Law of Surprise. Typically, he declares himself on the side of the Counterforce only after his death—blithering subversion through seances' "sensitive flames."

In the gross masochistic ritual framed and directed by Pointsman to keep Pudding manageable, the Brigadier comes to the Mistress of the Night in part, we are to understand, out of a healthy revulsion against his daily routine and its colorless, odorless "fucking ... done on paper" (616). Beneath her role as mistress, Katje, whose masochism is also, like Pudding's, a need to contact earthliness and to "cry at pain" (662), may sympathize with the Brigadier's "need for pain, for something real, something pure. They have taken him so far from his simple nerves. They have stuffed paper illusions and military euphemisms between him and this truth, this rare decency, this moment at her scrupulous feet" (234). Indeed, we know by now that masochism may always imply a try for connection, unity, love; we have learned to read blackness, Earth, excrement, as life symbols—but this is to say that the vectors of our responses cross-point exceedingly delicately here, in the book's most nauseating scene. Our feeling for the "rare decency" of Pudding's revolt is partly dissolved by its sheer revoltingness. We should be mildly embarrassed to realize that a conditioned "critical" recognition of symbolic meaning has threatened to get our living imaginations all the way past a scene of real and graphic shit-eating and urine-drinking. And if the shit-eating is, symbolically speaking, Pudding's gesture of health,

90

still he is not excused from dying of a massive *E. coli* infection (533). At any rate, the expiatory ritual is wholly Pointsman's production: Their show, in no real way, therefore, subversive, and encased moreover in framing allusions. Katje, for example, continues her role as secondary Venus by playing Venus in Furs, from the novel of that name by Leopold Sacher-Masoch, father of sadomasochistic pornography. Pudding's ritualistic approach through the chambers, a series of tests he must pass, suggests the questor's approach to the Chapel Perilous in Grail romance;[23] the seven chambers through which he must pass may allude to the seven seals, seven trumpets, seven vials, of the Apocalypse of Revelation; the whole "passage" rite is surely at least Pointsman's private allusion to his fantasy labyrinth with the apocalyptic Minotaur at its heart. A copy of Krafft-Ebing and a Savarin coffee can— to remind Pudding of the character Severin in *Venus in Furs*—are among Pointsman's conscious plants of meaning. Pudding's experience of reading them is meant to assure him that he is passing, under control, from power to preterition, as his masochism demands.

On the level of the more abstract symbolisms of black-and-white, the ironies are indeed richly moireed: the white paper gaming that both fascinates and disgusts Pudding and that he here seeks to escape can *cause* wars that then activate, in the black mud of battlefields such as those he remembers, the archetype of the "Mistress" of pain-pleasure, who for Pudding is "Death, Fear, Ruined Youth, and the memory of all these."[24] Pudding hates bureaucracy's odorless whiteness, but the stinking, shitlike mud of Flanders in which his nostalgia locates "life" is an earthliness betrayed, polluted by war and murder, as the spa's mud is polluted by Greta's crimes. It is part of Richard Poirier's excellent point that, in Pynchon's world, men like Pudding will themselves *plot* certain "things that can happen": "Nearly from the outset, the people of Pynchon's novels are the instruments of the plots they then help promote. Their consequent dehumanization makes the prospect of apocalypse and the destruction of self not a horror so much as the final

---

23. Paul Fussell has noticed this in his *The Great War and Modern Memory* (New York: Oxford University Press, 1975), p. 332. By no means do I want to disparage the wonderful creativity and overall credibility of this fine book, but it is, I suppose, my duty here to point out one egregious mistake that Fussell makes during one of his many admiring references to *Gravity's Rainbow*. Discussing the scene (88–92) in which Roger Mexico and Dr. Pointsman walk along the Channel Beach, Fussell refers to these characters as "Roger Pointsman and Tyrone Slothrop"; he also incorrectly places the two, or three, of them in the Special Operations Executive (*The Great War*, p. 69).

24. This is Fussell's formula (*The Great War*, p. 331).

ecstasy of plotting and of power. In international relations the ecstasy is thermonuclear war; in human relationships it can be sadomasochism with skin itself as leather, leather a substitute for skin."[25]

The real-historical British wartime agency known as the Special Operations Executive—reactivated Great War veteran Brigadier Colin Gubbins, commanding—is clearly the inspiration for Pynchon's White Visitation, although *Gravity's Rainbow* also mentions the SOE separately, as "the Firm," as it was indeed called in life. As Paul Fussell describes this organization, "it enrolled dons, bankers, lawyers, cinema people, artists, journalists, and pedants. Of its executive personnel the [*Times Literary Supplement,* May 18, 1965] observed, 'A few could only charitably be described as nutcases.' Its research departments especially enjoyed a wide reputation for sophomoric bright ideas and general eccentricity.... It was said that ... outré departments staffed by necromancers, astrologers, and ESP enthusiasts worked at casting spells on the German civil and military hierarchy."[26]

This brings us to Pynchon's PSI Section, whose outré personnel—with "no secular aspirations at all" (76)—include Carroll Eventyr, Edwin Treacle, Rollo Groast, the Rev. Paul de la Nuit, Gavin Trefoil, the "psychometrist" Ronald Cherrycoke, who loves Nora Dodson-Truck, who thinks that she is the Force of Gravity. The reader will find it hard to keep all these people distinctly sorted out, nor is it too important to do so, since they are as essentially interchangeable as their rivals, the dull positivists (Aaron Throwster, Géza Rózsavölgyi, Milton Gloaming, Teddy Bloat, etc.) who work for Pointsman.

True-believing spiritualists and narrow positivists represent two opposite bad faiths: two over-easy, unearned solutions to the One/Zero problem, the choice between "another mode of meaning behind the obvious, or none" (*Lot 49,* 137). PSI Section, of course, accepts the paranoid One, the angelic orders; like Blicero (and like rocketman Wernher von Braun in the novel's equivocal headnote), they define "transcendence" as escape from Earth, "transformation" as a simple translation to some other order of being. We should note that such a belief jibes not at all with that sense of an earthly transformation, an affirmative blending of life and death, through which the rapturous Rilke of the Ninth Elegy comes to sponsor invisible Slothrop:

25. Richard Poirier, *The Performing Self* (New York: Oxford University Press, 1971), p. 25.

26. Fussell, *The Great War,* p. 328.

—Earth! invisible!
What do you charge us with if not transformation?
Earth, my love, I will. Oh believe me, I need
no more of your springtimes to win me.[27]

But PSI Section's people are spiritualistic pointsmen, "controls" and "media" men, who seek continuity as cathexes between two discrete "sides," this and the Other. In one of their typical exercises, Cherrycoke, handling the personal effects of the pilot Basher St. Blaise and his wingman, reads, in the "information pouring in through his fingers" (150), the psychic news of the Lübeck Angel—"fiery leagues of face, the eyes, which went towering for miles, shifting to follow their flight" (151) during the Palm Sunday raid. The narrator later speculates that, alike in the London that sent the air raid and the Lübeck that answered with V-2's, there was "the masochist's unmistakable long look that said *hurry up and fuck me*" (215): the angel, Gravity's Rainbow itself arcing below, as sadomasochist pimp. The echo is of Slothrop's New England towns waiting, watching the sky these three hundred years, "slender church steeples poised up and down all these autumn hillsides, white rockets about to fire ... *yes the great bright hand reaching out of the cloud*" (29).

But the narrator remains basically noncommittal about all this spiritualist stuff, framing it when and as he needs to, in a variety of moods and voices. Sometimes he does play, at least, at believing in angels who act as astral pointsmen to route, not only hardware to Earth, but authorized archetypes into dreams: "Kekulé's dream here's being routed now past points which may arc through the silence, in bright reluctance to live inside the moving moment, an imperfect, a human light, over here interfering with the solemn binary decisions of these agents, who are now allowing the cosmic Serpent ... to pass" (411). But the agnostic "points which *may* arc" jostles the true-believing "*is* being routed," half-camouflaged in its contraction. With the One/Zero problem we seem doomed to wander always, if we are intellectually honest, with Roger Mexico and Oedipa Maas, between binary solutions, "like walking among matrices of a great digital computer, the zeroes and ones twinned above, hanging like balanced mobiles right and left, ahead, thick, maybe endless. Behind the hieroglyphic streets there would either be a transcendent meaning, or only the earth" (*Lot 49*, 136).

In *V.*, the One and the Zero solutions come cryptically scrambled

27. Rilke, Ninth Duino Elegy, lines 68–71.

together in the weird radio signals, "sferics," that Kurt Mondaugen's equipment pulls down out of the air above German Südwest. The message is DIGEWOELDTIMSTEALALENSWTASNDEURFUALRLIKST; removing every third letter yields an anagram of KURT MONDAUGEN; the rest spells the line from Wittgenstein's *Tractatus*, "Die Welt ist alles was der Fall ist." *V.*'s critics have often misleadingly overemphasized the second of these messages at the expense of the first. In *V.*'s context the Wittgenstein line is indeed an announcement of void, waste, inanimation—the antiparanoid zero. But the other message plausibly seems a personal greeting to Mondaugen from sentient, even playful, angelic orders. Which does Mondaugen want it to be? In *Gravity's Rainbow* old "moon eyes" reappears, and in a connection that shows him to have opted, as most men would and do, for the One. He is now a rocket-mystic, having heard Puritanwise, in Südwest, the voice of his calling: to work on means for penetrating those heavens out of which angels have spoken his name. Further, Pynchon himself may be said to have been the true caller: Mondaugen, by leading his friend Pökler into the embryo rocket program in *Gravity's Rainbow,* may be fulfilling the true, secret purpose for which he was being prepared—created—in *V.* And more: the *V.* character who showed Mondaugen how to unscramble the sferics was Lieutenant Weissmann, who, as if speaking from knowledge of Pynchon's own plans for the later novel, in which he himself will be Captain Blicero, had told Mondaugen, "Someday we'll need you ... Specialized and limited as you are, you fellows will be valuable" (*V.*, 224).

*   *   *

Franz Pökler the rocket engineer is a Cartesian rationalist who thinks he prefers always to move "by safe right angles along the faint lines" (399). He might have been saved from Blicero's plotting by his politically canny wife Leni, but unfortunately the Pöklers, with symmetrically opposite psychologies, disengage and slide past each other: Leni leaves Franz in favor of Peter Sachsa, her spiritualist/revolutionist lover in Weimar Berlin. Leni manages to combine political (1920s Leftist) idealism with holist mysticism. Since, for her, "everything is connected" in politics as in the living universe, she disapproves of Franz's "pure," apolitical interest in rockets, according to which, for the sake of future "expeditions to Venus" (401), Franz justifies taking development funds from Nazis and blinks at the rocket's probable use as a weapon of war.

And Leni knows too that below Franz's "rational" self and self-image lies his very German vulnerability, like Blicero's, to "fantasy, death-wish, rocket-mysticism—Franz is just the type they want. They know how to use *that*" (154–55). Thus his dream of expeditions to Venus, ancient V-1 of the morning, is necessarily also a mystical and mas-ochistic dream of V-2; target and craft, victim and aggressor, morning- and death-star all fusing in a single inamorata that vamps him out of himself:

> He would become aware of a drifting away ... some assumption of Pökler into the calculations, drawings, graphs, and even what raw hardware there was ... each time, soon as it happened, he would panic, and draw back into the redoubt of waking Pökler.... Some-thing was out to get him, something here, among the paper. The fear of extinction named Pökler knew it was the Rocket, beckoning him in. If he also knew that in something like this extinction he could be free of his loneliness and failure, still he wasn't quite convinced ... So he hunted, as a servo valve with a noisy input will, across the Zero, between the two desires, personal identity and impersonal salvation. (405–6)

Political allegory: Pökler, a "Victim in a Vacuum" (414), is the Weimar German to whom it can seem that the fierce grids of poverty, necessity, and confusion might be escaped if one surrenders the "personal iden-tity" with which democracy burdens one to a promise of "impersonal salvation": the rocket is Pökler's Nazism. During the war, Pökler and his personal Führer, Blicero, maneuver in an office political power game whose stakes are, for Pökler, Ilse, and for Blicero, Rocket 00000. The relationship models the perverse power relations between totalitarian rulers and ruled and suggests as well the pervasive metaphor of inani-mate systems' "self-awareness," the rocket in flight parodying a "life," creating in turn its creators' personal lives as impersonal mechanisms, politics as technology as sadoinanimation as "Los[ing] Himself In His Work" (277).

Pökler's own metaphor for the office game is chess, with the board a complex moire of potential paranoias: Blicero sends Pökler to sit at Ground Zero at Blizna to be destroyed; Blicero arranges the tradition of the yearly visits with Ilse at Zwölfkinder in order that Pökler might be saved from the RAF raid on Peenemünde; Blicero uses a different "Ilse" each year. But simple rationalization, not paranoia, is Pökler's primary defensive instinct. Told that Ilse is a ward of the Reich, well, "He'd heard there were camps, but saw nothing sinister in it ... *they have qualified people there ... trained personnel*" (410). The perfect allegorical figure of his "good" countrymen, he gets through the war by applying to everything—the war itself, his work for it, his superiors' plotting, his fears for himself and for Ilse—that mania for "Analysis," the "gift of Daedalus that allowed him to put as much labyrinth as required between himself and the inconveniences of caring" (428). The humbler style of self-deception at least makes Pökler more sympathetic than Gerhardt von Göll, the type of the grandiose German, who thinks himself able to leap entirely off the chessboard. For Pökler, by contrast, it is only near sleep's magic interface that the timid old dreams of transcendence return, dreams now hopelessly compromised by the time, the time itself a "master fantasist" Nazi dream. Here Pökler's innocence acquires, ironically and pathetically, the imagery of rocket-test highs:

> Staring up at the electric scatter from this part of Peenemünde mapping across his piece of ceiling priorities, abandoned dreams, favor in the eyes of the master fantasists in Berlin, while sometimes Ilse whispered to him bedtime stories about the moon she would live on, till he had transferred silently to a world that wasn't this one after all: a map without any national borders, insecure and exhilarating, in which flight was as natural as breathing— but I'll fall … no, rising, look down, nothing to be afraid of, this time it's good … yes, firmly in flight, it's working … yes. (410)

The narrator asks, "Should he have told her what the 'seas' of the Moon really were? That there was nothing to breathe?" (410). He never does, since to do so would really be to betray his own idealist's dream, which also is that of lovely and livable heavens, of a science and technology purely good, purely to take us there. As we pity Pökler for his bottomless innocence and consequent helplessness against evil, we can admire his managing to turn even the rocket's deathly rainbow into a simple wishing-rainbow—a hope for an enchanted flight, in the way that, as an old movie freak, he must sometimes think of "Over the Rainbow," with Ilse as the young Judy Garland (279). This headnote to the reel "In the Zone," most of which is to take place in Germany, is surely meant to signify our removal Over The Rainbow, which is Gravity's Rainbow, from the blitzed London of the first reel.

Finally, when the perverse *Märchen*-land of the Nazi Oz crumbles, Pökler is at last permitted to find the continuities that his labyrinths had insulated him from: he visits the stacks of dead and near-dead at the Dora camp, only a few hundred meters from the Mittelwerke: "All his vacuums, his labyrinths, had been the other side of this. While he lived, and drew marks on paper, this invisible kingdom kept on, in the darkness outside ... all this time" (432). He marries the earthliness, slipping his wedding ring onto a woman's hand—"If she lived, the ring would be good for a few meals, or a blanket, or a night indoors, or a ride home" (433). He goes to wait in the ruins of Zwölfkinder for an Ilse who probably will not appear; there he sees the "wire mesh" of a crumbling plaster witch, the stilled latticework of the wheel, like guilty secrets of structure now opening out to the stars and sea. Frieda the pig is leading Slothrop this way. Pökler, here at the end of "his" frame, pages 397–433, the book's longest, silently drops into invisibility himself, out of the novel—except for a brief resurfacing, pages 575–77, to meet Slothrop and brush by him. Pökler was "never that interested," he says, in the Schwarzgerät, to the problem of accommodating which in the rocket his whole career had been directed, bound, and betrayed.

* * *

Russian Captain Vaslav Tchitcherine, like Pökler, is consistently unsure of his real relations to the plots that surround him; he is "held at the edge" (703) of all revelation. As readers we see, or think we see, that They mean to use Tchitcherine to destroy Enzian, who is the blackness that They fear—and that as long as Tchitcherine acts compliantly as Their instrumentality he moves also to crush out his own blackness, his Earth-trace. But to get him moving in this direction They have to administer a violent stimulus, a rape of narcotics: in V-Mann Wimpe's Moscow hotel room between the wars, the "German precision" of the steel hypodermic full of Jamf's synthetic drug Oneirine is Tchitcherine's "first taste—his initiation into the bodyhood of steel" (702). That They may thus use drugs as means to control had been clearly enough explained to him by Wimpe and later is intimated again by his encounters with Chu Piang, who is a "living monument" to the "classic hustle," the Opium Wars, that the British ran on nineteenth-century China. But out in Kazakhstan, smoking opium with Chu, Tchitcherine typically "can't connect" the "cut, faceted, polished and foiled molecules" (348) of Wimpe's I. G. with the "raw jumble of opium alkaloids" (348) that sensitize him, outside at night, to the raw starwinds and earthwaves of the Asian Open. Missing connections, the elegant signs and symmetries of paranoia, and tending instead toward openness, Tchitcherine has, as Pynchon continues the organic-molecular metaphor, "a way of getting together with undesirables, sub rosa enemies of order, counterrevolutionary odds and ends of humanity: he doesn't plan it, it just happens, he is a giant supermolecule with so many open bonds available at any given time" (346).

His father too had been open to indiscriminate bondings with blackness. During the Russo-Japanese War, the fleet on which the elder Tchitcherine was a sailor had docked in German Südwest to take on coal for the long voyage to the disastrous Battle of Tsushima. In the harbor, the coal dust had powdered the white sailors' faces, swarmed evilly in the arc lights; in this rape of blackness by white Europeans, the elder Tchitcherine had felt "too much meaningless power, flowing wrong ... he could smell Death in it" (351). He went AWOL, making his separate peace by living awhile "near the railroad," with the "honest blackness" of the Herero girl who became Enzian's mother.

In the 1920s and '30s, Captain Tchitcherine is inexplicably assigned to help the Stalinist state impose the rationalized Word—standardized literacy—on the nomadic Turkic peoples of Kazakhstan in Central Asia. This Russian Wild East penetrated by ordering power is a mirror-reflection of the American Wild West to which Puritan-descended whites came to play cowboys and Indians. Tchitcherine even has a Tontoesque sidekick, the Kirghiz Dzaqyp Qulan, whose father had been killed during a Kirghiz "rising" to which White Russian settlers responded "in full vigilante panic, surrounded and killed the darker refugees with shovels, pitchforks, old rifles, any weapon to hand. A common occurrence in Semirechie then, even that far from the railroad" (340)—"even that far" because the Semirechie railroad, like the railroad in Südwest past which Tchitcherine's father glided, like the fences thrown over American plains and over Squalidozzi's Argentine pampas, is a symbol of the net of rationalization, specifically as language, the Word, which Tchitcherine must throw over the Kazakh openness. The bureaucratic factionalism, here overtly a word-gaming, among the rival alphabetical committees in Tchitcherine's agency echoes the sectarian squabblings of "word-smitten" colonial Puritans, as in the case of William Slothrop's heresy on behalf of the preterites. It is one of Slothrop's and Tchitcherine's many secret points of connection that they both carry on the traditions of ancestors who secretly favored preterition in its fights against the tyrannies of the Word.

And yet it is with pleasure that Tchitcherine copies onto a page for the first time in history the beautiful song of the *ajtys*, the singing duel that is a "coming-together-of-opposites," boy-and-girl voices. He is proud of "the New Turkic Alphabet he helped frame" yet knows that "this is how [the songs] will be lost" (357). And the deep ambivalence here about activated word-magic is also, almost necessarily, the novelist's own: "On sidewalks and walls the very first printed slogans start to show up, the first Central Asian fuck you signs, the first kill-the-police-commissioner signs (and somebody does! this alphabet is really something!) and so the magic that the shamans, out in the wind, have always known, begins to operate now in a political way, and Dzaqyp Qulan hears the ghost of his own lynched father with a scratchy pen in the night, practicing A's and B's" (356).

Thus it is with a complex and "reflexive" irony that Pynchon word-frames Central Asia, a place and time he has never seen, in a descriptive language as exalted as any in *Gravity's Rainbow*: great cloud-and-steppe armadas of imagery massed to achieve a whole authenticity inside the word-bluff:

> In the summer, irrigation canals sweated a blurry fretwork across the green oasis. In the winter, sticky teaglasses ranked the windowsills, soldiers played *preference* and stepped outside only to piss, or to shoot down the street at surprised wolves.... It was a land of drunken nostalgia for the cities, silent Kirghiz riding, endless tremors in the earth ... because of the earthquakes, nobody built higher than one story and so the town looked like a Wild West movie: a brown dirt street, lined with grandiose two- and three-story false fronts. (338)

> Often he'll come outside to find his morning skies full of sheet-lightning: gusting, glaring. Awful. The ground shudders just below his hearing. It might be the end of the world, except that it is a fairly average day, for Central Asia. Pulse after heavenwide pulse. Clouds, some in very clear profile, black and jagged, sail in armadas toward the Asian arctic, above the sweeping dessiatinas of grasses, of mullein stalks, rippling out of sight, green and gray in the wind. An amazing wind. But he stands in the street, out in it, hitching his pants, lapel-points rattling against his chest, cursing Army, Party, History—whatever has put him here. (339)

The "history," once again here, is quite real: during this period Stalin began the "Likbez" literacy program, sending instructors such as Tchitcherine's Galina out from the cities to teach in the "red dzurt" schoolrooms on the steppes.[28] At Baku in 1927, as Pynchon correctly

---

28. The source of Pynchon's information about this literacy program and about the Baku conference is Thomas G. Winner, "Problems of Alphabetical Reform Among the Turkic Peoples of Soviet Central Asia, 1920–1941," in *Slavonic and East European Review* 31 (December 1952): 133–48.

reports, there was a conference, the VTsK NTA (Vsesoyhzhyy Tsentral'nyy Komitet Novogo Tyurkskogo Alfavita), to decide which alphabet should be made standard; bitter disputes, complete with the "religious angle" (354), erupted between Latinists and Cyrillicists. A Latinist Azerbaijan journalist who attended the conference, Mamed Aga Shakhtatinsky, probably donates to Pynchon the name of Shatsk, "notorious Leningrad nose-fetishist" (352); another delegate, Badjbildin, name-connects to "Igor Blobadjian" (353). As part of Stalin's program, Thomas G. Winner reports, "teams of folklorists traveled throughout Kazakhstan, recording well-known and half-forgotten epics and other folklore productions; frequently directly from the recitations of the elder *aqyns*."[29] Thus Tchitcherine and Dzaqyp Qulan ride out into "the great silences of Seven Rivers [which] have not yet been alphabetized" (340) to find the place of the boy-girl singing duel, where a silent shaman sits radiating "for the singers a sort of guidance. It is kindness. It can be felt as unmistakably as the heat from the embers" (357). The shaman eventually sings his rhapsody of the Kirghiz Light, very possibly a real "half-forgotten" epic theme, although I have not been able to verify it. The light is a blinding presence whose revelation enables the seeker to "sense all Earth like a baby" (358)—a whiteness that is, this time, benign. Tchitcherine's pilgrimage to it, recounted briefly and cryptically, seems "half-forgotten" at once in the novel. Tchitcherine will miss its rocket connection because "he is no aqyn, and his heart was never ready" (359); he is preterite, "held at the edge."

In the Zone, Tchitcherine's plot interferes in moire with the plots of Slothrop, Marvy, Squalidozzi, von Göll, and many others. Although the pattern calls on him to be Slothrop's enemy, he likes Slothrop and wants to be his friend; notices, moreover, their common psychic concern with blackness: "Rocketman, your timing is *fantastic*.... it's your Schwarzphänomen.... You don't even know about it" (513). He has heard Slothrop's sodium-pentathol talk of American blacknesses: negroes, shit 'n Shinola: the life-sign of blackness corrupted to death-sign by a white culture's manipulations of the Slothropian subconscious. Jamf and the Farben money that sent Slothrop to Harvard have put finishing touches on these shadow-inversions. In a perfectly analogous way, Jamf with Wimpe's and Oneirine's help activated in

29. Thomas G. Winner, *The Oral Art and Literature of the Kazakhs of Russian Central* Asia (Durham, N.C.: Duke University Press, 1958), p. 152.

Tchitcherine a black "mantic archetype" (702), defining it as enemy, so that Tchitcherine would be moved to seek out and obliterate Enzian: blackness not as brother but as hostile Other.

Or so the great plot appears. But Jamf, who seems to twitch all filaments of the plot, looks frequently like "a fiction, to help [Slothrop] explain what he felt so terribly" (738)—an intimation of one of Slothrop's Blackdreams: "JAMF ... I" (287). Tchitcherine's meeting with Wimpe for his cooption by steel is given only as "rumored" (344), and the narrator himself calls Wimpe "legendary" (344). The weird Comrade Ripov, who comes from Moscow ostensibly to explain everything to Tchitcherine, in fact only teases him with epistemological ambiguities and might in fact be Their agent, or an Oneirine hallucination—a "rip-off" of Tchitcherine's consciousness—or, worst of all, an independent delusion of Tchitcherine's, and there be no plot. If Jamf and Wimpe are only apocryphal, they only reify a great plot that all along has been a mirage, a paranoid projection by some or all of the characters, or by the narrator, a vast delusory They-system "to help explain" reality. And Tchitcherine in that case has all on his own decided to destroy his black half-brother— "or you are hallucinating ... Or a plot has been mounted against you ... Or you are fantasying some such plot, in which case you are a nut, Oedipa, out of your skull" (*Lot 49*, 128). Pynchon's essential demonstration is that to look at history from the inside is inevitably to see a complex and inscrutable shadow-moire of "objective" and "subjective" visions. The only escape from the funhouse may be to drop or die out of history: to touch Earth, lie down by flowing water, and become "invisible," as Tchitcherine and Slothrop—in a subtly understated, elegant, and eloquent final parallelism—at last both do. As Slothrop, before his climactic rainbow vision, lies down near the stream in the Harz that magically yields him his old harmonica, so Tchitcherine lies down by a stream under a bridge with Geli Tripping; all his bonds open out, Murphy's Law comes in the breeze, and all his previous missed connections have been but feeble foreshadowings of the one that, redemptively, he misses now. Enzian passes by on the bridge; Tchitcherine meets him, doesn't know him, bums a cigarette, chats, waves good-bye, and the beautiful paradox is that in finally passing his black brother, without knowing him, Tchitcherine does find blackness again and is reunited with Earth.

*   *   *

It is *Gravity's Rainbow's* frequent symbolic assertion that life's integrated blackness is the primordial King Kong that, unchained, could
somehow smash the white death-order that They call life. The gravita-
tion of blackness creates the deeper, holistic urges that They fear and
that Slothrop, Tchitcherine, Pökler must be conditioned away from.
"Blackness" here corresponds roughly to what Norman O. Brown—
surely a fair-sized influence on Pynchon—calls a "body consciousness," below genital organization and aggressive sexuality,
below self-other dichotomies, where the consciousness of life and death
are united: "We thus arrive at the idea that life and death are in some
sort of unity at the organic level, that at the human level they are separated into conflicting opposites, and that at the human level the extro-
version of the death instinct is the mode of resolving a conflict that does
not exist at the organic level. The neurosis remains, as it should be, a
human privilege."[30]

Quite obviously, the black Hereros of Südwest embody the mystique
of black, primeval wholeness: their villages have a fourfold symmetry,
arranging themselves around the kraals of the sacred cattle, each village
a mandala, a Jungian archetype of wholeness. The poorest Hereros, the
Ovatjimba, root in the earth for food; their totem animal, the aardvark,
does likewise.[31] A woman who seeks fertility may bury herself in an
aardvark hole, "to be in touch with Earth's gift for genesis" (316). Of the
supreme deity, Ndjambi Karunga, the boy Enzian thinks, "Ndjambi
Karunga is what happens when [he and Weissmann] couple, that's all:
God is creator and destroyer, sun and darkness, all sets of opposites
brought together, including black and white, male and female" (100).
The shipment of the Hereros to Europe by the colonizing Germans is an
exact analogue of the abduction from Earth of coal tars from which to
make synthetic colors, coal to build the steel rocket and fuel rocket-sys-
tems—Enzian as raw material for steel as for love, for steel-love:

> It began when Weissmann brought him to Europe: a discovery that
> love, among these men ... had to do with masculine technologies,

30. Norman O. Brown, *Life Against
Death* (Middletown, Ct.: Wesleyan University Press, 1959), p. 100. For a thorough
survey of the presence in *Gravity's Rainbow* of Brown's neo-Freudian ideas on
history as the reification of a psychological
mechanism of repression, see Lawrence
Wolfley, "Repression's Rainbow: The Presence of Norman O. Brown in Pynchon's
Big Novel," in *Critical Essays on Thomas
Pynchon*, ed. Richard Pearce (Boston:
G. K. Hall & Co., 1981), pp. 99–124.

31. See Olga Levinson, *The Ageless Land*
(Capetown: Tafelberg-Uitgewers, 1961),
p. 54.

with contracts, with winning and losing. Demanded, in his own case, that he enter the service of the Rocket ... Beyond simple steel erection, the Rocket was an entire system *won*, away from the feminine darkness, held against the entropies of lovable but scatterbrained Mother Nature. (324)

Like Katje, Enzian is a strong self entrapped by multiple frames: the Word from Rilke with which Blicero christens his lover; King Kong; the dark Nibelungen whose Earth-hoard is stolen by predator-heroes; the Christ-Messiah who offers his people a redemptive self-sacrifice; even (although not specifically mentioned anywhere in the novel) a weapon, the A-A rocket designed near the end of the war to try to break Allied air control, which was called the "Enzian."[32] Most readers, wishing him well, will want to understand positively his self-imposed "mission" to build Rocket 00001, the motivation of which is indeed a wish to defy Them, as They themselves acknowledge in setting out to "destroy the blacks" (615). But the Schwarzkommando effort to scavenge pieces of "white" rocket with which to build a "black" rocket is compromised, corrupted from within, by its own necessarily bureaucratized and mechanical nature; the enterprise is as obsessively politicized, self-conscious, *structured* as any Nordic moires it would shatter: "Call the [Zone Hereros] together, get up there say *My people, I have had a vision* ... no no but there *will* have to be more staff, if it's to be that big a search, quiet shifting of resources away from the Rocket, diversifying while making it look like an organic growth" (525).

"Making it look ... organic": here is the bureaucrat busily dissembling his purposes, and this could be Pointsman's language—in the Zone, clearly, there can be no true, truly regenerative Erdschweinhöhle. The splintering of the Empty Ones from the main mass of Schwarzkommando symptomatizes the general fragmentation and plotting: could Ombindi's men even be spies for Them, counter-intelligence? Meanwhile, from inside his Leader frame, Enzian can have fewer and fewer real connections with life, and when he does connect, "It hurts." "You just connected" (525): Christian has had to punch him in the face to break through. "You—play this holy-father routine," Christian says, "and inside that ego you don't even hate us, you don't care, you're not even *connected*" (525).

32. Similarly, the A-A research program, run by the Hermann Goering Research Institute in Braunschweig, was code-named "Fire Lily." The reader of *V.* will recognize the name of the horse ridden by the brutal Foppl during the Herero rebellion in Deutsch Südwest Afrika in 1905.

But the archly named Christian himself assumes that he will be first in an apostolic succession of guardians of Enzian's "text." There is every possibility that Enzian intends to consummate the Christ role by ascending in glory in Rocket 00001—to "revalorize," in Mircea Eliade's terms, a "celestial archetype of Creation,"[33] and so give his people a mythic impetus for the future. He never directly reveals, may never quite consciously formulate, these plans, but we can see the suggestive symmetry-axis linking Enzian and the sacrificial Gottfried through their common corrupter, Blicero. And there are hints:

> What Enzian wants to create will have no history. It will never need a design change. Time, as time is known to other nations, will wither away inside this new one. The Erdschweinhöhle will not be bound, like the Rocket, to time. The people will find the Center again, the Center without time, the journey without hysteresis, where every departure is a return to the same place, the only place. (319)

> Sitting now between a pair of candles just lit, his gray field-jacket open at the neck, beard feathering down his dark throat to shorter, sparser, glossy black hairs that go running in a whirl, iron filings about the south pole of his Adam's apple ... pole ... axis ... axle-tree ... Tree ... Omumborombanga... (321)

The Omumborombanga Tree was the Bushman-Herero World Tree, from which all things were born—the *axis mundi* in their myth of creation.[34] *Gravity's Rainbow* refers often to the World Tree archetype, frequently to make the rocket recall and express it; Christ's Cross, we are asked to recall, had been the "Tree" at the site of God's creation of Adam—the locus of the old Jerusalem and of the coming new, the axis of the world. If Enzian ascends along the rocket-axis, he may believe, he will draw down a timeless, Great Time inside which mundane time will "wither away": exemplary hero, he will become his people's new creator, actualizing a new mythic creation.

Yet his intermittent humor and self-deprecating embarrassment may express his reluctance to being "self-conned as any Christian" (321) by virtue of all these temptations to grandiosity. There seems to be a possible alternative to Enzian's crucifixion: he may realize instead the shy,

33. The theory of the development of "cosmogonic" myth referred to here is *passim* in much of the work of Mircea Eliade; see particularly *The Myth of the Eternal Return; Cosmos and History*; and *Myths, Dreams and Mysteries*. I return to the theme in Chapter 6.

34. See the *New Larousse Encyclopedia of Mythology* (London: Hamlyn Publishing Group Ltd., 1959), p. 476 (in the chapter by Max Fauconnet, "Mythology of Black Africa").

vague counter-desire he sometimes expresses to go only a little way "up," to stand modestly "outside" history and watch it from a height. Near the end, Katje finds him in such a mood (656 ff.)—wanting to be, in this odd way, preterite again. He had told Slothrop: "We have a word that we whisper, a mantra for times that threaten to be bad. Mba-kayere. You may find that it will work for you. Mba-kayere. It means 'I am passed over.' To those of us who have survived von Trotha, it also means that we have learned to stand outside our history and watch it, without feeling too much" (362).

Either the mantra will save him for preterition, or Enzian will reach apotheosis, Blicero's rule over him culminating in final, orgasmic ascent. If the latter, he will finally join *Gravity's Rainbow*'s class of those "elected," ironically, to be pure preterite victims of power—Pynchon's near-sainted, slaughtered innocents, whose best exemplars are the children, Ilse, Bianca, and Gottfried. This sacrificial class includes also Jessica Swanlake, maneuvered helplessly by Pointsman away from Roger Mexico and into opportune linkage with Jeremy Beaver; perhaps Kevin Spectro, one of the adepts of the Pavlovian Book, a kind doctor killed by a rocket hit on St. Veronica's Hospital; certainly Tantivy Mucker-Maffick,[35] Slothrop's friend, who like Yossarian's friend Dunbar in *Catch-22* one day simply "is disappeared"—"They did it. Took his friend out to some deathtrap, probably let him fake an 'honorable' death … and then just *closed up his file*" (252). There is also a would-be victim, Klaus Närrisch, who tries grimly but unsuccessfully to die for Der Springer and Springer's grandly unstated "intentions." He is Pynchon's elementary comment—*närrisch* means "foolish"—on German obedience.

Gottfried, the purest of victims, is as passively devoid of character, inside the movie archetype of the waif/porn star, as inside the Hansel frame, and as, at the final ascent, inside Weissmann's engineered symbolism and Pynchon's own many allusive impositions. To discuss the symbolic connections of the ascent, one feels, is to differentiate a symbolic rainbow out of the blinding whiteness of this climax of novel, of homosexual eroticism, of intricate orchestrations of imagery. The ascent

35. Mucker-Maffick's name combines two Britishisms: the familiar *muckin' about* and the less familiar verb *maffick*—the latter defined in a phrase dictionary as "to celebrate an event extravagantly." It derives from the exultation that took place in London on May 18, 1900, when Mafeking, long beseiged by the Boers, was relieved. The two names combine in a suggestion of riotous though good-humored drinking, which is most appropriate for Slothrop's friend.

will furnish a mythos, the narrator says (again, after Mircea Eliade), for the future Raketen-Stadt, with Rocket as Cross or Tree, "the axis of a particular Earth, a new dispensation, brought into being by the Great Firing" (753). From here we are invited to embark on a tour through regions described famously by Sir James Frazer, Jesse Weston, and Jung—and incidentally to watch a collective parody of all the Modernist literature that has undertaken to guide the same tour. The figure of risen Christ connects archetypally with that of the ancient Near Eastern year- and fertility-god, dead and buried with the vegetation in fall, resur- rected in spring: an ascending life-energy that communicates among levels of being, the phallic rocket in positive, creative aspect. This is, roughly, Jung's "Mercurius" archetype (see Chapter 6), an axis of bind- ing energy within creation that unifies the whole, and whose root mean- ing is wholeness.[36] Mercurius was expressed in the Roman Mercury, descended from the Pelasgian-Greek Hermes, a chthonic deity, his totem the snake, his symbol the phallus, who relayed life's energies between Earth and underworld. The narrator imagines a rocket cycle with a chthonic phase, the rocket beginning "Infinitely Below The Earth And Going On Infinitely Back Into The Earth it's only the *peak* that we are allowed to see" (726). Anthropomorphized as Homer's beautiful youth, messenger to the gods, Hermes functions also as patron of thieves and of invisible subterfuge, and guide of spirits to Hades. At Hades' gate, journey's end, stood the monstrous dog Cerberus, and here Pynchon plucks a string lightly: while ascending, Gottfried remembers "the last dog's head, the kind dog come to see him off" (759). One hundred pages earlier, in a different connection, "it is the kind Dog, the Dog no man ever conditioned, who is there for us at begin- nings and ends, and journeys we have to take, helpless, but not quite unwilling" (655). Gottfried, further, is gagged with a white glove, which, says the narrator, is "the female equivalent of the Hand of Glory, which second-story men use to light their way into your home: a candle

36. Jung incorporates in this Mercurius figure a great deal of hermetic and al- chemical lore. For example, Mercurius, or Hermes, is analogized to the alchemist's crucible fire: "In alchemy the fire purifies, but it also melts the opposites into a unity. He who ascends unites the powers of Above and Below and shows his full power when he returns again to earth." See my Chapter 6 for more evidence that these Jungian investigations underlie Pynchon's Rocket 00000 and the sacrifice of Gottfried. See, further, Jung's "*filius philosophorum* who is often depicted as a youth or hermaphrodite or child…. This being ascends and descends and unites Below with Above, gaining a new power which carries its effect over into everyday life" (*Mysterium Coniunctionis*, vol. 14 of *Collected Works of C. G. Jung* (Princeton, N.J.: Bollingen Series 20, Princeton Uni- versity Press, 1970), pp. 227 and 228.

in the dead man's hand" (750). In hermetic lore, the Hand of Glory, the dried, stiffened hand of a corpse, was a talisman of invisibility, which the cat burglar could carry to cause doors of houses to spring magically open, as if for Mercury, god of thieves.

As Blicero's lover, consecrated to a rapturously erotic death inside the phallic rocket and its Imipolex, Gottfried also activates the myth of Tristan and Iseult—if, following Denis de Rougemont, we interpret the myth as an expression of that secret "passion" allied to death wish, a passion that the Age of Courtly Love imagined as seeking to smash through the proprieties and taboos that the society (King Mark in the legend) imposes between lovers. Gottfried von Strassburg, the premier poet of Tristan in the German Middle Ages, may give Gottfried his name. And "Kabbalist spokesman Steve Edelman" tells us (753) that the rocket corresponds, further, to the Kabbalists' mystic Tree or Body of God, the stages of which the soul negotiates in process of ascent through concentric "spheres" of creation.[37]

Inside the rocket, Gottfried wears "white slippers with white bows" (750)—and Weissmann, outside, ceremoniously names off the firing switches in their fourfold symmetry. In eighteenth-century French Freemasons' circles, apparently, there was an initiation ceremony for the grade of Masonic Master:

> The Lodge was opened with the Te Deum, followed by prayer.... After the opening the Grand Inspector led forward the Dove of the Rite, who was a young boy or maiden, clothed in white and wearing white slippers ... the Dove was breathed upon three times by the Master ... and was then placed in a Tabernacle and locked in. A state of lucidity in the Dove was supposed to be induced so that he or she could receive messages from the Seven Angels, whether as regards the fitness of the Candidate or on any matters which might be proposed at the will of the Masters. One of these proceeded to circumambulate the Lodge, making four circles with his sword in the air at the four cardinal points. He traced also with chalk a large circle in the center.[38]

Did the Dove sometimes fake it, consciously, perversely making up

---

37. Jung, *Mysterium Coniunctionis*, p. 23: "The Cabala develops an elaborate hierosgamos fantasy which expatiates on the union of the soul with the Sefiroth of the worlds of light and darkness, 'for the desire of the upper world for the God-fearing man is as the loving desire of a man for his wife, when he woos her.'" The internal quote is from the *Zohar*, a Kabbalistic text, and carries a footnote wherein Jung is reminded of "the psychotic experiences of Freud's Schreber."

38. Waite, *Freemasonry*, pp. 95, 96.

his own "messages"? Why doesn't Pynchon "characterize" his people better? For the Masons, the Dove couldn't possibly fake it. He had no inside, no independent impulse; he was a pure instrumentality of the rite. Gottfried may indeed turn out to be the exemplary hero for a new dispensation in which, encapsulated by our systems and rocketed far from concrete life, we are unable to feel each others' realities; when we will have forgotten even organic death, that other death possible in *Gravity's Rainbow*, a merging of flowing water in water, sap in sap. The self either may break clear of all frames, dissolving in the outside (Slothrop), or it may be crushed out of being by external pressures, by too much imposed, unreal, abstract definition (Gottfried). Neither of these deaths may be pleasant to contemplate, but the first certainly is the more "natural" in Pynchon's universe and carries much emotional assent there. Meanwhile, we listen to McClintic Sphere's and SHROUD's gentle advice: "Keep cool but care. It's a watchword, Profane, for your side of the morning" (*V.*, 345). To keep cool but care is to make connections, coolly but caringly, on all our open bonds, to include and not to preclude the senses of other lives, of life.

Us

I will not discuss Slothrop separately: as the closest thing the book offers to a central character, he is involved in nearly all other characters' stories and will keep showing up here as he does in the novel. I isolate his progress for other sorts of scrutinies later in this book. With a name that immediately suggests "sloppy," "slob" (although it has other etymologies, too) he is, like Benny Profane, the schlemihl head of a preterite cast of which the only respectable-looking member in *Gravity's Rainbow* is Roger Mexico, the man who tries, too late, to rescue Slothrop from dissolution. In the judgment of his foe and foil Pointsman, Mexico looks like a choirboy and talks like a metaphysical anarchist, a priest of those powers of randomness that threaten Pointsman's mechanical-causal universe. Mexico's receptivity to surprise has of course an allotropic relation to the perspective of twentieth-century science and mathematics, which deal with reality probabilistically. Excluded middles, as in *Lot 49* (136), are "bad shit"—but "to Mexico belongs the domain *between* zero and one—the middle Pointsman has excluded from his persuasion—the probabilities. A chance of 0.37 that, by the time he stops his count, a given square on his map will have suffered only one hit, 0.17 that it will suffer two" (55).

Roger and Jessica, in their unauthorized occupancy of a little house in a stay-away zone, effect a partial Frederick Henry-like withdrawal from the war, finding, below all Their moires, a clearable space for love, a region where souls and things are continuous and need not even be separately named: "She is his deepest innocence in spaces of bough and hay before wishes were given a separate name to warn that they might not come true.... You go from dream to dream inside me. You have passage to my last shabby corner, and there, among the debris, you've found life. I'm no longer sure which of all the words, images, dreams or ghosts are 'yours' and which are 'mine.' It's past sorting out. We're both being someone new now, someone incredible" (177).

This rehetoric is not sentimental, since it is not, like true sentimentality, based in a complacency of the imagination. Rather, it warns that the condition of love as defined by Roger and Jessica is most unstable, a frail sound-shadow in the whirling obsessiveness of Their world. In the "cold fieldmouse church" on Christmas Eve, Roger's face flushes pink, certainly not from conventional piety—from what, then? Jessica wonders whether he is only hot, or only embarrassed to be here—or whether he is responding to the fact of so much tender preterite life crushed together here (like the oil in the lamps) by the war outside: "his eyes more glowing than the lamplight alone can account for—isn't it? or is that how she wants it to be?" (129). Two pages later, when the infant Christ is visited by the sinister kings, "Is the baby smiling, or is it just gas? Which do you want it to be?" (131). The honest imagination must forever wander in the moire between radical choices, One and Zero. Does the Christmas Star's light announce love, or is it a prophecy of history's rerouting toward Christian Europe's death-dispensation? The Magus of T. S. Eliot's wonderful poem may feel the same ambiguous immanence in the Star's blue-black moment:

> Were we led all that way for
> Birth or Death? There was a Birth, certainly,
> We had evidence and no doubt. I had seen Birth and Death,
> But had thought they were different; this Birth was
> Hard and bitter agony for us, like Death, our death.
> We returned to our places, these Kingdoms,
> But no longer at ease here, in the old dispensation,
> With an alien people clutching their gods.
> I should be glad of another death.[39]

39. T. S. Eliot, *Journey of the Magi* (New York: Harcourt, Brace & World, 1936), lines 35–43.

Roger and Jessica's love, in the face of such radical indeterminacies, may be holist "magic." But to break it, differentiate it, all Pointsman has to do is whisper to Jessica a counter-spell, the talismanic word of the rationalized postwar world: "Security. Her magic word, her spell against demons" (709). She leaves Roger for Jeremy Beaver, for safe British rocket work, and Roger must draw back "into his single envelope" (629). Hereafter he takes on the role of Counterforce zany and is less clearly individualized than before, the Lawrentian paradox being that selflessness of the kind offered by love defines and honors the self. Without love, we are like the Inamorati Anonymous of *Lot 49*, anonymous losers read out of human connection.

When Pointsman insists on believing in causal connections between new rocket falls and distributions already achieved, Mexico has to tell him, "That's the Monte Carlo fallacy" (56). PSI Section's psychics merely choose different sorts of dogmas to satisfy the same "one clear need" (40) to explain *causally* the penetrations of this world from the "Other Side" by way of Slothrop's hardons. Mexico admits that this basic human need for models to supply coherence to events is *"His need too, all right"* (40)—but is redeemed by his insistence that wishful thinking and arbitrary dogmatizing will not do; in the absence of "evidence" there is nothing for it but to apply the Poisson equation, which is not a causal model or metaphorical belief system but merely a statistical description of observed randomness. In this intellectual integrity Mexico is quietly seconded by other characters, mostly shadowy, English "ghosts ... beneath the eaves" (138), in the first, British, reel. Osbie Feel, who may be a cartoon of a young sixties doper, evades dogma through drugs and finally penetrates chaos too far—near the end of the book he is on heroin, self-destroyed—but meanwhile likably steers Katje toward the Counterforce. Lab technician Webley Silvernail sympathizes with the captive lab rats: "I would set your free, if I knew how. But it isn't free out here" (230). The quiet Kevin Spectro, for his part, asks, "When you've looked at how it really is ... how can we, any of us, be separate?" (142). The question is also Thomas Gwenhidwy's: "What if [the preterites are] all Jews, you see? all scattered like seeds? still flying outward from the primal fist so long ago" (170). This mad Welshman, whom the narrator compares to Fluellan in *Henry V*, loves food and drink, children, and the preterites' brave persistence under plots. One of the novel's most good-humored passages describes the subversive bugs who invade his larder and "unify" its stocks: "The bugs can be heard, loud as mice, munching through Gwenhidwy's paper sacks, leaving streaks and footprints of shit the color of themselves behind. They don't seem to go much for soft things, fruits, vegetables, and such, it's more the solid lentils and beans they're into, stuff they can gnaw at, paper and plaster barriers, hard interfaces to be pierced, for they are agents of unification, you see. Christmas bugs" (173).

And Gwenhidwy validates his own faith in preterite survival by popping up, with the likewise long-forgotten Carroll Eventyr and Ensign Morituri, at the Counterforce's Gross Suckling Conference after the war. The three bare names, bobbing up like corks, witness that the zone may at any time produce surprise and magic survivals. The German boy Ludwig, chasing his lost lemming Ursula, clearly at first looks doomed, a lemming himself, bound for some cliff; but he quietly follows the armies, selling himself for sex, until "he has found [Ursula] at last and after all and despite everything" (729). By so enjoying the happy ending, the happily leering narrator mocks himself and yet still makes his point. Surprise can happen; "to expect any more, or less, of the Zone is to disagree with the terms of the Creation" (729). Geli Tripping, in fact, not only survives but rescues Tchitcherine with her, conjuring him into love and away from having to recognize Enzian when they meet. Even for Ilse Pökler, a hint goes, there may be "change, and departure ... help when least looked for from the strangers of the day, and hiding, out among the accidents of this drifting Humility, never quite to be extinguished, a few small chances for mercy" (610).

More tough and active preterites flash briefly into and through visibility, Pynchon comparing them explicitly to subnuclear particles speeding in bright picoseconds of life. Blodgett Waxwing proffers Slothrop a zoot suit and then disappears again into the underground flux. Albert Krypton, the name alluding both to a rare, "invisible" gas and to Superman's planet, escapes the MP's and comes to rest briefly at Putzi's, where he again disappears sometime during another MP incursion; we have only just met these characters. Frau Gnahb careens over the Baltic in her black-market boat, days very clearly numbered, singing, as a sea chanty, some of *Gravity's Rainbow's* most likable verse:

I'm the Pirate Queen of the Baltic Run, and
   nobody fucks with me—
And those who've tried are bones and skulls,
   and lie beneath the sea.
And the little fish like messengers swim in and
   out of their eyes,

Singing, "Fuck ye not with Gory Gnahb and her
desperate enterprise!" (497–98)

Of these preterite good guys, the most hard-pressed, the most terribly
worn by his preterition, is Säure Bummer, former cat burglar, now drug
dealer and doper: "Face long worked at by leaps from second-story
windows, 'first rubdowns' under gloved and womanish fists in the pre-
cinct stations ... black light from the pavements of boulevards at night
finely wrinkled ... sans-serif Us at the entrances to the underground
stations point in smooth magnetism at the sky to bring down steel
angels of exaltation, of languid surrender—a face that in sleep is awesomely old, abandoned to its city's history" (437).

His scenes are constantly broken off by hostile incursions, but Säure
defines his heroism when raiding MP's scream, "You will show me your
papers!" and "Säure smiles and holds up a pack of Zig-Zags, just in
from Paris" (442). His first name is the German for "acid," since in his
cat-burglar days he had carried around a bottle of acid with which to
threaten cops (had he also had a Hand of Glory, for invisibility?). With
"Bummer," the name is a drug pun to reiterate that on the whole his life
has been a preterite bum trip, indeed. In his long arguments with the
musician Gustav Schlabone, Säure supports Rossini ("lovers always
get together, isolation is overcome" [440]) against Gustav's Beethoven,
orchestrator of Teutonic grandeur. But Gustav really, or also, thinks he
sees in Beethoven the beginning of a "German dialectic ... culminating
with dodecaphonic democracy, where all notes get an equal hearing"
(440); Pynchon alludes to the twelve-tone "row" of Arnold Schönberg,
with "democracy" as equality of opportunity, unity, among all the keys,
black and white, of the keyboard. Gustav is later found at the Krupp
banquet, playing one of the kazoo "inner voices" in the "suppressed
quartet from the Haydn Op. 76, the so-called 'Kazoo' Quartet in G-Flat
Minor" (711). He interrupts himself to help Mexico and Bodine with
their subversion and thus comes officially over to the Counterforce.
Säure's other hangers-on, Trudi and Magda, would sympathize, since
they also promote touch, sensitivity, union: "A Mutt and Jeff routine,"
they "travel around in the city whenever they can, by way of interven-
ing, if only for a minute, in people's minds" (442).

Of Pynchon's small group of holdover characters from his other novels, the only one who plays a prominent role both in an earlier book and
in *Gravity's Rainbow* is Seaman Pig Bodine—and the differences
between the Pig of *V.* and the Seaman Bodine of *Gravity's Rainbow* are

partial touchstones of the differences between the novels as wholes. In *V.,* Pig is always vividly painted as The Gross Sailor, lying, for example, on Rachel Owlglass's couch, letting "one thick furry arm fall to the floor with a dull thump ... eyes still closed ... slobbering beer. It ran out of the corners of his mouth, formed brief pools in the bushy caverns of his ears ... right foot had begun to wobble, roughly in time with the music ... 'There's nothing I love ... Than good shitkicking music' " (*V.,* 116–17).

V. emphasizes the grotesque hairiness; Pig's fist clutching a quart of beer "looked like a badger with pituitary trouble" (*V.,* 116). But in *Gravity's Rainbow* he is said only to have "an orangutan look to him" (369), and the physical description throughout is muted. Further, although in *V.* neither Pig nor anyone else is really interested in any drug but alcohol, when Bodine first appears in the later novel, ensconced at the Chicago Bar, he is singing "The Doper's Dream," immediately announcing what will be his book-long gee-wow preoccupation with dope. America's late 1960s, it is perhaps relevant to notice, intervene between the two novels, and in *Gravity's Rainbow* cannabis and hallucinogens give underground life a manner that is stonedly quite self-aware, rather more intelligent, and more highly stylized and radicalized than any analogous subversions in *V.* The book is no mere glorification of drug use; drugs are "mindless pleasures," held at all times in a tight ambivalence. Symptoms and symbols of preterition, of ways in which good guys may escape a rationalized life, drugs are also, like paranoia, a tactic by which to evade whatever real chances there may be to make practical assaults on Their evil. The same general ambivalence holds with regard to the preterites' tendencies to place faith in magic or in the worship of charismatic cult figures. Bodine is a celebrant of the mythos of John Dillinger (see also Säure Bummer, 436); he reminds Slothrop of the strange, beautiful, mythic crowd scene that took place outside the Biograph Theater in Chicago when the FBI gunned Dillinger down:

> gate, *everybody* was there. They were taking off clothes, tearing checks out of checkbooks, ripping off pieces of each others' newspaper, just so they could soak up some of John Dillinger's blood. We went crazy.... They wouldn't want you thinking he was anything but a "common criminal"—but Their head's so far up Their ass—he still did what he did. He went out socked Them right in the toilet privacy of Their banks. Who cares what he was *thinking* about, long as it didn't get in the way? (741)

The more Their rigidifying of human conduct proceeds, the more radical, mindless, anarchic, ineffectual, or "criminal" will mythic figures and gestures of opposition become. So Pig himself changes, in the space since *V.*, from stereotypical hell-raising sailor to obscurely heroic, spaced-out rebel, headed for rarefied legend. In *V.* his talk veers only once out of sailor grossness, and then only to Whole Sick Crew–induced existentialist jargon (*V.*, 118); but in *Gravity's Rainbow* he is prophetic, possessed of a savvy, flip eloquence:

> "Just a humble guy," the swarthy doughboy of the deep scratching in his groin after an elusive crab with a horn finger, rippling in the ballooning pleats and fabric of his [extravagant zoot suit's] trousers, "just a freckleface kid from Albert Lea, Minnesota, down there on Route 69 where the speed limit's lickety-split all night long, just tryin' t' make it in the Zone here, kind of a frecklefaced kid used a safety pin through a cork for a catwhisker and stayed up listened to the voices coast to coast before I was 10 and none of them ever recommended gettin' into any of them *gang wars*, bud*dih.*" (710–11)

He can mourn powerfully over "losing" Slothrop, now on the last edge of visibility: "*But somebody's got to hold on, it can't happen to all of us—no, that'd be too much ... Rocketman, Rocketman. You poor fucker*" (741). If he believes at such a moment in the talismanic magic of Dillinger's blood, so must we believe in the nobility of the belief, without forgetting its unreality: "Do you—please, are you listening? This thing here works. Really does. It worked for me, but I'm out of the Dumbo stage now, I can fly without it. But you. Rocky. You ..." (741).

Bodine himself is fading here, like Rocketman, rollicking toward invisibility: fading as all the characters might do, if set free enough, loosed amid Earth's entropic forces that level energies and disperse selves: "She's still with you, though harder to see these days, nearly invisible as a glass of gray lemonade in a twilit room ... still she is there" (577). I have not seen it noticed in criticism that *Gravity's Rainbow* never gives Bodine a first name, never says "Pig," only "Seaman Bodine." Perhaps Pynchon wants readers themselves to make the closed-loop connections—from here back to the prosaic Pig of *V.*, perpetually AWOL from shipboard, and forward again to *Gravity's Rainbow*, in whose world pigs are everywhere, loose, magically AWOL from organized slaughter. They are cult animals, of all beasts the closest to Earth. The narrator even apologizes, "sorry pigs, nothing personal" (707), for imagining a drooling infant in a picture, the Gross Suckling, clutching a hamhock. The pig Frieda and her traveling companion Slothrop, the pig-suited Plechazunga, seem somehow the distant objects of William Slothrop's old kindness and pity, as he had herded his pigs, with their "untroubled pink eyelashes and kind eyes" (555), over the Berkshires to Puritan Boston. All the novel's elaborate hierarchies and moires are grounded here, where the pigs root, "at home with the Earth, sharing the same gift of life" (555).

Pig Bodine is the last human shape before reaching the wordless domain of the animals, who are speechless and nameless, whom language hasn't detached from Earth. Pynchon's own language, like Rilke's, is unfailingly kind to animals, framing a few individual beasts with names attentively right: Wolfgang the chimp, Frieda the pig, Ursula the lemming, Wernher the owl, Grigori the octopus. These names parody "characterization," of course, as a trapping device—for Pynchon's human, named characters also want to diffuse their shapes and names, as the novel's system opens out to the world, quiet resonances on the air, in the mind, in history's collective self-consciousness. "Still she is there," once art has activated her, a permeation of being in Being—"You'll never get to see her. So somebody has to tell you" (472). So somebody, this magnificent novelist, has.

4

Max Weber,
the Spirit of Capitalism,
and *Gravity's Rainbow*

The Mass Society

Accepting his party's nomination for president in 1976, Jimmy Carter attacked, as *Newsweek* paraphrased him, "an unidentifed 'elite.' This unnamed 'they,' he charged, 'never stand in line looking for a job when unemployment prevails,' never lack a place to sleep when 'a confused and bewildering welfare system' fails, never suffer from inferior education, but send their children 'to exclusive private schools.' They benefit from 'an unfair tax structure—and tight secrecy always seems to prevent reform.'" Carter's successful campaign was marked throughout by just such a skillful combination of classic American populist rhetoric with newer sorts of insinuations, the tones of what we may pseudo-journalistically call the New Paranoia. As shared during the 1970s and early 1980s between news media and their publics, this mode of mind feels most comfortable—or best entertains itself—in believing that the American contemporaneity in some way shows forth the workings of a vague power elite. The media have melodramatized not only the main events of Vietnam and Watergate, but also CIA plots against leaders of foreign countries, drug experiments by federal agencies on unknowing subjects, high-level-conspiracy theories of the 1960s assassinations, the roles of large oil companies in energy crises, welfare and nursing home management scandals, and certainly outriding capers by such people as Spiro T. Agnew, Robert Vesco, J. Edgar Hoover, and John Mitchell. That Carter himself could bid for "inside" power by mediating himself as an "outsider" to power seems, together with the fact of journalism's happily noting the ploy, some sort of "inside" joke, in turn; in the New Paranoia, no one feels safely outside the texture.

As I have already tried to show, Pynchon's fiction plays constantly with just such vertiginous inside-looking-out epistemologies. When it is vaguely called topical, what is usually meant is that the sense of powerlessness, of one's experience as an "appearance" directed by controls from above—such as Pynchon's characters, narrator, and readers all feel congruently, evokes the New Paranoia of daily life. The topicality depends in part also, to be sure, on our fleeting glimpses in *Gravity's Rainbow* of real, familiar power elite figures—Walter Rathenau, J. Edgar Hoover, Allen Dulles, anachronistic Nixon, et al.; Pynchon's Chemical Instrumentality for the Abnormal, Committee on Idiopathic Archetypes, and Committee on Incandescent Anomalies all say CIA. But Pynchon's subversive, preterite characters, below their jesters' disguises, are also contemporaries of ours, and the novel's world, in short, is a surrealistically refracted society of the masses—one that fits quite well, incidentally, de Tocqueville's description, around 1835, of a possible future state of American hyperdemocracy, "where all things are out of their mutual connections, where virtue is without genius, and genius without honor; where the love of order is confounded with a taste for repression, and the holy rites of freedom with a contempt for law; where the light thrown by conscience on human actions is dim, and where nothing seems to be any longer forbidden or allowed, honorable or shameful, false or true."[1]

In C. Wright Mills's prescient *The Power Elite*—quite likely an "influence" on Pynchon—the modern masses are the pitifully disinherited heirs of that rational community of informed, active "publics" envisioned by Enlightenment social theory. Masses, unlike publics, do not really give ideal impulse and direction to a political process, do not contribute ideas to any power dispensation, do not engage in dialogue with each other; rather, they passively receive such values, opinions, and stereotypical habits of mind as will make them most pliable to the uses of power. The power elite themselves, who are leaders more or less interchangeably of government, corporate business, and the military, are bound together by "intimate sensibilities shared with one another";[2] lacking coherent morality, ideal goals, or any fineness of sensibility such as the eighteenth century demanded of men of power, they can "come readily to define themselves as inherently worthy of what they possess ... to believe themselves 'naturally' elite"[3] by virtue

1. Alexis de Tocqueville, *Democracy in America*, ed. Richard D. Heffner (New York: New American Library, 1956), p. 35.

2. C. Wright Mills, *The Power Elite* (New York: Oxford University Press, 1956), p. 15.

3. Ibid., p. 14.

of the very fact that they monopolize power. The mass society is thus two interpenetrant, interdependent, but nonetheless paradoxically quite closed systems, the lower one being a "mediated" reality inside which a man may be trapped, defined, by his merely mechanical, instrumental functions. Such a man, says Mills,

> does not gain a transcending view from [any] media; instead he gets his experience stereotyped, and then he gets sunk futher by that experience. He cannot detach himself in order to observe, much less to evaluate, what he is experiencing, much less what he is not experiencing. Rather than that internal discussion we call reflection, he is accompanied through his life-experience with a sort of unconscious, echoing monologue. He has no projects of his own: he fulfills the routines that exist. He does not transcend whatever he is at any moment.... He is not truly aware of his own daily experience and of its actual standards: he drifts, he fulfills habits.[4]

In *Gravity's Rainbow* Pynchon underlines constantly, with help from the metaphor of Gödel's Theorem, the proposition that it is impossible to judge anything accurately inside a closed system, from a standpoint that is itself inside the system—the proposition simultaneously finding further metaphors in and applying itself to the worlds of sociology, science, epistemology, ethics, aesthetics, and metaphysics.[5] And in *Lot 49* the printed-circuit-like streets of the closed system of San Narciso/America leave Oedipa Maas asking "how had it ever happened here, with the chances once so good for diversity?" (*Lot 49*, 136).

By this stage in my study it should be clear that these worldly sociological matrices of the secular paranoias that I discuss in this chapter are far from being the whole imaginative story—even the whole of the paranoid's imagination's concerns—in *Gravity's Rainbow*. But Pynchon after all has celebrated his friend Richard Fariña's novel as having shown "exactly what, in this bewildering Republic, is serious and what cannot possibly be"; for *Gravity's Rainbow*, for "republic," read "post-Renaissance West," reading as synecdoches such matrices as post-1871 Germany, Puritan Massachusetts, and post–World War II America. In this chapter, accordingly, I describe some models of secu-

---

4. Ibid., p. 322.

5. Cf. also Herbert Marcuse's argument that the "benevolent totalitarianism" of advanced industrial society creates a closed "universe of discourse" from inside which no criticism in terms of outside values is possible. For Marcuse, technology itself is the all-comprehending "medium"; in this medium "culture, politics and the economy merge into an omnipresent system which swallows up or repulses all alternatives" (Marcuse, *One-Dimensional Man* [Boston: Beacon Press, 1964], p. xvi).

lar-paranoid themes of the New Paranoia, as suggested to Pynchon's imagination by some of the work of the great German sociologist Max Weber. Although Pynchon's uses of Weber have so far been more widely discussed in the criticism than most other aspects of *Gravity's Rainbow*, and although the Weberian themes themselves are fairly familiar, still, in view of the great prominence of their place in Pynchon's vision, it seems wise to look at some length and in a Pynchonian light at the Weberian concepts of bureaucracy and charisma and at Weber's sociological readings of seventeenth-century Puritanism. The chapter closes by tracing *Gravity's Rainbow*'s uses, in a Weberian, paranoiac, and New Paranoiac light, of the history of the I. G. Farben cartel of modern Germany.

Charisma and Routinization: The Zone

The popular senses in which the term *charisma* has come to be widely used exfoliate from Weber's original sense, in which the word denotes a property of leadership and authority over masses of people as exerted by the heroic, presumably exalted or "chosen" leader whose claim to extrarational inspiration is taken by his followers as authoritative and absolute. "The natural leaders in distress have been holders of specific gifts of the body and spirit; and these gifts have been believed to be supernatural, not accessible to everybody":[6] that Christ and Hitler are both beautifully exemplary charismatics reminds us that this definition is quite "value-neutral." In Pynchon, charisma can dovetail with preterition, as in Slothrop's case, in that for Weber charisma is transient, evanescent, fated to be "passed over" by history in the long run. It moves men only so long as it can keep providing "miracles" to validate its claims and attain its ends. When the miracles fail, or when the charismatic leader is "deserted by God" and abdicates his role, charisma is subsumed in existing, stable, and self-sustaining authoritarian patterns. In history the two chief of these, according to Weber, have been the traditional-patriarchal and the rational-bureaucratic, the latter increasingly being the dominant pattern of social and political organization for the twentieth century.

Weber's is one of those intellectual canons whose tag-terms Pynchon

6. From Weber's *Wirtschaft und Gesellschaft*, in *From Max Weber: Essays in Sociology*, trans. and ed. H. H. Gerth and C. Wright Mills (New York: Oxford University Press, 1958), p. 245.

teasingly scatters around in *Gravity's Rainbow,* so that we may be tempted to try to explain events there in terms of these special conceptual frames. Géza Rózsavölgyi speaks hopefully to Pointsman of a postwar future in which "personalities could be replaced by abstractions of power.... There should be no room for a terrible disease like charisma.... Its rationalization should proceed while we had the time and resources" (81). Joseph Ombindi of the Empty Ones asks Enzian whether he would not say that the absorption of the Hereros into the prewar German state represented "in Max Weber's phrase ... a 'routinization of charisma'" (325). Enzian's reply—misleadingly, for the formulation within its own terms is quite valid—is " 'Outase' ... which is one of many Herero words for shit, in this case a large, newly laid cow turd" (325). The bisexual Thanatz sees in the rocket "a Max Weber charisma ... some joyful—and *deeply* irrational—force the State bureaucracy would never routinize, against which it could not prevail ... cruel, hard, thrusting into the virgin-blue robes of the sky ... Oh, so phallic" (464–65). Thanatz and Ombindi each have a valid enough perspective, Weber's, on *Gravity's Rainbow's* reality—since the Nazi system can indeed be said to have routinized the charismatic Earth-energies of the Hereros, and since, postwar, They want to bring the rocket, Their own charismatic Frankenstein assembly, safely back within frames of rational power. Also, Slothrop may conveniently be seen, as Joseph Slade sees him, as "a charismatic hero without a following";[7] his half-conscious quest for the rocket and dim desire to preserve it for preterite uses are, in these terms, attempts to prolong charismatic, as opposed to rational-bureaucratic, energies in the Zone.

Most charismatic people and objects in *Gravity's Rainbow* are thus, after Weber, "routinized"—although another alternative exists in paranoia's suspicion that charisma may simply be deliberately extinguished: "There's people in high places," Major Marvy tells Tchitcherine, "wanna wipe them suckers [the Schwarzkommando] out, *now*" (565). Or, in yet another alternative, They may decide simply to ignore individual heroism, mystery, magic, ignoring it being tantamount to obliterating it, since to be "unauthorized" is in Their terms not to exist: charisma and preterition alike here attain to invisibility. This crushing or ignoring out of existence is the fate of Weber's "pure" charismatics, those rare beings "absolutely opposed to ... objectified form,"[8] who

7. Joseph Slade, *Thomas Pynchon* (New York: Warner Paperback Library, 1974), p. 210.   8. Weber, *Wirtschaft und Gesellschaft,* p. 262.

tend toward an "unavoidable separation from the world."[9] Another Weberian term, "pariah," denotes outsiders of this invisible kind; members of pariah castes (diasporic Jews, Indian untouchables) are tolerated for economic reasons but are held off from intercourse of any nonutilitarian kind with the elite. When Roger Mexico crashes Pointsman's business conference, the assembled executives over whom he literally pisses are slow to react, "still not quite willing to admit that this is happening, you know, in any world that really touches, at too many points, the one *they're* accustomed to" (636).

Spontaneity, mystery, magic, surprise, all attributes of "pure" charisma, may thus either fade because nobody is looking or else be routinized—the latter rather after the manner of comicbook heroes trapped inside the frame-panels that mediate their new identities as mass-merchandized articles. Leslie Fiedler has argued that Superman, Plasticman, et al., in that they reify deep archetypal patterns of imagination, express genuine and violent folk-impulses, and that this is why, despite their "framing" in comic books, they can arouse the fear and hostility of neo-Puritan middle classes:

> The comic books with their ... heroes ... are seen [by middleclass masscult] as inheritors, for all their superficial differences, of the *inner* impulses of traditional folk art. Their gross drawing, their poverty of language cannot disguise their heritage of aboriginal violence, their exploitation of the ancient conflict of black magic and white. Beneath their journalistic commentary on A-bomb and Communism, they touch archetypal material: those shared figures of our lower minds more like the patterns of dream than fact.... They are our not-quite machine-subdued Grimm, though the Black Forest has become, as it must, the City; the Wizard, the Scientist; and simple Hans, Captain Marvel.[10]

In *Gravity's Rainbow*, however, all charismatic heroes of whatever kind eventually lose their effectiveness, because, by Weber's theory, "it is the fate of charisma, whenever it comes into the permanent institutions of a community, to give way to powers of tradition or of rational socialization. This waning of charisma generally indicates the diminishing importance of individual action."[11]

The formulation nicely explains why, when Gottfried's sacrifice pro-

9. Ibid., p. 248.

10. Leslie Fiedler, "The Middle Against Both Ends," in *Mass Culture*, ed. Bernard Rosenberg and David Manning White,

pp. 537–47; quote from p. 541.

11. Weber, *Wirtschaft und Gesellschaft*, p. 253.

ceeds, the old superheroes, long since "framed" as now Gottfried himself is being terminally framed, arrive too late to stop it: "Superman will swoop boots-first into a deserted clearing, a launcher-erector sighing oil through a slow seal-leak, gum evoked from the trees.... The colors of his cape will wilt in the afternoon sun, curls on his head begin to show their first threads of gray ... Submariner and his gang will run into battery trouble ... Plasticman will lose his way among the Imipolex chains ... 'Too Late' was never in their programming" (751–52).

Incarnated as Rocketman, Slothrop obviously expresses his charismatic potential—and, in the light of Weberian theory, his death wish. In earlier, better days, imagines the narrator, the moire of his fate had perhaps brought him into alignment with two other doomed charismatics, Malcolm X and John Kennedy:

> It is nice to think that one Saturday night, one floor-shaking Lindy-hopping Roseland night, Malcolm looked up from some Harvard kid's shoes and caught the eye of Jack Kennedy (the ambassador's son), then a senior ... did Red suspend his ragpopping just the shadow of a beat, just enough gap in the moire there to let white Jack see through, not through to but through *through* the shine on his classmate Tyrone Slothrop's shoes? Were the three ever lined up that way—sitting, squatting, passing through? Eventually Jack and Malcolm both got murdered. Slothrop's fate is not so clear. It may be that They have something different in mind for Slothrop. (688)

And then down the Roseland toilet thinking of Jack Kennnedy, who might have retrieved somehow the mouth harp Slothrop has dropped, "violated gravity somehow" (65), while Malcolm X (alias Red the shoeshine boy, working off at the Roseland his "sin of being born the color of Shit 'n Shinola" [688]) had watched from above. The narrator even thinks he hears, all the way from New York, the accompaniment of Charlie "Yardbird" Parker, the great alto sax player, on "Cherokee"— "His bird's singing" already menaced by a surrounding culture of Muzak, ubiquitous supermarkets' "groggy wash of the endlessly, gutlessly overdubbed strings" (63). It would appear that the self-destructive Bird was one of Weber's "pure" charismatics, preferring extinction to routinization: "Down inside his most affirmative solos honks already the idle, amused dum-de-dumming of old Mister fucking Death he self" (63).[12]

12. When Bird Parker died in 1955, a doctor estimated his age, on the basis of his medical condition, to have been between fifty and sixty; actually it was thirty-four. Cause of death could have been lobar pneumonia, a perforated peptic ulcer,

Charisma, however, is very seldom pure, is rather almost always corruptible, co-optible. When Roger Mexico and Seaman Bodine, zoot-suited, set out to subvert a Krupp banquet with a Disgusting Dinners Drill, the preposterous degree of their success, and the amazingly puerile nature of the drill itself, are meant to color the episode as fantastically unlikely as any comicbook miracle: "Sir Hannibal Grunt-Gobbinette is threatening, between spasms of yellow bile foaming out his nose, to bring the matter up in Parliament" (716–17). More to the point than such preterite wish-fantasy is the narrator's cool explanation of why the Counterforce, as a matter of fact, will fail. Not only must its operations remain by definition irrational, hence disorganized, but its individual members "are as schizoid, as double-minded in the massive presence of money, as any of the rest of us, and that's the hard fact. The Man has a branch office in each of our brains, his corporate emblem is a white albatross, each local rep has a cover known as the Ego, and their mission in this world is Bad Shit. We do know what's going on, and we let it go on. As long as we can see them, those massively moneyed, once in awhile. As long as they allow us a glimpse, however rarely. We need that. And how they know it" (712–13).

More technically, not only does security (Jessica Swanlake's "spell against demons" [709]) allure by its promise of a participation in bureaucratized power, hence of a release from charismatic responsibilities, but those already in power positions will, for their parts, very willingly bring charisma "inside," because

> they wish to see their positions transferred from purely factual
> power relations into a cosmos of acquired rights, and to know that
> they are sanctified. These interests comprise by far the strongest
> motive for the conservation of charismatic elements of an objectified
> nature within the structure of domination.... [Furthermore,] after
> its routinization, [charisma is] a suitable source for the legitimate
> acquisition of sovereign power by the successors of the charismatic
> hero. Routinized charisma thus continues to work in favor of all
> those whose power and succession is guaranteed by that sovereign
> power, and who thus depend upon the continued existence of such
> power.[13]

Weber's point, a very Pynchonesque one, is that charisma and bureau-

---

cirrhosis of the liver, a massive heart attack, or any combination of these. Bird had been a heroin addict since about age fifteen and an acute alcoholic through most of his adult life. Even granted that jazz musicians generally do not tend to lead healthful lives, the case for a special self-destructiveness here seems fairly clear.

13. Weber, *Wirtschaft und Gesellschaft*, p. 262.

cratic organization are not finally dichotomous, either/or phenomena, but that there is dialectic and interdependence between them. After routinization, charisma's followers become good law-abiders within institutionalized authority (e.g., Christians in their churches). On the other hand, "bureaucratic control has inevitably at its apex an element which at least is not wholly bureaucratic,"[14] and from this apex emanates the final irrationality that covertly drives the system: Pynchon's "They" are assumed to be animated or enslaved by a rocket mystique of Their own, a higher power of the mysticisms or paranoias that bind and blind preterite characters. Weber, politically an aggressive Gross Deutscher, understood the Imperial German State as providing the final charismatic (nationalistic) impetus for the rationally efficient war effort of 1914–1918; he would have found in the Second War's German state, perhaps, an even better example of the relationships, since it was from the charismatic apex of Hitler and Nazism that the entire totalitarian state dispensation, another highly organized war effort, and a fiendishly "calculated" program of genocide, at last depended.

Pynchon's Zone extrudes temporarily in history as a sort of ahistorical chaos—a Rilkean openness suddenly made manifest by the destruction of the old bureaucracies and of the charismas behind or above them. Conditions there imply some fleeting chance for that freedom that Weber defined as the knowing of options: among possible models, metaphors, myths, for the understanding of life, a play of choices for history. "There are no zones," Schnorp, the black-market pastry entrepreneur, tells Slothrop, "no zones but the Zone" (333)—and "a second chance," recapitulating the primeval one, for economic organization: "You have had a glimpse of the Ur-Markt" (335). But in fanatic pursuit of the balloon that Schnorp and Slothrop ride into a cloud—airscape symbol of indeterminacy, of an absence of grid coordinates—are Marvy's Mothers in a reconnaissance plane. Incipient grids of air-traffic lanes are already "one more overlay on the Zone ... defining invisible corridors-in-the-sky" (620); plots are working, They are reimposing control. The preterite now must act quickly if their liberated charismas are to unite for the creation of a new, more humane history. Instead, the preterite flounder, unable, schlemihl-like, to overcome the ambivalences left in them by their former routinizations, unable to

14. Weber, *Wirtschaft und Gesellschaft*; quoted in Herbert Marcuse, "Industrialization and Capitalism," in *Max Weber* *and Sociology Today*, ed. Otto Stammer (New York: Harper & Row, 1971), p. 147.

organize to "play Their game" (638), which *is* organization. The rocket, itself an orphaned charisma, awaits appropriation by the former rocket technicians, the Schwarzkommando, who are its charismatic "children," but Enzian sees his mission darkly, and rocket and children separately are reroutinized from above, before their charismas can merge. Slothrop tries to recover the *papers* that in the old days had given him rank and identity; he seeks a discharge alike from the old institutional structure and from his new charismatic freedom, and does not learn to ask "What th' fuck are *papers*, anyhow?" (623) until it is too late for him, as for Superman.

In fact, Slothrop's long history of *paper*-conditioning announces another major Weberian image/symbol in *Gravity's Rainbow*. The Slothrop family had made its original fortune by logging off New England hillsides until they had gone to "necropolis, gray with marble dust" (27)—had routinized the "living green" of the trees to paper's "dead white" (268). When Broderick Slothrop sold Tyrone to I. G. Farben, the Slothrop paper, as a consequence of the deal, went to make worthless Notgeld such that "you carried marks around in wheelbarrows to your daily shopping and used them for toilet paper, assuming you had anything to shit" (284). White paper, like white porcelain toilets, bespeaks the repression of "shit," of the organic: it creates false value, particularly as money ("money in the Puritan sense—an outward and visible O.K. on [the elect's] intentions"—652). It also mediates literacy, including the all-governing scriptural Word of Puritanism. In these skeined senses—"Shit, money, and the Word, the three American truths" (28)—paper means a repressive rationality; it is a "medium," in McLuhanesque terminology, for the covert "message" of bureaucratic control—for the rules, regs, files, that effect the differentiation of life. "It is not death that separates these [preterite] incarnations, but paper: paper specialties, paper routines. The War, the Empire, will expedite such barriers between our lives" (130).

And "paper specialties," aided by the bureau-jargon word "expedite," glances at two distinctive traits of the highly developed bureaucracy as defined by Weber: its creation of a cult of the "professional," the trained expert, and, correlatively, its jealous possessiveness about "professional secrets": "Every bureaucracy seeks to increase the superiority of the professionally informed by keeping their knowledge and intentions secret. Bureaucratic administration always tends to be an administration of "secret session": insofar as it can, it hides its knowledge and action from criticism.... The concept of the "official secret" is the specific invention of bureaucracy, and nothing is so fanatically defended by the bureaucracy as this attitude."[15]

Ironically, it is just such attempts of mature bureaucracies to keep their systems closed that inevitably comes to work, Weber thought, *against* the ideal of "equality" that inspirits, however vaguely, that very democracy that of all political systems is the one most likely to promote the growth of bureaucracies. Weber's maximally bureaucratized state brings about, eventually, "the *levelling of the governed* in opposition to the ruling and bureaucratically articulated group."[16] Its paper-mediated ethic for preterite use is that, in Roger Mexico's paraphrase, "we are meant for work and government, for austerity: and these shall take priority over love, dreams, the spirit, the senses and other second-class trivia" (177).

And yet, Pynchon implies, since bureaucracies more often co-opt than exclude charismas, professional cultisms might always be routinized traces of once-charismatic, "magical" forces; bureaucracy reifies in its own nature its own *irrational* love of the ideal of rationality. And this ideal, Weber set out to show in *The Protestant Ethic and the Spirit of Capitalism,* may in itself be a transformation of a sacred dogma that informed radical seventeenth-century English Protestantism: "Theologically based categorization degenerated into secular classification which assumes, for secular ends, theological sanctions."[17]

The Puritan Word

The English Calvinists of the Westminster synod of 1647 provided the Puritan movement's authoritative definition of the elect and the reprobate (Pynchon's "preterite," the "passed over"):

> Chapter III (of God's Eternal Decree), No. 3. By the decree of God, for the manifestation of His Glory, some men and angels are predestinated unto everlasting life, and others foreordained to everlasting death....
>
> No. 5. Those of mankind that are predestinated unto life, God before the foundation of the world was laid, according to His eter-

15. Weber, *Wirtschaft und Gesellschaft,* p. 233.

16. Ibid., p. 226.

17. Joseph Krafft, " 'And How Far-

Fallen': Puritan Themes in *Gravity's Rainbow*," *Critique* 18 (1977): 55–73; quote from pp. 56, 57.

nal and immutable purpose, and the secret counsel and good pleasure of His will, hath chosen in Christ unto everlasting glory, out of His mere free grace and love, without any foresight of faith or good works, or perseverence in either of them, or any other thing in the creature as conditions, or causes moving Him thereunto, and all to the praise of His glorious grace....

No. 7. The rest of mankind God was pleased, according to the unsearchable counsel of His own will, whereby he extendeth, or with-holdeth mercy, as He pleaseth, for the glory of His sovereign power over His creatures, to pass by, and to ordain them to dishonour and wrath for their sin, to the praise of His glorious justice.[18]

Replacing the earlier, truly "catholic" conception of a church sodality as a collection of sinners equally open to grace, the Puritan dichotomy absolutely divided "preterite" mankind, who labored hopelessly under Adam's sin, from the tiny minority of the elect, for whom alone it had been given Christ to die and who received salvation by the arbitrary "grace" of an absolutely transcendent, inscrutable God. The church by definition was any gathering of the elect, although no one even within this "visible" communion could take completely for granted the fact of his election to the "invisible" one. One did not *earn* salvation, much less have it mediated to him by priestly hierarchies, since ontologically there was a profound separation between man and God, as, on earth, between saint and reprobate; Puritanism "den[ied] gradation and assert[ed] a break between the human and the divine, with only the word as bridge."[19]

The mystical Word, sparking the gap between God and man, manifested itself not only in scripture but also as the private sign or inner light looked for by the Puritan saint to confirm his grace and also in the minister's eloquence from his pulpit: "Behind the uttered words of the preacher vitalizing the revealed word of the Bible, hovers the Word itself, the Holy Spirit that will enter the soul of man and help him in his unbelief."[20] By a mundane word-system of doctrinal language, by scripture citation and pious talk, the system of Puritan piety was kept closed: words rationalized the faith in the Word, scripture-mongering

18. Westminster Confession, 5th official ed. (London: n.p., 1717), quoted in Max Weber, *The Protestant Ethic and the Spirit of Capitalism*, trans. Talcott Parsons (New York: Charles Scribner's Sons, 1958), p. 100.

19. Larzer Ziff, *Puritanism in America: New Culture in a New World* (New York: Viking Press, 1973), p. 6.

20. Ibid., p. 29.

meanwhile providing explications for history as well as for mundane phenomena, the whole process constituting a feedback to close the reflex arc. These are Pynchon's proto-paranoid "WASPs in buckled black, who heard God clamoring to them in every turn of a leaf or cow loose among apple orchards in autumn" (281).

That eloquence, and advanced literacy and learning in general, were so prized by the "word-smitten" Puritans (207), and that these Puritans at the same time, and in the name of the Word, so repressed so many non-Puritan forms of life, suggests Pynchon's own ambivalence about complex uses of language in general. The sense of the perilous, both/ and freedom of play between transcendental and rationalized, rationalizing words can become a major tension, a "Puritan mystery" (267), ubiquitous in Pynchon's work. In *The Crying of Lot 49*, Oedipa Maas surveys from a hilltop the "printed circuitry" of San Narciso's housing tracts, imagining that "words were being spoken" (*Lot 49*, 13). They may be the narcissistic dream-words of the closed culture's television frequencies, or, alternatively, like the epileptic's "pure piercing grace note announcing his seizure" (*Lot 49*, 69), they may herald a redemptive Word, some ultimate revelation—the secret of Tristero, the nature of Inverarity's will—to transform the American system. Slothrop's London fear of the rocket is partly a metaphysical dread of the nothingness of which V-2 seems to whisper: "a Word, spoken with no warning into your ear, then silence forever ... no, no bullet with fins, Ace ... not the Word, the one Word that rips apart the day" (25). But the rocket also variously serves all the novel's characters, including Slothrop, as quasi-religious Text, Tower, or Word: the "Key," for example, that Enzian's men hope will give them back their freedom. Pynchon's "dark" critics err in taking his Entropy metaphor too literally and linearly, since closed systems are not necessarily homogenized forever at maximum equilibrium; they may always be opened out, entropically destabilized again by White Visitations from outside. If the rocket is a symbol or reification of the death energies of the very system that it might now rip apart, then, the implied question goes, is apocalypse a suicidal gesture from inside, or is it perhaps a redemptive irruption from outside?

One of the novel's myriad, almost invisible inquiries to this effect is a simple song line, when Slothrop, as one of those "whom the old Puritan sermons denounced as 'the glozing neuters of the world,' " is invited to sing:

How-dy neighbor, how-dy pard!
Ain't it lone-ly, say ain't it hard,
Passin' by so silent, day-after-day, with-out, even
   A smile-or, a friendly word to say? Oh let me
Tell ya buddy, tell ya ace,
Things're fal-lin', on their face—
Maybe we should stick together part o' the way, and
Skies'll be bright-er some day!
Now *ev'*rybody— (676–77)

A second reading reveals that "now ev'rybody—" telegraphs the novel's last line; its interruption on page 760 is due presumably to the fall of the final rocket on "this old theater." Thus, does "Skies'll be brighter some day" imply, as the pop song diction would have it, some happy ending or dispensation of love, or does the line in its false-bottomed drawer really offer a prophecy of technologized Puritanism's Last Judgment on itself, and terminal whiteness? The language of *Gravity's Rainbow*, as much in these covert fluxions as in any paraphrasable "meaning," asserts that images, ideas in general, and certainly historical potentialities have punning depths, like words. Pynchon's well-known reverence for the "high magic to low puns" (*Lot 49*, 96) ultimately expresses his sense of the both/and indeterminacy of events; it is simply not metaphysically tenable to be causal-deterministic, Pavlovian, controlling, "Puritan."

      *   *   *

That Puritanism became a successfully ongoing worldly system is partly due, Weber claimed, to its famous "work ethic." *The Protestant Ethic and the Spirit of Capitalism* describes the belief that the saint must incessantly "labour in a calling" on earth, doing God's work and hoping to gain from God a sign of grace. Although private profit was not the explicit end of one's labor, and although it surely would have been sinful to waste profits in mere self-indulgence, it was, at the least, tempting to see in the degree of one's private profit a measure of God's favor:

> The usefulness of a calling, and thus its favour in the sight of God,
> is measured primarily in moral terms, and thus in terms of the
> importance of the goods produced in it for the community. But a
> further, and, above all, in practice the most important, criterion is
> found in private profitableness. For if that God, whose hand the

Puritan sees in all the occurrences of life, shows one of His elect a chance of profit, he must do it with a purpose. Hence the faithful Christian must follow the call by taking advantage of the opportunity.[21]

Weber identifies this inner imaginative alignment of personal diligence, "rational matter-of-factness," as needed to make diligence show a profit, and personal sanctity as impelling the characteristic Puritan "asceticism." Rational sobriety had the merit also of protecting the Puritan from the corruptions of the world's entropic disorganization: from vanities, follies, sensual snares; from relict paganism as symbolized in maypoles, Morris dances, and Christmas trees; from secular art forms like the Shakespearean theater.[22] In short, "that powerful tendency toward uniformity of life, which today so immensely aids the capitalistic interest in the standardization of production, had its ideal foundation in the repudiation of all idolatry of the flesh."[23]

The connection between piety and purposeful rationality, Weber continues, persisted, particularly in America, even after the theological middle term—rational labor as validating spiritual salvation—had dropped away. When he visited the United States in the first decade of this century, Weber monitored the sociological expressions of evolving neo-Puritanism, giving his report in "The Protestant Sects and the Spirit of Capitalism."[24] The strongest social allegiances of American businessmen, he found, were not to "catholic" social bodies, with admission open to all, but to neo-Protestant "sects": groups whose applicants had to prove themselves against vague criteria of "worth" in order to be admitted. In secular organizations like boys' clubs, college fraternities, Freemason chapters, and metropolitan businessmen's clubs, the circular judgments ran, one is worthy of admission, hence one is admitted, hence one is generally worthy and trustworthy, especially for business purposes. In southern rural communities, where

21. Weber, *The Protestant Ethic*, p. 162.

22. "When Shakespeare was twenty-three a book was published in London which described actors as 'fiends that are crept into the world by stealth,' 'sent from their great captain Satan (under whose banner they bear arms) to deceive the world, to lead the people with enticing shows to the Devil.' The author also describes them as apes, hell hounds, vipers, minotaurs, painted sepulchres, dogs and of course caterpillars, and his book is most suitably entitled *A Mirror Of Monsters*" (Marchette Chute, *Shakespeare of London* [New York: E. P. Dutton & Co., 1949], p. 54n).

23. Weber, *The Protestant Ethic*, p. 169.

24. In Gerth & Mills, *From Max Weber*, pp. 302–23.

secularization had not proceeded as far, "admission to the Baptist congregation is recognized as an absolute guarantee of the moral qualities of a gentleman, especially of those qualities required in business matters."[25] This very bourgeois ethic, Weber noted again, can operate in democracies to further the growth of bureaucratization in ultimately undemocratic directions. Pynchon concludes that the linkage between bureaucratic organization, the earlier predator ethic of capitalism, and the original piety of the Puritans creates one side, the blind side, of the contemporary dichotomy between Them and Us, Hothouse and Street (cf. *V.*), systems managers (with "no right at all to be where they are" [521]) and rootless poor/crazy/young. The saints of a charismatic religiosity have become, in Weber's words, "specialists without spirit, sensualists without heart; this nullity imagines that it has attained a level of civilization never before achieved."[26]

In a little North Sea town near Cuxhaven, Slothrop puts on a Pig-Hero costume to help village kids commemorate Donar's, or Thor's, once having sent a giant pig, Plechazunga, to repel a Viking invasion. "The old gods, even by the 10th century, still had some pull with the people. Donar hadn't quite been tamed into Saint Peter or Roland"; and so the town's Roland statue, behind which the pig-suited Slothrop hides, is "a particularly humorless, goggle-eyed, curly-headed, pinch-waisted specimen" (568). When the MP's come to break up the party and its inevitable black-market dealings, forcing Slothrop to flee, the implication is clear that the real and long-term enemy of pagan pluralism, pagan charisma, was not the Vikings (men of the North though they were), but a methodical, Rolandesque, dogmatizing Christianity and now its military-industrial heirs. If paganism, as Pynchon seems to assume here, could accommodate multiplicity and connect life with life, then Christianity, and its caricature, Puritanism, allowed no such complexities or ambivalences—hence the denunciations by the "old Puritan sermons" of those who, like Slothrop, are "so divided, so perfectly unable to come down on one side or another" (676–77).

In the stories of Katje Borgesius's ancestor Frans van der Groov and Tyrone Slothrop's ancestor William, the novel provides two much more fully developed set-piece studies of Puritanism in historical action. Frans participates in the extermination of the world's only living dodo

25. "The Protestant Sects"; in Gerth & Mills, *From Max Weber*, p. 305.

26. Weber, *The Protestant Ethic*, p. 182.

population, on the island of Mauritius in the seventeenth century. In the act, in a densely beautiful passage, he is seen "framed" as in an old painting darkening under its varnish:

> Once he sat all day staring at a single white dodo's egg in a grass hummock ... he waited for scratching, a first crack reaching to net the chalk surface: an emergence. Hemp gripped in the teeth of the steel snake, ready to be lit, ready to descend.... It was then, if ever, he might have seen how the weapon made an axis potent as Earth's own between himself and this victim, still one, inside the egg, with its ancestral chain, not to be broken out for more than its blink of world's light. There they were, the silent egg and the crazy Dutchman, and the hookgun that linked them forever, framed, billiantly motionless as any Vermeer. (109)

The undetonated Word, a white flash to unite destroyed and destroyer, waits in the hard "steel snake"—this snake cruelly mirror-reversing the positive sign of the symbol of carbon chemistry's "ancestral chain," the coiling Great World Serpent of Life. The Puritan party has found that it can make practical use of other beasts—like, sadly, the pigs they have brought from Holland, who root out and eat dodo eggs—but the dodoes lack both any obvious usefulness and any chance for that acquisition of language that would have meant, in the narrator's phrase, a "chance of co-opting them in to what their round and flaxen invaders were calling Salvation" (110). Hopelessly outside the divine scheme, they are "ill-made ... so ugly as to embody argument against a Godly creation" (110). Yet Frans acquires doubts: seeing that the colony will founder, he wonders, "if [the Puritans] were chosen to come to Mauritius, why had they also been chosen to fail, and leave? Is that a choosing, or is it a passing-over? Are they Elect, or are they preterite, and doomed as dodoes?" (110).

Familiar dichotomies having begun to blur, Frans must restructure his rationalizations for continuing to kill dodoes. He fantasizes their becoming useful—"Sanctified now they will feed us, sanctified their remains and droppings will fertilize our crops" (111)—by virtue of their receiving "a miracle: a Gift of Speech" (110):

> Ranked in thousands on the shore, with a luminous profile of reef on the water behind them, its roar the only sound on the morning, volcanoes at rest, the wind suspended, an autumn sunrise dispensing light glassy and deep over them all.... *For as much as they are the creatures of God, and have the gift of rational discourse, acknowledging that only in His Word is eternal life to be found* ... And there are tears of happiness in the eyes of the dodoes. They are all brothers now, they

and the humans who used to hunt them, brothers in Christ, the
little baby they dream now of sitting near, roosting in his stable,
feathers at peace, watching over him and his dear face all night
long. (110–11)

The Pynchonian marker-word "dear," as it floats to the surface of this
passage, confirms that Frans despite himself has an intuition of his
"brotherhood," indeed, with all other life. But as filtered through
Puritanism and receiving its language from it, all that is likely to come
from this intuition is the cloudy feeling that his gun's "axis" somehow
"links" Frans with that which he kills. The anticipation of Captain
Blicero and his sadomasochistic rocket is clear. The dodoes and the
Dutch colony, in the end, do indeed die—in real history as in the novel.

The book-long Progress of Puritan-descended Tyrone Slothrop is a
running parody of the ideal, Bunyanesque one,[27] his drivenness to
make it proposed as an obscure birthright: "He hangs at the bottom of
his blood's avalanche, 300 years of western swamp-Yankees, and can't
manage but some nervous truce with their Providence.... Ruins he goes
daily to look in are each a sermon on vanity.... Slothrop's Progress:
London the secular city instructs him: turn any corner and he can find
himself inside a parable" (25). The modern Slothrop's doubts about the
hoary Puritan "Providence," doubts more radical than those of Frans
van der Groov, reduce it to a vague superstition of Slothrop's luck, often
hard to believe in even as such: "Hey *Providence*, what'd you do, step
out for a beer or something?" (378). Although in the early, paranoid
stage of the Progress, often enough, "The hand of Providence creeps
among the stars, giving Slothrop the finger" (461), the later, antiparanoid Slothrop completely inverts the Bunyanesque model by
wholly losing, not validating, his faith in transcendental ideas of order.
And, in a most significant inversion of the Puritan jargon, the "grace"
that experience is constantly said to demand of him, of all the preterite,

27. One very sly little checkpoint along
the way of the parodic Progress is the nasal
erection that Slothrop gets with Trudi (439),
referring probably to Freud's idea that the
body's extremities can be sublimated sub-
stitutes for the phallus: covert explication
of the English Puritan fashion for large ears
and noses. In *A Tale of a Tub*, Swift, too,
made good use of the English Non-Con-
formists' ear- and nose-fetishes (1704):
"It is held by Naturalists, that if there be
a Protuberancy of Parts in the Superior
Region of the Body, as in the Ears and
Noses, there must be a Parity also in the
Inferior: And therefore in that truly pious
Age [of the Puritan Commonwealth], the
Males in every Assembly, according as
they were gifted, appeared very forward in
exposing their Ears to view, and the
Regions about them."
See also Norman O. Brown, *Life Against
Death* (Middletown, Ct.: Wesleyan Univer-
sity Press, 1959), for a Freudian treatment,
with due respects to Swift, of phallic ears.

is no rigid state transcendentally given, but a kind of inner, improvisatory, fast-footed cool, as Seaman Bodine explains: "A-and it doesn't even matter why *we're* doing this, either. Rocky? Yeah, what we need isn't right reasons, but just that *grace*. The physical grace to keep it working. Courage, brains, sure, O.K., but without that grace? forget it" (741).

The speech may be meant as a reductive Bodinification of Hemingway's solemn "grace under pressure"; simultaneously, and quite seriously, the "grace" ethic of *Gravity's Rainbow* perhaps feels itself as some higher power of *V.*'s "keep cool but care." In any case, grace is now clearly preterite, not elect, property; preterition needs "a community of grace, a gift of persistence" (265), that it may survive the "graceless expectations of old men who watched … you lindy-hop into the pit by millions, as many millions as necessary" (472).

The first American Slothrop, and *Gravity's Rainbow*'s kindest guardian ghost, is William Slothrop, a mess cook on the fictional ship *Arbella*, which arrived at the Massachusetts Bay Colony in 1630. The narrator imagines William's stews, spilled on deck, being shaken off "the indignant shoes of the more elect" (204),[28] these messes subtly recalling the banana peel that had caused Miklos Thanatz to slip overboard from the decadent *Anubis* to join the preterite "Humility." Just so, William Slothrop, "sick and tired of the Winthrop machine" (554), deserts and goes west, beyond the Berkshires, to the good company of his preterite pigs:

> [William] and his son John got a pig operation going—used to drive hogs right back down the great escarpment, back over the long pike to Boston, drive them just like sheep or cows. By the time they got to market those hogs were so skinny it was hardly worth it, but William wasn't really in it so much for the money as just for the trip itself. He enjoyed the road, the mobility, the chance encounters of the day—Indians, trappers, hill people—and most of all just being with those pigs. They were good company. Despite the folklore and the injunctions in his own Bible, William came to love their nobility and personal freedom, their gift for finding comfort in the mud on a hot day—pigs out on the road, in company together, were everything Boston wasn't, and you can imagine what the end of the journey, the weighing, slaughter and dreary pigless return back up

28. In this passage, "more elect," quite nonsensical in Puritan theological terms, implies that among the Puritans of Massachusetts there was already an incipient decadence in the direction of secular hier- archies such as would characterize the oligarchical rule. Joseph Krafft has noticed this implication of "more elect" in his paper, " 'And How Far-Fallen.' "

into the hills must've been like for William. Of course he took it as a parable—knew that the squealing bloody horror at the end of the pike was in exact balance to all their happy sounds, their untroubled pink eyelashes and kind eyes, their smiles, their grace in cross-country movement. (555)

Several commentators have already noted[29] that William Slothrop connects to Thomas Pynchon's own Puritan ancestor William Pynchon, a prominent member-sharer in the party that arrived aboard the *Jewell* at Massachusetts Bay in April 1630.[30] William Pynchon had a plantation at "Rocksbury," Massachusetts, where he engaged in farming and sea commerce. Because, like the famous renegade Thomas Morton of Merrymount, he violated the law against trading firearms to Indians, and because of the barrenness of the soil on Boston Neck, Pynchon moved west into the Connecticut Valley, leading the first permanent English settlement party into "Agawam," the site of the current Springfield, where he bargained peaceably and successfully with the Indians for land rights in 1636. Commissioned to furnish the Connecticut Valley settlements with food, he traded for Indian corn; a long dispute with a rival, Captain John Mason, seems to have been provoked by the differences between the two men's ways of dealing with Indians, Pynchon's conciliatory, Mason's aggressive and brutal. Twice Pynchon was brought to trial on charges of manipulating the corn trade for his personal gain and at the expense of the settlements. He was convicted and his power greatly reduced, but he was at last vindicated when the Roxbury Church and the Massachusetts General Court intervened in his favor.

What did finally doom Pynchon's New World career was his book, *The Meritorious Price of Our Redemption*, published in England and

---

29. Among the critics who have at least mentioned the historical William Pynchon are Joseph Slade in "Escaping Rationalization: Options for the Self in *Gravity's Rainbow*," *Critique* 18 (1977): 27–37; Matthew Winston in "The Quest for Pynchon," *Twentieth Century Literature* 22 (1975): 278–87; and Jules Siegel, in a gossipy, humorless, ridiculously self-aggrandizing article, "Who Is Thomas Pynchon and Why Did He Take Off With My Wife?," *Playboy* 24 (March 1977): 97, 122, 169, 170, 172–74.
Mark Richard Siegel, apparently misreading the Winston article, calls William Slothrop "a real New England Pilgrim

who arrived in the same fleet as Pynchon's own ancestor William": *Pynchon: Creative Paranoia in "Gravity's Rainbow"* (Port Washington, N.Y.: Kennikat Press, 1978), p. 60.

30. For some historical sources on the career of William Pynchon, see footnotes to the articles cited above. My brief account below follows two old, perhaps inadequate sources: Ezra Hoyt Byington, *The Puritan in England and New England* (Boston: Roberts Brothers, 1896), and Mason A. Green, *Springfield, 1636–1886, History of Town and City* (Springfield, Mass.: C. A. Nicholas & Co., 1888).

indeed, like William Slothrop's book *On Preterition*, "among the first books to've been not only banned but ceremonially burned in Boston" (555)—Pynchon's book on the Common in 1650. *The Meritorious Price* discussed the meaning of Christ's vicarious atonement, taking issue with the Bay Colony's prevailing interpretation, a fiercely severe one that asserted that Christ went unwillingly to his sufferings that divine wrath might be diverted from sinful men, divine justice be satisfied, and the elect redeemed. Pynchon's argument to the contrary was that Christ had acted willingly, "mediatorially," and that universal redemption can come because "as Adam's disobedience ruined the world, so Christ's perfect obedience, as our mediator, redeemed the world."[31] Christ "did not suffer the wrath of God, but He did the will of God."[32] In William Slothrop's *On Preterition*, an elect pig survives the slaughter in Boston specifically in order to "validate all the ones who'd had to [die]" (555). "William argued holiness for these 'second Sheep,' without whom there'd be no elect" (555). The heresy of both Williams, then, is to argue that election emerges dialectically from preterition, and for the sake of it; that election is not ontologically *other*. In both cases, real and fictional, "the Elect in Boston were pissed off about that" (555). William Pynchon had to recant and, clearly doomed to be banished from Massachusetts (as had been Roger Williams, who followed the case with interest), sailed back to England, leaving his son John behind.

The very early America of both Williams is, like the cleared space of Tyrone Slothrop's Zone, a region where "all the fences are down, one road as good as another, the whole space ... cleared, depolarized, and somewhere inside the waste of it a single set of co-ordinates from which to proceed, without elect, without preterite, without even nationality to fuck it up" (556). Each of the two Slothrops in his context in *Gravity's Rainbow* offers a "fork in the road ... singular point" (556) for historical choice to jump from. Had America not jumped the wrong way from William Slothrop's point, the narrator asks, "Might there have been fewer crimes in the name of [elect] Jesus, and more mercy in the name of [preterite] Judas Iscariot?" (556). The question crosses the interface of the fiction and attaches itself to Pynchon's own ancestor's time, and hence to the America that we know. The backgound condition that underlies real and fictional history—the "waste" of the passage above, the word not yet internally punctuated, frame-differentiated, to any

31. Quoted in Byington, *The Puritan*, p. 207.

32. Ibid., p. 208.

meaning by any Tristero or other system—might bring forth either unified life or life's terminal wastage, either of which, it is Pynchon's proposal about the texture of history, may yet, may tomorrow, emerge.

The Capitalist Word

For an imagination inside the twentieth century, what does it mean to model history in terms of the Weberian bureaucracy metaphor? *Gravity's Rainbow*'s use of various orders of fact and fantasy surrounding the history of the I. G. Farben cartel of Germany suggests one sort of answer. During the frame that begins on page 518, Enzian rides his motorcycle through the bombed-out wreckage of the Jamf Ölfabriken Werke A.G., a Farben plant for making synthetic gasoline by hydrogenation of coal. At another such plant, the Leunawerke, he will find Pavel of the Schwarzkommando getting high by sniffing "leunagasolin." Laszlo Jamf is the novel's creation, as is the oil plant named for him, but the Leunawerke was one of the installations really built by the I. G. so that Hitler could conduct his war without undue concern about fuel supplies. Enzian, here penetrating the weird moire that is Farbenmade history, acquires by some paranoid osmosis what seems to him "an extraordinary understanding" (520): the Jamf Werke "is *not a ruin at all. It is in perfect working order.* Only waiting for the right connections to be set up, to be switched on ... modified, precisely, *deliberately* by bombing that was never hostile, but part of a plan both sides—'*sides?'*—had always agreed on" (520). It follows that

> this War was never political at all, the politics was all theater, all just to keep the people distracted ... secretly, it was being dictated instead by the needs of technology ... by a conspiracy between human beings and techniques, by something that needed the energy-burst of war, crying "Money be damned, the very life of [insert name of Nation] is at stake," but meaning, most likely, *dawn is nearly here, I need my night's blood, my funding, funding, ahh more, more* ... The real crises were crises of allocation and priority, not among firms—it was only staged to look that way—but among the different Technologies, Plastics, Electronics, Aircraft, and their needs which are understood only by the ruling elite....
>
> Yes but Technology only responds (how often this argument has been iterated, dogged and humorless as a Gaussian reduction, among the younger Schwarzkommando especially), "All very well to talk about having a monster by the tail, but do you think we'd have had a Rocket if someone, some specific somebody with a name

and a penis hadn't *wanted* to chuck a ton of Amatol 300 miles and blow up a block full of civilians? Go ahead, capitalize the T on technology, deify it if it'll make you feel less responsible—but it puts you in with the neutered, brother, in with the eunuchs keeping the harem of our stolen Earth for the numb and joyless hardons of human sultans, human elite with no right at all to be where they are." (521)

The passage is difficult because, as usual, Pynchon mixes rhetorical signals: it is impossible to say which side of the argument, if either, is the more nearly correct. The younger Schwarzkommando argue persuasively for human choice, free will, as ultimately driving history— but who is that stigmatizing the argument as reductive and "humorless"? Against it, Enzian's "paranoid terror" (522) offers its usual imaginative seductions, even a mesmeric Dracula metaphor positing a wholly dehumanized, thus immortalized, historical process that sucks the blood or blood-money of the passive preterite. The view that modern history is a complete dominion of instrumentalities is a popular one, since, as the younger Schwarzkommando point out, it allows us to trade our responsibility for a comfortable masochism or diverting spectacle. Charles A. Reich, for example, looks bestsellingly in at the door of the executive suite to find that "there is no one there ... What looks like a man is only a representation of a man who does what the organization requires. He (or it) does not run the machine; he *tends* it."[33]

Or try Weber again: "Economic forces [are] interested in the emergence of military conflagrations *per se*, no matter what be the outcome for their own community.... A lost war, as well as a successful war, brings increased business."[34] This is echoed in *Gravity's Rainbow*: "The real business of the War is buying and selling" (105). In short, technology as monster-by-the-tail is a most seductive view psychologically as well as, in part, empirically.

But on the whole, *Gravity's Rainbow* takes neither side, demonstrating instead that, since paranoia and antiparanoia both exclude middles, both are in the end simplistic, "bad shit" (*Lot 49*, 136). There *are* recognizable human elites who seek to blow up blocks full of civilians, but They and Their unconscious agents, like Pökler, act for the most narrowly self-deceptive and fuddled of reasons, and that is because they *are* in a measure slaves, not masters, of the systems they have made. An

33. Charles A. Reich, *The Greening of America* (New York: Bantam Books, Inc., 1971), p. 107.

34. Weber, *Wirtschaft und Gesellschaft*, pp. 167, 168.

inconspicuous grace note in Enzian's speech refers to history as a "conspiracy between human beings and [their own] techniques"—and not, therefore, a conspiracy quite among humans, or quite among things. The both/and formulation also is C. Wright Mills's:

> Do the elite determine the roles that they enact? Or do the roles that institutions make available to them determine the power of the elite?.... The view that all of history is due to the conspiracy of an easily located set of villains, or of heroes, is also a hurried projection from the difficult effort to understand how shifts in the structure of society open opportunities to various elites and how various elites take advantage or fail to take advantage of them. To accept either view—of all history as conspiracy or of all history as drift—is to relax the effort to understand the facts of power and the ways of the powerful.[35]

As the "facts" about the I. G. Farben cartel outcrop throughout *Gravity's Rainbow,* the characters, preferring, as usual, conspiracy theory to drift theory, connect the dots toward paranoid visions. Readers mongering scholarship may connect the same dots toward apparent historical testimony: Pynchon of course insists that any discussions of historical structures like the I. G. must appear as a crosslit moire of many plots on both sides of a "fictional" interface. Joseph Borkin is within his rights, anyway, to describe the cartel as "a mighty industrial colossus. So huge were its assets admitted and concealed, so superior its technological know-how, and so formidable its array of patents that it dominated the chemical business of the world. I. G. fortified this commercial leadership by constructing a maze of cartels whose members included such industrial giants as Kuhlmann of France, Imperial Chemical Industries of Great Britain [ICI: Pynchon's "Icy Eye"], Montecatini of Italy, Aussiger Verein of Czechoslovakia, Boruta of Poland, Mitsui of Japan, and Standard Oil (New Jersey), Du Pont, and Dow Chemical of the United States."[36]

At its height the cartel controlled about 350 German firms, had linkages with more than 500 foreign firms, and was the biggest and strongest industrial organization in the world. That such an empire should have grown up so quickly in Germany supports Pynchon's positing of "the German mind" as a particularly salient expression of the Western post-Renaissance mania for analysis, framing, labyrinth-building,

---

35. Mills, *The Power Elite,* pp. 24, 27.

36. Joseph Borkin, *The Crime and Punishment of I. G. Farben* (New York: Free Press, 1978), p. 1.

bureaucratization. The Friedrich Bayer Company of Elberfeld, later a major I. G. partner, achieved early success by its "tedious, meticulous experimentation, in which a thousand little facts were wrenched from nature through co-ordinated massed assault ... a procedure which illustrated the method and spirit introduced into scientific inquiry by the rising industrial laboratory of the late nineteenth century."[37] The great chemist Justus von Liebig trained chemists August and Carl Clemm, whose early aniline dye company, Chemische Fabrik Dyckerhoff, soon became the Badische Anilin- und Soda-Fabrik of Ludwigshafen (BASF), which grew to be the most powerful Farben member.[38] Max Weber pointed to Liebig's research laboratories at Giessen University as an example of the early bureaucratization in Germany of scientific research and of technology.[39] We note that, as a student, Franz Pökler lives on Liebig street in Munich; that "Liebig was at the University of Giessen when Kekule entered as a student" (411); and that it is given to Pökler to know that it was Kekule's "dream of 1865 ... that revolutionized chemistry and made the IG possible" (410). Another "succession" from Liebig to the I. G. is plotted by Walter Rathenau's spirit-voice at Sachsa's seance: "Tyrian purple, alizarin and indigo, other coal-tar dyes are here, but the important one is mauve. William Perkin discovered it in England, but he was trained by Hoffmann, who was trained by Liebig. There is a succession involved. If it is karmic it's only in a very limited sense ... another Englishman, Herbert Ganister, and the generation of chemists he trained ... Then the discovery of Oneirine. Ask your man Wimpe" (166).

From historical Perkin and Liebig to fictional Wimpe and Jamf and dreamlike Oneirine; from live Rathenau to his spirit-voice in a seance: at the time, the progression from colors "given" in nature to those synthesized from coal tars might have felt just this creepy, oneiric. And so, indeed, must have felt the facts gathered by Senator Truman's investigating committee in 1942—in the midst of America's war with Germany—regarding "arrangements" made in 1939 between I. G. Farben and Standard Oil (New Jersey), expanding their first arrangements of

37. John J. Beer, "Coal Tar Dye Manufacture and the Origins of the Modern Industrial Research Laboratory," in *The Development of Western Technology Since 1500*, ed. Thomas Parke Hughes (New York: Macmillan Co., 1964).

38. The chairman of BASF throughout the period of Nazi rule was Hermann Schmitz, whom Pynchon (*GR*, 565) miscalls *Carl* Schmitz, perhaps confusing him with Carl Bosch, Schmitz's mentor and predecessor as head of the I. G.

39. Weber, *Wirtschaft und Gesellschaft*, pp. 223, 224.

1927/1928. Sometime in the 1930s, I. G. had sold Standard the world patent rights (exclusive of Germany) to the coal hydrogenation process, while Standard turned over to I. G. two percent of Standard's entire common stock: "The parties negotiated their agreement in the manner of two great powers forging a treaty to divide the world into separate spheres of influence. They agreed to observe the sovereignty of each in their respective fields [oil and chemicals]."[40] By the "Hague Memorandum" of September 1939, with the war in Europe already on, the I. G.'s American patents reverted to the safekeeping of Standard, and Standard transferred much valuable technical information to the I. G., pressing for a reciprocal transfer of I. G. data, particularly on the Buna rubber manufacturing process. But I. G. released only the Buna patents, withholding the technical information that Standard needed to make effective use of them; the Nazi government seems to have been satisfied that the German advantage in rubber technology was safe for any coming war between the United States and Germany. Frank Howard of Standard stated in a memo from The Hague that the two companies had done "our best to work out complete plans for a modus vivendi which would operate through the term of the war whether or not the U.S. came in."[41]

In Pynchon's Zone, any throwaway line may encrypt just such real-historical data: Major Marvy complains to Tchitcherine, vaguely, "You ain't got General Electric breathin' over your shoulder, fella. Dillon, Reed ... Standard Awl ... shit ..." (565). And "Too many tungsten filaments would eat into available stockpiles of the metal ... and disturb the arrangement between General Electric and Krupp about how much tungsten carbide would be produced, where and when and what the prices would be. The guidelines settled on were $37–$90 a pound in Germany, $200–$400 a pound in the U.S. This directly governed the production of machine tools and thus all areas of light and heavy industry. When the War came, some people thought it unpatriotic of GE to have given Germany an edge like that. But nobody with any power. Don't worry" (654).

But even though the gaudiest paranoid air castles might thus be secret caricatures of the truth, the reader of *Gravity's Rainbow* learns quickly to think of "I. G. Farben" chiefly as a convenient designation or construct, an objective correlative for our paranoid reading skills and for charac-

---

40. Borkin, *The Crime*, p. 57. 41. Quoted in Borkin, *The Crime*, p. 92.

ters' paranoid feelings; when "I. G." appears, there is no telling whether what we could call a *fact* lies beneath it. Slothrop's vague undergraduate fantasy that "Harvard's there for other reasons. The 'educating' part of it's just sort of a front" (193) makes us remember his father's deal with the I. G., the profits of which went to send him to Harvard. As he hits Zürich, a lit clock tower

> connects to Ivy League quadrangles in his distant youth, clock-towers lit so dim the hour could never be read, and a temptation, never so strong as now, to surrender to the darkening year, to embrace what he can of real terror to the hour without a name…. it was vanity, vanity as his Puritan forebears had known it, bones and heart alert to Nothing, Nothing underneath the college saxophones melding sweetly, white blazers lipsticked about the lapels, smoke from nervous Fatimas, Castile soap vaporizing off shining hair, and mint kisses, and dewed carnations. (267)[42]

College life '30s style has a thin, kaleidoscopic scrim, and Slothrop's fear of the "Nothing" beneath it is a reprise of his childhood dread of whatever lay behind the flaring Northern Lights. In *V.* Hugh Godolphin penetrates, as he thinks, the gaudily iridescent skin of his fabulous Vheissu. " 'What did you see?' asked Signor Mantissa…. 'Nothing,' Godolphin whispered, 'It was Nothing I saw' " (*V.*, 188). The paranoid metaphysician fears the rupturing of the plot, or the void, One or Zero, up through *Maya's* gaudy, bright surface; we seem far at this point from any real, worldy power conspiracy. And yet Slothrop's Zürich fantasy continues this way:

> there are ex-young men, here in this very city, faces Slothrop used to pass in the quads, who got initiated at Harvard into the Puritan Mysteries: who took oaths in dead earnest to respect and to act always in the name of *Vanitas*, Emptiness, their ruler … who now according to life-plan such-and-such have come here to Switzerland to work for Allen Dulles and his "intelligence" network, which operates these days under the title of "Office of Strategic Services." But to initiates OSS is a secret acronym: as a mantra for times of immediate crisis they have been taught to speak inwardly *oss … oss*, the late, corrupt, Dark-age Latin word for bone. (267–68)

42. The first time I read this passage and the paranoid fantasy immediately following it—with its Ivy League quadrangles, clock tower, shadows and leaves underfoot—I "saw" with what seemed complete certainty what Pynchon's memory-source had been: the Arts Quad at Cornell University, flanked by Goldwin Smith Hall, home of the English department, and dominated by the clock tower of Uris Library. Pynchon, of course, was an undergraduate at Cornell. I don't know why I remain so sure that he had this specific scene in mind when he wrote the passage describing a Harvard memory of Slothrop's.

Puerile Vanitas worshipers, grown up to be puerile government gofers, *do* keep faith, though of course they don't know it, with Vanitas—the OSS being, as it appears, a "lightly concealed entranceway" (*Lot 49*, 135) to the real, if paranoiacally interpreted, I. G. order. "Intelligence" is in ironic or paranoid quotation marks because Allen Dulles, chief of the OSS operation in Switzerland, was also a partner in the law firm of Sullivan & Cromwell (nowhere mentioned in *Gravity's Rainbow*), which handled legal affairs for the General Aniline and Film Corp., of Binghamton, New York, also known as American I. G. Chemical Corp., a property of I. G. Farben.[43] The I. G. concealed its ownership of the American firm not only throughout the war, but well into the 1970s, by using a Swiss holding company, I. G. Chemie, as a cloak. A similar Swiss puppet firm, Psychochemie A.G. or Grössli Chemical Corporation, is the nominal employer of Laszlo Jamf at the time of his experiment with Infant Tyrone Slothrop. It should be repeated that paranoias like this are apposite to Pynchon's novel, not literally as secret solutions to history, but as compelling historical hallucinations. They are refractions of, framings or zonings for, Zone and twentieth-century history as felt from inside. They are visions, therefore, that tend to actualize real history. To understand and watch as they do so is to be one's self, in turn, paranoid, and to further the process—to help "make" paranoid history.

One early book about clandestine corporate activities in the Zone, and probably one of Pynchon's undiscovered source works, is J. S. Martin's *All Honorable Men* (1950): Marvy's casual "Dillon, Reed" (565) can lead us there. During the 1930s, Dillon, Reed & Company of Wall Street handled American transactions for the German steel trust Vereinigte Stahlwerke. There is in existence a memo, J. S. Martin vaguely reports, between Dillon, Reed and the German combine, signed by William Draper, later commanding general of the Economics Division of the American Control Council Group for Occupied Germany, a group whose task was to decartelize the Zone. The civilian Martin, as he resigned in disillusionment from the group in 1947, complained to journalists of "the pressure of specific American companies like General Electric and General Motors to prevent decartelization changes in Ger-

---

43. The closest that *Gravity's Rainbow* comes to being explicit about these connections—even though the full effect of the passage I have quoted depends on them—is to mention in passing (579) the

Agfa photographic plates, manufactured by General Aniline, in connection with their use by the German film industry during its golden period in the 1920s.

many that might affect their properties and business interests."[44] Although complete decartelization was the official policy of SHAEF and of the Truman administration, "The plants of the favored firms were all decked out with priorities and ornamented like Christmas trees.... Military government officials were supposed to work out their economic programs without disturbing anything.... We had not been stopped in Germany by German business. We had been stopped by American business."[45] General Draper, asked in January 1946 why shares of I. G. Farben, supposedly a disbanded company, were doubling in price on the Munich stock exchange, "smiled wryly and remarked that the speculators must be 'buying a piece of the Control Council.'"[46]

J. S. Martin's self-consciously breezy account of early allied scavengings in the Zone for industrial secrets lets us see, by contrast, with how much cannier self-consciousness Pynchon has spun what is eerily the same moire, from history, paranoia, and art:

> Major Tilley and the Standard Oil investigation which he was making for Phil Amram dropped from sight for a few days while the Major's party searched in the field for records. But I heard from him again when I joined my group at Essen on May 23. Colonel Kellam handed me a note from Major Tilley, dated from Frankfurt the week before: "Dr. Bütefisch, chief of I.G. Farben synthetic oil production, Leuna, has admitted that Dr. Hahn, his deputy, has hidden papers, including secret documents and letters from and to Ringer, at the following address: Bad Sachsa, Haus der Dynamit A.G."
>
> Bad Sachsa showed on the map as a point in the midst of the Harz Mountains, a few miles from the Devil's Pulpit on the Brocken, a traditional site of the Witches' Sabbath. The Hitler Youth had revived the legend and held Walpurgisnacht celebrations annually on May first. We had reports that in the same area numbers of SS troops had declined to celebrate V-E Day and were playing come-and-get-it with units of the Fifth Armored Division. As we got together our party of ten to make the circuit of the Harz, looking for records of Krupp, Mannesmann, the Stahlwerke Verband, and the Standard Oil-I.G. Farben correspondence, an officer of the Ninety-Fourth said to hell with the regulations and made me put a pistol in a shoulder holster under my field jacket.[47]

Surely Slothrop, invisible, lurks nearby: only a few days earlier he had

44. J. S. Martin, *All Honorable Men* (Boston: Little, Brown & Co., 1950), p. 218.

45. Ibid., p. 219.

46. Borkin, *The Crime*, p. 158.

47. Martin, *All Honorable Men*; I have lost the page number.

been with Geli Tripping up on the Brocken, amid "relics of the latest Black Sabbath ... Kriegsbier empties, lace undergarments, spent rifle cartridges, Swastika-banners of ripped red satin" (329). Schwarzkommando units live (315) in the old mine shafts—the fatuously coded "Haus der Dynamit"—near Bad Sachsa, and Bad Sachsa gives Leni Pökler's lover Peter Sachsa his name. Pavel of the Schwarzkommando sniffed leunagasolin at the Leuna plant run by Bütefisch, who got six years for slavery and mass murder at Nürnberg. Major Tilley, if we just squint a little, obligingly fades into Major Marvy.

On the other hand, there is the story of what happened, during the April 1945 hiatus, at the huge I. G. Farben headquarters building in Frankfurt.[48] For the few days between its evacuation by Farben officials and the arrival of United States forces, the building was occupied by a large crowd of DP refugees, who looted tons of I. G. documents and set them on fire to heat the building and to cook food. The Americans had to mount a complex trucking operation to salvage what was left of the papers in order to try to extract any useful intelligence from them. Did the DP's use Their secret documents for toilet paper as well? And was Pynchon's failure to use this ideal crystallization of his symbolism out of the reality of the times a deliberate shadowing of a part of the moire, or did he just miss the data?[49]

Yet again, few readers, while becoming engaged in the most engaging but surrealistic, quite fantastic Story of Byron the Bulb, are likely to feel much need to believe in the historicity of "Phoebus," the sinister

48. This building was spared from bombing, by the common account, on orders from Eisenhower, who wanted to use it as a United States Army headquarters—which today, as the Abrams Building, it still is.

49. The story is told in Josiah E. Du Bois, *Generals in Gray Suits* (London: Bodley Head, 1953), pp. 37, 38. Further, Khachig Tölölyan has done much research on the real-historical truth of the last days of the war and first days of the peace, the time during which semiofficial Allied scavenger squads operated in the Zone to gather pieces of rocket data. He finds, not surprisingly, that Pynchon has very intricately intermingled historical truth with his fiction, especially with regard to the symbolic constellation of "shit, money, and the Word," as in Du Bois's story of the preterite occupation of the Farben build-

ing. The most interesting of Tölölyan's instances concerns the technical rocket manuals that Pynchon has Slothrop study at the Casino—manuals "salvaged by the Polish underground from the latrines at the training site at Blizna, stained with genuine SS shit and piss" (*GR*, 211). In truth, Tölölyan reports, a British intelligence officer, Geoffrey Gollin (mentioned only once, noncommitally and in another connection, in *GR* [240]), received authorization from the Russians to search Blizna after its liberation. There he indeed found rocket papers in an SS latrine, where the fleeing Germans had tried to "flush" them out of sight. See Tölölyan, "War as Background in *Gravity's Rainbow*," in *Approaches to Gravity's Rainbow*, ed. Charles Clerc (Columbus: Ohio State University Press, 1983), pp. 31–67.

light-bulb cartel, which seeks to reduce the average lifetime of bulbs, "run pretty much by International GE, Osram, and Associated Electrical Industries of Britain, whch are in turn owned 100%, 29% and 46% respectively, by the General Electric Company in America" (649). But Phoebus was, in fact, a cartel partnership, begun in the 1920s between Osram G.m.b.H., the German electrical firm owned by Siemens & Halske and by German GE, and International General Electric. In 1934 A. F. Philips, head of Dutch Philips, a later cartel partner, wrote to Clark Minor of General Electric: "There seems to exist in various territories a growing tendency to supply lamps for higher voltages than in the past.... This, you will agree with me, is a very dangerous practice and is having a most detrimental influence on the total turnover of the Phoebus Parties.... After the very strenuous efforts we made to emerge from a period of long-life lamps, it is of the greatest importance that we do not sink back into the same mire."[50]

The Pynchonesque "mire" substantiates the narrator's account of the cartel's character and helps explain its reaction to the quasi-miraculous bulb-snatchings by the preterite, which protect Byron's immortality: "[Phoebus's] stonefaced search parties move out into the streets" (651).

The Story of Byron the Bulb itself, in the Colonel's Haircut frame-passage that encloses it (640–55), reminds us that naked light bulbs have been burning all along, sub rosa, in quiet corners of *Gravity's Rainbow*; here, for the first time explicitly, Pynchon identifies their eerie light as a major element in his symbolic design. The story is first, and obviously, a parable of preterition, like the earlier stories of Frans van der Groov's dodoes and William Slothrop's pigs. Each of the dodo/pig/light-bulb preterite populations is imagined—in sadly unreal fantasies within fantasies—as giving rise to a charismatic figure (articulate dodoes, Messiah-pig, immortal Bulb) whose election for subversive, redemptive purposes is set against the debased neo-Puritan sense of "election" to serve entrenched power: in Babybulb Innocence, Byron dreams of large-scale mass subversions, "gonna organize all the Bulbs, see, get him a power base in Berlin, he's already hep to the Strobing Tactic.... gonna get Herbert Hoover, Stanley Baldwin, all of them, right in the face with one co-ordinated blast" (648–49). But of course he learns that the preterite have already been too much divided by Them, and charisma itself is too ambivalent, ever to effect such mass heroism. Byron in the end feels himself "condemned to go on forever, knowing the

50. Quoted in Martin, *All Honorable*   Men, pp. 147, 148.

truth and powerless to change anything. No longer will he seek to get off the wheel. His anger and frustration will grow without limit, and he will find himself, poor perverse bulb, enjoying it" (655).

He remains, though, awake, aware, and watchful: as he burns now over the colonel's haircut and secretly guides its course, he has burned, we are now told, over Franz Pökler's bunk at Nordhausen, moving among and perhaps giving shape to the black-and-white dreams of rocket-transcendence. There is no telling where else he has been in the novel, where incandescent light generally comprehends and encloses the human net:

> Franz now will be home from the rocket-field, blinking under the bulb as Frau Silberschlag delivers Leni's last message. Messages tonight, borne on the light of Berlin ... neon, incandescent, stellar ... messages weave into a net of information that no one can escape. (165)

Here Pynchon owes much to Marshall McLuhan:

> The electric light is pure information. It is a medium without a message, as it were, unless it is used to spell out some verbal ad or name ... it is the medium that shapes and controls the scale and form of human association and action. The content uses of such media are as diverse as they are ineffectual.... Indeed, it is only too typical that the "content" of any medium blinds us to the character of the medium.[51]

Pure media for McLuhan are thus continuous, "contentless" information, "totally radical, pervasive, and decentralized";[52] what happens "under" or "in" their light is merely projected human contents. The poor Neukölln glassblower who is afraid of the dark keeps Byron burning all night because "Light, in his dreams, was always hope: the basic, mortal hope" (651), but Byron himself is indifferent to this "symbolic" content. And thus electric light may, in Pynchon's terms, carry, comprehend, or symbolize the great message, the secret: that all reality may be continuous, that all things may connect, below the net and behind the Word. Bernie, Brenda, and Benito the Bulbs, and the human preterites who keep rescuing Byron from Phoebus, share wordlessly this most vital of information: "The light bulb ... has become one of the great secret ikons of the Humility, the multitudes who are passed over by God

51. Marshall McLuhan, *Understanding Media*, pp. 8, 9.   52. Ibid., p. 9.

and history. When the Dora prisoners went on their rampage, the light bulbs in the rocket works were the first to go" (299).

During the haircut at which Byron presides, Eddie Pensiero, the amphetamine addict, models the colonel's hair in obsessive patterned "frequencies." Eddie is constantly shivering and can pick up and respond to—cf. Pirate Prentice's gift—the shivers of other people as well. It seems that his shivers here, and therefore the colonel's hair patterns, respond to the movie-frame-like "succession of electric peaks and valleys" (642) of Byron's burning, which depend in turn on the speed with which Paddy McGonigle, another enlisted man, cranks the generator. But all the time Byron is "dictating the muscular modulations of Paddy McGonigle's cranking tonight, this is a loop here, with feedbacks through Paddy to the generator again" (647). Meanwhile someone invisible out in the night—we can hardly doubt that it is Slothrop—is playing a blues on a mouth harp. Blues notes as "bent" through harmonica holes and through the feedback loop establish a ground continuity and sympathy with Byron's secret "pain-radiance" (655), and, as the colonel tilts his throat up, "Eddie Pensiero, with the blues flooding his shaking muscles, the down, mortal blues" (655), prepares apparently to stab the jugular—and the frame suddenly ends. The whole feedback loop, the "net of information that no one can escape," is secretly intruded by influences from outside, and the haircut ends, or probably ends, in this violence because it obeys the urgings of Preterite Blues: the secret communion of "invisible" beings, Slothrop on the harp, and Byron, now at last striking the subversive blow that he had dreamed of back in Babybulb Heaven.

The optimism of Marshall McLuhan for humankind, for human kindness, in the "global village" of instantaneous communications, comes in like everything else for some gentle debunking in Pynchon—for example, Slothrop as teenaged "electrofreak" rhapsodizing to his straight old man about "a clean, honest, purified Electroworld" where life might be entirely escaped (699). But I think that Pynchon is somewhat attracted to this hope: a culture united by instantaneous electronic feedback just might, if the right choices are made, if the right news from outside is properly attended to, improve finally on the old mechanical, linear, machine-bureaucratic culture of analysis and rationality, synthesis and control. The intuition of this technological form of connectedness could suggest to us, Pynchon implies, a whole sympathy that might lay the Puritan ghost. In the next chapter I elaborate on some aspects of science that, for Pynchon, issue in this cybernetic vision of a possible future.

5

The Culture of Science
in *Gravity's Rainbow*

Course Prerequisites

By "culture of science" I mean also those cultures of mathematics, philosophy, and historical studies that I examine here, as demanded by *Gravity's Rainbow's* own integrated examinations. While, one must assume, it is just barely possible to tear the scientific/philosophical/cultural-historical thematic family out of its connections with others of the novel's such families—the matters of this book's other chapters—it seems quite impossible to discuss Pynchon's science in isolation from his philosophy or his history. This chapter, accordingly, is long, preposterously ambitious in its synthetic attempts, nervous, amateuristic. And, if the subject of Pynchonian science makes us feel most unguarded, it may be best to try to examine the reasons for that sense of unguardedness before proceeding.

One obvious if regrettable reason is that the metaphorical language of science often seems largely opaque to literati, perhaps the majority of us, who, in the age of the dichotomous Two Cultures of C. P. Snow, are guilty of a shameful ignorance of the culture of science. "What is the Second Law of Thermodynamics about?" The question, Snow justifiably says, is the scientific equivalent of "Have you read a work of Shakespeare's?"[1] But trained analysts of literature who would be in the least uneasy with thermodynamics will inevitably feel unsettling sensations when they confront Pynchon's scientific displays and arrays in *Gravity's Rainbow*—cross-referenced signs, equations, imageries from the alien culture that seem to flash, flicker, wink, chat cozily at each other, like console lights on some hugely complacent, narcissistic, gently sarcastic

1. C. P. Snow, *The Two Cultures: And a Second Look* (Cambridge, Eng.: At the University Press, 1965), p. 14.

computer. Perhaps it is this discomfort that has preconsciously led some critics to charge that Pynchon's renowned erudition, particularly in his science, is largely faked: a tinselly, overgeneralized, whiz-kid patter. Mitchell S. Ross, for one, complains of Pynchon's "uncanny ability to regurgitate the indigestible stuff that is force-fed to undergraduates"[2] —with the further dubious implication that such a procedure if really practiced must automatically bar the work from achieving serious artistic ends. Ross deserves a reply, and there are, I think, several valid, interrelated replies.

First, we can admit that Pynchon's erudition is frequently thin, overly self-conscious, too clearly ripped untimely from general reference works; the learning unquestionably is wide but not necessarily deep— as Pynchon himself, in his introduction to *Slow Learner*, has recently taken pains to point out.[3] Yet it is hard to see how a novel that so aspires to be "about" a culture's entire connectedness could afford, practically, to back every erudite bet as it goes, even if we think that such backing of bets is crucial for its artistic success. Those who now complain of Pynchon's being unreadable by virtue of his excessive formal braininess would perhaps find his novels untouchable if the novels managed somehow fully to flesh out each skeleton of allusion. A second reply to Ross is to observe that there is, among writers with ambitions as large as Pynchon's, a long tradition of inspired intellectual amateurism. Goethe the amateur naturalist wove dubious optical, biological, and geological theories into his work and picked unwinnable fights with Newton; and Joyce and Eliot surely were not, in any narrowly academic sense, *experts* in the philosophy, science, and mythography they so beautifully systematized. Finally there is the fact, pointed out by Alfred Harbage for Shakespeare's case, that the faker's art may often be artfully pressed to the service of characterization: "Anyone who has written even a routine piece of fiction is aware of the necessity of faking—of using strategically his bits of technical knowledge so that his lawyers will seem like lawyers, his doctors doctors, his priests priests, and so on. The bits expand in the reader's imagination into a comprehensive body of knowledge...."

2. See Mitchell S. Ross, "Prince of the Paperback Literati," *New York Times Magazine*, February 12, 1978.

3. "People think I know more about the subject of entropy than I really do," Pynchon says, for instance, in this introduction, and goes on the say that his understanding of entropy, such as it was, and gleaned amateurishly as it was from Norbert Wiener and Henry Adams, made the story "Entropy" "too conceptual, too cute and remote," such that the characters "die on the page." He is right.

The naive response is to identify the presumed knowledge of the characters with the actual knowledge of the author, when often, in such cases, the part of the iceberg of knowledge which shows is the only part which exists."[4]

We might object that Pynchon's learning is not, like Shakespeare's, primarily in the service of characterization; rather it seems to ask to be taken seriously in itself, to propose itself as central to the author's thematic design. Meeting this, we encounter what may be called a reflexive or metathematic point of the novel itself about the nature of "objective" bodies of knowledge. Pynchon's narrator is a "subject" of consciousness who represents a thoroughly contemporary mode of defensive awareness of the elusiveness of "objectivity," even in science; beyond its verifiable ground of flat data, Pynchonian science, faithful to real contemporary science at its most profound theoretical levels (I am thinking of quantum physics), is not so much a matter of "fact" as of a self-consciously metaphorical system arising *out of* apparent fact. Pynchon means to propose that science, no less than other metaphorical systems, is a dynamic subjectivity interrelating the images, myths, and synthetic methods of human experience. Accordingly, when synthetic consciousness is self-aware in Pynchon, it is usually self-ironic and scuffling, and yet at the same time possessed fantastically by some dream of erectable order. In his 1966 essay on Watts, Pynchon points to the immigrant Simon Rodia, who spent his vagrant Los Angeles life constructing out of "busted glass, busted crockery, nails, tin cans, all kinds of scrap and waste ... the famous Watts Towers, perhaps his own dream of how things should have been: a fantasy of fountains, boats, tall open-work spires, encrusted with a dazzling mosaic of Watts debris."[5] From the waste heaps of plastic "synthetics," consciousness shuffles new syntheses, "kicking endlessly among the plastic trivia, finding in each Deeper Significance and trying to string them all together like terms of a power series ... to bring them together, in their slick persistence and our preterition ... to make sense of, to find the meanest sharp sliver of truth in so much replication, so much waste" (590).

The quest is essentially too schlemihl-like to feel very seriously "academic" and thus constitutes a parody of academics' quests at their least

4. Alfred Harbage, *Conceptions of Shakespeare* (New York: Schocken Books, 1968), p. 24.

5. Thomas Pynchon, "A Journey Into the Mind of Watts," *New York Times Magazine,* June 12, 1966.

imaginative, most objectifying extremes. But the raw materials of any scientific or intellectual quests will indeed be found in those undergraduate courses that Ross complains of, however the stuff must be force-fed, and seem indigestible, to business administration majors. These raw materials are the possessions alike of Pynchon, his narrator, and, ideally at least, his critics, the latter almost inevitably operating out of those very liberal arts institutions from which Pynchon himself has remained in such long and, surely, ambivalent exile.

In order to reach his fictive synthesis of that culture of science whose sign will be the V-2, Pynchon must take for granted some knowledge of the great seminal ideas and father-figures out of the seminal century of modern science: the seventeenth. A quick review, then, of course prerequisites—of some of the elements of the systems of Galileo, Kepler, Leibniz, Descartes, Newton—seems called for in an introductory class like this one as this chapter begins.

In the period immediately preceding Newton and Leibniz's century, the Copernican heliocentrism first seriously destabilized the thousand-year dispensation of scholastic philosophy and church theology, which had arrayed a vast system of signs in a mysticized structure centered on man as the soul of God's purpose in a moral creation. Galileo, by wielding the new tools of the age—mathematical method, empirical observation, experimentation—helped undermine the teleological cosmos by perfecting and cannily using (not inventing) the telescope. Moving bodies, Galileo showed, will continue to move at constant velocity if unperturbed; they have, that is, a mathematically explicable "inertia" of movement and are not obligated by their being "soulless" to come to rest, as the classical Greeks and medieval scholastics alike had thought. Galileo's later discovery of the gravitational constant of acceleration prepared the way for Newton and also furthered the gradual realization that mathematics, and not teleological animism, was the right language for describing the movements of heavenly spheres.

The heliocentrist Johannes Kepler, working largely with data collected by the great empiricist Tycho Brahe, derived the famous three laws of planetary motion: that the orbits of planets are ellipses (not, as the schoolmen had learned from the Pythagoreans, circles, the teleologically "perfect" shape); that the orbital speed of a planet varies proportionately with its varying distance, along the ellipse, from the sun; and that a planet's period of revolution is proportional to its overall orbital distance from the sun. For Kepler, generally, "All certain knowledge must be a knowledge of ... quantitative characteristics, perfect knowledge is always mathematical."[6] Yet—and this is of interest to Pynchon, who is aware of the Jungian study of Kepler by the twentieth-century physicist Wolfgang Pauli—Kepler adhered to heliocentrism in part because it seemed to validate a private system of his in which the solar system mystically figured forth the Trinity, with the sun as God the Father, the outer circumference of the system as the Son, and the mathematical forces that bind all together as the Holy Spirit.

With Newton's *Principia Mathematica* of 1687, all such residual mysticisms as Kepler's were finally and, it seemed, irrevocably cast out of the scientific purview. With the help of his invented mathematical tool, the calculus, Newton built up the intricate openwork and mosaic complexity of his system of the world, whose governing principle was universal gravity: "Every body attracts every other with a force directly proportional to the product of their masses and inversely proportional to the square of the distance between them." Yet, unable to see how "forces" like that of gravity could behave immaterially, i.e., could propagate through a vacuum without the mechanical impact of matter, Newton felt compelled to postulate a super-rarefied fluid, the "ether," filling all space; force in a vacuum seemed simply incommensurate with the completely mechanistic materialism of Newton's system. Newton, this is to say, could not explain the inner *nature* of gravity and when not etherizing could only call gravity "a general law of nature": "For these mathematical laws are manifest qualities, and their causes only are occult."[7] But Newton's positivism, his emphasis on the supremacy of experimental data, his distrust of all metaphysical-smelling hypotheses, defined the tone of the physics of the succeeding two centuries, for which space was absolute, other, subject indefinitely to quantification and differentiation—and finally, through these projective methods, to conquest.

The lesson of seventeenth-century science, then, was the essentially mathematical and empirical nature of Nature. The mind was thrown into a new and highly ambivalent relation to nature: seeing limitless possibilities for learning to understand better what lay outside itself, mind saw also that a mathematicized nature in no sense *needed* mind's understanding or was a function of it. Robert Boyle, the first serious student of the physics of gases and a deeply religious man, wrote, at

6. E. A. Burtt's paraphrase of Kepler in Burtt, *The Metaphysical Foundations of Modern Science* (New York: Doubleday Anchor Books, 1954), p. 67.

7. Newton in his *Optiks*, quoted by Burtt, *Metaphysical Foundations*, p. 222.

once assertively and uneasily, "I see no necessity that intelligibility to a human understanding should be necessary to the existence of an atom, or of a corpuscle of air, or of the effluviums of a lodestone."[8] In formal philosophy, cognately, Leibniz's *Monadology* pictured reality as a network of point-monads, unable to intercommunicate, subject interchangeably and simultaneously to external regulatory control by God. The *cogito* of Descartes defined human consciousness as isolated and self-referential: one could only *know* with certainty the fact of one's own existence as "thinking," while matter, body, *res extensa*, the objective world, could be taken as real as a matter merely of inference. God would not deceive us by making matter *seem* so real if it were not real. Cartesian externalities, including animal and plant life and one's own body, were automata, governed purely by mathematical laws, subsisting in "primary" qualities—mass, velocity, mathematical relations—while "secondary" qualities, such as color, sound, odor, were the phantasmagoric diversions of the imprisoned consciousness.

E. A. Burtt generalizes on the humbling effects of the new science and philosophy for the seventeenth century:

> Now the great Newton's authority was squarely behind that view of the cosmos which saw in man a puny, irrelevant spectator (so far as being wholly imprisoned in a dark room can be called such) of the vast mathematical system whose regular motions according to mechanical principles constituted the world of nature. The gloriously romantic universe of Dante and Milton, that set no bounds to the imagination of man as it played over space and time, had now been swept away. Space was identified with the realm of geometry, time with the continuity of number. The world that people had thought themselves living in—a world rich with colour and sound, redolent with fragrance, filled with gladness, love and beauty, speaking everywhere of purposive harmony and creative ideals—was crowded now into minute corners in the brains of scattered organic beings. The really important world outside was a world hard, cold, colourless, silent, and dead; a world of quantity, a world of mathematically computable motions in mechanical regularity. The world of qualities as immediately perceived by man became just a curious and quite minor effect of that infinite machine beyond.[9]

But to share Pynchon's sense of the psychology of modernity is to feel the onesidedness of this sketch. There is another possible post-Carte-

---

8. Quoted by Burtt, ibid., p. 186. 9. Ibid., pp. 238, 239.

sian mood, one that opposes (without negating) all these humilities and abasements. If during the seventeenth century man had become a fugitive subjectivity lost in despiritualized nature, still, *thinking, creating* man, who once had been locked in his place in a stagnant teleological scheme, could now feel himself great in potential, strong in realizable will. The Romantic movement, in fact, later charged intellectual man with having attained, following his divorce from nature, "a 'self-centered' soul, which transfers the center of reference from the whole to its individual and acquisitive self."[10] And Romanticism sometimes found in its own desire to heal the Cartesian split by the reintegration of self with nature, a new, Faustian danger—that of swallowing nature whole in a complete subjectivism, supremely idealist egotism. One sense in which *Gravity's Rainbow* is a "romantic" evaluation of history, including the history of Romanticism, is that it is concerned with the dialectical tension between two drives, both realized or at least realizable in science: mind's wish to reintegrate itself with nature and its simultaneous wish imperialistically to swallow nature whole by epistemologies and technologies for the "abstraction" of concrete reality. These impulses, in Pynchon, are related as Yin and Yang: as benign science and its (at best) ambiguous technological issue; as imaginative synthesis and I. G. Farben Synthetics; as life and film; as Eros and Thanatos.

Indeed, Romanticism was not and is not, as is sometimes claimed, simply "hostile" to science; rather, its holism seeks to make new connections between scientific and other metaphorical modes for the expressions of fundamental imaginative impulses. Richard Poirier suggests that Pynchon may answer Wordsworth's Romantic call, in the preface to *Lyrical Ballads,* for a holist poet of nature *and* of rational science, able to "carry sensation into the midst of the objects of science itself."[11] Poirier's Pynchon is at his most "important" when he insists that

> all systems and technologies ... partake of one another. In particular, science directs our perceptions and feelings whether we know it or not, even while, as literary people, we may like to imagine that it is literature that most effectively conditions how we feel.[12]

10. M. H. Abrams, *Natural Supernaturalism* (New York: Norton Library, 1973), p. 295.

11. Wordsworth quoted in Richard

Poirier, "The Importance of Thomas Pynchon," *Twentieth Century Literature* 21 (1975): 151–62.

12. Ibid., p. 157.

Our modern modes of synthesis and analysis

> are not merely impositions upon consciousness. They are also a
> corporate expression of consciousness; they express *us* all as much
> as do the lyrical ballads. They express us more than does our late
> and befuddled resistance to them. Put another way, the visual and
> audible messages offered on the film *Citizen Kane* tell us no more
> (and no less) about modern life than do the movie projector which
> shows the film or the camera which made it. These machines are a
> product of the human imagination which, if felt as such and studied
> as such, refer us to the hidden nature of human feeling and human
> need.[13]

Among *Gravity's Rainbow*'s characters it is Leni Pökler who most
strongly intuits this, what she roughly calls "parallelism" of systems, as
of what is outside and inside rational consciousness, although, in her
central argument on the point with Franz, mere words fail her, and she
resorts to a metaphor from Cartesian geometry: " 'Not produce,' she
tried, 'not cause. It all goes along together. Parallel, not series. Metaphor. Signs and symptoms. Mapping on to different co-ordinate systems, I don't know' " (159). Of course, Leni chooses the allusion to the
geometry in which points are referred to as a "co-ordinate system" of
mutually perpendicular axes, x and y, to appeal to her rationalistic husband, who must move "always by safe right angles along the faint lines"
(399). But the Pöklers are arguing about the consciously rationalistic
Franz's *irrational* love for the movies—specifically for the confusedly
mystical filmic products of German Expressionism. That there might
exist, in Leni's approximate sense, "parallels" between pre-Fascist
socioeconomic conditions, pop-cultural forms, and the contempo-
raneous "co-ordinate systems" of Einstein and the theoreticians of
quantum physics reminds us in turn of *Lot 49*'s implication of a parallelism between our own time and the other, the first, great age of modern science, the seventeenth century. The time of militant Puritanism,
with its doctrine of an absolute ontological gap between God and man,
was the time also of the Cartesian/Newtonian dualism as felt as "co-
ordinate" with the messages being brought by the "new perspectives
[telescopes]" that "begin to tell tales," in Sir Thomas Browne's words in
Urn Buriall. And the melodramatists of the Jacobean stage whose work
Pynchon parodies in *The Courier's Tragedy*, by "Richard Wharfinger,"
appealed hardly less luridly to their audiences than did the Weimar
moviemakers to theirs; the seventeenth-century English audiences,

13. Ibid., pp. 158, 159.

Pynchon remarks in *Lot 49*, and he could as well remark of the 1920s Germans of *Gravity's Rainbow*, were "preapocalyptic, death-wishful, sensually fatigued, unprepared, a little poignantly, for that abyss ... that had been waiting, cold and deep, only a few years ahead of them" (*Lot 49*, 44). Overlay these two ages of profound scientific advance, the seventeenth and twentieth centuries, and understand why Roger Mexico, invading Pointsman's conference of I. G. executives who sit plotting the postwar power dispensation, scents Wharfingerian "hoods, eye-slits, gold paraphernalia, the incense and thighbone scepter" (636).

It is already a critical commonplace to remark, in one or another connection, that Pynchon is "deeply ambivalent" about Western civilization as reified idea of order. The ambivalence has its roots in the feeling that the systematizing, framing impulse, while nearly synonymous with thought itself, is yet felt to betray some deeper ideal of "freedom." Systems express and define us; any idea of cognitive or mythic life without them is a contradiction in terms. Systems are beautiful, Simon Rodia's towers are beautiful; and yet systems also vitiate "nature" and "freedom," whether we make them ourselves, consciously, or simply take them as "found." For Poirier, Pynchon is thus "a great novelist of betrayal, and everyone in his books is a betrayer who lets himself or herself be counted, who elects or who has been elected to fit into the scheme of things. But they are the worse betrayers who propose that the schemes are anything more or less than that—an effort to "frame" life in every sense—or who evade the recognition of this by calling it paranoiac."[14]

Recognition—the exceedingly difficult job of discerning from the *inside* the lines of the force-fields that bind us—remains our only practically possible freedom: the Weberian freedom that consists simply in the realistic awareness of whatever options remain open to us *within* our condition. One practical "message" of *Gravity's Rainbow* with regard to science is that we, today's nation of starers, choose scientific illiteracy—evade recognition—only at our own great cost. Ask one of us about the current NASA program to explore deep space and the planets, and we are likely to ask righteously why the government "doesn't spend all that money for solving the *real* problems—you know, the ones here on Earth." But if it is a real problem, for example, to learn what quantities of hydrocarbons our industrial system may safely burn without causing disastrous harm to Earth's atmosphere and Earth's life, it is

14. Ibid., pp. 161, 162.

likely to be imperative that we send probes into the Venusian atmosphere, where, apparently, runaway effects of an excess of CO_2 have
turned the planetary surface into a 1000-degree inferno. If the impulse
we feel to burn hydrocarbons to fuel the present industrial system is,
like the system itself, an inheritance from the age of the Protestant ethic
and the spirit of capitalism, then surely it would be intelligent of us to
remember that Galileo, during the same age, stared at the moons of
Jupiter, the cloudtops of Venus, and wondered, purely, what these
worlds might be like. The message out of Tchitcherine's Haunting that
"everything is connected" (703) states also the Haunt of Pynchonian
consciousness—the axiom that all fabrications, in science, art, myth,
technology, *both* have always concealed *and* might always reveal the texture of history to those—all of us—who live inside that texture.

*   *   *

From these introductory remarks on the seventeenth century, our
class moves quickly past the two centuries of unchallenged Newtonian
rule and into the late nineteenth century, when, with the work of Faraday, Clausius, Gibbs, Clerk Maxwell (with his Demon), and other students of energy systems and "fields," science began to edge up on its
next profound revolution. With that revolution we reach scientific contemporaneity: the work of the builders of quantum physics and of
cybernetic technology; the Surprise Theorem of Kurt Gödel. The course
then proceeds, interdisciplinarian, to some philosophical systems of
the late nineteenth century, which feedback-loop-connect, again, with
the Pynchonian history of science. More loopings will implicate the
Romantic movement and Pynchon's transformations of central Romantic ideas; we then move forward again, through some aspects of German cultural history that culminate, for Pynchon, in Weimar movies,
Nazism, and Captain Blicero's V-2. Finally, a brief consideration of
Slothrop's Progress under the aspect of the Pynchonian Rainbow sign
sends us out of the course in a more or less positive mood.

A History of Automata

"The thought of every age is reflected in its technique":[15] having

15. Norbert Wiener, *Cybernetics, or Con-*   *Machine*, 2d ed. (Cambridge, Mass.: MIT
trol and Communication in the Animal and the   Press, 1961), p. 38.

announced this axiom, Professor Norbert Wiener of MIT, best-known of the founders of the eclectic postwar science of cybernetics, devotes the first chapter of his book *Cybernetics* to a discussion of how three successive ages of modern science imagined the ideal automaton, or man-machine. For the seventeenth and eighteenth centuries, Wiener shows, the automaton was a clockwork mechanism; for the nineteenth, a heat engine; for the twentieth, an electronic device operating from its environment through the exchange of information (cybernetic "feed-back"). In both Wiener's and Pynchon's explications of the history of scientific thought, these man-machine toys offer one way of tracking the course of history-as-science-as-technologized metaphor.

During the age of Newton, the Leibnizian monads, and Cartesian dualism, the age also of the development of the first really accurate clocks and navigational instruments, "the automaton becomes the clockwork music-box, with the little effigies pirouetting stiffly on top."[16] Each little figure is passive, its motions directed by a harmony tightly, mechanically preestablished; and yet the movements of the whole look as "natural," effortless, as, say, the social caste arrange-ments of neo-Classical Europe. As science refined and perfected New-ton's mechanics, the eclipses, ecliptics, precessions of sidereal spheres were calculated, triumphantly, for centuries into the future; the astron-omer Laplace could even fantasize an omniscient information-collect-ing machine, or a God, which, aware of every disposition of every particle in the universe at a given instant, could know the future to the end of all ages. The calm complacency of the model, its fantastic prom-ise of safety from any qualitative enigma, is evoked sometimes in Pynchon's fiction by spectacles of groups of people unable, for whatever reason, to intercommunicate, yet locked, like Leibniz's monads, into some grand scheme that operates from above them to keep them in phase. The seventeenth-century code word "predestined" (from Puritan doctrine) identifies the model when Oedipa Maas wanders into a roomful of dancing deaf-mutes, each dancing "whatever was in the fellow's head," and "how long, Oedipa wondered, could it go on before collisions became a serious hindrance? There would have to be col-lisons. The only alternative was some unthinkable order of music, many rhythms, all keys at once, a choreography in which each couple meshed easy, predestined" (*Lot 49*, 97).

Pointsman wants to explain the coincidence of Slothrop's hardons

16. Ibid., p. 40.

with rocket hits on the hypothesis of universal "stone determinacy"; as much for the Pavlovian as for his nominal opposites among the mystics of PSI Section, this vague faith in a predestinarian One blends toward the paranoiac belief in the one plot that manipulates men and events, as passive effigies, toward their last end. It is to the metaphysical and Protestant theological thought of the seventeenth century that men of Pointsman's mind owe the anachronistically "living hypothesis"[17] by which they justify to themselves their control of effigy lives—Slothrop's, Prentice's, Katje's, Pudding's.

But by the early nineteenth century, physical scientists had begun to learn to think, not alone in terms of the outward, mechanical relations of matter, but also in terms of—in Newton's old derogation—"occult" manifestations: dynamics, fluid relations, evolutions, and "fields" of force. Oersted's unification of electricity and magnetism made of "electromagnetism" an entity that seemed in its nature as much connected with the spaces between matter as with Newtonian mass itself. Faraday discovered the process of electrolysis, by which chemical compounds could be formed or dissociated by an electric current—and Faraday's name is significantly dropped in a passage of *Gravity's Rainbow* concerning this dangerous intimacy between matter and force: the encounter of the sentient pinballs from the planet Katspiel with the naked solenoids in Lyle Bland's Masons' defective pinball machines. After Cats'-Plays of pure force have tormented the little Newtonian spheres below the pinball deck, they return to their fellows in the offshoot slot,

> sobered, a few, having looked into the heart of the solenoid, seen the magnetic serpent and energy in its nakedness, long enough to be changed, to bring back from the writhing lines of force down in that pit an intimacy with power, with glazed badlands of soul, that set them apart forever—check out the portrait of Michael Faraday in the Tate Gallery in London, Tantivy Mucker-Maffick did once, to fill up a womanless and dreary afternoon, and wondered then how the eyes of men could grow so lambent, sinister, so educated among the halls of dread and the invisible. (584–85)

These glazed badlands are distinctly nineteenth-century ones: "educated" recalls Henry Adams's quest after such mysteries, and the passage generally, with its London drear and old portrait gallery, forms

17. William James's term in "The Will to   Believe," 1896.

one point of a delicate stencil, traceable here and there in the novel, outlining an elder, daguerreotyped age of thought:

> a numbered cosmos, a quaint, brownwood- paneled, Victorian kind of Brain War, as between quaternions and vector analysis in the 1800's—the nostalgia of Aether, the silver, pendulumed, stone-anchored, knurled-brass, filigreed, elegantly functional shapes of your grandfathers. These sepia tones are here, certainly. (726–27)

The stencil underlies, like a nostalgic memory-stratum, much more in the book than is apparent at first glance. Pirate Prentice, on the opening page and in the midst of World War II, dreams "the fall of a crystal palace" (3). Inasmuch as this alludes to the great Crystal Palace, later destroyed by fire, that housed the London Exposition at Hyde Park in 1851, the dream refers cryptically to the collapse of an old scientism under new forces that have built the Raketen-Stadt of the twentieth century, partly by transforming scraps of that heaped intellectual rubble itself. And this new order too, runs the implication, is an elaborated and mortal Crystal Palace—the modern power station out Pirate's window is "crystals grown in morning's beaker" (6)—which is itself marked to become gaudy debris. Such precisely is the sort of brown fatalism that possessed Pynchon's old prof from *V.*, Henry Adams, as he stood facing the Dynamo at the Exposition in Paris in 1900 and knew himself to be standing at a crucial switchpoint along the historical "track of the energy." "Henry Adams had stared aghast at Power," remembers Callisto in the story "Entropy." Somehow, Adams felt, the force that would drive the imminent twentieth century age of "multiplicity" could be linked with that ancient force, which Adams, Newtonlike, called "occult," of the Virgin of Chartres, architectress of "thirteenth century unity." Pynchon's Adamsian Lady V. is, of course, an architectress mostly of chaos, and yet the center of all her novel's stenciled, paranoid dreams of order. At home alike at Adams's Chartres and Pynchon's Malta, Florence or Test Stand VI (Peenemünde), the Lady evokes the pre-1914 educated suspicion that, in Adams's words, "Chaos was the law of nature; Order was the dream of man."[18]

In "Entropy" (1960),[19] Pynchon begins what will be his long explora-

18. Henry Adams, *The Education of Henry Adams* (New York: Modern Library, 1931), p. 451.

19. "Entropy" was first published in the *Kenyon Review* in 1960; it is reprinted in *12 From the Sixties*, ed. Richard Kostelanetz (New York: Dell Publishing Co., 1967), and in the 1984 *Slow Learner* collection.

tion of the mystery encoded, for late nineteenth-century students of science and history, in the word *force,* particularly in the thermodynamic concept of Entropy.[20] In the fast-evolving science of thermodynamics, entropy was first defined qualitatively by Clausius, then quantitatively by Gibbs and Boltzmann, who, working from the new realization of the molecular (discontinuous) structure of gases, derived equations that described entropy's "flow." (In "Entropy" this and more scientific background is given, in full undergraduate pomp, by an author quite as self-consciously erudite as the character Callisto, who functions as his erudite-amateur mouthpiece.) The term *entropy* paraphrases the Second Law of Thermodynamics by denoting the tendency of all matter and energy within a closed system to mix, to lose heterogeneity—all differences between separate regions within the system being erased by the aggregated effects of chance movements of particles, until the system attains a statistical equilibrium state where energies do not form discrete vectors, and perfect kinetic disorder—maximum entropy—reigns. In its most highly generalized sense, entropy signifies disorder: a straight flush will nearly always lose its ordered integrity when the deck is reshuffled; a glass of hot water in a cool room will raise the temperature of the room, losing its own identity as a region of discrete heat, until the glass/room system attains a uniform temperature and maximum entropy. Further, the fact that the uniform temperature is a *later* state of the system—the glass will always grow colder and the room hotter, never vice versa, with time—signifies that entropic processes are "irreversible," one-way in time: the increase of entropy distinguishes the past from the future. Nineteenth-century physics here discovered its need for a *statistical* mathematics: the old Newtonian mechanics, having been meant to describe systems, like the solar system, with very few individual members, were appropriate only for time-reversible processes (a film of the celestial motions run backwards looks just as probable as one run the "right" way; *GR,* 204). But the statistical probabilism that addressed myriads of small behaviors in time-irreversible systems implied that an entropic "arrow of time" marked a universal dynamic tendency toward general disor-

20. In defining entropy in some detail as I do here I risk, I suppose, seeming to take as novel a concept now almost venerable. Extended definition *does* still seem advisable for any study of Pynchon—but see, e.g., the chapter entitled "Entropy" in Tony Tanner's *City of Words: American Fiction 1950–1970* (New York: Harper & Row, 1971) for a survey of the many uses to which a great many modern fiction writers have put this now rather trendy concept.

ganization and final chaos. The physicist Josiah Gibbs in fact posited an inevitable "heat death" for the universe, when galactic fires and vacuum's cold everywhere will have averaged out: "something like limbo," Pynchon's Callisto says, "form and motion abolished, heat-energy identical at every point." In the phylogenic century of Darwin, Hegel, Goethe, the optimisms of neo-Romantics and of the builders of industrial systems found their dialectical answer in such dark thermodynamic thought-experiments. Adams wrote that "at the accelerated rate of progression since 1600, it will not need another century or half century to turn thought upside down. Law in that case would disappear as theory or *a priori* principle and give place to force. Morality would become police. Explosives would reach cosmic violence. Disintegration would overcome integration."[21]

In "Entropy," the vaporous decadent Callisto is immobilized by his fear of the Gibbsian heat death; he stays permanently inside the little counter-entropic "hothouse" he has made for himself, in a second-story Washington, D.C., apartment, as an enclave against the leveling forces outside—the first of Pynchon's many systems "closed" by virtue of having been obsessively elaborated from inside. In his bed, Callisto cradles a dying bird against his body, hoping to sustain the bird's life by entropic transfer of heat. The bird's death, apparently, is to signal catastrophe—that is, that no more heat transfer is possible, increase of entropy having everywhere reached its end. From bed, Callisto dictates his memoirs to his faery-exotic mistress, Aubade, who tends an exotica of hothouse plants and checks frequently on the thermometer outside the window: for days now, ominously, the temperature has been perfectly steady, at 37 degrees Fahrenheit. Despite his foolishness, Callisto is allowed to propose in the memoirs the sociocultural entropy metaphor to which Pynchon will point seriously in later work: "in American 'consumerism' ... a similar tendency from the least to the most probable, from differentiation to sameness ... a heat-death for his culture in which ideas, like heat-energy, would no longer be transferred, since each point in it would ultimately have the same quantity of energy; and intellectual motion would, accordingly, cease."[22]

This is a fair description of the white Los Angeles of Pynchon's Watts essay and of the generalized "America" whose homogenous aspect

21. From a 1905 letter by Adams to the historian Henry Osborn Taylor, quoted by Lewis Mumford in his *The Pentagon of Power* (New York: Harcourt Brace Jovanovitch), p. 232.

22. Pynchon, "Entropy," in Kostelanetz, ed., *12 From the Sixties*, p. 28.

makes Oedipa Maas ask, "How had it ever happened here, with the chances once so good for diversity?" (*Lot 49*, 136). But, as the absurd Callisto and some of Pynchon's critics fail to see, the entropy metaphor also may be read in a way that implies some hope even for such maximally homogenized systems. In the Watts essay, the black ghetto and, in *Lot 49*, the Tristero System surround the leveled-out regions, promising or threatening some redemption—perhaps, as seen from inside, a form of apocalypse. No system anywhere short of the total Gibbsian cosmos can be regarded as forever closed: they may always open or be opened out to larger systems. Heat deaths resurrected by violent irruptions or "White Visitations" from outside will merge, in turn, in more general stases, wherein the same possibility is again immanent: a nest of "levels" to be slowly unfolded, whether or not to any ultimate Gibbsian end, by circumambient angels, if we believe in such things.

Throughout Pynchon's fiction one may find such images of nested systems and of their quasi-mystical "openings-out," interpenetrations. "Noise," for example, leaks up through the floor and into Callisto's upstairs hothouse from the downstairs, high-entropy region where "Meatball Mulligan's lease-breaking party was moving into its 40th hour"—quite as *Gravity's Rainbow*'s preterite and elect worlds leak into each other, and as, in *V.*, Stencil's romantic quest and Profane's random yo-yoing finally dovetail as narratives. And since the frames between as within these fictional systems are permeable, Meatball's party may be regarded as continuous with later zany, high-entropy Pynchon parties—with those of the Whole Sick Crew, or the one at Putzi's, or the one aboard the *Anubis*, where "the same old shit ... [is] going on [as] back at Raoul de la Perlimpinpin's place, and for all Slothrop knows it's the same party" (463). If, as Pynchon seems glad to admit in *Slow Learner*, the vice of "Entropy" is the over-selfconsciousness of amateurism that leads the author to design a pat internal form to model an abstract idea, still the story's feelings about ideas of order and disorder are already complexly mixed. Meatball finally decides to reverse entropic disorganization by cleaning up the apartment, evicting the drunks, helping the girl who has fallen asleep in the shower to get into bed, while, upstairs, Aubade suddenly slams her fist through the window, turning with bleeding hands "to face the man on the bed and wait with him until the moment of equilibrium was reached, when 37 degrees Fahrenheit should prevail both inside and outside." Too much orderedness is answered by an incursion of "natural" chaos, an equivocal winter chill that refreshes, while too much chaos calls up a commendable housecleaning impulse ("a pain in the neck," Meatball thinks, "but probably better ...").

Life's fear of entropic processes seems most acute when objects undergoing them seem revealed, suddenly, as "alive," their time-arrows in effect becoming lifelines of automata, man-machines. In comic vein, Pynchon likes to propose the apparent hostility of inanimate objects to the designs of schlemihls as a diagnostic phenomenon in schlemihl lives: "But there is a mad exuberance, as with inanimate objects which fall off of tables when we are sensitive to noise and our own clumsiness and don't *want* them to fall, a sort of wham! ha-ha you hear that? here it is *again*, WHAM! in the cephalopod's every movement" (187). Indeed, although *V.* makes much of the horror of the absolutely inanimate Other, Pynchon's characters, increasingly through the canon, ask themselves whether the more frightful thing, antiparanoiac, is the otherness of the inanimate world, or, paranoiac, the very "life-likeness" of the malign behaviors of Things. When Things, most seriously death-dealing things like the rocket, seem to have will and intent, the projection signifies a tidal attraction between the partly dehumanized humans of a Thingified culture and that culture's purely mechanical reifications. Blicero's masturbatory joy when the rockets fall back from launch and destroy their technician-launchers echoes the rocket's own joyful "screaming across the sky," which merges in turn with the screams of its human victims. And Katje, following her indenture to Blicero, can tell Slothrop: "Between you and me is not only a rocket-trajectory, but also a life. You will come to understand that between the two points, in the five minutes, *it* lives an entire life" (209).

Katje's speech makes quite explicit, at last, the conceit of rocket-as-automaton. As the potential energy stored in its fuel is converted to kinetic energy in burning, the rocket ascends against gravity—i.e., it "lives," precisely in the fashion of the ideal man-machine of the nineteenth century, which, as Wiener explains, is the heat engine: "The automata which are humanly constructed and those other natural automata, the animals and plants of the materialist, are studied from a very different aspect in the nineteenth century than in the seventeenth and eighteenth centuries. The conservation and degradation of energy are the ruling principles of the day. The living organism is above all a heat engine, burning glucose or glycogen or starch, fats and proteins into carbon dioxide, water, and urea."[23]

The living organism at birth, this is to say, is in a state of low entropy, of intricate cellular differentiation and organization; the organism takes in the highly structured organic molecules of its food—thus raising minutely the entropy of its biometric environment—and reconstitutes these materials to maintain its structures, "burning fuel" in this way until its final opening-out at death, when all structured materials are sent back to be broken down in the larger organic flux. Death, the loss of the hothouse organism's coherence, thus represents the attainment of the maximum equilibrium state for the system of organism plus environment: "The stable state of the living organism is to be dead."[24] The automaton rocket ascends to reach its lowest entropy, its peaking of life against Earth's leveling force, at Brennschluss; there, fuel exhausted, the engines cut off and the rocket "dies," to be gathered, inanimate, back to "the entropies of lovable but scatterbrained Mother Nature" (324).

Considered, then, as a closed, dynamic system for the conversion of potential to kinetic energy, the rocket iconizes the fact of the twentieth century's inheritance of nineteenth-century imaginative technique. In the manner of its preflight construction, the rocket, like an organic life, is "an entire system won" (324) from scatterbrained nature, "from the debris of the given" (413): from iron ore, oxygen, hydrocarbons. And no less clearly than these Earth materials are co-opted for rocket uses, so are the black Hereros co-opted by the white Germans, the technological and human processes in parallel connoting the counterentropic progress of the life of white, Northern, Germanic, generally "Western," culture- and empire-elaboration. Grandiosely, as if to Wagnerian music, the rocket ascends on the strength of the potential energies stored in it after their artificial sorting from black Earth matrices: coal for its steel, Herero lives for its assembly. When and if it apocalyptically falls, the fall will mean death for all aboard the culture; and yet, after these raw materials return to Earth, to maximum entropy and regenerative darkness, there will eventually be new life—or else, or also, new "assembled" automaton-reifications of life. Most generally, then, Pynchon posits, with Henry Adams, that the life-force in this sense *is* the force of mind as will-to-order, and hence a force pointing to

23. Wiener, *Cybernetics*, p. 41.   24. Ibid., p. 58.

death, such that the exercise of the life-force is inevitably accompanied by mind's reflex horror of orderings once achieved:

> Unable to define Force as a unity, man symbolized it and pursued it, both in himself, and in the infinite, as philosophy and theology; the mind itself is the subtlest of all known forces, and its self-inspection necessarily created a science which had the singular value of lifting [Adams's] education, at the start, to the finest, subtlest, and broadest training both in analysis and synthesis....
>
> During a million or two of years, every generation in turn had toiled with endless energy to attain and apply power, all the while betraying the deepest alarm and horror at the power they created.[25]

The omnivorous symbolism of Melville's White Whale is recapitulated, and even pushed a step further, by Pynchon's rocket—designated acutely by Poirier as "Moby Dick and the *Pequod* in one."[26] V-2 is not only nature's raw chaos of all-colors or of no-color behind which the final secret of One or Zero lurks; it is, as well, mind's attempt to project itself, as counterentropic ordering impulse, onto the chaos; further, its deathliness is the sign of mind's dread of order once projected: mind's suspicion that its own characteristically energetic life is, somehow, a pernicious fiction or deep subversion of a universal creation pledged helplessly to the increase of disorder. Life, Wiener says, "finds its home" in "local enclaves whose direction seems opposed to that of the universe at large and in which there is a limited and temporary tendency for organization to increase"[27]—the eddy of low entropy, individually and collectively, being life itself. Life and all its patterned works are anomalous, impermanent, beautiful phantasms; towers will fall, but the obsessiveness that built them is a life impulse, and all towers, like the rocket, like Pynchon's novel, monumentalize life's glorying itself, because of its deep distrust and fear of itself: life's grandiloquent bluff.

*   *   *

"If the seventeenth and early eighteenth centuries are the age of clocks, and the later eighteenth and nineteenth centuries the age of

25. Adams, *Education*, pp. 476, 497.

26. Richard Poirier, "Rocket Power," *Saturday Review: The Arts* 1 (March 3, 1973): 59–64; quote from p. 60.

27. Norbert Wiener, *The Human Use of Human Beings: Cybernetics and Society* (New York: Avon Books, 1950), pp. 20, 21.

steam engines, the present time is the age of communication and control."[28] By his discussion of the earlier automata in the first chapter of *Cybernetics*, Wiener prepares the ground for his examination, to which the rest of his book is given, of the twentieth century as a time when life and machines have tended increasingly to form a single closed system. The intimacy between life and its machine creations, it is easy to feel, has developed so far that the very ontological distinction between them is on the point of blurring. This very blurring is a major theme developed in *V.*—often, in fact, developed no more subtly there than in fashionable decryings of the advance of "smart machines" in the mass society. "Me and SHOCK are what you and everybody will be someday ... None of you have very far to go," the plastic humanoid SHROUD tells Benny Profane (*V.*, 266, 267). Such fears are of course real and contribute largely to Pynchon's vision; but, as shown particularly in *Gravity's Rainbow*, there is another, more positive and far more subtle way of regarding the increasing cloture of the system of men and machines. Considering what he has famously called the worldwide "extension of the human nervous system" in electronic media, Marshall McLuhan hints at this way by observing *both* the hope implicit in the phenomenon *and* the danger of the imagination's lagging too far behind its progress: "We actually live mythically and integrally, as it were, but we continue to think in the old, fragmented space and time patterns of the pre-electronic age.... In the electric age, when our central nervous system is technologically extended to involve us in the whole of mankind and to incorporate the whole of mankind in us, we necessarily participate in depth in the consequences of our every action. It is no longer possible to adopt the aloof and dissociated role of the literate Westerner."[29]

In both McLuhan's and Wiener's thought-systems, whose terms and imageries are complementary here, life defines itself essentially by the exchange of intelligence, "messages," with the environment, rather than merely by the passive reception of raw materials or "forces" from outside. Smart machines are here now because we have come to understand smartness itself, and not any preestablished mechanical harmony or any thermodynamic process, as life's diagnostic attribute. What is exchanged among forms of life and among automata, cybernetics calls *information*. The quantum of information is a single decision between

28. Wiener, *Cybernetics*, p. 39.

29. Marshall McLuhan, *Understanding*

Media (New York: McGraw-Hill Co., 1964), p. 4.

two binary alternatives; the "content" of each mediating signal is the intelligible "message." Cybernetic automata are those machines built to take in and process a flux of messages from the outside; *feedback* is the familiar term for the process. In such devices as home thermostats, electronic "eyes" that open doors for approaching people, radar-controlled antiaircraft systems such as were developed by Wiener and his associates for World War II, and increasingly "lifelike" generations of computers, electronic receptors are analogous to living sense organs, internal information-processing circuitries to brains, and information-storage capacities to living memory. An Earth united by such lifelike processes is neither a passive arrangement of gears nor a thermodynamic engine running inevitably and depressingly down, but, ideally, a resonant informational system that keeps up its own life and in which "relations stop nowhere," as in William James.

Cybernetics defines an *informational* entropy that is precisely reciprocal to thermodynamic entropy. The flow of information from one place to another will always be subject to distortion by "noise," the general term subsuming all factors that would dilute or scramble the message, the susceptibility of the message to noise distortion increasing with the amount of information improbably packed in. In "Entropy," thus, Callisto's hothouse is a highly organized "message" about his obsessive mental contents; its pristine order is disturbed, as intense concentration may be disturbed, by noise from outside, in this case the amplified music that pierces up through the floor. In the same story, Meatball Mulligan commiserates with his friend Saul, whose wife Miriam has just left him after an argument over—by now it is pop-psych jargon—Marital Communications: "Tell a girl: 'I love you.' No trouble with two-thirds of that, it's a closed circuit. Just you and she. But that nasty four-letter word in the middle, *that's* the one you have to look out for. Redundance. Irrelevance, even. Leakage. All this noise. Noise screws up your signal, makes for disorganization in the circuit."

In the three novels, and in *Gravity's Rainbow* especially, the history of characters generally is, as the narrator says of Herero history, "one of lost messages" (322); a major purpose of Pynchon's art is indeed to display human life as a running phenomenology of ambiguous signals, missed opportunities, failed perceptions—and this whether in individual cases we blame the apparent jamming of messages on entropy, private insensitivities of the receivers, or Their malign agency. The zone Hereros remember dimly an old Südwest myth of the "sly hare who nests in the Moon" (anyone who looks for it can really see it), who might transmit "Moon's true message," presumably one of peace or felicity; but, in the long Herero exile, "The true message has never come" (322). McLuhanesque trees near Berlin have "branches like dendrites of the Nervous System fattening, deep in twittering nerve-dusk, in preparation for some important message" (364), and soon, echoingly, Slothrop and Säure get stoned under an upended tree stump that is "a giant nerve cell, dendrites extended into the city … Signals coming in from all directions" (367). They play Rocketman, though, and miss whatever message might have arrived from the dark. In the surrealistic fantasy flowering from the colonel's haircut (642 ff.), the sinister speech by "Mister Information" to "Skippy" alludes first to the Percy Crosby cartoon strip *Skippy*, of 1920s–1945 vintage.[30] More centrally, we are meant paranoiacally to feel that Mister Information's information has been deliberately jammed (since what he says seems to be purely what They want Skippy to hear), and thus that the monologue somehow connects to the atmospheric phenomena that have been puzzling the colonel this late summer of '45, and whose meaning, as it happens, *we* know: "But these sunsets out here, I don't know. Do you suppose something has exploded somewhere? Really—somewhere in the East? Another Krakatoa? Another name at least that exotic … the colors are so different now…. Is the sun's everyday spectrum being modulated? Not at random, but systematically, by this unknown debris in the prevailing winds? Is there information for us? Deep questions, and disturbing ones." (632) Later, Slothrop finds a tattered fragment of newspaper headline that once had delivered the same information, but weathering, increase of entropy, has degraded it so that now, like the colonel, he can't "read" it: only $\frac{MB\ DRO}{ROSHI}$ (693) remains from "bomb dropped … Hiroshima."

Paranoiacs' plot-information, as typically mediated by paper, is often a matter of intelligence in the word's most reductive (military/corporate) sense. Ironically, we may even yet miss it, although we actively

---

30. The Skippy/Percy Crosby allusion is an interesting one of Pynchon's "lightly concealed entryways" to corridors leading far outside the novel, yet always in touch with it. Skippy, like Orphan Annie, led a schlemihl's life, always threatened by evil forces of change, which meant, for the politically reactionary Crosby, Rooseveltian changes in the direction of liberalism, urbanism, and the homogenized Global Village. Crosby, and his cartoon strip, became more and more politically preachy and belligerent; Crosby drank too much, had marital and legal troubles, and attempted suicide; finally he became a full-blown paranoiac. In the veterans hospital to which he had been committed he seemed perfectly lucid and "normal" much of the time but was quite as psychotic as Freud's Dr. Schreber. One imagines even that Crosby himself could have composed Mister Information's sinister speech to Skippy in *Gravity's Rainbow*.

seek it: "In runs a short but spunky secretary ... and commences belting Roger in the shins with the excess-profits tax records from 1940 to '44 of an English steel firm which happened to share a patent with Vereinigte Stahlwerke for an alloy used in the liquid-oxygen coupling for the line running aft to the S-Gerät in A4 number 00000. But Roger's shins are not set up for this kind of information." (632)

Slothrop obsessively searches and deals for papers containing "this kind of information," since he might thus learn his history; with his Zürich informational connection, Semyavin, he has this conversation:

> "What is it you're after?"
> "Uh, information?" ...
> "Oh. Another one." ... A tragic sigh.
> "Information. What's wrong with dope and women? Is it any wonder the world's gone insane, with information come to be the only real medium of exchange?" (258)

Pynchon uses Wiener to help make the point that information of this kind, as words on paper to be bought and sold, is constellated with that other mercantile-Puritan value, money. After the informational score from Semyavin, a chorus line of Loonies on Leave descends on Slothrop, and one Loony, maybe a secret friend, confides: "You can spot right away what's wrong, everyone promises ya somethin' fer nothin', right? yes now oddly enough, that's the main objection engineers and scientists have always had to the idea of ... perpetual motion or as we like to call it Entropy Management" (260). No more in the information-dealing game than in the universe according to thermodynamics does anyone ever really get something for nothing: dealing in information for money is in itself a participation in Their game of "shit, money, and the Word—the three American truths." Wiener writes of the characteristically American misconception that, since "a thing is valuable as a commodity for what it will bring in the open market.... The fate of information ... is to become something which can be bought and sold."[31] Writing in 1950, he is thinking of the Cold War cult of "know-how," of "atomic secrets" regarded as national treasures to be jealously locked into safes. The truth, of course, is that information by its nature is mobile and bodiless and will as a matter of course penetrate everywhere—neo-Puritans of the sect of McCarthy to the contrary notwithstanding. It is because They try hopelessly to deal in, compete for, and hoard information that, according to Wiener,

31. Wiener, *Human Use*, pp. 154, 155.

each terrifying discovery merely increases our subjection to the need of making a new discovery. Barring a new awareness on the part of our leaders, this is bound to go on and on, until the entire intellectual potential of the land is drained from any possible constructive application to the manifold needs of the race, old or new. The effect of these weapons must be to increase the entropy of this planet, until all distinctions of hot and cold, good and bad, man and matter have vanished in the formation of the white furnace of a new star.[32]

"The entropy of this planet" will increase in the apocalyptic event, it is Wiener's sense, because inanimate weapons, shattering at their "deaths," do not, as dead organic things do, release any materials or information capable of reintegration into the wider life-system. When, like the rocket, the weapons are controlled from inside by information-processing systems, they are, in a quite horrible sense, "lifelike" without being living, the cybernetic automata of the present. When the informational hoard is destroyed in detonation's "white furnace," the wastes left behind are a wreckage of that negative entropy by whose original theft the Earth has been a little impoverished of life's energies.

V-2 is a cybernetic automaton chiefly in that a feedback-looped "control … for the first time was … put inside" (30). *Gravity's Rainbow* accurately describes (239, 301) the rocket's cybernetic "brain," a revolutionary information-processing device that was called (creating a most fortuitous pun for the novel's purposes) the I. G., for inertial guidance device. With its use, in Frederick Ordway's words, "everything needed to obtain the required impact accuracy would be within the missile itself. It utilized gyroscopes, accelerometers, and an analogue computer to furnish data to position the jet vanes during powered flight for maintaining trajectory control."[33] So, in flight, "was the Rocket's terrible passage reduced, literally, to bourgeois terms, terms of an equation such as that elegant blend of philosophy and hardware, abstract change and hinged pivots of real metals which describes motion under the aspect of yaw control:

$$\theta \, \frac{d^2\phi}{dt^2} + \sigma^* \frac{d\phi}{dt} + \frac{\delta L}{\delta \propto} \, (s_1 - s_2) \propto \; = \; -\frac{\delta R}{\delta \beta} \, s_3 \, \beta\,"$$

(239)

32. Ibid., p. 176.

33. Frederick I. Ordway III and Mitchell R. Sharpe, *The Rocket Team* (New York: Thomas Y. Crowell, 1979), p. 40.

A fellow amateur, reputed to have majored in mathematics,[34] clarifies this equation for me. θ is the desired yaw angle, preset as a "control." ϕ is the missile's range; the differential

$$\frac{d^2\phi}{dt^2}$$

is the change in the actual yaw angle with reference to an absolute axis
fixed by gyroscopes. The third additive term refers to the continuous
change in the weight of the rocket as its fuel is consumed. On the other
side of the equal sign, R is the distance from the rocket to the Earth's
center; β the angle between the local horizontal and the direction of
flight; δ a velocity ratio

$$\frac{V}{Vc}$$

where

$$\frac{d\phi}{dt}$$

As the readings of continuous changes in all these parameters are integrated by the guidance device, a continuous negative feedback operates
to keep the yaw angle—the deviation of the rocket's position from the
tangent to the parabolic curve—within the limits of safety for the trajectory. In short, V-2 can ascend against gravity because it can integrate
these data "inside"; it is an automaton, not only in the nineteenth-century sense, by virtue of being a heat engine that burns fuel, but also in
the twentieth-century sense, by virtue of being a closed informational
system.

And further, just as the uses of human and mineral materials as
"fuel" are parallel within the thermodynamic-automaton model, the
use (by the larger technological system that built the rocket) of expendable human lives, human "information," and the in-flight use (in this
sense the destruction) of information by the I. G. device are mirror-
analogues. Like the rocket/I. G. device system, the larger technological
system, as long as it lives, remains closed, taking only to itself, "pre-

34. My thanks to Mr. Roy Benson,   Cornell University.
formerly of the physics department of

serving, possessing, steering between Scylla and Charybdis the whole way to Brennschluss. If any of the young engineers saw correspondence between the deep conservatism of Feedback and the kinds of lives they were coming to lead *in the very process* of embracing it, it got lost, or disguised—none of them made the connection" (239). Indeed, to "make a connection" is to go imaginatively outside a closed system, to learn a language other than negative feedback. Steve and Charles, the General Electric apparatchiks who pull an inspection tour of the Nazi Toiletship, are two such "young engineers" and perhaps originate in Pynchon's days of working for Boeing Aircraft: "Look at that *Charles*, you can't pick your search team, not if you're just out of school and here I am, in the asshole of nowhere, not much more than a gofer to this—what is he, a fag? What am *I*? What does GE want me to be? Is this some obscure form of company punishment, even, good God, permanent *exile*? I'm a career man" (449).

What he is, in fact, is the GE bureaucracy's "servomechanism." McLuhan's is the precise diagnosis:

> To behold, use or perceive any extension of ourselves in tech-
> nological form is necessarily to embrace it. To listen to radio or to
> read the printed page is to accept these extensions of ourselves into
> the personal system and to undergo the "cloture" or displacement
> of perception that follows automatically. It is this continuous
> embrace of our own technology in daily use that puts us in the
> Narcissus role of subliminal awareness and numbness in relation to
> these images of ourselves. By continuously embracing technologies,
> we relate ourselves to them as servomechanisms.[35]

A medium at a London seance foreshadows these realizations about the rocket when, cryptically in this early context, she says, "It's control.... For the first time it was *inside*, do you see. The control is put inside. No more need to suffer passively under 'outside forces'—to veer into any wind" (30). Dr. Pointsman, fearing the mysterious process by which Slothrop's hardons seem to transmit information from outside to the world inside mechanical/causal science and the bureaucratized service of government, asks "what new pathology lies Outside now?" (144) and reminds all interested inside parties that "*we must never lose control*" (144). Since internal pointsmen of closed informational systems cannot accept the possibility that any preterite outside may infiltrate and destabilize the closed systems, these deep conservators share

---

35. McLuhan, *Understanding Media*, p. 46.

the fate—their subconscious awareness of which Pynchon calls their death wish—of finally going down with their systems, when these systems run out of material and informational life-resources to steal, hoard, and destroy in use. One passage in *Gravity's Rainbow*, atypically, moralizes directly:

> Taking and not giving back, demanding that "productivity" and "earnings" keep on increasing with time, the System removing from the rest of the world these vast quantities of energy to keep its own tiny desperate fraction showing a profit: and not only most of humanity—most of the World, animal, vegetable and mineral, is laid waste in the process. The system may or may not understand that it's only buying time. And that time is an artificial resource to begin with, of no value to anyone or anything but the System, which sooner or later must crash to its death, when its addiction to energy has become more than the rest of the World can supply, dragging with it innocent souls all along the chain of life. (412)

The language—simple for once, even rather sophomorically sloganeering—knowingly telegraphs the clichéd concern, post-*Gravity's Rainbow*, with an energy crisis; but "energy" here addresses the waste, not just of oil resources or of the famous environment, but of life's whole pool of counterentropic "information." The subject is our addiction, not simply to petrochemicals and machines, but also to habits of thought and of valuation and judgment as old and as self-reinforcing as technologized Progress itself in its three triumphant, post-Newtonian centuries.

*   *   *

In the passage from page 412 quoted above, there also lurks a persistent Pynchonian icon of any would-be sorter of information inside a system: Maxwell's Demon, a pixie of real scientific thought whose haunting of Pynchon's fiction from the beginning is, by this date, well known and well documented. The Demon, however, is important enough in this thematic context to justify a brief if redundant notice here. James Clerk Maxwell, the great nineteenth-century quantifier of electromagnetic and thermodynamic phenomena, posited the following hypothetical case of the large-scale violation of the Second Law of Thermodynamics—the principle that "entropy will always increase." Imagine, he said, a rectangular box with impermeable walls, inside which a known quantity of gas is distributed at maximum equilibrium.

Imagine, running down through the box, an impermeable partition containing a tiny gate or trap door. The door is controlled by a small device, or tiny intelligent being, able to distinguish faster-moving from slower-moving molecules in the gas. As each fast molecule approaches, the Demon lets it pass through the trap door into one half of the chamber; the slower molecules he concentrates in the other half. Since heat is a function of the speed of molecular movement, the Demon will in this way be able to "unmix" the gas, to lower the entropy of the system: one half of the box will contain a high concentration of fast molecules and so will be hotter than the other half. If the heat differential drives a heat engine attached to the box, the whole system will constitute a perpetual motion machine, as long as the Demon keeps sorting; mechanical work will have been generated from inside—something for nothing—in direct violation of the Second Law.

Wiener observes that "it is simpler to repel the question posed by the Maxwell Demon than to answer it."[36] One of Maxwell's purposes in inventing the apparent absurdity of the Demon, then challenging physical theory to explain why it was absurd, may have been to illustrate the nature of the statistical determinism whose mathematics had become necessary to physics with the discovery of the molecular nature of matter. Statistical "laws" that describe gas behaviors are essentially probabilistic, transcending the *strict* determinism that would have to account separately for each individual collision. The Demon is probabilism's subverter; the impossibility of his agency, if proven, the vindication of probabilism's necessity. But the deeper reasons for the Demon's impossibility were, as a matter of fact, inaccessible to Maxwell and his contemporaries, since they involve both the "coupling" of thermodynamic with cybernetic entropy and the quantization of energy such as has only been understood after 1900. These deeper reasons, however, are the ones most pertinent to Pynchon's symbol. The Demon first operates by virtue of his collection of *information* about the velocities of the molecules; the production of work is thus directly proportional to the quantity of information monitored, used, and destroyed. As long as the Demon himself interacts with the gas by taking in information about it, he is "coupled" with the gas system, and, since the entropy loss in the gas is overbalanced by the entropy gain from the destruction of information, the entropy of the total system continues to increase, preserving the Second Law. Further, in order to "see" the molecules, the Demon

36. Wiener, *Cybernetics*, p. 57.

must have light or some other form of radiant energy; by this additional coupling, the impacts of light quanta (photons) on the molecules will so disturb their behaviors as to jam the Demon's messages well beyond the degree of precision he needs to function as sorter. That is, "all coupling is strictly a coupling involving energy, and a system in statistical equilibrium is in equilibrium both in matters concerning entropy and those concerning energy. In the long run, the Maxwell Demon is itself subject to a random motion corresponding to the temperature of its environment, and, as Leibniz says of some of his monads, it receives a large number of small impressions, until it falls into 'a certain vertigo' and is incapable of clear perceptions. In fact, it ceases to act as a Maxwell Demon."[37] The Demon, Wiener adds, may conceivably persist in his function, in a state of "metastability," for a short while—just as an organic life persists metastably, for as long as it lives, against universally increasing entropy. But in the end the Demon is a born loser, and this, for Pynchon's symbolic purposes, is the centrally germane fact about him.

In *Gravity's Rainbow* the Demon appears less saliently than in *The Crying of Lot 49*, confining himself for the most part to quick, leering glimpses out from between interstices. Friedman and Puetz plausibly suggest that he is the thief who makes off with Slothrop's uniform (i.e., "sorts" the ongoing plot): "From way down the hall, a tiny head appears around a corner, a tiny hand comes out and gives Slothrop the tiny finger" (199). The narrator briefly fantasizes that Maxwell in inventing the Demon had wanted to warn the world against "personnel like Liebig" who would sort, bureaucratize from inside, the energies of science. In general in the novel, the Demon is equated metaphorically with system-mongering Theys, who are born losers: Theirs presumes to be a perpetual motion machine, a self-contained technological universe always "ascending"; but eventually, wider "couplings" will open the system, entropy *will* increase, the rocket fall. The Demon meanwhile presides metaphorically over all forms of Their Demonic compulsion to build systematic artifices in ultimate malice toward life—and yet, in the very building, seductively to mimic life's essential activity. Men can thus easily be conned and co-opted into becoming semblances or "servomechanisms" of nonlife; Wiener puts it thus:

> When human atoms are knit into an organization in which they are
> used, not in their full right as responsible human beings, but as

37. Ibid., p. 58.

cogs and levers and rods, it matters little that their raw material is flesh and blood. *What is used as an element in a machine, is an element in a machine.* Whether we entrust our decisions to machines of metal, or to those machines of flesh and blood which are bureaus and vast laboratories and armies and corporations, we shall never receive the right answers to our questions unless we ask the right questions.[38]

The final sentence of this passage may lie behind Pynchon's Proverb for Paranoids, 3: "If they can get you asking the wrong questions, they don't have to worry about answers" (251).[39]

Pynchon thus arrives, with Wiener, at what amounts to an ethical imperative: a humanity that would remain humane has an urgent need carefully to distinguish between organic life and its counterfeits, the automata, plot-networks and systems with the appearances of "lives of their own." And the novel's very first scene has affirmed, as the reader will realize at some point, the essential difference between life and non-life: the secret that organic life collectively *does* subvert informational entropy, after all, by sending DNA molecules bearing "messages" down through the species' genetic, collective histories. As Pirate Prentice and his friends cook their banana breakfast,

> there grows among all the rooms, replacing the night's old smoke, alcohol and sweat, the fragile, musaceous odor of Breakfast ... taking over not so much through any brute pungency or volume as by the high intricacy to the weaving of its molecules, sharing the conjurer's secret by which—though it is not often Death is told so clearly to fuck off—the living genetic chains prove even labyrinthine enough to preserve some human face down ten or twenty generations ... so the same assertion-through-structure allows this war morning's banana fragrance to meander, repossess, prevail. (10)

The rooftop "bananery" is a "hothouse" of life, floored with humus in which "anything could grow" (5) and sealed against a hostile outside of "icefields ... and a cold smear of sun" over which an incoming rocket arcs. Symbolically, the hothouse is an entire Earth full of life, and the winter outside is the surrounding inanimate cosmos. Life collectively is an *open* informational system, having no boundedness short of the

---

38. Wiener, *Human Use*, p. 254.

39. Cf. also Mister Information to the colonel: "Mister Information *always* answers questions." Colonel: "For what he's making, I'd even question answers" (646).

interface of the whole Earth with the cosmos. And—the final subversion, and this gorgeous passage's widest implication—perhaps even here, as at all other Pynchonian interfaces, there occurs leakage, a certain secret surprise of penetration. Evolution since Darwin has been defined as the net statistical product of the adaptations of life forms to "random" mutations of genetic materials, accidents that are now thought to be caused by the impacts on living genes of the flux of subnuclear particles that fills all space and rains down through the atmosphere onto the Earth. In this fundamental connection with the cosmic outside and with chance may lie life's innermost secret, the source of its dynamism of change. And in the behaviors of the subnuclear particles themselves lies, as only lately understood by theoretical physics, a kind of principle of surprise whose ultimate sanction Pynchon sometimes invokes for his definition of living Being as a continuous adaptation to indeterminacy. These remarks can provide my own interfacing with the next fascinating topic.

Surprise Physics

Even to step most gingerly into the very exciting but abstruse domain of quantum physics is to feel the shoes of one's amateurism pinch tightly. Of the two main components of the revolutionized physical thought of the early twentieth century, the relativity and quantum theories, it is the latter that Pynchon's fiction employs more gainfully. Unfortunately, quantum physics is also the harder of the two to understand and discuss in nonmathematical ways. The physicist E. J. Zimmerman, in fact, identifies the very impossibility of grasping quantum-mechanical reality in terms of everyday models as one of the three most essential characteristics of that reality, the other two being its irremediable probabilism and its assumption that matter/energy is fundamentally discontinuous, quantized.[40] *Gravity's Rainbow* offers few overt references to the new physics, but, thanks to many indirect ones, the quantum world picture provides deep-basement congruencies with other, more obvious mataphorical functions at work in the novel. Here I will display these congruencies, having first done my best to paraphrase the essential outlook of the new physics.

At the end of the nineteenth century the Newtonian mechanics, still

40. See E. J. Zimmerman, "Time and Quantum Theory," in *The Voices of Time*, ed. J. T. Fraser (New York: George Braziller Inc., 1966), pp. 479-99.

largely intact, continued to dominate the scientific imagination. The Gibbsian thermodynamics (already discussed) of molecular systems was kept within the Newtonian purview by the assumption that individual molecular motions obeyed strict deterministic laws, however their aggregated effects might have to be dealt with statistically. The mildly unsettling concept of "fields" had been introduced, primarily by Faraday's work on electromagnetism and by Maxwell's electromagnetic theory of light. But "fields" were precariously explained by the neo-Newtonian assumption that some quasi-material "ether," filling all space, was the medium for the forces that could still be regarded as propagating by the mechanical impact of matter. The ether was to be rendered completely untenable by the famous Michelson-Morley experiment, which demonstrated that ether does not exist. The finding, which led Einstein directly to special relativity, revived the action-at-a-distance quandary that had so disturbed Newton. *Gravity's Rainbow* briefly evokes a "nostalgia of ether" (726–27), remembering how cruelly, after 1900, "the assumption of a Vacuum in time tended to cut us off from one another. But an Aether sea to bear us world-to-world might bring us back a continuity, show us a kinder universe, more easygoing" (726). And because the nineteenth century, before its fall from ether-innocence, sometimes discussed an "ether *wind*," Pynchon can further allude indirectly to the old ether model by showing us Frans van der Groov "warp[ing] a skein of dreams into Pirate's own, heretical dreams, exegeses of windmills that turned in shadow at the edges of dark fields, each arm pointing at a spot on the rim of a giant wheel that turned through the sky, stop and go, always exactly with the spinning cross: 'wind' was a middle term, a convention to express what really moved the cross ... and this applied to all wind, everywhere on Earth" (620–21).

To such earnest attempts to preserve mechanical/causal models of linkages between discrete properties of systems, compare the quantum-mechanical and relativistic outlooks engendered respectively in 1900 by Planck and in 1905 by Einstein, in which, to quote the physicist Werner Heisenberg,

> the whole objective description of nature in the Newtonian sense, in
> which determinate values are attributed to the defining elements of
> a system, such as position, velocity, and energy, had to be aban-
> doned in favor of a description of observational situations, in which
> only the probabilities of certain outcomes could be given. The
> words in which we allude to atomic phenomena therefore became

problematic. It was possible to speak of waves or particles, and necessary to realize at the same time that this expedient by no means involved a dualistic description of the phenomena but rather an absolutely unitary one; the meaning of the old terms became somewhat blurred.[41]

Max Planck, in discovering the quantization of energy, introduced a new constant of nature, h, the "quantum of action"—and it is only because the value of h is unimaginably miniscule (6.6256 × 10^{-27} erg-seconds) that in our macroworld we fail to see the ultimate "grainedness" of all natural processes. In the new quantum epistemology, light can be understood either as particulate—a stream of discrete electromagnetic quanta, or photons—or as a wave function giving the mathematical shape of distributed probabilities of finding a given photon in one or another region of space. In 1924 Louis de Broglie proposed that, more generally, *every* bit of apparent "matter" might somehow "correspond to" a wave function, or "matter wave relation," whose wavelength would be equal to Planck's constant divided by the product of the particle's mass and velocity. In this view, "particles" are point concentrations of somethingness within standing matter-wave orbits expressing quantized energy states; as much as it "is" a particle, a moving electron "is" the wave-mathematical summation of the distributions of its positions; its manifestation as particle is in some mysterious way a function of its having been looked for under that ideal aspect. De Broglie's matter-wave model was soon supplemented by the wave-mechanics of Erwin Schrödinger and by a mathematical scheme of Werner Heisenberg's called matrix mechanics; these models were found to be mutually supportive and, in 1926, were synthesized into the theory then first generally called the quantum mechanics, representing already a vastly profound application and broadening of Planck's original description of quantization.

It now became possible to identify "fields" as manifestations of the wave nature both of matter and energy, complementary to the particle nature: clearly, subatomic entities could no longer be thought of as "things" on the analogy of Newtonian planets, bullets, billiard balls. The familiar concepts of "waves" and "particles" now are seen not as competing either/or alternatives for the literal denotation of fundamental entities, but as both/and models, or metaphors, expressing equally some underlying, "absolutely unitary" reality. They are *appearances:* the

41. Werner Heisenberg, *Across the Frontiers*, trans. Peter Heath (New York: Harper Torchbooks, 1974), p. 157.

principle of the oddly "idealist" orientation of quantum theory is that how an entity manifests itself in experiment depends on the manner of the experiment and on our ways of manipulating the quantum equations. We investigate not a material, but a mathematical ground of reality.

A main pillar of the new physics that is of much metaphorical use to Pynchon is the Uncertainty Principle of Heisenberg. It asserts that we cannot know simultaneously and to an indefinite degree of precision *both* the position *and* the velocity (or momentum) of a given particle; as our knowledge of one of these properties grows more precise, the other blurs in proportion:

$$\Delta p \times \Delta q \geq \frac{h}{2\,\mathrm{pi}},$$

where p is momentum, q position, and Δ denotes "uncertainty of." The relation applies also to other pairs of fundamental properties; in fact, in its most general form the Uncertainty Principle says that for every characterizing quantity A there exists a quantity B such that it is impossible to know both quantities simultaneously below a certain horizon. The principle adumbrates a "looseness of play"[42] in the universe, a fluid indeterminacy underlying all macroscopic appearances of precisely determined interlockings of variables. Wesley Salmon's discussion of radioactive decay sketches one good example of the effects of such discoveries on even such a fundamental commonsense notion as causality in time. Each unstable nucleus of uranium, at some time during the element's slow self-conversion to lead, emits an alpha particle. Inside the nucleus, before the event, the alpha particle hits the nuclear wall about 10^{21} times each second and has, with each hit, one chance in 10^{38} of escaping: this means statistically that it will escape sometime within about a billion years. But, where the question of the determinacy of separate events is no longer begged (as it was in Maxwell's time), the inquiry after what "causes" a given nucleus to release its particle on a given occasion turns out to be strictly meaningless:

> When we ask why the alpha particle escaped on that particular trial, having failed on countless other occasions, the answer is simply that there is a probability of about 10^{38} of such an outcome on any given bombardment of the wall. That is all there is to it. Perhaps you

42. Sir James Jeans's resonant phrase (1937), quoted in Victor Guillemin, *The* *Story of Quantum Mechanics* (New York: Charles Scribner's Sons, 1968), p. 232.

want to say that there must be some reason for the success of this
trial and the failures on others, but we do not yet know what it is.
According to quantum mechanics, however, that is not the case. We
are, according to that theory, dealing with an irremediably indeter-
ministic process.[43]

Erwin Schrödinger, more generally, speaks of quantum mechanics'
postulation of

> the lack of individuality of a particle, or even of an atom. If I observe
> a particle here and now, and observe a similar one a moment later at
> a place very near the former place, not only cannot I be sure
> whether it is "the same," but this statement has no absolute mean-
> ing. This *seems* to be absurd. For we are so used to thinking that at
> every moment between the two observations the first particle must
> have been *somewhere*, it must have followed a *path*, whether we
> know it or not. And similarly the second particle must have come
> from somewhere, it must have *been* somewhere.... In other words
> we assume ... that we could have kept our particle under *continuous
> observation*, thereby ascertaining its identity.
>
> This habit of thought we must dismiss.... Observations are to be
> regarded as discrete, disconnected events. Between them are gaps,
> which we cannot fill in.[44]

As good readers of Pynchon and of this brief discussion will already
have seen, the terms and imageries of quantum theory have large functions within Pynchon's metaphorical system, although usually the
entryways to them are more closely guarded than are entryways to, say,
Weberian, filmic, or Jungian underground lines. The opening may be a
single, coyly emphasized word, say Uncertainty:

> barn-swallow souls, fashioned of brown twilight, rise toward the
> white ceiling ... they are unique to the Zone, they answer to the
> new Uncertainty. Ghosts used to be either likenesses of the dead or
> wraiths of the living. But here in the Zone categories have been
> blurred badly. The status of the name you miss, love and search for
> now has grown ambiguous and remote, but this is even more than
> the bureaucracy of mass absence—some still live, some have died,
> but many, many have forgotten which they are. Their likenesses will
> not serve. Down here are only wrappings left in the night, in the
> dark: images of the Uncertainty. (303)

43. Wesley C. Salmon, "Determinism
and Indeterminism in Modern Science,"
in *Reason and Responsibility*, 3d ed., ed. Joel
Feinberg (Encino, Calif.: Dickenson Publishing Co., 1975).

44. Erwin Schrödinger, "Causality and
Wave Mechanics," in *The World of Mathematics*, 4 vols., ed. James R. Newman
(New York: Simon & Schuster, 1956), 2:
1056.

In war-survivors' agonized searches for lost relatives, "categories have been blurred badly": motes of humanity once as real to themselves and to others as solids to Newton "have forgotten which," dead or alive, they are. Faces flaring in passage now have only that fugitive sort of "visibility" where either/or distinctions have no fixed meaning; the Zone's "new Uncertainty" renders DP's, as the narrator says explicitly elsewhere, both "particle and wave" (398): particulate point-solutions in a wavelike, controlled "bureaucracy of mass absence" (and might not the last two words pun on the masslessness thought to characterize some kinds of elementary particles?). There is a choice of apposite metaphors: we may identify Their bureaucratizing governance of life either with the old cause/effect scientism that overlies a more general quantum reality, or, within quantum terms themselves, with deterministic wave functions that somehow express the indeterminate flux below. Preterites, anyway, pay a price virtually in their sense of ontological reality for the grace of feeling themselves remaining invisible, particulate, indeterminate as to precise velocity and position. Enzian is partly jaunty and partly despairing when he tells Slothrop how easily the Schwarzkommando might escape (or "be escaped") from deterministic wave functions—"our chances of being right here right now are only a little better than even—the slightest shift in the probabilities and we're gone—schnapp! like that" (362).

As the incipiently paranoid Slothrop stands by the roulette wheel in the Casino Hermann Goering, he senses that "Their odds were never probabilities, but frequencies *already observed*" (208). But, since waveform "frequencies" *are* probabilities averaged through time, Slothrop, however justified his paranoia is on other grounds, here signifies his misunderstanding, rather like Pointsman's, of the relations of probability functions to the random events they subsume. Although such functions ("odds") are calculable, and in this statistical sense determined, their ground data, the particulate movements "below" them, really may be random. The wheel is not fixed for individual trials, cannot be, and Slothrop may (and does) escape the Casino by surprise, as the alpha particle may escape the uranium nucleus at any unforeseeable time. Pointsman's fear of Mexico's Poisson equation, despite its *looking* deterministic, is a correct intuition that the equation does not imply any mechanism whereby rocket strikes determine each other. And Mexico's individuated domain "between zero and one" (55) offers real—precisely because random—chances for freedom, love, escape from Their determined waveforms: "He'd seen himself as a point on a moving wavefront, propagating through sterile history—a known past, a projectable future. But Jessica was the breaking of the wave. Suddenly there was a beach, the unpredictable ... new life. Past and future stopped at the beach" (126).

For Pynchon, in fact, human lives are properly better, more truly, conceived as free particles in liberatingly random flux: critics who flatly observe that in his fiction "human lives are conceived as waveforms," hence that he is detached, cold, etc., miss the moral imperative because they miss the sense, explicated by Neils Bohr's Complementarity Principle, of the both/and potentialities in preterition. All manifest energy, reality, *is both* wave and particle; how entities shall *appear* and function depends on how they are looked for, how the "experiment" frames them. Compassion, as well as the understanding of Their enterprise, consists of learning to see the potential for freedom below "Their odds," Their waveform-equations for life; we must learn to ask of humanity's flux, after Norbert Wiener, "the right questions."

Slothrop, cruising the Berkshire roads, does not stop for the roadside girls he thinks he is out to pick up, but rather remains inside the "metal and combustion" (471) frame of his car—backward glances in the steel rearview mirror falsely seeming to him to allow "the day's targets more reality than anything that might come up by surprise, by Murphy's Law, where the salvation could be" (471). But the narrator here reminds us that, in fact, one may stop anytime for concrete life, for particularity; that surprise is immanent in reality; that in all preterite passages, indeed, "there is Murphy's Law to consider, that brash Irish proletarian restatement of Gödel's Theorem—*when everything has been taken care of, when nothing can go wrong, or even surprise you ... something will*" (275).

The theorem, published in 1931 by the Czech mathematical logician Kurt Gödel, "destroyed the hope of finding a consistent and complete formal axiomatic system for mathematics."[45] By a technique of manipulating numbers and "meta-numbers" assigned to propositions in axiomatic systems, Gödel showed that any such system must contain at least one proposition that is unprovable within the system's own terms. This amounts to a statement that in mathematics, as in the universe of thermodynamics, there can be no closed systems that are indefinitely self-sustaining. And just as They in Their function as Maxwell Demons must fail when They try to sort human energies from inside, so, in Their

45. James R. Newman ed., *The Harper Encyclopedia of Science*, rev. ed. (New York: Harper & Row, 1967).

metaphorical aspect as mathematicians who calculate lives within rigid systems of axioms, They go also against a deep—an ultimate—grain.

It is hardly Pynchon's notion uniquely that because the new physics seems to enshrine indeterminacy and a new uncertainty about the terms of creation, it can loosely be thought of as cognate with other systems of knowing, including mystically tending ones. This is all the more true since its subjective "idealism," in speaking of how mind at once mines and mimes reality, seems to modify old Cartesian dichotomies between subject and object, mind and matter, systematizers and systems "objectively" known. Among many eminent theoretical physicists who have written on these wider matters, it is a feeling and hope—more than any clichéd affirmation of "common interests" among scientists, metaphysicians, and theologians—that by virtue of the immense profundity of its kind of awareness, this new system can endorse other forms of the search for, in Heisenberg's Platonic term, "the One":

> Having pointed out with the utmost clarity the possibilities and limitations of precise language, [Plato] switched to the language of poetry, which evokes in the hearer images conveying understandings of an altogether different kind. I shall not seek to discuss here what this kind of understanding may mean. These images are probably connected with the unconscious mental patterns the psychologists speak of as archetypes, forms of strongly emotional character that in some way reflect the internal structure of the world. But whatever the explanation for these other forms of understanding, the language of images and likenesses is probably the only way of approaching the "one" from more general domains. If the harmony in a society rests on a common interpretation of the "one," the unitary principle behind the phenomena, then the language of poetry may be more important here than the language of science.[46]

And here for his part is the quantum physicist Bernard d'Espagnat questioning the assumption, for quantum events, of the invariance of "Einstein separability"—the familiar deterministic principle that connections and influences between events must be propagated at a finite speed never exceeding that of light. It is his point that Einstein separability may turn out to be our own ether myth; entities at these ultimate levels may interact, rather, in some acausal, "instantaneous" way, "the

46. Heisenberg, *Frontiers*, pp. 120, 121.

One" in such a case being a texture of (in Jung's term) synchronistic relations: "The violation of separability seems to imply that in some sense all these objects constitute an indivisible whole."[47] An acausal ground of this kind appears to Pynchon, I think, to sow hints of itself in events of the macroscopic world; I discuss more of these matters in my next chapter. Meanwhile, I discuss another allusive system that Pynchon uses to point to them.

Surprise Philosophy

Gravity's Rainbow, I have been saying, implicitly takes the quantum mechanics as a present, scientific mode of Western culture's long argument with itself over the relations between inside and outside, subject and object, mind and matter: the duality that first emerged axiomatically in the seventeenth century. Pynchon charges that Western science and technological enterprise since Descartes and Newton have been informed, most unfortunately, by what A. N. Whitehead called the Fallacy of Misplaced Concreteness: the assumption that outer realities that the mind necessarily sees "framed" in categorical fictions are indeed there in precisely that way, independent and other. One of the symbolic burdens of Pynchon's Rainbow is to remind us that what appears to exist in this "concrete" way may in fact exist only relationally, as a chance intersection of scattered facts (sunlight, moisture, the laws of optics) with a mobile observer. The Rainbow points, as does the quantum-mechanical vision and as does Eastern mysticism in general, toward what Alan Watts calls "the relational character of the world." Like a fundamental particle, a rainbow

> is "void" because it has no independent existence of its own.... The universe is not ... *composed* of independent things, that is, as human thought ordinarily fragments it: but the universe disposes itself as things ... Man cuts himself off from the universe and loses his sense of his original body by considering himself as an "I" which *has* these experiences, standing back from them just as one looks at a picture. To empty (*wu*) the heart (*hsin*) is to stop standing back from experience and to see, not that one *has* it, but that one *is* it.[48]

I return to the East in Chapter 6 but trace here, virtually over the Rain-

---

47. Bernard d'Espagnat, "The Quantum Theory and Reality," *Scientific American* 241 (November 1979): 128–40; see p. 140.

48. Alan W. Watts, *The Two Hands of God: The Myths of Polarity* (New York: George Braziller, 1963), pp. 70, 71.

bow-sign and with aid from Pynchon's metaphorical uses of Newton's calculus, this process-metaphysics and its connections with some antecedents in Whitehead, Bergson, and William James.

The Rainbow alludes in one Galilean and three Newtonian senses to the first days of modern science. The parabola obeys Galileo's description of the path of ballistic projectiles; the rocket's subjection to gravity is a subjection to Newton's law; the diffraction of white light into the rainbow spectrum was first described by Newton during his work in optics; the arc of the flight path can be mathematicized by the calculus procedures elaborated by Newton (separately by Leibniz) out of the work of predecessors. In *Gravity's Rainbow*'s calculus, further, the tiny differentiations of Δx along the Cartesian axis under the curve are assimilated to movie frames—with such further allusions as the one to the "blinding color" of a movie projector's beam over the heads of movie starers (472) completing a subtle triangulation of Newtonian optics with the already familiar calculus-film connection.

In this latter image, preterite starers sit motionless under the beam as if themselves melded out of the rainbow colors arcing above them. In nature, rainbow colors precede and underlie whiteness (as particulate life may be said to underlie quantum wave functions); *color* for Pynchon in general bespeaks life in healthily differentiated variety, even polymorphous perversity, while whiteness is often the deathly "integration" of life, the bleaching and screaming at the heart of the firestorm. And yet differentiation is at the same time "bad" if understood as referring to how the preterites are cut off by Them from mutual connection, "condemned to separate rows, aisles, exits, homegoings" (663). Such subtly equivocal connotations of "color" and integration/differentiation appear as early in Pynchon's work as the 1964 *Saturday Evening Post* story "The Secret Integration"—wherein a cute little gang of white middle-class children try in whatever ways they can think of to subvert the safe, rectilinear world of the adults of Mingeborough, Massachusetts, the Slothrop family's hometown.[49] Their leader, an intellectual prodigy

49. This story folds into *Gravity's Rainbow* in the frame-spliced section of the latter called "The Occupation of Mingeborough," where we meet the townsfolk one generation back from those in the short story. Slothrop's brother Hogan serves in the Pacific in World War II but "will come home" to court a girl named Marjorie, losing out finally to one Pete Dufay; "She and Dufay will have a daughter named Kim"—of the story—"and Kim will have her braids dipped in the school inkwell by young Hogan, Jr." (744)—also a child in the story.

"The Secret Integration" also anticipates the later novel by giving us houses with Faces; preterition metaphorized as a junkyard (see also *Lot 49*); a mild idolatry

named Grover Snodd, answers his friend Tim Santora's question "What's integration mean?" in this way:

> "The opposite of differentiation," Grover said, drawing an x-axis, y-axis and curve on his greenboard. "Call this function of x. Consider values of the curve at tiny little increments of x"—drawing straight vertical lines from the curve down to the x-axis, like the bars of a jail cell—"you can have as many of these as you want, see, as close together as you want."

> "Till it's all solid," Tim said.

> "No, it never gets solid. If this was a jail cell, and those lines were bars, and whoever was behind it could make himself any size he wanted to be, he could always make himself skinny enough to get free. No matter how close together the bars were."

> "This is integration," said Tim.

> "The only kind I ever heard of," said Grover.[50]

The relevant mathematical terminology is punningly most apt for Pynchon's world: the set of all *real* numbers is composed of an infinity of *rational* numbers, which can be matched with definite points on a number line, and a higher-order infinity of *irrational* ones, such that between any two rational numbers, no matter how close together they lie, is an infinite number of irrationals. Earlier, in preparation for Grover's jail-cell metaphor, an alcoholic black jazz musician whom the boys have befriended is hauled away by white cops to the town jail—and Grover knows that life, irrationality, "color," might always slip away from a white rationality's grid-repressions.

Grover keeps his own faith with "color" by continually planning subversions, "yelling at walls" around him, as the adults' delta-x's keep trying futilely to reach a point—a solid wall—as limit. The kids' parents make anonymous hate calls to the black family, the Barringtons, who have recently moved into the suburb. The children, however, gladly accept young Carl Barrington into the gang, partly because he seems always, Grover thinks, to impart "color" to things, make them seem more alive. Pynchon here employs the clichéd irony of children's inno-

---

of black jazz musicians; even a pipe with a bowl carved in the shape of Churchill's head, complete with a cigar out of which smoke issues—Jeremy Beaver smokes one of these (*GR*, 707).

50. "The Secret Integration" may be found in the *Saturday Evening Post* 237 (December 19, 1964) and in *Slow Learner*.

cence in racial and racist matters to cause the obvious pun on "integra-tion" to escape even Grover until very near the end:

> "Integration also means white kids and colored kids in the same school," Grover said.
>
> "Then we're integrated," Tim said. "Hey."
>
> "Yeah. They don't know it, but we're integrated."

But saved for the end also is a less predictable, quite uninnocent irony here. "They don't know it"; the integration is secret, because the Bar-ringtons really have no children, as the white parents gratefully note. Carl is imaginary, a joint fantasy of three of the gang, and thus the first of Pynchon's "invisible" preterite characters: "Carl had been put together out of phrases, images, possibilities that grownups had some-how turned away from, repudiated, left out at the edges of towns, as if they were auto parts in Etienne's father's junkyard." Sifting through the desolate junkpile of imagination's *waste*, Grover, Tim, and Etienne have constructed, after Simon Rodia of Watts, a colored fantasy-tower, secretly integrated, of imagination itself. There are already here, then, as far more elaborately in *Gravity's Rainbow*, two both/and symbolic senses of the colored Rainbow curve: the free, natively integrated curve of free life and lives, prior to and opposed to linear treatment; and the artificially differentiated, then reintegrated reflex curve of the calculus, movies, and of deterministic control. The latter, *calculated* curve is men-tioned offhandedly as another of Grover's nemeses. Because his teach-ers had noticed an abnormal skewing of the curve of grade distributions, they had been able to catch Grover at his "racket" of doing his friends' homework for a dime an assignment: " 'You can't fight the law of averages,' Grover said, 'you can't fight the curve.' "

In *Gravity's Rainbow* we learn that Franz Pökler had watched films of rocket models falling when dropped from Heinkel airplanes (407) and, connecting the images of film frames and the delta-t's of calculus, had realized that Blicero might extend these techniques for differentiating the curve "past images on film, to human lives" (407). And if Pökler is a full, sympathetic portrait of the good German falling half-consciously and half-willingly under Nazi control, the syndrome is seen even more clearly in the case of the ex-rocket engineer Klaus Närrisch, who is the cartoon-resonance of the portrait. Taken by Gerhardt von Göll, Slothrop, and Frau Gnahb to the wrecked rocket center at Peenemünde, Närrisch is left behind there to be killed (as everyone thinks) by

Tchitcherine's men. Although he does not understand "Springer's *full* intentions in the affair," he can reflect solemnly, as he waits in a concrete drainage pipe to be tracked down and shot, that "it is reasonable ... that he, being smaller, he should be the sacrifice, if it helps Springer survive, even survive another day ... wartime thinking, ja, ja ... but too late to change" (516).

At this moment we know that Springer is a babbling idiot on sodium amytal. It is no paranoiacally plotted affair, only a chaos of von Göll's and Slothrop's humbling that has brought Närrisch here. His complete resignation to what, ironically, is a *delusion* of his coherent control is Pynchon's comment, of course, on the Führer-Prinzip—but in Närrisch's consciousness the metaphor comes in technocybernetic form. The rocket's I. G. control device, Närrisch remembers, carried along "A fixed quantity, A," representing the desired velocity at the moment of Brennschluss; the device also sensed the rocket's acceleration, and, via the calculus integration and (at some stages in the technology) a feedback loop with the ground trackers, the real velocity, B, was monitored. When B coincided with A, the rocket caused its own "death," shutting off its engines, the pure ballistic then falling by gravity to a desired location in London. As Närrisch's "hunters" approach his hiding place, he masochistically sighs that "B, b-sub-N-for-Närrisch, is nearly here— nearly about to burn through the last whispering veil to equal 'A'" (518). The Rainbow prepares to bend; the Brennschluss-cusp is the death of the rocket-child. Raptly he contemplates the "reflex" process: "Up till assigned Brennschluss velocity, 'v_1' electric-shocked as any rat into following this very narrow mazeway of clear space—yes, radio signals from the ground would enter the Rocket body, and by reflex—literally by electric signals traveling a reflex arc—the control surfaces twitch, to steer you back on course the instant you'd begin to wander off" (517). As the "you" finally, fully assimilates his human course to the rocket's inanimate one, we are to recall servomechanistic Pökler's playing the demanded role of disinterested technician for Blicero, by way of negotiating for Ilse: "Any deviations into jealousy, metaphysics, vagueness would be picked up immediately: he would either be corrected back on course, or allowed to fall" (417).

Grover Snodd, who keeps a half-conscious faith in the possibilities of the true life-curve even while feeling his life being determined by the other species of curve, is closer to representing a normatively moired pattern of human conduct than are these German engineers of Gravity's Rainbow. And yet those Pynchon characters who thus submit masochistically or paranoiacally to control are not just isolated neurotics; they are so numerous in the fiction because theirs is the way that seems easiest to that part of permanent human nature that, in Eliot's phrase, "cannot bear very much reality," cannot accept a responsible freedom in all its indeterminacy. And it is also Pynchon's point that passivity under control is especially likely to flourish in a technological Age of Control that mass passivity has helped to actualize in the first place. How naturally the seductive sense of a predestinarian/paranoid "journey's end" to our lives can arise from life's flux is suggested, in quite another context, by William James:

> We live, as it were, upon the front edge of an advancing wave-crest, and our sense of a determinate direction in falling forward is all we cover of the future of our path. It is as if a differential quotient should be conscious and treat itself as an adequate substitute for a traced-out curve. Our experience, *inter alia*, is of variations of rate and direction, and lives in these transitions more than in the journey's end. The experiences of tendency are sufficient to act upon— what more could we have *done* at those moments even if the later verification comes complete?[51]

In denying modern philosophy's general assumption that there exists fundamentally a subject/object duality, and in positing "pure experience," empirically sensed, as the real ground of being instead, William James is close to another philosopher, Henri Bergson, who, like James and like Alfred North Whitehead, has had an influence on Pynchon's work that has gone so far almost entirely unnoticed.[52] In speaking, for example, of "the cardinal difference between *concrete* time, along which a real system develops, and that *abstract* time which enters into our speculations of artificial systems," Bergson, like James in the passage just quoted, and like Pynchon, calls the Newtonian/Leibnizian calculus to his metaphorical aid and gives us a mathematicized metaphysics:

> What does it mean, to say that the state of an artificial system depends on what it was at the moment immediately before? ... The instant "immediately before" is, in reality, that which is connected with the present instant by the interval dt. All that you mean to say,

51. William James, *Essays in Radical Empiricism* (1912) and *A Pluralistic Universe* (1909) (reprint ed., New York: Long, Green & Co., 1943); quote from *Essays*, p. 69.

52. James W. Earl, in an essay on *Gravity's Rainbow*, does briefly mention Bergson's "cinematographical illusion"—the movie-metaphor

of experience as differentiated and "framed"— as well as Bergson's Pynchonesque theory of comedy in "Laughter" (1900). See James W. Earl, "Freedom and Knowledge in the Zone," in *Approaches to "Gravity's Rainbow,"* ed. Charles Clerc (Columbus: Ohio State University Press, 1983), pp. 229–50.

therefore, is that the present state of the system is defined by equations into which differential coefficients enter, such as ds/dt, dv/dt,
that is to say, at bottom, *present* velocities and *present* accelerations.
You are therefore really speaking only of the present—a present, it
is true, considered along with its *tendency*.[53]

In *Gravity's Rainbow* (301) we are reminded that one of the problems that
the integral calculus was formulated to solve was measuring the
instantaneous "tendency" of a projectile along its path: knowing acceleration at that instant, to find velocity and distance. The rocket's I. G.
device "sensed acceleration first" (301), then integrated from acceleration (meters per second per second) back to velocity (meters per second), then integrated again back to distance (meters). Thus to freeze the
rocket's "life" in frame-differentiated segments of what Bergson would
call "abstract time" is in effect to stop time: "to integrate ... is to operate
on a rate of change so that time falls away: change is stilled... 'meters
per second' will integrate to 'meters.' The moving vehicle is frozen, in
space, to become architecture, and timeless. It was never launched. It
will never fall" (301).

This answers Bergson: "When the mathematician calculates the
future of a system at the end of time t, there is nothing to prevent him
from supposing that the universe vanishes from this moment till that,
and suddenly reappears. It is the t-th moment only that counts—and
that will be a mere instant. What will flow on in the interval—that is to
say, real time—does not count, and cannot enter into the calculation."[54]
Bergson sees as an indictment of the differentiating, "geometrical"
method of Western philosophy the perplexity of that philosophy, "as
soon as it opened its eyes," with the famous paradox of Zeno's arrow (to
which Pynchon surely means to allude in the passage of *Gravity's Rainbow* just quoted). Mathematically, Bergson explains, the arrow is considered "motionless in each point of its course [and must therefore be]
motionless all the time it is moving."[55] His solution is to say that the
mathematical frame-arbitrations that seem to create the paradox are, in
the first place, only mental projections, unreal overlays on real duration. The arrow's curve is in essence as undivided "as the sweep of the
hand" in an arc—and surely it is possible that Pynchon is thinking of
this simile when he has Pökler show Ilse the shape of the rocket's path,

53. Henri Bergson, *Creative Evolution*,
trans. Arthur Mitchell (New York: Herny
Holt & Co., 1911), pp. 21, 22.

54. Ibid., p. 22.

55. Ibid., p. 308.

"motioning with his hand, the parabola trailing behind encompassing testing stands, assembly buildings, drawing them together" (409).

Analogous to Pynchon's indeterminate or "irrational" flux between frame-arbitrations, Bergson's "real duration" is that out of which life emerges as a continuously creative *act:* "Continuity of change, preservation of the past in the present, real duration—the living being seems, then, to share these attributes with consciousness. Can we go further and say that life, like conscious activity, is unceasing creation?"[56] Mere "geometrical" intellect, which, Bergson admits, properly does and practically must express itself in science and mathematics, is yet unable by its nature to understand biological evolution and life's vital relation to time. Having imagined time as differentiated in segments, intellect "is obliged next to reunite [the segments] by an artificial bond,"[57] which bond is "the idea of a formless *ego*, indifferent and unchangeable, on which [intellect] threads the psychic states which it has set up as independent entities."[58] Because intellect prizes static forms, the whole of Western science and philosophy since Plato's ideal forms has taken for granted that framed models of reality necessarily correspond to objective reality— Whitehead's Fallacy of Misplaced Concreteness. Bergson, again like Pynchon, metaphorizes the reflex arc as a "cinematographical mechanism"; the mind, ego-threading its views of forms at separate Δt's, then blurring them, thereby "persuaded itself ... that it imitates by its instability the very movement of the real."[59] But in fact, writes Bergson, finally, intellect and inert matter alike are "weighted with geometry" and by their natures *descend*—as the dead rocket to its last delta-t—while life and consciousness *ascend*—as Gottfried's still-living heart beats through the final ascent before Brennschluss. Is it prohibitively far-fetched to suggest that Pynchon remembered Bergson in using "Ascent" and "Descent" as titles for the final two frame-spliced segments of *Gravity's Rainbow?*

The "process philosophers" Bergson, James, and Whitehead may, at any rate, help us to understand better the effects and the implications of Pynchon's style of connectedness—and this whether or not we think that Pynchon himself has consulted them and means us to follow. To show how easily the vision of, say, James can be mapped onto the style, here is a typical descriptive-rhapsodic-paranoid passage from *Gravity's Rainbow*:

56. Ibid., p. 23.

57. Ibid., p. 3.

58. Ibid.

59. Ibid., p. 307.

Everybody you don't suspect is in on this, everybody but you: the chaplain, the doctor, your mother hoping to hang that Gold Star, the vapid soprano last night on the Home Service programme, let's not forget Mr. Noel Coward so stylish and cute about death … Walt Disney causing Dumbo the elephant to clutch to that feather like how many carcasses under the snow tonight among the white-painted tanks, how many hands frozen around a Miraculous Medal, lucky piece of worn bone, half-dollar with the grinning sun peering up under Liberty's wispy gown, clutching, dumb, when the 88 fell—what do you think, it's a children's story? There aren't any. The children are away dreaming, but the Empire has no place for dreams and it's Adults Only in here tonight, here in this refuge with the lamps burning deep, in pre-Cambrian exhalation, savory as food cooking, heavy as soot. And 60 miles up the rockets hanging the measureless instant over the black North Sea before the fall, ever faster, to orange heat, Christmas star, in helpless plunge to Earth. (134–35)

To the reader reasonably at home here there will appear myriads of connections, relations, among all these signs, images, beauties, and terrors: connections seeming instantaneously to crystallize over the surface, like branching frost, seeming both to be paranoid impositions and to show forth some ground continuity of experience. And William James explicates:

> The concrete pulses of experience appear pent in by no such definite limits as our conceptual substitutes for them are confined by. They run into one another continuously and seem to interpenetrate. What in them is relation and what is matter related is hard to discern. You feel no one of them as inwardly simple, and no two as wholly without confluence where they touch. There is no datum so small as not to show this mystery, if mystery it be. The tiniest feeling that we can possibly have comes with an earlier and a later part and with a sense of their continuous procession.[60]

It is out on such limbs of reflexive imagination, over such rainbows, that life, its experience, its perception of living relations, perpetually climbs. Pynchon's writing, with all its heat and mobility, its downright aggressive reverence for all that must perforce be *seen* on the climb, is hard breathing set to the music of the style of connectedness.

Rainbow, Romanticism, and Reich

During the late seventeenth century, when Newton in England was systematizing the calculus, Leibniz in Germany also was doing so,

60. James, *A Pluralistic Universe*, p. 282.

apparently without knowledge of Newton's work. Because Newton delayed the publication of that work for some years, a dispute arose over priority, Leibniz being accused of plagiarism, and English and German mathematicians, having jealously taken sides, curtailing communications. It is to Leibniz, not to Newton, that Pynchon attributes the development of the calculus, proposed as manifesting "this strange connection between the German mind and the rapid flashing of successive stills to counterfeit movement, for at least two centuries—since Leibniz, in the process of inventing calculus, used the same approach to break up the trajectories of cannonballs through the air" (407). So runs one of Pynchon's paraphrases of a rather familiar indictment of the German impulse to analyze, systematize, differentiate, name—and yet the English scientific historian William Dampier complains, also familiarly, that "the German mind, from Leibniz onward, has always sought to construct a broad rational theory of the Universe before examining any part of it." The holist, idealist thrust leads, by the stereotype, to a kind of schizoid dualism in that it works against what Pynchon in another place calls "the German mania for name-giving, dividing the Creation finer and finer, analyzing, setting namer more hopelessly apart from named" (391).

It is a quite remarkable fact about a novel so wholly American in its general personality that nearly all of its most important sources, father figures, oracular voices, and invited guests are German-speaking: from the mythological Nibelungen, Gottfried von Strassburg's Tristan and other ancients resurrected by Wagner, to Leibniz, Goethe, and Wagner himself, through Rilke, Freud, Jung, Max Weber, and the great twentieth-century physicists (Planck, Einstein, Heisenberg), to Rathenau, Stinnes, and the men of I. G. Farben, to the Weimar moviemakers, all the way through National Socialism and to Rocketman Wernher von Braun—"Yes, sort of *German*, these episodes here" (240), the narrator says at one point, and could say at almost any point. In general, *Gravity's Rainbow* uses the "German" tension between integrating and differentiating to define post-Romantic German history as on the whole a synecdoche for post-Renaissance "Western" history. The German mind and its works are enabled, for example, to comprehend the rationalizing *and* mysticizing impulses of the Germanic peoples of England and Holland and of Anglo-Puritan America. It seems advisable thus to sketch some courses of modern German imaginative history, connecting them—via Pynchon's semisubmerged allusions—to *Gravity's Rainbow's* more general historical themes.

Early Romanticism in Germany, as elsewhere, was egalitarian, Utopian, "liberal" in its main spirit and in its politics—when it had any conscious politics. The Revolution in France had seemed at first to signal the death of what was plausibly a sociopolitical reification of Newton's mechanical universe: the neo-Classical order of Europe, with its rigid system of caste, its static absolutism, its spurious decorousness of polished forms. Since the *Sturm und Drang* time when Goethe's novel of Young Werther had inspired a rash of suicides in university towns like Jena and Heidelberg, Romanticism was characteristically a rather dreamy and adolescent mystique—and Pynchon evokes its survival in Franz Pökler's arrested imaginative development (as Leni thinks) during prerocket days: "She knows about the German male at puberty. On their backs in the meadows and mountains, watching the sky, masturbating, yearning. Destiny waits, a darkness latent in the texture of the summer wind. Destiny will betray you, crush your ideals ... dress you in the gray uniform of another family man, and without a whimper you will serve out your time, fly from pain to duty, from joy to work, from commitment to neutrality. Destiny does all this to you" (162).

The Romantic tradition of obligatory *Wanderjahre* in youth addressed, of course, exactly this problem of the fear of, and secret longing for, inevitable rationalization. One *Wanderjahre* work of German Romantic literature, Adalbert von Chamisso's *The Marvelous Tale of Peter Schlemihl* (1813), gave the term *schlemihl*, borrowed from old Yiddish sources, to general literary tradition, and hence finally to Pynchon's *V.* The tale moreover provides one minor frame for Slothrop's peregrinations. Peter Schlemihl is a restless young man who impulsively sells his shadow to an old man, the devil, who rolls it up out of the grass, puts it in his pocket, and walks away with it. Horrified now at his lack of a shadow, Schlemihl wanders homeless through the great world in cloak and seven-league boots, botanizing, zoologizing, and searching for love. Since the shadow, as Thomas Mann observes, implies "human belongingness,"[61] Peter Schlemihl, and Romantic youth in general, is doomed to a hopeless yet ennobling quest to get back, immediately to nature, ultimately to human society. Wandering in the hills, the outcast obscurely becomes a Holy Fool—like Slothrop, from whom the devilish Jamf has stolen the "shadow": Slothrop's birthright of belongingness to American culture. The unconscious trace of this "shadow" is in the

61. See the essay "Chamisso" in Mann's   A. Knopf, 1947).
Essays of Three Decades (New York: Alfred

"Blackwords" that Slothrop babbles under Pointsman's sedation, words that connote what Pynchon defines as standard American neuroses about shit, death, Negroes: thus equivocally shadowless, Slothrop gravitates toward a terminal invisibility, achieved at last when he lies down by the stream in the Harz. And meanwhile Blicero's rocket arcs above: erected systems, as products of the frame-differentiation of unitary reality, soar away from the earthly gravity of the gentle Romantic landscapes of Chamisso, Tieck, Eichendorff, the brothers Grimm, from which landscapes they take their inspiration, sometimes consciously (e.g., Blicero's perverse Hansel and Gretel *Märchen*).

Pynchon may be seen to have adapted several central aspects of Romantic thought into a Transformational Romanticism, as I call it, that stands as uniquely approved for the Zone. The novel first enthusiastically takes up the central Romantic belief in a dynamic, "organic" nature, continuously surprising. The sense of the wondrous variety and anisotropy of the world's fine detail activates the Pynchonian ethic of acute sensitivity to preterite life and to humble fact, as the same intuition brought forth the Romantics' demand that the soul try to know the connectedness of things by paying as close attention to the concrete world as to the ideal. The reverent awareness of the organic nature of Nature served the Romantic goal of healing man's Fall from the Garden of primordial integration;[62] the Romantic tradition assumes that, since the Fall, essential duality has prevailed. Romantic landscapes are alternately, or simultaneously, sublime and gentle, grand and subtle, mountained and valleyed, as the self is conceived as at once strong and weak, purposeful and torn, of Earth and of heaven, good and evil. The Romantic glorification of individual energy, originality, genius, assumes the self's duty to attempt self-transcendence by channeling the passionate aspiration of instinct, or of "intuition" (or, in the English Romantics' misleading term, "reason") toward reintegrating the self with the world.

But in Pynchon the Transformational status of Romantic nature, Romantic self, and the Romantic quest is, as the narrator would say, not so clear. Nature for the Romantics was full of signs of its own yearning back toward man's fallen spirit; the mysticization of landscape, strong in Germany well before its co-option by racist nationalism, signified the

62. M. H. Abrams, my major source in these matters, shows in *Natural Supernaturalism* how such common Romantic analogues for man's predicament as that of the scriptural Fall sublimated, in a secularizing age, Judeo-Christian scriptural symbols.

belief in nature's wish that man rejoin his spiritual matrix. But in Pynchon the sense of nature's meaning or message has fallen prey to the oscillation between One and Zero—between belief in the void of inanimate fact and belief in the mystical order of being where souls dwell in stones. And the One/Zero problem is quite intimately germane to the problem of how to conceive of the Transformational Romantic self. I have argued that Pynchon shares Bergson's and James's assumption that subject and object and their duality are not, after all, ontologically fundamental truths, postlapsarian or otherwise, but are merely illusions, fictions or metaphors for naming the "Double Lights" that seem, from inside, to compose the moire of experience. If knower and known are only Yin/Yang appearances unfolded from something deeper, from a continuum that "knows" itself and is sentient "in" itself, then, as against such a ground, the autonomous Romantic self is simply not *real* for Pynchon as it is for, say, Wordsworth or (the most extreme case) Byron. In *Gravity's Rainbow*, in fact, the Romantic self comes in for explicit deflation, appearing as the Coleridgean albatross, a fiction of mere "self-interest" to be hung aroung preterite necks, or, better, to be placed "Radio-Control-In-The-Head-At-Birth"-wise (542) in preterite minds: "The Man has a branch office in each of our brains, his corporate emblem is a white albatross, each local rep has a cover known as the Ego, and their mission is this world is Bad Shit" (712–13). Slothrop, disentangling himself from or dying away from the plot, "plucks the albatross of self now and then, idly, half-conscious as picking his nose" (623); by near the end, his former illusion of an integral self has become "one plucked albatross ... Only feathers" (712).

But the moire of experience as *felt* is as real for Pynchon as for the Romantics, whether or not the subject/object lamps, flats, reflectors behind the moire are taken as real. Romanticism, in sum, finessed the question of the ontological "truth" of the self. Although it glorified and exalted the self, it did not do so at all in the spirit of radical idealisms for which the self alone was real, but celebrated the self rather as the sum of concrete experience: a microcosm, yet also an epistemological prison. With reference to Wittgenstein's definition of self in the mathematical sense as "the limit of its world," and to *Lot 49*'s Randy Driblette "projecting" his self like the machine at the planetarium, William Plater accurately defines the Pynchonian self as "closed within its projection of a world. The world as it is and as it is created come together in the self, in the 'I' and eye of the observer. From his earliest stories to *Gravity's*

Rainbow Pynchon explores the self that is all that is the case.... In the variety and complexity of their projections, these characters begin to suggest the limits of the world, and the isolation of the self."[63]

The planetarium metaphor in turn suggests Pynchon's concern with history, in which we find ourselves always immersed, as fully "made." Paranoiacally to project self is, of course, to make plots; one's private plots and the publicized plots of others together create self's experience of the "network of all plots" (603) that is visible history. In *V.*, Evan Godolphin speaks to his friend the Gaucho of this general human predicament and of human beings' "communion" within it; the realization of the communion, he sees, is the truth that had all along been encoded in his father's fantastic myth of Vheissu:

> I thought Captain Hugh was mad; I would have signed the commitment papers myself. But at piazza della Signoria 5 I was nearly killed in something that could not have been an accident, a caprice of the inanimate world; and from then till now I have seen two governments hagridden to alienation over this fairy tale or obsession I thought was my father's own. As if this condition of just being human, which had made Vheissu and my boy's love for him a lie, were now vindicating them both for me, showing them to have been truth all along and after all. Because the Italians and the English in those consulates and even that illiterate clerk are all men. Their anxiety is the same as my father's, what is coming to be my own, and perhaps in a few weeks will be the anxiety of everyone living in a world none of us wants to see lit into holocaust. Call it a kind of communion, surviving somehow on a mucked-up planet which God knows none of us like very much. But it is our planet and we live on it anyway. (*V.*, 178)

As surely as this passage parodies Faulkner, old Godolphin's Vheissu-quest, Stencil's V-quest, and Slothrop's rocket-quest transformationally parody the Romantics' self-consciously "transcendental" quest after the absolute. Further, Vheissu's real historical message is that, as we hide from the apocalypse that we fear and (as Evan does *not* see) secretly desire, we erect exactly such fictions as will, shared among us, *make* preapocalyptic history. Evan forgives his father the paranoid quest, since he now sees that questing is in this sense nearly synonymous with living, with building a self. At the same time, the passage is quite busy implying that there is something pathetic, lost, not to mention self-

63. William Plater, *The Grim Phoenix: Reconstructing Thomas Pynchon* (Bloom-   ington: Indiana University Press, 1978), p. 19.

destructive, about our necessary "communion" within the terms of merely necessary fictions.

If there is another and better kind of quest, it differs radically from the quest by ascent, by systematizing and structure-building. M. H. Abrams shows that the Romantics' conception of man's final, ideal state of reintegration has as its analogue not the original, wordless Garden, but a secular city of the enlightened and apotheosized consciousness, a worldly New Jerusalem on a higher spiritual plane than the Garden, since consciousness, with its intellect, arts, and sciences, will have intervened in the struggle to reachieve wholeness. At the same time, consciousness is both a fruit and symptom of the original Fall. In Pynchon, the city at the end of intellect's road of ascent becomes the horrific Expressionist Raketen-Stadt. The positive reintegrative fantasy most often celebrated by the rhetoric is, rather, that of a plunge back "below" differentiation, back to Earth and wordlessness: Tyrone and William Slothrop's, Bodine's, Squalidozzi's anarchic wish for a relinquishment of history, rather than for a further educative ascent throught history: "At least one moment of passage, one it will hurt to lose, ought to be found for every street now indifferently gray with commerce, with war, with repression ... finding it, learning to cherish what was lost, mightn't we find some way back?" (693).

The lyricism is lovely, but the answer to the question is no, we mightn't: it is with conscious deceit that Gerhardt von Göll promises Squalidozzi, "I can lead you back to the Garden you hardly remember" (388). In wistful passages such as the one above, the authorial, or narratorial, voice protects itself, by virtue of its very fragility and beauty, against von Göll's hard reality from without, as against its own irony from within. That is to say, it admits that the dream of the Garden is an unrealizable wish-fantasy. Pynchon's anarchism, if we choose to call it that, is not realistic enough to be practically programmatic, "political"; it is rather, as George Levine has designated it, "prepolitical."[64] Pynchon is much less possessed of illusion than were the Romantics who, believing in ascent, took Bastille Day as the first of the Last Days of earthly injustice. No anarchic miracle of surprise with promise of lasting results, but a very "determined" world war, has temporarily opened the 1945 Zone, and the next age, as we and Pynchon know, will

64. See the last paragraph of George Levine, "Risking the Moment: Anarchy and Possibility in Pynchon's Fiction," in *Mindful* *Pleasures: Essays on Thomas Pynchon,* ed. George Levine and David Leverenz (Boston: Little, Brown & Co., 1976).

not be in any sense Utopian but rather Weberian, a "rationalized power-ritual," in Roger Mexico's phrase (177).

In Romanticism, Morse Peckham writes (and he could be speaking of Pynchon's world), "man can be understood only in terms of his history, and reality can be understood only in terms of the history of man's dealings with the world."[65] And since, as Peckham continues, " 'Spirit' is the term many Romantics used for the interpretational tension from subject to object, and reality, therefore, is the history of Spirit,"[66] science, therefore, is also a history of spirit—a metaphorical means, good as any, for showing man's need for reconnection with organic nature. Tags sometimes quoted to show the "hostility" of the early Romantics to science—Wordsworth's "we murder to dissect," Blake's prayer to be kept from "Newton's sleep," Keats's complaint that Newton had killed the rainbow by dissecting its beauty—show only, in fact, the Romantic distrust of *Newtonian* science. Shelley and Goethe were among the Romantics who were avid amateur scientizers, in part because they thought that science could offer a means, at once intuitional and intellectually respectable, for correcting Newtonianism's stifling overvaluation of mathematics and mechanism as keys to the possible knowledge of nature. *Gravity's Rainbow*, according to Slade the work of "a Goethe in greasepaint,"[67] is indeed close to Goethe's *Faust* in that in both of these works, with or without the greasepaint, the authors entertain an enormously active respect for science, a dutiful amateurism in its pursuit, and a belief that its place must necessarily be central in any truly encyclopedic articulation of culture. As Pynchon informs the whole central nervous system of *Gravity's Rainbow* with metaphors from physical science, Goethe in part defines the meaning of *Faust II* by deploying there his own avid partisanship in the scientific debates of his day.[68]

Like his namesake Fausto Maijstral in *V.*, Goethe's Faust undergoes an evolution of spiritual states: the late Goethe of Part II, as born-again

65. Morse Peckham, *The Triumph of Romanticism: Collected Essays* (Columbia: University of South Carolina Press, 1970), p. 46.

66. Ibid.

67. Slade, *Thomas Pynchon*, p. 239.

68. My favorite example of this practice of Goethe's is the debate, in a Greek (i.e.,

"Classical") setting, between Thales and Anaxagoras over the question of whether Earth owes its creation to water or fire (*Faust II*, Act II, iii). Anaxagoras, favoring fire, speaks for the Plutonists (or Vulcanists) of Goethe's time; Thales more or less defeats him, since Goethe shared the view (incorrect, as it turned out) of those geologists who were Neptunists.

Classicist, explains the earlier, Romantic Faust of Part I as having embodied certain extremely dangerous tendencies of Romantic subjectivism, as having wanted that "infinite" knowledge of absolute nature whose attainment would mean his total release from concrete life, the incorporation of the universe inside Faustian will, object inside subject. But Part II opens with an Adamic birth in a garden of a "new" Faust who, waking after a long sleeping-off of his old self, of the Romantic effects of Part I, has a vision, first of a waterfall, then of an attendant rainbow. Goethe's poetry of the rainbow defines now for Faust his essential earthliness, his inner relation with the permanence-in-change of life's closed system:

> Yet how superb, across the tumult braided, The painted rainbow's changeful life is bending, Now clearly drawn, dissolving now and faded, And evermore the showers of dew descending! Of human striving there's no symbol fuller: Consider, and 'tis easy comprehending— Life is not light, but the refracted color.[69]

"Refracted color" points, as in Pynchon, to the transient shapes, individual lives, that make dropleting falls through the arc; and as white light is immanent in "painted" colors, the neo-Platonic forms that Goethe believed to underlie earthly phenomena are immanent everywhere in the entropic life-system's curve. For Goethe, pure forms remain inaccessible to the senses, therefore to the understanding, and therefore, properly, inaccessible to a science that must stop short of transcendent abstraction. The experience of "color"—of revealed appearances—thus constitutes the ultimate limit of our possible *real* contact with nature. And this contact, ideally, is always full length: subjective "human striving" toward nature takes the symbolic shape of a reflex arc that is perfectly coincidental with the entropic curve that is its object, with nature itself. Goethe's belief, then, was in the given, objective identity of the world with its subjective presence in mind: in a "perfect correspondence between the inner nature of man and the structure of external reality, between the soul and the world."[70]

Pynchon's narrator habitually yearns after a fixed belief, and sometimes rapturously affirms one, in this absolute Goethean congruency between outside and inside. Among the characters, it is mostly the gen-

69. Goethe, *Faust*, trans. Bayard Taylor (Boston: Houghton Mifflin Co., 1898), vol. 2, p. 7.

70. Erich Heller, *The Disinherited Mind: Essays in Modern German Literature and Thought* (New York: Farrar, Straus & Cudahy, 1957), p. 30.

tle and powerless ones who wisely do not "differentiate as much ... between Outside and Inside" (141). For example, kind Kevin Spectro suggests timidly to Pointsman that the cortex may be "an interface organ, mediating between Outside and Inside, but *part of them both*" (141-42). Three times in the novel, at least, Pynchon's Rainbow sign seems to summon the Goethean waterfall/rainbow—and, in each case, both/and effects show how easily the integration of life with living imagination may be corrupted by history's perverse, differentiating *uses* for life. In one of the Rainbow sign's aspects, the mythological Great World Serpent—"beautiful serpent, its coils in rainbow lashings in the sky" (721)—it is "given" in a dream to Friedrich August von Kekule, mediated, if we believe the narrator's fantasy, by sinister pointsman-angels of the other side who now would reveal to history the molecular structure of benzene. From this plotted point (in 1865) will branch the chemical synthetics industry and the Farben cartel with its means to ends of synthesis and control. Next, a waterfall/rainbow, refracted and scattered, appears to Pökler when, before the Great War, his parents take him to see the Rhine cataract at Schaffhausen: "All around them were clouds, rainbows, drops of fire. And the roar of the waterfall" (160). The memory surfaces—opportunistic pointsmen/angels, it may be, having again intervened—when Pökler first meets the rocket, Kurt Mondaugen's primitive model, at Berlin Reinickendorf in 1929. When this rocket explodes on its test stand, Pökler ducks behind "concrete barracks and earthworks 40 feet high," the narrator observing that "these were the kind of revenents that [later] found Franz, not persons but forms of energy, abstractions" (161). It is clear that rocket history from now on will be impelled by an incest of abstracting Newtonian impulses with the obscure rocket mysticism whose signs in Franz Leni Pökler will recognize.

The Goethean rainbow appears, at last, pretty much undisguised, at a point near the end of Slothrop's Progress. The reader will feel the radiant vision here as a crux in the novel's imaginative life. Slothrop, wandering in the Harz, plucking the feathers of his albatross-self, approaching the reintegration with Earth that will destroy his historical cohesion, suddenly "sees a very thick rainbow here, a stout rainbow cock driven down out of pubic clouds into Earth, green wet valleyed Earth, and his chest fills and he stands crying, not a thing in his head" (626). But—as I noted in my introduction—to complete the sense of the vision's both/and significance we must look ahead to a still later vision: the message of Hiroshima as mediated to Slothrop by a black-and-white newspaper scrap showing "a giant white cock, dangling in the sky straight downward out of a white pubic bush" (693). The white death's-cock of the rape of the Earth—reversing the sign of the rainbow-cock's fecundation—is culminating history's black-and-white fever dream; its shape is that of the downward fall of the determined arc, of death's "fucking [such as is] done on paper" (616). In the narrator's earlier words, "It is the parabola. [Slothrop and Katje] must have guessed, once or twice—guessed and refused to believe—that everything, always, collectively, had been moving toward that purified shape latent in the sky, that shape of no surprise, no second chances, no return. Yet they do move forever under it, reserved for its own black-and-white bad news certainly as if it were the Rainbow, and they its children" (209).

This passage makes a good transfer-point out of earlier German Romanticism and into its late transformation in Rilke—for "No second chances, no return" alludes to Rilke's "Once, only once," a line that haunts *Gravity's Rainbow* and is identified at one point as "one of Their favorite slogans" (413). But the line understood this way is a trap, for, in Pynchon's uses of it, it is a both/and. We should not, as some Pynchon critics seem to do, accept the "dark" reading of the line—Their reading, and Blicero's—to the effect that since individual life is transient, then death is "all," and affirmation of death—our acquiescence in our use, instrumentalization, waste—is inevitable or imperative. The Rainbow in its bending back to Earth symbolizes the cloture of the life-system and the individual life's impermanence but does *not* therefore speak of any real despair. For Rilke, earthly life is enough, as the jubilant passage that is the line's source shows clearly: "But because being present is so much, because it seems that what is here is in need of us, this fading world has strangely charged us. Us who fade the most. *Once* to everything, only *once*. *Once* and no more. And we too, *once* to have been, if only this *once:* to have been of the earth seems beyond revoking."[71]

Although this context "affirms" death in the reductive sense that it evokes human mortality, the reader is tone-deaf who hears in the passage any rejection of life and consequent worship of death. Erich Heller compares (with obvious qualifications) the Rilkean willing of affirmation out of the sense of the oneness of life and death to a similar willing in Nietzsche, whose Superman's Dionysian joy issues from the sorrow of a "positivistically self-contained world" in eternal recurrence.

71. Rainer Maria Rilke, *The Duino Elegies*, trans. Stephen Garmey and Jay Wilson (New York: Harper Colophon Books, 1972), Ninth Duino Elegy, lines 10–16.

Although superficially they sound quite opposite, Rilke's "once, only once" and Nietzsche's eternal return are identical in essential meaning, Heller contends; it is nice to believe this, for an appropriate Nietzschean echo is present in the narrator's rapturous hymn to "The World ... a closed thing, cyclical, resonant, eternally-returning" (412).

*   *   *

In that the post-Romantic nineteenth century saw, not only in Germany, but everywhere in the West, a rapid acceleration toward the present extreme state of specialization of knowledge, bureaucratization of imagination, the period was one of a rapidly widening gap between Romanticism and philosophical idealism on the one hand, and a practical and increasingly materialistic science and technology on the other, the latter in its extreme form banishing subject, mind, altogether from the field of reality: "The application to living beings of the principles of the conservation of matter and energy led to the exaggerated belief that all the various activities, physical, biological, and psychological, of the existing organism would soon be explained as mere modes of the motion of molecules, and manifestations of mechanical or chemical energy.... it was in Germany that his development of *Darwinismus* was most prevalent."[72]

The materialistic outlook seemed increasingly to sanction urbanization and Satanic Mill industrialization, the sway of what Weber called patriarchal social authority in the Reich, and the charismatic militarism of the rational and rationalizing Prussian state. At the same time, philosophical idealism, *Volk*-mysticism, and transcendental Romanticism enjoyed polymorphous vogues in Wilhelmine Germany. There were, that is to say, "idealists" of all sorts who chose to remain outside the constricting frames of mechanized and materialized life. Bismarck's Second Reich, after its stabilization, disappointed all manner of idealist thinkers—including, politically, those *gross-Deutsch* Germanic mystagogues who had been frustrated by Bismarck's *klein-Deutsch* policy of expelling Austria from the Reich; including, culturally, pan-Europeans who had been alienated by the 1870/1871 treatment of France; and including, philosophically, radically idealistic monists who moved

72. Sir William Cecil Dampier, *A History of Science* (Cambridge, Eng.: At the University Press, 1961), p. 316.

toward inverting materialism by altogether denying the objective world. These philosophical monisms, by asserting ideal couplings of subjective will with transcendental egos and world-spirits, such that the concrete reality so prized by the early Romantics was left entirely behind, were well situated to act as hosts for later parasitical doctrines of National Oversouls, the Nazi embrace of Fichte being a well-known case in point.

And quite as Fichte, Nietzsche, Wagner were at last kidnapped into the Nazi pantheon, the perversely misconstrued Rilke—the *Elegies* "just off the presses" (99)—is tucked lovingly inside Weissmann/Blicero's pocket when this future Nazi arrives in Südwest in 1922. This is another of Pynchon's demonstrations of the ease and the subtlety with which healthily "colored" visions can be debased, enlisted in paranoiac black/ white moires. During the period of German history that culminated in Weimar, the period from Goethe's Rainbow to the first dreams of Gravity's, early Romanticism had somehow become a pan–Germanic/racist mysticism, or (in George Mosse's term) "New Romanticism," which opposed its quasi-organicist *Kultur* of blood, soil, and race to the urbanized civilization of the machine. There was thus a moire of love-hate relations between extreme forms of the two very "opposites" whose strengths Goethe had separately feared: egoistic Romanticism and abstracting Newtonianism, both threatening, Goethe thought, to lead man beyond concrete experience and into unearthly forms of megalomania. The opposites are, in this sense of the final identity of their tendencies, final collaborators. Although nineteenth-century mysticisms of *Volk* are conventionally claimed to have evolved, somehow all on their own, into the Nazi system, Pynchon's own more complex and credible thesis, of which Goethe would have approved, is that twentieth-century German conditions issued from the interplay between *Volk*-ish charisma and technologized rationality. V-2 thus makes an ideal Nazi icon in that it represents a final perverse synthesis of forces—high-technological means applied to *Volk*-charismatic ends— whose long dialectical wrestle the Great War itself appears hardly to have perturbed at all, and by its disappointing results may well indeed have intensified.

The Second Reich's "secret Germany" (as some adherents called it) expressed itself sometimes in renascent paganisms that came flickering up through the grid of rationalized Church Christianity: the publisher Eugen Diederichs's Sera Circle typically mingled pagan, Christian, and foreshadowed Nazi imagery in the rites of a "revived" Germanic sun cult, a yearly festival featuring ritual dancing under the sign of a red banner with a gold sun in its center. In Pynchon's Blicero there persists this odd phase-state of the German mind: the rocket-launching plat-forms his unit builds in Holland resemble "a rude mandala, a red circle with a thick black cross inside, recognizable as the ancient sun-wheel from which tradition says the swastika was broken by the early Chris-tians, to disguise their outlaw symbol" (100). Such rites of the Germanic mystique found particular favor, before 1914, with German youth: the Wandervogel organization, founded in 1901 as a boys' hiking and nature club, readily became, as it spread over the country, a plastic-deformable movement against all establishments of the fathers. Con-scious Wandervogel politics varied across the spectrum, but all cells aggressively idealized nature, soil, soulfulness, and the spiritually exal-ted *Bund* of youth. One of the movement's favorite painters, Karl Höpp-ner or "Fidus," foreshadowed the homoerotic and generally the vulgar aspects of Nazi art by depicting nude youths standing in stylized attitudes of aspiration on sun-drenched cliffs, amid vague prospects. Blicero in pre-1922 days has a Wandervogel friend, the graceful, athletic Rauhandel, who plays a sort of Annabel Leigh to Gottfried's later Lolita: "Haven't you wanted to murder a child you loved … As he looks up at you, at the last possible minute, trusting you, and smiles, and purses his lips to make a kiss *just as the blow falls* across his skull … isn't that best of all?" (671).

The citizens of the 1920s inflation, of Leni Pökler's street, are steeped in the Weimar Republic's own chief expression of "New Romanticism," the Expressionist movement in art and film, to such an extent that Leni can notice that the reality of the street itself appears somehow to have leaked out from a film (by Ufa, the German movie conglomerate of the time): "Rudi, Vanya, Rebecca, here we are a slice of Berlin life, another Ufa masterpiece, token La Boheme student, token Slav, token Jewess, look at us: the Revolution. Of course there is no Revolution, not even in the Kinos" (155).

Weimar Expressionism expressed, vaguely, a "free-floating, aimless militancy"[73] of dissatisfaction with republican forms and norms. There was no formal statement of doctrine, but the art partook decadently of the standard "romantic" fascinations with violence, madness, and the fear/love of death. It practiced a surrealist technique influenced by Cubism, Dada, and atonal music; believed in earthliness as against

73. Walter Laqueur, *Weimar: A Cultural His-* tory (New York: G. P. Putnam's Sons, 1974).

urbanism, and in destiny; was antiscientific, antidisciplinarian, self-conscious and utterly without humor. It was essentially synchronous, as Pynchon shows, with the general state of mind ("blame that some-thing-in-the-air, the Zeitgeist. Sure, blame it" [578]) that was causing diverse occultisms to mushroom busily in Weimar cellars (e.g., at Peter Sachsa's seance), these reaching back in turn to the nineteenth-century vogues for spiritualism, Germanic paganism, theosophy, Rosicru-cianism, Freemasonry. As Franz Pökler walks the Weimar Street or "street-theater" (399) to paste up movie bills, Pynchon's film makes of the street a "stark Expressionist white/black" (393) fantasy too:

> It was well after dark and bitter cold by the time his paste bucket was empty and the ads all put up to be pissed on, torn down, swastikaed over. (It may have been a quota film. There may have been a misprint. But when he arrived at the theatre on the date printed on the bill, he found the place dark, chips of plaster littering the floor of the lobby, and a terrible smashing far back inside the theatre, the sound of a demolition crew except that there were no voices, not even any light that he could see back there … he called, but the wrecking only went on, a loud creaking in the bowels behind the electric marquee, which he noticed now was blank.) (160)

Siegfried Kracauer interprets the nocturnal Weimar Street as pre-sented by Expressionist movies as a symbolic domain of threatful surprise, of the misrule of chance; its prevailing imageries of whirling circles and of the light of carnival (as in the seminal *Cabinet of Doctor Caligari*, 1920) suggest an all-licensing, preauthoritarian chaos into which one may plunge to lose one's self in destructive delights. In Pynchon's fiction, the preterite street is consistently opposed (cf. *V.* and "Entropy") to the hothouse of paranoia and other self-projective/protec-tive strategies; the Pöklers grow estranged because Leni's natural ele-ment is the surprise, the chance, of the street, while Franz's is the hermetic rocket-hothouse. Since the street is *prior* to the hothouse, Franz must pass through its black/white moire, as above, before he can reach Mondaugen and the primitive rocket, his entryway to his hothouse; he will reach Reinickendorf just after pausing at the deserted theater. Pökler, moreover, bears a suspicious resemblance to the hero of Karl Grune's 1923 film *Der Strasse* (a film *not* mentioned in *Gravity's Rain-bow*)—in which a restless middle-class burgher, lured by the circling lights outside his window, deserts his wife serving soup in the parlor and wanders outside into a lurid plot of street violence, crime, dec-adence, chaos. His return at the end to wife and soup signifies (if we share Kracauer's view of the film) a reembracing of faith in order, sub-mission, respectability: a faith that will lead him willingly into the Nazi hothouse. This and other Expressionist films, contends Kracauer, pre-pared the middle classes for Nazism by reinforcing the bourgeois pref-erence for order, order at any price, over chaos, One over Zero, plot over indeterminacy.

Pynchon, further, alludes to the likelihood that Fritz Lang's *Die Nibelungen*—*GR*, 159, 578–79—called up in its Weimar audiences the same vague *Volk*-ish mystique as did Wagner's opera in its nineteenth-century audiences—with Lang's gorgeous gunmetal sets and wooden charac-terizations implying, in Kracauer's judgment, the "triumph of the orna-mental over the human." Much the same point applies to von Cserepy's *Fridericus Rex* (1922), the idealized film biography of Frederick the Great that, like *Der Strasse*, goes preterite in Pynchon's novel unless we count "The rage then was all for Frederick" (394). Pynchon and Kracauer both find in Lang's 1921 *Der Müde Tod* (Weary Death, alternatively titled Des-tiny) the morbid expression of a death mystique that, in *Gravity's Rainbow*, proves irresistible to the control-addict Närrisch. Preparing to die, När-risch thinks of this film, although "he's forgotten the ending, the last Rilke-elegiac shot of weary Death leading the two lovers away hand in hand through the forget-me-nots" (516). And the narrator at this point leaps beyond German contexts to show us, of all people, John Dillinger, leaving the Biograph Theater to be killed in the FBI ambush, and finding "a few seconds' strange mercy in the movie images that hadn't quite yet faded from his eyeballs—Clark Gable going off unregenerate to fry in the chair, voices gentle out of the deathrow steel, *so long, Blackie*" (516).

Inasmuch as Pynchon wants to make of the movies an exemplary case of how our own created media, presuming to "mediate" between our-selves and the world, in fact vitiate the realities *an sich* of self and world, we may invert current movie-ad jargon to say that Dillinger "is" Gable, his "eyeballs," the mediatory interface between outside and inside, world and self, here corresponding to the film's interface/mediation between life and art/fantasy.

Franz Pökler, staring, likewise "is" the actor Rudolph Klein-Rogge in Lang's 1925 *Metropolis* (with Klein-Rogge ushering in, according to Pynchon, a movie archetype, King Kong's, here just beginning its long career):

> Klein-Rogge was carrying nubile actresses off to rooftops when
> King Kong was still on the tit with no motor skills to speak of. Well,
> one nubile actress anyway, Brigitte Helm in *Metropolis*. Great movie.

> Exactly the world Pökler and evidently quite a few others were
> dreaming about those days, a corporate city-state where technology
> was the source of power, the engineer worked closely with the
> administrator, the masses labored unseen far underground, and
> ultimate power lay with a single leader at the top, fatherly and
> benevolent and just, who wore magnificent-looking suits and
> whose name Pökler couldn't remember, being too taken with Klein-
> Rogge playing the mad inventor that Pökler and his co-disciples
> under Jamf longed to be—indispensible to those who ran the
> Metropolis, yet, at the end, the untameable lion who could let it all
> crash, girl, State, masses, himself, asserting his reality against them
> all in one last roaring plunge from rooftop to street. (578)[74]

Pökler will indeed assume the role of "indispensible" engineer to
Blicero, but will, unlike Klein-Rogge, be routinized in the role and
never enjoy the Konglike, charismatic plunge from towering hothouse-
structure to street. Such a plunge is a joy reserved for the charismas
from which bureaucratic systems depend—here, for the Nazism that
Pökler will serve in his bureaucratized indenture to the rocket. The 1945
Götterdämmerung will at last justify Goethe's fear for the end of
abstracted mysticism in megalomania, mad self-reference: "Man in his
Promethean, Faustian imaginative power ... isolating himself in the solipsistic universe of total sacrilege."[75]

The novel evokes the Germanic *Liebestod*, not only in this charismatic
mode but also as another, even sicker mystique: a quiet longing to follow what is conceived, as in *Der Müde Tod*, as the beckoning of "tender,
wistful, bureaucratic Death" (579) into some obscurely erotic labyrinth.
The masturbating Pointsman imagines himself voluptuously penetrating the labyrinth of his death-dealing work in search of the orgasmic
Minotaur; Gerhardt von Göll, mesmerized, pilots his moving camera
dolly down the endless corridor-mazes of King Ludwig's Herrenchiemsee palace.[76] In both the charismatic and passive-masochistic

74. This accurate evocation of Lang's
Metropolis is, clearly, *Gravity's Rainbow's*
admission of the indebtedness of its own
Raketen-Stadt to the film. *V.* owes it a debt
as well: in the film the mad inventor Rot-
wang infuses an automaton he has built,
the "Bad Maria," with the spirit of the living Good Maria, whom he has abducted
to his laboratory. To watch the scene is
inevitably to think not only of Frankenstein's monster, but also of the gradual
immachination of the Lady V.—the Bad

Maria being to the living one as the
automaton Bad Priest is to earlier
V-incarnations.

75. Frank D. McConnell, *Four American
Novelists* (Chicago: University of Chicago
Press, 1977), p. 168.

76. The latter image is probably meant
also to recall first that the decadent, homosexual king so adored in nineteenth-century Bavaria had also heard voluptuous

modes, Blicero "identifies" (98) with the dead youth of Rilke's Tenth
Elegy: a languid spirit who, led by a female "Lament," begins an ascent
to a mountain peak beyond the commercialized City of Pain that is the
world. In the poem, the youth leaves behind both the "money which
breeds itself / ... all its golden genitals, / the whole works, the facts" and
the world of life, "the *real* world, where children play, and lovers hold
each other."[77] But Blicero, typically missing the pained Rilkean
ambivalence, feels only a "lager of Yearning" (98) for the "transformation" that awaits the youth at the peak. Here, at the "interface between
one order of things and another" (302), Blicero thinks, Rilkean angels
will bend to pluck the youth off to a white, transcendent remove from
the hated earthly "cycle of infection and death" (724)—the Rainbow
cycle that is in fact what Rilke's poem *really* celebrates, affirming life and
death together.

Pynchon's numerous references to "German" mysticisms of points,
peaks, cusps, and singularities acquire auxiliary allusions from mathematics and physics. The "singular point" is the lightning strike; the
limit of the delta-t; a "singularity" at which physical laws are transcended (a modern instance is the singularity of infinite gravitational
force at the center of a black hole); or "even, according to the Russian
mathematician Friedmann, the infinitely dense point from which the
present Universe expanded" (396). Another one of the problems that
Newton intended his calculus to solve was finding the center of mass of
any solid body—and Pirate Prentice intuits that it is in the "hidden cen-
ters, inertias unknown" (302) of falling bodies that all their deathliness
may be mystically felt as gathered: "What if [the Rocket] should hit
exactly—ahh, no—for a split second you'd have to feel the very point,
with the terrible mass above, strike the top of the skull" (7).

In his central rhapsodic improvisation on the theme of the mystic
transfer from life to death across a cusp (396), the narrator collects
images among which that of Hitler's mountain eyrie at Berchtesgaden
most perversely recalls Rilke's mountain peak; and Pynchon gives his
imaginary Expressionist-porn film the name *Alpdrücken* in the belief,
surely, that the "Alp" in this word for "nightmare" derives from some
ancient German ambivalence about mountain peaks at whose "lumi-
nosity and enigma ... something in us must leap and sing, or withdraw

---

whispers of death in these palace mazes,
and second, a point in passing, that the
Weimar films had been the world's first to
perfect the use of the continuously moving

camera in filming.

77. Rilke, Tenth Duino Elegy, lines
30–32, 39.

in fright" (396). During the Weimar era of cinema, as Siegfried Kracauer reports, there was a group of mountain movies—*Im Kampf den Bergen* (Struggle With the Mountains, 1921), *Berg des Schicksals* (Peak of Destiny, 1924), *Der Heilige Berg* (The Holy Mountain, 1927)—that made a cult of intrepid climbers who would ascend to peaks where destiny (most often, their deaths) lay in wait; Kracauer connects the mysticized peak-and skyscapes in which these films indulged with the opening shots of majestic clouds out of which Hitler's plane descends toward the Nürnberg rally in Leni Reifenstahl's famous propaganda film *Triumph of the Will* (1934).

"Do all these points imply, like the Rocket's, an annihilation?" (396). Quite as significant for the novel as the humorless mystic solemnity of the question is Pynchon's answering reductive fantasy of the plucking-off-from-the-peak as the kind of rescue King Kong could have used: "You're *way* up there on the needle-peak of a mountain, and don't think there aren't lammergeiers cruising there in the lurid red altitudes around, waiting for a chance to snatch you off. Oh yes. They are piloted by bareback dwarves with little plastic masks around their eyes that happen to be shaped just like the infinity symbol … out to nab you, buster, just like that sacrificial ape off of the Empire State Building, except that they won't let you fall, they'll carry you away, to the places they are agents of" (664).

In a similar subversive move of Pynchon's, the calculus, and the parabola that it describes, are mystically worshipped by the Nazi architect Etzel (= "Attila") Ölsch, but the character is quite preposterous, his death wish chiefly signified by his eagerly puffing on what he knows to be an exploding cigar (300). Some writers have claimed that Pynchon does not on the whole undercut the novel's pervasive peak-mysticism but rather means the Blicerean, sky-pointing, life-transcending mystique as sympathetic, as "true," and Blicero's interpretation of Rilke therefore as correct. But the Rainbow-curve, with its thermodynamic and Goethean linkages, signifies quite otherwise. Sky aspiration in general is itself a both/and, but the ease with which it can turn into Nazi ballistics shows once again the general ease of aspiration's corruption: in so disliking Gravity's rule, Blicero, for Pynchon, is simply *wrong* (and is incidentally false to Rilke). The complement to this impulse to thrust self-assertively toward angelic orders is the masochistic desire, once no angels are discerned, for a self-destructive Brennschluss and plunge to "delicious and screaming collapse" (578). The Nazified screaming-across-the-sky, because it denies all concrete referents of the Rilkean wish to remain "simply here, simply alive" (230), will turn back to annihilate myriads of other lives, with its own.

Lance Ozier discusses Pynchon's peak, cusp, and Brennschluss imageries in a substantial paper,[78] where he also rightly suggests that in *Gravity's Rainbow* not all mysticisms of "transcendence" are to be viewed as corrupt, perverse; the judgment attaching to them depends on whether the "transcendence" remains earthly—a flowing out of the self, toward other life—or whether it aims for the sky. As George Levine nicely explains, Leni Pökler's "death wish"—her loss of fear during street riots where "Δt approaches zero" (159)—is essentially positive, since it is based not on any abstracted denial of concrete life, but, quite the contrary, on the "moments of possibility" felt as immanent in each particulate image of life:

> The flash of knees under pearl-colored frock as the girl in the babushka stoops to pick up a cobble, the man in the black suitcoat and brown sleeveless sweater grabbed by policemen one on either arm, trying to keep his head up, showing his teeth, an older liberal in a dirty beige overcoat, stepping back to avoid a careening demonstrator, looking back across his lapel how-dare-you or look-out-not-*me*, his eyeglasses filled with the glare of the winter sky. There is the moment, and its possibilities. (158–59)

The ritual of the demonstration, the narrator notes, is "pre-choreographed exactly where it is" (158): this would seem to be the same claim that Pynchon made much earlier for the "choreography" of the Watts riot, during which, Pynchon's 1966 essay says, each person somehow knew where he had to be, what he had to do, all together enacting a unity not imposed clockwork-wise from above but arising organically, mysteriously, from within. Levine's comments on Leni's riot scene pick up, as well, its implicit warning to critics and readers that we not over-"abstract" critically beyond concrete moments as *given* in a fiction, or, for that matter, in the world:

> The moment, however systematized our reading of it, suggests almost infinite possibilities and particularities, and ... any verbal efforts to locate it will pass over far more than can be chosen.... Thematic analysis is inescapable and essential ... but the moments are there beyond any patterns into which they may be made to fit. Pynchon can be so intellectualized that we ignore how deeply, viscerally painful, indeed nauseating, he can be: we ignore too what I

78. Lance Ozier, "The Calculus of Transformation: More Mathematical Imagery in *Gravity's Rainbow,*" *Twentieth Century Literature* 21 (1975): 193–210.

regard as his most astonishing and overwhelming power, to imagine love out of the wastes of a world full of people helpless to love.
These qualities live in the moments, not in the patterns. For his
characters and, I think, for us, the challenge is to penetrate the
moments as they come and then find a way to live with them.[79]

In the novels a genuine self-transcendence in the direction of unity, connectedness, with other life may be experienced, so long as the
experience is sought on Earth, where other life in all its particularity *is*.
Franz, irrationally wanting to fly, participates rationally nevertheless in
the Nazi abstractedness; Leni, by contrast healthy in her deepest
instincts, knows that the true possibilities for love and life persist in the
affirmation, even sometimes to death, of the "anarchist miracle" (*Lot 49*,
89), of the street.

If this discussion can show anything important about Pynchon's
Rainbow sign, it shows, I hope, that this grandest one of the both/and
signs characteristic of the style of connectedness is extremely suggestive of the mystical nature of Pynchon's vision. In my introduction,
too, I have suggested the affinities of the Rainbow's polyvalency of sig-
nification with the workings of Jungian dreams. Still, to work here on
the level at which discrete "meanings" may be isolated, I close this
chapter by sketching how the geometrical/geographic figure that is
Slothrop's Progress is specified by the Rainbow sign and how, as so
specified, the Progress gathers nearly all the major code-words of
which Pynhcon weaves the style.

At the end of the Progress, Slothrop "disappears," i.e., becomes
"invisible" to history and to the novel, by escaping the frames with
which these have confined and defined him. Meanwhile, though, the
name/game/frames are extraordinarily various—and if Slothrop is all at
once a movie-spy-melodrama hero, a neo-Puritan Pilgrim, a free charismatic, a thermodynamic "life," a quantum particle, a (Peter) Schlemihl,
a Grail-questing knight, a sacrificial year-god, Tannhäuser, and the Fool
of the Tarot deck, his Progress itself is an earthly and inverted "shadow"
or parody of the Blicerean rocket's parabola arcing over the novel.
Slothrop begins in London, where V-2 for its part has "died," and he
ends in the Harz, necessarily somewhere near Nordhausen, where V-2
had been "born." Both in that his path remains fixed to Earth and in
that it peaks at a *southern*most point (the Casino on the French Riviera),
it inverts and parodies the form of the Blicerean quest for "transcen-

79. Levine, "Risking the Moment," in   *Mindful Pleasures*.

dence" as symbolized by the firing of the final rocket skywards and toward the *North* Pole. As, outside the narrative, Slothrop travels from London to the Casino, he remains, in this inverted "ascent," under Pointsman's control. But after escaping from the Casino, the escape being his Brennschluss point, he "falls" uncontrolledly northward again. Of the opposite-signed code terms that may be attached to the x and y axes framing this curve/flight path/life, the following is a quick review:

Control	Freedom
Entropy loss	Entropy gain
Ascent	Descent
Self	Selflessness
Visibility	Invisibility
History	Timelessness
Differentiation	Integration
Probability wave	Free quantum
Abstraction	Concrete experience
Routinization	Charisma
Whiteness	Greenness or blackness
Determinacy	Surprise
Grace (Puritan sense)	Preterition
Instrumentalization	Grace (Pynchon's sense)
Paranoia	Antiparanoia

Of course, each pair of terms implies all the others; of the last pair, though, something more may be said, by way of pointing to further details in the Progress. When, during his veering fall into the zone, Slothrop feels himself to be entering an "anti-paranoid part of his cycle," antiparanoia being "a condition not many of us can bear for long" (434), Pynchon gives us a vivid image to show the insubstantiality of most paranoid fictions: "Part of the ceiling, blown away ... is covered now with soggy and stained cardboard posters all of the same cloaked figure in the broad-brimmed hat, with its legend DER FEIND HÖRT ZU ... well right now Slothrop feels ... the whole city around him going back roofless, vulnerable, uncentered as he is, only pasteboard images of the Listening Enemy left between him and the wet sky" (433–34).

For Slothrop, as for most of us, paranoid fictions personal or communal are preferable to that "wet sky": "Either They have put him here for a reason, or he's just here. He isn't sure that he wouldn't, actually, rather have that *reason*" (434). Thus, rather than have to feel "uncentered," he capers soon into what the narrator calls Peenemünde's "holy Center" and there makes his closest approach to the rocket. But surprise intervenes again, and he misses seeing it where it secretly lies "over the embankment, down in the arena ... waiting in this broken moonlight" (510)—"and likewise groweth his Preterition sure" (509). The embankment recalls the "revetment" behind which Pökler had crouched at the Reinickendorf test station—but Pökler then had begun moving willingly *toward* the rocket. Here Slothrop is moving, despite himself, *away* from the hidden V-2's "lost message." And since the loss of a "center," or plot, or hothouse, on which to hang the self is in effect a relinquishment of self, Slothrop's accelerating loss of time-boundedness and coherent image is defined with help from the calculus: " 'Temporal bandwidth' is the width of your present, your *now*. It is the familiar 'Δt' considered as a dependent variable. The more you dwell in the past and in the future, the thicker your bandwidth, the more solid your persona. But the narrower your sense of Now, the more tenuous you are. It may get to where you're having trouble remembering what you were doing five minutes ago, or even—as Slothrop now—what you're doing *here*, at the base of this colossal embankment" (509).

The death that Slothrop dies, to Rilkean strains, in integrating with Earth, is perhaps an example of what Rilke called "*der grosse Tod*," the Great Death that ripens inside each separate person, that prepares itself for him and "finds" him and is the completion and explanation of his individual life. By contrast, "*der kleine Tod*," the Little Death, is the mass, impersonal, standardized and meaningless death brought about by mass control—the rocket's victims screaming amid the fireburst. Control, then, "elects" men to the Little Death; to be preterite from *that*, however Slothrop may fear preterition, is to discover one's unity with an Earth where lives, souls, are not scattered in separate wreckages but are recycled, "returned," to the organic round. Although it had seemed originally that Christ's Star had come to promise the possibility of a *grosse Tod* for each individual life, Pynchon wants to imply that the deathliness of a Christianized course of history lay latent also, both/ and, in the same star. At the rocket's first appearance in the skies of *Gravity's Rainbow*, Pirate Prentice calls it "a new star, nothing less noticeable" (6); the church choir in the beautiful Evensong set piece sings Christ's praise and promises even while the V-2's are falling outside, "ever faster, to orange heat, Christmas star, in helpless plunge to Earth" (135). And yet one of the images Pynchon seems most to love is that of the first piercing of the sky by the Evening Star, as here, in the hopefully named Rue Rossini in Zürich: "Just for the knife-edge ... there comes to Slothrop the best feeling dusk in a foreign city can bring: just where the sky's light balances the electric lamplight in the street, just before the first star, some promise of event without cause, surprises, a direction at right angles to every direction his life has been able to find till now" (253). Since he has just escaped from the Casino and will proceed, after this Brennschluss, "at right angles" to his life's prior history of secret control (as the rocket literally changes direction after its Brennschluss-cusp), his intuition here is correct: this first star does signal the onset of his antiparanoid free-fall to Earth. But it may also be, like the "star" at the very end of the book, really "*not a star*," but "falling, a bright angel of death" (760); available too is the irony that, in point of astronomical fact, the Evening Star is not a star, but Venus, consistently in the novel an archetype of V-ness, hence too of the rocket.

There is yet further dazzling complexity about the Star: when Gottfried, ascending in the 00000, notes the engine exhaust-fires below his feet just before they cut off at Brennschluss, he thinks of the paradox that

> The true moment of shadow is the moment in which you see the point of light in the sky. The single point, and the Shadow that has just gathered you in its sweep...
>
> Always remember.
>
> The first star hangs between his feet.
>
> *Now*— (760)

Not, here, a redemptive wishing-star brightness, but rocket exhaust; not, here, a redemptive organic blackness, but the chill darkness that falls across Eliot's Hollow Men, the Shadow of Whitman's "lovely and delicate death," the rocket seen from above is Gottfried's *grosse Tod*, the destiny that his life with Blicero has been preparing, while at the same time, seen from below, it is Slothrop's, everyone's, promise of *kleine Tod*, perversely "integrative" destruction. The two stars are here fixed as one on the "knife-edge": Blicero had bidden Gottfried remember "the edge of evening ... the long curve of people all wishing on the first star ... Always remember those men and women along the thousands of miles of land and sea" (759–60). And below him now falls the horizon-curve, somewhere along which is Slothrop, wishing. Pynchon's symmetries are remarkable, not just for their inventiveness, but for their subtle care and completeness, their sense of responsibility to themselves. Which side of the Star, of the Shadow, the Point, does one feel one's self living on? In the novel, just for each knife-edge of the experience of it, the choice seems free.

6

The Gods of
Gravity's Rainbow

One Over Zero

In a dim Moscow hotel room, between the wars, I. G. Farben Verbindungsmann Wimpe, the cartel's sythesized-opiate pusher, shows
Tchitcherine a hypodermic full of Laszlo Jamf's "Oneirine theophosphate":

> (Tchitcherine: "You mean *thio*phosphate, don't you?"
> Thinks *indicating the presence of sulfur* ...
> Wimpe: "I mean *theo*phosphate, Vaslav,"
> *indicating the Presence of God.*) They shoot up. (702)

The inconspicuous vowel shift that suddenly renders "God" immanent
in the molecule (although Tchitcherine's "insane rush" will turn out to
be "ungodly" [702]), is one of those little now-you-see-it tricks by which
the style of connectedness intimates the nearness of certain vague presences whose nature I explore in this final chapter. To the mystery,
mysticism, oneiromancy, and "magic" to be felt everywhere in *Gravity's
Rainbow*, the first entryways, as we would expect, are such words
through whose frames we feel bending incursions, like notes through
harmonica holes, of numinous realms outside, where all meanings, all
metaphors, somehow are one. Later in this same scene, for further
example, the narrator tells us, "Young Tchitcherine was the one who
brought up political narcotics. Opiates of the people" (702). But, Wimpe
implies, the religious "opiate" defined by Marxism maps somehow
onto this hypo's literal contents, with which the I. G. will narcoticize the
preterite—opiate of the powerless, after Marx after all, as *theo*phos-
phate. And the literal *point* of the needle that is injecting the drug "is"
also one of those metaphorical points, such as the two men have just
been discussing, where by deciding between alternative tracks for his
life a man becomes uniquely "real ... the time between doesn't matter"
(702); the steel needle "is" also Tchitcherine's switchpoint, Wimpe as

pointsman, to the coming war's "bodyhood of steel" (702). When such word-switchpoint moments seem to intrude from some mega-advantage above the grid of causality, even narrative time linearity may blur: the Oneirine Haunting that follows directly on the page from the two men's shooting-up seems also, or "really," to be happening years later, when Comrade Ripov, in body or as hallucination, appears to set Tchitcherine straight on Their purposes for his life and for rocket history's, although both lives' courses remain as Haunted, ambiguous, as before.

That "drug-epistemologies" (528), mystical intimation, paranoid terrors, may possibly point to transcendental realities is at least, in Pynchon, a sort of constant background of suspicion—readers being left, not much assisted, to think what they will of any Other Kingdoms implied when words like molecules act hallucinogenically: as when Wimpe's theophosphate is said to call up a paranoia that "like other sorts of paranoia … is nothing less than the onset, the leading edge, of the discovery that *everything is connected,* everything in the Creation" (703).

Here, though of course the statement feels crucial for the whole novel, we, like Tchitcherine, are "held at the edge" of a terminally clouded veil: What is "everything"? What is "connected"? Like Oneirine-summoned "mantic archetypes," like the Kirghiz Light, like the "pure piercing grace note" announcing a seizure in epilepsy (*Lot 49,* 69), the code clause seems to gesture toward, but ultimately to occlude, some central truth that, if it could appear, would burn an "overexposed blank" in the film of consciousness (*Lot 49,* 69). Thus Pynchon's stylistic convention, convenience, and serious assertion is that veiled "perceptions" of what may be transcendent truths are (to borrow a metaphor from the culture of science) like the visible trains of ionized matter surrounding, implying, the flights of invisible particles in bubble chambers. Mystical/paranoiac feelings characteristically trail behind themselves nervous, compulsive, word-diddling scholarships of "explication" that do not at all touch the inexplicable: " 'Mantic archetypes' (as Jollifox of the Cambridge School has named them), will find certain individuals again and again, with a consistency which has been well demonstrated in the laboratory (see Wobb and Whoaton, 'Mantic Archetype Distribution Among Middle-Class University Students,' *J. Oneir. Psy. Pharm.,* XXIII, pg. 406–53)" (702).

The reader of *Gravity's Rainbow,* faced with the basic Pynchonian One/Zero problem, may at least plausibly share my feeling that at its heart the novel opts for the One—for some One. Beyond the "last whispering veil" (518) of self-consciously self-occluding language, there does reside some mystical donnée that, in the Jamesian sense, we must *give* Pynchon, although, it is true, the donnée seems devilishly hard to locate and define, obscured deliberately as it is by the cheap imitations, petty subversions, and dummy scholasticisms that are meant at the same time to point to its "edge." Not enough of Pynchon's critics have yet approvingly noted, as did Robert Sklar six years before *Gravity's Rainbow* was published, both that the "backbone" of Pynchon's work is science and that the hard vertebrae are threaded by a nerve of feeling of a kind quite other than scientific: "At the heart of Pynchon's imagination lies not science and technology, not the parody and wild humor which are so much a part of his style, but a sense of mystery, a vision of fantasy, that expresses itself in dualisms, in images of surface and depth, of mirrors, of secret societies and hidden worlds."[1]

Unfortunately, these terms are clumsy in their attempts to denote Pynchon's mystical element; since here we are moving away from the realm of the Word, it is not paradoxical that Alfred Kazin does better with his vague "something": "The key to Pynchon's brilliantly dizzying narratives is the force of some hypothesis that is authentic to him but undisclosable to us. There is a felt mystery, a communicable unsolidity, to our human affairs.... *The Crying of Lot 49* is ... the fable of the wild-goose chase that *something* now sets up for minds that still seek order, source, tradition, divinity."[2]

Kazin—also writing before *Gravity's Rainbow*—correctly sees that the paranoid patterns of Pynchon's characters' *searches* for an unnameable "something" beyond them are finally to be distinguished (if possible) from what may be real outer signs of a real "something" whose influence, in turn, feeds back into the psychological inside, silently warping or guiding the textures of searches. For what may be incursions of this mysterious order, one of Pynchon's favorite code words is "magic": "what keeps [Oedipa] in her tower is magic, anonymous and malignant, visited on her from outside and for no reason at all" (*Lot 49*, 11). This "magic" at the end of the first chapter of *Lot 49* is apt suddenly to mystify the reader who has been having no trouble understanding Oedipa's solipsist plight, her Rapunzel-like imprisonment in the tower of her subjectivity, from out of which she spins a tapestry into the void,

1. Robert Sklar, "The New Novel, USA: Thomas Pynchon," *Nation* 205 (September 25, 1967): 277–80; quote from p. 278.

Novelists and Storytellers from Hemingway to Mailer (Boston: Atlantic Monthly Press, 1971), p. 277.

2. Alfred Kazin, *Bright Book of Life:*

"and the tapestry was the world." The magic, mysteriously peopling that void after all, destabilizes the understanding accustomed enough to such solipsist plights in twentieth-century literature and life. Safer ground is offered at once: literary and scientific allusions comfortingly to connect Oedipa's task with Henry Adams's in the *Education*, the task being (in Pynchon's paraphrase of Adams) to "examine this formless magic ... measure its field strength, count its lines of force" (*Lot 49*, 11). But no such counting, framing, rationalizing techniques, as familiar either in life or in art, will quite cause the "magic" to down. In much the same way, Tchitcherine's story, though of course most improbable, gives no trouble to readers who accept the novel's congenital cartoonishness of plot. All seems well up to the point, near the end, when Tchitcherine's blood-hunt for Enzian is not resolved, but apparently dissolved, by the intervention of "magic": Geli Tripping invokes Kabbalistic angels as she makes love to Tchitcherine just before he encounters Enzian, "pacing her orgasm to the incantation ... naming the last Names of Power" (734), preventing the men from recognizing each other, preventing murder, while the narrator comments offhandedly, "This is magic. Sure—but not necessarily fantasy" (735). Commonplace magic, apparently, is not "fantasy"—and, if not real witchcraft and real angels, what is it exactly that saves Enzian from his so massively "plotted" fate?

The narrator remains consistently cryptic about the difference between magic and fantasy, but E. M. Forster—relevantly here, I think—distinguishes in *Aspects of the Novel* between two properties that prose fictions may have, which he calls "fantasy" and "prophecy."[3] Prophecy, he writes, is not meant "in the narrow sense of foretelling the future" but as indicating the novelist's constant, necessarily vague "reaching back" to a sense of an "infinity" attending all things. Prophecy's "face is toward unity, whereas fantasy glances about. [Prophecy's] confusion is incidental, whereas fantasy's is fundamental."[4] As regards both the magnitude and the kind of distances that the two kinds of fictions ask readers to travel, here are Forster's witty discriminations:

> [Fantasy and prophecy] are alike in having gods, and unlike in the gods they have.... Therefore on behalf of fantasy let us now invoke all beings who inhabit the lower air, the shallow water, and the

3. See chapters 6 and 7 of E. M. Forster, *Aspects of the Novel* (New York: Harcourt, Brace & World, 1955).

4. Ibid., p. 136.

smaller hills, all Fauns and Dryads and slips of the memory, all
verbal coincidences, Pans and puns, all that is medieval this side of
the grave. When we come to prophecy, we shall utter no invocation,
but it will have been to whatever transcends our abilities, even
when it is human passion that transcends them, to the deities of
India, Greece, Scandinavia and Judaea, to all that is medieval
beyond the grave and to Lucifer son of the morning.[5]

The light-fantastic is the spirit that causes fairies to hover, as around Dr.
Slop's bag, around the author's chronology, around the author's intentions themselves, in *Tristram Shandy*, Forster's exemplary "fantastic"
novel, where "confusion is fundamental." But if in a prophetic *Gravity's
Rainbow* some sort of holist vision, instead, is fundamental, then the
"something" that saves Enzian is at last an undivided property of the
universe, not necessarily fantasy, i.e., not merely any fortuitous cor-
rectness of Geli's faith in the Kabbala or of anyone's in another mystical
system.

Here, though, we face immediately the problem of how to reconcile
Pynchon's prophetic One with the novel's own kind of "fantasy," meaning not only its variously preposterous mystical systems but also the
pratfalls, Marx Brothers sequences, nonsense messages, low puns, rubber cocks, oracles out to lunch. We must feel all these things as existing
not just as their likes in Sterne do, for their own sweet sakes and for
sweet confusion's, but also in order that they might shadow forth, somehow, the something that infinitely attends them. To this problem
Pynchon's complex deployments of the code words "song" and "magic"
may provide a key. Preterition's low-comic world, which is fantasy's
province, is protected "magically," claims the narrator, by "song," as
Rocketman is by his cape: "While the nobles are crying in their nights'
chains, the squires sing. The terrible politics of the Grail can never
touch them. Song is the magic cape" (701). The Grail-questing elect,
who practice an absolutely unreal dichotomization between Their own
world and the "magical" one, are bound in their nights'/knights' chains
of "politics," humorlessness, solemnity, deafness to song. But the preterites' song, besides being a mindless pleasure, is also a signature of
the deep connection of preterition with an invisible flux, with the One.
At this point and in this sense the song of low fantasy merges with, is
validated by and contained in, the higher, prophetic song.

In fact, Forster identifies a general stylistic trait vaguely called "song"
as characteristic of prophetic novels: *Moby Dick*, for example, gives us

5. Ibid., pp. 109, 110.

throughout "the sensation of a song or sound," as do indeed all the prophetic novels of the only consistently prophetic novelists Forster professed to be able to think of: Emily Brontë, Dostoevsky, Melville, Lawrence. If he is right, then in order to catch the prophetic note in a fiction's style we must at some point stop talking and simply listen, at length. Here then is the larger part of one of *Gravity's Rainbow's* most exalted passages, the frame-segment called "Streets," which for me is one of the book's high points, and, for that matter, a high point in the novelistic literature of this century:

> But in each of these streets, some vestige of humanity, of Earth, has to remain. No matter what has been done to it, no matter what it's been used for....
>
> There were men called "army chaplains." They preached inside some of these buildings. There were actually soldiers, dead now, who sat or stood, and listened. Holding on to what they could. Then they went out, and some died before they got back inside a garrison-church again. Clergymen, working for the army, stood up and talked to the men who were going to die about God, death, nothingness, redemption, salvation. It really happened. It was quite common.
>
> Even in a street used for that, still there will be one time, one dyed afternoon (coaltar-impossible orange-brown, clear all the way through), or one day of rain and clearing before bedtime, and in the yard one hollyhock, circling in the wind, fresh with raindrops fat enough to be chewed ... one face by a long sandstone wall and the scuffle of all the doomed horses on the other side, one hair-part thrown into blue shadows at a turn of her head—one busful of faces passing through in the middle of the night, no one awake in the quiet square but the driver, the Ortsschutz sentry in some kind of brown, official-looking uniform, old Mauser at sling arms, dreaming not of the enemy outside in the swamp or shadow but of home and bed, strolling now with his civilian friend who's off-duty, can't sleep, under the trees full of road-dust and night, through their shadows on the sidewalks, playing a harmonica ... down past the row of faces in the bus, drowned-man green, insomniac, tobacco-starved, scared, not of tomorrow, not yet, but of this pause in their night-passage, of how easy it will be to lose, and how much it will hurt....
>
> At least one moment of passage, one it will hurt to lose, ought to be found for every street now indifferently gray with commerce, with war, with repression ... finding it, learning to cherish what was lost, mightn't we find some way back?
>
> In one of these streets, in the morning fog, plastered over two

slippery cobblestones, is a scrap of newspaper headline, with a wirephoto of a giant white cock, dangling in the sky straight downward out of a white pubic bush. The letters

MB DRO

ROSHI

appear above with the logo of some occupation newspaper, a grinning glamour girl riding astraddle the cannon of a tank, steel penis with slotted serpent head, 3rd Armored treads 'n' triangle on a sweater rippling across her tits. The white image has the same coherence, the hey-lookit-me smugness, as the Cross does. It is not only a sudden white genital onset in the sky—it is also, perhaps, a Tree....

Slothrop sits on a curbstone watching it, and the letters, and girl with steel cock waving hi fellas, as the fog whitens into morning, and figures with carts, or dogs, or bicycles go by in brown-gray outlines, wheezing, greeting briefly in fog-flattened voices, passing. He doesn't remember sitting on the curb so long staring at the picture. But he did.

At the instant it happened, the pale Virgin was rising in the east, head, shoulders, breasts, 17° 36' down to her maidenhead at the horizon. A few doomed Japanese knew of her as some Western deity. She loomed in the eastern sky gazing down at the city about to be sacrificed. The sun was in Leo. The fireburst came roaring and sovereign. (693–94)

In this passage, a microcosm of *Gravity's Rainbow,* key words and images, with erudite footnotings attached, click beautifully in their couplings, although of course the mechanical sounds are not what one listens for when seeking "song." Yet, since the couplings and bondings are perhaps among song's preconditions, they should be briefly noted. We move from a predictable irony regarding army chaplains, regarding religion and war, to invocations of "Earth" vs. I. G. Farben synthetics (the holy afternoon's color is "coaltar-impossible"); to glimpses of preterite faces framed in their passage by tour-bus windows, plus a passing snatch of song from that preterite instrument, the harmonica; to the cybernetic jamming of the headline's message of Hiroshima; to image-codes for the pseudo-sexuality of machines; to mythic associations, Cross and Tree, for the mushroom cloud; to the cloud, finally, as "pale Virgin," clearly the V-3 whose coming the dialectic of Pynchon's whole work has implied, here a kind of negative Great Mother Goddess ("some Western deity"). These points and others, connected, give us a blue-pencil sketch of the novel, and here we might want to say that the song resides "not in any of these by itself, but in their connectedness." But connectedness, insofar as it expresses itself in such connect-the-dots games, is itself a veil, an artifice or paranoia—at best a series of hints for those "held at the edge." We may try to talk vaguely of the "tone" of the passage, but there is not one, but a shower of tones: angry, wistful, elegiac, fantastic, horror-stricken, comic, wistful again, horror-stricken again. Like the words that denote them, the tones are controlled and conditioned, "framed," merely, at last. My feeling is that if Pynchon's "song" is anything real, and if we may say that it surfaces at any specific points, the oracular sentence "The sun was in Leo" is one such point. That at the time of Hiroshima the sun was in Leo is of course simply a fact, and to remark it here may be just to practice "astrology." But, if so, how is it that this sentence can release "floods of our emotion," to quote Forster on a similarly strategic sentence in Dostoevsky? To be a believer in systematic astrology, or to assume Pynchon is, cannot begin to explain the effect of transcendent *meaningfulness* about the juxtaposition of Hiroshima with the zodiacal sign of blood and aggression. Somewhat analogously, *Hamlet*'s song depends on no literal belief in ghosts, though the play's plot requires its ghost. Pynchon's song also lies, I think, in the fact of Slothrop's being allowed to "see" distantly, but not to understand, the pale Virgin; it lies in calling the fireburst "sovereign"; it lies in the almost invisible ambiguity of the "it" in "at the instant it happened." That I feel myself here growing even more vague than usual means either that I am talking nonsense or that Pynchon is writing it, or that indeed what is happening in the writing where I think I hear it is "song" in Forster's sense, the passage releasing its flood, leaving mere words-as-counters behind.

On this subject of Forsterian "prophecy," it should be added that of Forster's two specifications for the attitude of the *reader* toward prophetic writing—"humility" and "suspension of the sense of humor"—the second may cause some problems here. That it would seem, to understate, inappropriate for Pynchon's readers to suspend their sense of humor may mean chiefly that Forster's sense of the workings of prophetic fiction needs some expanding to fit this new case. Because he employs *both* fantastic and prophetic notes, Pynchon is quite unlike the pure prophets in Forster's small sample, all of whom, relatively, lack humor. That his prophetic visions, unlike theirs, may seem *essentially* qualified by mediating entanglements with fantasy, Pynchon mixes his mystical signals, often asking us in one place to take some mystical system seriously for what, apparently, it reveals (for example, the spiritualism that calls up Walter Rathenau's voice in Sachsa's seance), and then in another place making complete and obvious fun of the same system (see the scene in which Nora Dodson-Truck is "suckered into seances that wouldn't fool your great-aunt" [639]). Or, more subtly, we are given "mystical" passages that both do and do not allow themselves to be taken straight, their tone flickering across a "quicksilver edge" (713) between Revelation and cut-up rather in the manner of the familiar black-and-white drawing of what is either a chalice or a pair of profiles about to kiss:

> But each of the Sephiroth is also haunted by its proper demons or Qlippoth. Netzach by the Ghorab Tzerek, the Ravens of Death, and Hod by Samael, the Poison of God. No one has asked the demons at either level, but there may be just the wee vulnerability here to a sensation of falling, the kind of very steep and out-of-scale fall we find in dreams, a falling more through space than among objects.... The Ravens of Death have now tasted of the Poison of God ... but in doses small enough not to sicken but to bring on, like Amanita muscaria, a very peculiar state of mind ... They have no official name, but they are the Rocket's guardian demons. (748)

The choice to take smirking parody, alone and always, as the essential tone of all the novel's mystical passages is the choice to take the novel generally as nihilistic, absurdist, wholly psychopathological in its interest: a choice of Zero as opposed to One, the commoner choice, my rejection of which I have already tried to make plain. Yet, it should also be stated, there is an equal-and-opposite danger in taking the "One" in Pynchon too uniformly seriously or literally, or, as in the case of a recent study by Douglas Fowler, too reductively. Fowler's *A Reader's Guide to "Gravity's Rainbow"*—the first of what surely will be a series of "reader's guides" to Pynchon—is cleverly written, pertinently researched, and full of excellent comments on individual scenes and effects. But Fowler's general view of the novel is finally so trivializing that it is hard to see why he regards it as "great" enough to be worthy at all of such minute interpretive efforts. Constantly, heavily emphasizing Pynchon's use of the conventions of Gothic horror thrillers, Fowler makes of the sense of Pynchon's One something so suffocatingly literal as to give us a *Gravity's Rainbow* that takes as its central *donnée* "a War of the Worlds ... where the basic energy ... derives from the clash between this world and what I will abbreviate as The Other Kingdom—between our world of logic and rationality and the five senses and a nightmare world that has begun to penetrate and to threaten it.... We must recognize that Pynchon does not use fairytale magic or supernatural event in a merely psychological way, or as a metaphor only. His Other Kingdom is never directly described, but it is potent and malign."[6]

In this view, paranoia is the characters' surest insight, paradoxically because it is not paranoia at all, but a real, waking reprise of childhood's archetypal nightmares-that-always-come-true. Repeatedly Fowler captions the whole of Pynchon's fiction with *Lot 49*'s reference to "magic, anonymous and malignant." Correctly taking this to point to something real outside the self, Fowler sees in it a warrant to ignore almost completely the ("merely") psychological and metaphorical functions of ideas of order in Pynchon, to ignore *Lot 49*'s own definition of metaphor, the central business of the imagination, as "a thrust at truth and a lie, depending on where you are" (*Lot 49*, 95). Of course Pynchon adopts (therefore also parodies) Gothic fictions, "doing" Romantic Gothicism as he does comic books, spy melodrama fiction, classical myth, science, movies—but it hardly follows that in essence the novel *is* Gothic fiction, with all the same *données*. Pynchon is surely "interested in magic," as Fowler says, but he is not therefore uninterested in the human psychology that *creates* various, finally all unverifiable, magical fictions. Between one dead end and another, even an absurdist, nihilistic Pynchon seems preferable to one who believes that by offering old Boris Karloff reruns he can tell a whole truth about history, mind, reality.

*   *   *

In this section, then, I try to define how the manifestations of "magic" in *Gravity's Rainbow* connect, first, inside, with the psychology of human needs, and also outside, with whatever One may be felt as creating the field in which magic can operate—magnetizing the magic onto itself. How do magic "cathexes" (one of Freud's favorite terms) operate to connect the One with (one of Jung's) the psychic archetype of the self? The question leads me finally to state my sense that of all of *Gravity's Rainbow*'s sources and "influences" it is Jung whose vision most closely, in general, resembles Pynchon's. Indeed, much in the same way as Jung's system is taken either as too mystical for its scientific pretensions, or too scientific, "merely psychologizing," for a system that takes

6. Douglas Fowler, *A Reader's Guide to*   Ardis, 1980), pp. 10, 11.
"Gravity's Rainbow" (Ann Arbor, Mich.:

the real mysticisms of history so seriously, so Pynchon is often found either too mystical for a writer who wants to chronicle contemporary predicaments honestly, or too savvily self-subversive for one who would have us feel, more or less seriously, so many prophetic insights, so many "shivers and voids" (587).

The Jungian axiom that most alienates religionists is that any apparently transcendental phenomena we experience—dreams, visions, religious or shamanic revelations, parapsychological happenings, etc.—are in fact projections of the activities of an autonomous personal and/or collective unconscious. They express numinous archetypes issuing from the deep psychic structure, i.e., from the self, the totality of the unconscious psyche. Yet also in Jung, to alienate Pointsmanlike empiricists, is a second axiom, to the effect that the very *fact* of a deep, transrational nature in man does finally imply some order, *in fact* transcendental, that subsumes all things inside and outside the self. In the very autonomy of the unconscious, as in the indeterminacies discerned by the New Physics, Jung felt this transcendental reality, calling it a "psychoid" field, the ultimate matrix both for the self (the psychic realm) and the material universe. Jung believed further—as Pynchon also seems to—in the classical mystics' axiom that the ineffable One can never be apprehended directly: even the archetypal symbols called up by psychic-projective processes are already mediations, obscurings, of native "psychoid" reality. Mythologies and religions in their received forms have therefore, like other projected systems, no literal or final claims to authority, though they are greatly significant as *psychic* facts. Jung's reproach to "naive-minded" people who dogmatize about framed versions of the ineffable—in a sort of mystically-minded reprise of Whitehead's Fallacy of Misplaced Concreteness—might be directed as well to Fowler-like critics of Pynchon, who take the map for the territory:

> It is ... impossible to demonstrate God's reality to oneself except by using images which have arisen spontaneously or are sanctified by tradition, and whose psychic nature and effects the naive-minded person has never separated from their unknowable metaphysical background. He instantly equates the effective image with the trancendental *x* to which it points.... But ... it must be remembered that the image and the statement are psychic processes which are different from their transcendental object; they do not posit it, they merely point to it.[7]

7. C. G. Jung, *Answer to Job*, 2d ed. (Princeton, N.J.: Bollingen Series, Prince- ton University Press, 1969), p. xv.

I will refer often to the connections between Pynchon's uses of real-historical mystical systems and Jung's explications of these same systems as manifesting "psychic processes." What must be emphasized here is that, for both Jung and Pynchon, the systems are interesting primarily as psychic or psychological concepts; interesting in that they typify mind's own bootstrap attempts, first on the level of archetypes, then on that of dogma, to grasp with words and images that whole in which mind remains embedded, of which mind itself is a shard or "declined" manifestation.

An important corollary of these observations is that there is no *intellectual* imperative by which Pynchon demands that readers or characters believe in his One, whatever forms we may dimly perceive it to take. Since no one can know with certainty whether a transcendental background exists—whether mystical intimations do somehow show forth a One, or are wholly projections, or are malignly plotted "appearances"—we may, in good enough faith, leap at Zero, becoming antiparanoid or nihilistic. Alternatively we may choose, as I am maintaining that Pynchon himself has chosen, to leap at a form of faith in a One; or else we may be content, with Roger Mexico and Oedipa, to wander indefinitely, agnostic, among "zeros and ones twinned above ... ahead, thick, maybe endless" (*Lot 49*, 136). But, in light of this impasse, what is of real importance in Pynchon's novels is the *ethical* imperative that might generally be said to run, Know your state, know it in relation to whatever evil surrounds you, and find your freedom in resisting Their incursions on life. In the present context, the imperative begins with the insistence that we try hard to distinguish between what *could* be real signs of real transcendental orders, on the one hand, and Their paranoiacally ordered, counterfeit systems, on the other. The secular orders that They have set up, Their paranoid history as a We-They moire of control, dominance and submission, represent merely—in Jungian terms—the sick, unindividuated condition of a collective Western psyche that has chosen death and separation over healthy integration and that has reified this "shadow" impulse in and as secular life. We must distinguish Their patterns, projected from inside the funhouse that We and They inhabit, from what the patterns mimic, a possibly real other order. To fail, as for example Fowler fails, to see in this way through Their Halloween masks, is to miss Their wholly human nature and Their human—therefore combatible—evil. The second part of the imperative, then, is the demand that we refuse passivity, avoid easy, paranoid senses of victimization; it is the claim that we must choose, instead, moral activity; join, in some sense, a Counterforce; and try at least to affect—if not completely to effect—our lives' fates. Mexico, while remaining agnostic in transcendental matters, knows that, in his life's foreground, how he chooses to deal with Them, how he goes operational with his choice, matters deeply for his freedom and conscience: "Which is worse, living on as Their pet, or death? It is not a question he has ever imagined himself asking seriously. It has come by surprise, but there's no sending it away now, he really does have to decide, and soon enough.... Letting it sit for awhile is no compromise" (713). Edward Mendelson, also citing this passage, notes Pynchon's demand, implied everywhere in his novels, that preterites make conscious *choices* out of realistic assessments of their "interests."[8] That is to say, life's business in Pynchon's world is not, finally, mindless pleasures, but the cultivation of hair-trigger sensitivities to "real tasks and [needs for] purposive choices."[9]

Pynchon as mystic may believe in an ultimate Oneness to give the metaphysical lie to Their illusion of paranoid separation, but Pynchon as moralist meanwhile condemns the paranoid cop-out, which is passivity, *mere* mindless pleasures, and that includes merely escapist indulgence in mysticism. Such, I think, is the imaginative place of the One in *Gravity's Rainbow:* a tempering background for *ethical* life, never an excuse to avoid existential decisions, ethical choices, or historically effective action. While considering the many mystical systems that Pynchon's learning has furnished him for use in the novel, I will try to work slowly through them, toward the sense of the One they variously imply and conceal—but without losing touch, I hope, with those concurrent features of Pynchon's work that place him among the most dedicated historicists and most intense moralists among living writers.

The Way of the Tower

In Rilke's Seventh Duino Elegy there runs a passage that celebrates the vaulting "towers"—the immediate symbolism is of Gothic cathedral towers—that men have built out of their passionate imaginings of other orders:

O marvel, Angel, for *we* are this,
we, O great one. Tell them we did such things; my own breath

---

8. See Mendelson's introduction to his edited *Pynchon: A Collection of Critical Essays* (Englewood Cliffs, N.J.: Prentice-

Hall, 1978), pp. 1–15.
9. Ibid., p. 13.

is too short for the praising of it. So we have not then
entirely neglected our world-space, this generous allotment,
these spaces of *ours*....
But a tower was great, was it not? O Angel, it was,—
great even next to You? Chartres was great—[10]

Adjust for contextual and tonal differences, and the human impulse
whose reification is regarded here is the same one that Pynchon regards
as he faces Simon Rodia's Watts Towers and thinks, perhaps, of Newton's System of the World. And as "we know by now" (747), the rocket
as "tower" is a general symbol for all real and possible, splendidly
ordered, gargoyled, too often mad, fruits of the human will to imagine
some structure in the ineffable secrets above or behind the world. Late
in *Gravity's Rainbow,* the narrator reads Blicero's Tarot, "exactly as [the
cards] came up" (746), and—

> Of 77 cards that could have come up, Weissmann is "covered," that
> is his present condition is set forth, by The Tower. It is a puzzling
> card, and everybody has a different story on it. It shows a bolt of
> lightning striking a tall phallic structure, and two figures, one
> wearing a crown, falling from it. Some read ejaculation, and leave it
> at that. Others see a Gnostic or Cathar symbol for the Church of
> Rome, and this is generalized to mean any System which cannot
> tolerate heresy: a system which, by its nature, must sooner or later
> fall. We know by now that it is also the Rocket.
>
> Members of the Order of the Golden Dawn believe the Tower
> represents victory over splendor, and avenging force. As Goebbels,
> beyond all his professional verbalizing, believed in the Rocket as an
> avenger. (747)

The tower symbol here again suggests the compulsively elaborated
nature both of any manmade systems "read" and of the solemn reading
themselves; for example, Goebbels, in a solemn act of reading/naming,
turns what had been the A4 into the V-2, hoping thus to *create* a "*Ver-
nichtungs-*" or "*Vergeltungswaffe*" (destruction or revenge weapon). That
the reductively sexual reading of the Tower card is treated so dis-
respectfully amounts to Pynchon's rejection (as earlier, through
Hilarius in *Lot 49*) of the system of Freudianism—but some systematic
readings may on the other hand have real validity: Pynchon has furnished thermodynamic and cybernetic metaphors fully to sanction the
rocket's identification as "system which, by its nature, must sooner or
later fall." And yet the juxtaposition of this with the coy "we know by

10. Rainer Maria Rilke, *The Duino Elegies,* (New York: Harper Colophon Books, 1972),
trans. Stephen Garmey and Jay Wilson   Tenth Duino Elegy, lines 75-79, 81, 82.

now ..." reminds us again that readings are not just the Tarot gypsy's or propagandist's game, but also the novel-reader's and -critic's, and that we are playing it now. Meanwhile, the connections busily being made among Tarot, Christian, heretical Christian, and Golden Dawn symbolic systems carry forward Pynchon's main business, that of creating a very complexly mixed sense of what connectedness means. We see that among this jerrybuilt Babel of signs, some at least may be real intimations of a transcendental field in which there are activated, through these "shards," unitive archetypal meanings.

Separate books by the English mystic A. E. Waite on the Tarot, the Kabbala, and Freemasonry have clearly been of much use to Pynchon. Consider, for example, Pynchon's "Kabbalistic Tree of Life," on which "the path of the Tower connects the sephira Netzach, victory, with Hod, glory or splendor.... Netzach is fiery and emotional, Hod is watery and logical. On the body of God, these two Sephiroth are the thighs, the pillars of the Temple, resolving together in Yesod, the sex and excretory organs" (748). For "pillars of the Temple" see Waite's *Encyclopedia of Freemasonry* under the heading "Kabbalistic Tradition and Masonry," under which, in turn, the subheading "Of Spiritual Building" adumbrates the equation between esoteric-spiritual and worldly-practical senses of the Masonic "craft." Masonic mythology springs from a seed story of the mysterious murder of a Master Builder by four unknown assassins while this original Mason was carrying out his commission to build the Temple of Solomon. In the later esoteric symbology, the Temple is the stone-towered embodiment of the Masonic Brotherhood's store of wisdom and of the store of the Kabbalists, once Temple/Tower is assimilated, as Waite suggests, to Tree of Life/Body of God: "We find ... after what manner, according to mystic Israel, Solomon's Temple was spiritualized; we find profound meanings attached to the two Pillars J and B; we find how a Word was lost and under what circumstances the chosen people were to look for its recovery."[11]

The Lost Word of Masonry is a mysterious formula of the Masonic Master, toward the recovery of which every Speculative (esoteric) Mason still theoretically directs his quest. For his Kabbalistic connection, Waite assimilates this Lost Word to the Hebraic tradition's True, Holy Name of God (*GR*, 590), of which the Holy Tetragrammaton J-H-V-H is an incomplete fossilization. Pynchon transforms for his own pur-

---

11. A. E. Waite, *A New Encyclopedia of Freemasonry*, 2 vols. (New York: Weather- vane Books, 1970) 1: 417.

poses this Kabbalistic/Masonic lore of the Word, the Name of the One that transcends and rebukes the appearances of the Many. Among its echoes in Pynchon are the Divine Word of Puritanism, mystically immanent in the preacher's words from the pulpit; the white-visiting Word of the epileptic, heard during the fit but later forgotten; the Word of Nothingness that Slothrop fears he will hear when the rocket hits him; the Word, the Text, the Key that Enzian seeks "among the wastes of the World" (525). In this and other cheerful cribbing from Kabbalistic, Masonic, and other mystical systems, Pynchon's mystical impulse calls up an attendant, framing, parodic and self-parodic system of its very own. The paranoid atmosphere of the novel is in part a function of the general mystics' notion that their systems' "fallen" words and images are at once betrayals of Oneness and coded "thrusts at truth" back in the One's general direction. As Waite testifies, mystic initiates' words, when directed "downward," must become, in self-defense, as "veiled" as any paranoiac conspirator's: "If it is to be asked: What is the connection between the loss and dismemberment which befell the Divine Name JEHOVAH and the Lost Word in Masonry, it is obvious that I cannot answer, except in a veiled manner; but every ROYAL ARCH Mason knows what is communicated to him in the Supreme Degree."[12]

I will quote a bit more of Waite's prose, since it beautifully expresses the mystical, quasi-paranoid manner of mind that so fascinates Pynchon—the mystic's way, oddly vague and precise at once, of rushing headlong to interlock "meanings" syncretically, yielding a style of connectedness that is the black-sheep blood-relative of Pynchon's own:

> The world for the Kabbalists was full of palaces and sanctuaries, while visible creation ... was viewed as the House of Adonai, the abode of the Indwelling Glory.... the outward Sanctuary was transfigured by many meanings, so that it was now the body of man enlightened by the abiding spirit—which was also the understanding of the Law; and now Celestial Jerusalem; how the destruction ... of the material city signified the Secret Doctrine laid waste by the advocates of the letter, or again the chosen nation, the peculiar people delivered into the hands of idolators; and finally ... how the external city and its holy places were symbols of the primeval world before the serpent ascended into the Tree of Life.... the Rosicrucian Fraternity also symbolized a sacred city and house not made with hands; while at the very period when the wonder and rumour of the ZOHAR first astonished the academies and synagogues of Spain there fell that Order of Knights Templars which speculation has

12. Ibid.

> always accredited with the design of restoring Zion.... The Office
> and mission of the Church itself may be similarly regarded, for this
> is also a city of many palaces, which—in virtue of inherent vitality—
> builds itself up from within and is improved and beautified forever
> by the continual transmutation of its living stones.[13]

Waite here suggests a sociohistorical process of rationalization that imitates in ground plan the metaphysical One-Many structure: a slow declension of original "magic" into a system of ritualizing cults and cells, thence ultimately into "Paranoid Systems of History." Although Freemasonry's origins are unknown, the movement may be traced back at least as far as religious associations formed by the architects of Tyre, who, under the name of the Dionysiac Fraternity, built temples in Asia Minor; certainly, anyway, as Pynchon says, "The Magic in these Masonic rituals is very, very old" (588). It is Pynchon's announced hypothesis or mock-hypothesis that "way back in those days, it *worked*" (588)—gave real access, one guesses, to some transcendental reality. But in Europe Masonry split into the mystical cells of Speculative Masonry, on the one hand, and the simple "businessmen's clubs" (587) of the Craft Masons, on the other. These latter became routinized such that any originally incorporated magic charismas were reduced to mere latencies: "As time went on, and [Masonic magic] started being used for spectacle, to consolidate what were only secular appearances of power, it began to lose its zip. But the words, moves, and machinery have been more or less faithfully carried down over the millennia, through the grim rationalizing of the Word, and so the magic is still there, though latent, needing only to touch the right sensitive head to reassert itself" (588).

In this passage, the obvious drug-resonances of "sensitive head" remind Pynchon's reader that by partaking in the effects of the novel's own "magic" code words he may become an adept of the novel's own system. Similarly, we have learned that a "mouthorgan," which carries preterites' "silver chances of song" (63), is a magical object (Slothrop's harmonica, dropped down the Roseland toilet, magically finds him again in the Harz)—but the novel's "grim rationalizing" is such that Lyle Bland's blandly unmagical Masonic lodge is in "Mouthorgan, Missouri" (587). Even worse, after G-man Melvin Purvis guns down John Dillinger, They let him feel "between his lips the penis of official commendation" (516): the endpoint of the decadence of the mouth-organ

---

13. Ibid., pp. 421, 422.

image. About the mysterious Masonic code-image of the All-Seeing Eye, or, in *Gravity's Rainbow*, the "strange single eye crowning the pyramid," A. E. Waite says, "The ... symbol is concerned with the watch and ward of Providence, 'Whose eye never slumbers or sleeps.' ... But it is an Eye also which 'pervades the inmost recesses of the human heart ... [while] beyond the limits of these familiar intimations ... one of the Secret Rituals which are not of Masonry ... has this sentence: 'It is called the Closed Eye of the Unknown Darkness,' by allusion to the darkness of Unmanifest Spirit."[14] But Pynchon's system is happy enough to employ the Eye in the following characterization of Masonry as among the typical, really historical, paranoid systems:

> Non-Masons stay pretty much in the dark about What Goes On, though now and then something jumps out, exposes itself, jumps giggling back again, leaving you with few details but a lot of Awful Suspicions. Some of the American Founding Fathers were Masons, for instance. There is a theory going around that the U.S.A. was and still is a gigantic Masonic plot under the ultimate control of the group known as the Illuminati. It is difficult to look for long at the strange single eye crowning the pyramid which is found on every dollar bill and not begin to believe the story, a little. (587)

Constitutional paranoiacs among readers are very slyly courted by the "reflexive" properties of this writing, which itself works precisely by laying down awful suspicions, then jumping back giggling. And on the next page:

> We must also never forget famous Missouri Mason Harry Truman, sitting by virtue of death in office, this very August 1945, with his control-finger poised right on Miss Enola Gay's atomic clit. (588)

To tag Truman as a *Missouri* Mason implies that visible history somehow was connected with Lyle Bland's Masonic lodge, hence with *Gravity's Rainbow*'s entire mock-paranoid system of history, now "validated" beyond the fictional frame.

For paranoid systems of history, Pynchon insists, *are* real and actualize real history, however delusive the original paranoid contents. Anti-Masonic paranoia has of course a long tradition in Jesuitical circles; the "theory going around" that the eighteenth-century Bavarian Illuminati directed and direct a malign conspiracy remains a central tenet of John Birch Society faith. And there is, of course, the past and

14. Ibid., p. 21.

present phenomenon of paranoiacally tinged revivalist Christianity; D. H. Lawrence recalls from his childhood that "Down among the uneducated people you will still find Revelation rampant ... the capital letters of the name: MYSTERY, BABYLON THE GREAT, THE MOTHER OF HARLOTS AND ABOMINATIONS OF THE EARTH thrill the old colliers today as they thrilled ... the underground early Christians [to whom] Babylon the Great meant Rome.... and great was the satisfaction of denouncing her and bringing her to utter, utter woe and destruction."[15] The visions of St. John of Patmos in his imprisonment can surely be read as expressing excellently the Tower-pathology such as, Norman Cohn writes, is "commonly to be found in individual cases of paranoia. The megalomaniac view of oneself as Elect, wholly good, abominably persecuted yet assured of ultimate triumph; the attribution of gigantic and demonic powers to the adversary; the refusal to accept the ineluctable limitations and imperfections of human existence ... the obsession with inerrable prophecies ... systematized misinterpretations ... ruthlessness directed toward an end which by its very nature cannot be realized— toward a total and final solution."[16]

Cohn's last two words grimly suggest with what ease mystical tower-systems can issue in those real systems of history that oppress and may at last destroy us. Below, for a while, I review a few more tower arcana as they are deployed—always with these dark resonances—in *Gravity's Rainbow*.

*　　*　　*

In Kabbalism Pynchon finds the doctrine of the ten mystic Sephiroth: points or regions on the symbolic Body of God that is, as a whole, the symbolic outline of universal, "fallen" creation. The lowest of these, Malkuth, lies closest to Earth on the Tree/Tower/Body, as Leo Schaya explains: "As passive and receptive principle, the end-point of the influx of all the emanations of the *Sefiroth* ... called the "woman" or the "wife," the "queen" of the divine "king".... she manifests, in the midst of the cosmos, the unity of the divine emanations ... of which she then

15. D. H. Lawrence, *Apocalypse* (New York: Viking Compass Book, Viking Press, 1966), pp. 10, 11.

16. Norman Cohn, *The Pursuit of the Millennium* (London: Secker & Warburg, 1957), pp. 309, 310.

represents the descent or direct revelation, [and] is called *shekhinah*."[17] Thus, since Malkuth suggests Earth, the female principle, and the mutability of the organic world, Greta Erdmann can identify herself with Shekhinah/Malkuth when she tries to lure a Jewish child to the edge of the black mud pool at Bad Karma, wanting to drown him, and "burlesquing ... in heavy Yiddish dialect.... 'I wander all the Diaspora looking for strayed children. I am Israel. I am the Shekhinah, queen, daughter, bride, and mother of God. And I will take you back, you fragment of smashed vessel, even if I must pull you by your nasty little circumcised penis—'" (478)

Here, extremes of tower corruption, as anti-Semitism and Nazism (the scene takes place just as the war is beginning), mingle with acknowledgments of Kabbalism's holistic impulse and with the novel's own Earth-Mother mystique, which elsewhere also frames Greta. Pynchon again both adapts and parodies Kabbalism in his later assimilation of Malkuth, as Earth/mud/organic sign, to shit, in Slothrop's surrealistic late date to meet someone "in the Male Transvestites' Toilet ... station metatron, quadrant Fire, stall Malkuth ... the usual Hour. Don't be late" (680). And Geli Tripping invokes this same "Great Metatron" when she wants to save Tchitcherine: the Angel Metatron, premier messenger of the Kabbala, who represents "the whole of God's spiritual descent ... the great universal mediator,"[18] appears to be the Kabbalistic transformation of Jung's "Mercurius" archetype. And it may have been Jung who gave Pynchon his lead to the Kabbalistic "Qlippoth, Shells of the Dead" (176), which in the novel are what remain of the souls of men picked clean, in life, "by the needle-mouths of death-by-government" (176). Late Kabbalistic philosophy, Jung reports in *Answer to Job*, contained the idea of an "abysmal world of 'shards,'" which are "ten counterpoles to the ten *sefiroth*," the evil backside of God.[19] Accordingly, in the novel, "each of the Sephiroth is also haunted by its proper demons or Qlippoth," and "the different Qlippoth can only work each his own sort of evil ... (what, a dialectical Tarot? Yes indeedyfoax)" (748). "Tarot," in this connection, because of the Golden Dawn doctrine that the Major Arcana of the Tarot deck correspond to connections among the Sephiroth on the Body of God—as, by common syncretic procedure along the Way of the Tower, the four

17. Leo Schaya, *The Universal Meaning of the Kabbalah* (Baltimore: Penguin Books, 1973), p. 58.

18. Ibid., p. 121.

19. Jung, *Answer to Job*, p. 19n.

Tarot suits are connected with the four Tetragrammaton letters, which Kabbalism connects with the four Aristotelian elements:

J - fire - rods

H - water - cups

V - air - swords

H - earth - pentacles

The Tetragrammaton reaches, in turn, for the Earth's four winds and four primary metals (gold, silver, copper, iron), these three groups, having made twelve, conveniently marrying the Zodiac. Tower systems revel in interconnectedness, Robert Graves's homemade syncretic system in *The White Goddess* being Pynchon's exemplary "scholarly quest" of the kind (*V.*, 50).

The Tarot cards that Pynchon's narrator uses for Blicero's reading may be found illustrated, just as described in the novel, in Waite's *The Pictorial Key to the Tarot*—a work that, belittling the deck's common uses for mere fortune-telling, defines the Tarot symbols, instead, as archetypal intimations of a secret "Doctrine Behind the Veil": "The Tarot embodies symbolical presentations of universal ideas, behind which lie all the implicits of the human mind, and it is in this sense that they contain secret doctrine, which is the realization by the few of truths embedded in the consciousness of all, though they have not passed into express recognition by ordinary men."[20]

The "ordinary" preterite passengers forced to continue on Pynchon's bus tour through Their worldly system cannot linger behind, though they would like to, to learn what is being revealed to the old men who sit in shaded courtyards "shuffling the ancient decks oily and warm, throwing down swords and cups and trumps major" (413). It is in Waite's book that Pynchon finds (as he acknowledges, 738) his instruction in the "Celtic style" of laying out and interpreting the Tarot array; he also alludes, this time veiledly, to Waite's deck in the paranoid/Puritan/rocket image of "the great bright hand reaching out of the cloud" (29)—a design motif of all four of Waite's Aces.

Then, surely, any twentieth-century novelist who dramatizes a Tarot reading invites readers to revisit *The Waste Land*, there to receive a push

20. A. E. Waite, *The Pictorial Key to the Tarot* (New York: Samuel Weiser, Inc., 1973), p. 59.

toward the source that Eliot cited for his own Tarot lore, Jesse Weston's *From Ritual to Romance*. The now well-known thesis of this book is that the Tarot symbology is derived neither from the Grail legend of medieval Christian romance nor from Celtic folklore (although both of these contribute overlays), but from an archaic vegetation- and fertility-cult of the pre-Indo-European Aegean, Near East, and India: a young year-god, who is son, brother, husband or lover of the Great Mother Goddess, is slain, ritually lamented, and buried or scattered in the fields in fall, then rises in spring to ascend again to the Mother, the myth standing ultimately for "a constantly recurring cycle of Birth, Death, and Resurrection, or Re-Birth, of all things in Nature."[21] Weston links the symbolism of Tarot suits backward to the sexual symbology of the fertility cult, then forward again to the Grail legend. For example, in the suit of Swords, Christianity saw the lance that pierced Christ's side, allowing the blood to fill the holy chalice or Grail—the Tarot suit of Cups—while at the same time "Lance and Cup (or Vase) were in truth connected together in a symbolic relation long ages before the institution of Christianity, or the birth of the Celtic tradition. They are sex symbols of immemorial antiquity and world-wide diffusion, the Lance, or Spear, representing the Male, the Cup, or Vase, the Female, reproductive energy."[22]

The rocket that Slothrop chases is intermittently called a "Grail"; his penis-lance is conditioned to tilt at the V-ness, Great Mother Goddess, or Grail-Cup, which is V-2. And since the Fool of the Tarot deck, and therefore Slothrop-as-Fool, is assimilable to the sacrificial year-god, Frank McConnell can plausibly regard Slothrop's eventual "scattering" (742) "as a grim version of the ancient *sparagmos*, the scattering and breaking down of the god Osiris, of Adonis, of the Son of Man in Isaiah, as a sacrificial death which may not guarantee, but at least establishes the chance for a birth and rebirth of the fertility of the human world."[23]

Indeed, the one of the Tarot Major Arcana that is of most prominent note in *Gravity's Rainbow* is Arcanum number zero, the Fool—consistently a background for Slothrop in his role as "holy Fool," as schlemihl and Peter Schlemihl, and in his final "invisible" preterition. In one of our

21. Jesse L. Weston, *From Ritual to Romance* (Garden City, N.Y.: Doubleday Anchor Books, 1957), p. 36.

22. Ibid., p. 75.

23. Frank D. McConnell, *Four Postwar American Novelists* (Chicago: University of Chicago Press, 1977), pp. 196, 197.

very last glimpses of him, he may be playing "Harmonica, kazoo" for a
rock band called "The Fool"—the name is as apt for Slothrop, "knowing
his Tarot" (742), as it is anachronistically clever for "an English rock
group" (742). For the record jacket photo, in which Slothrop's unidentifi-
able face may appear, the group poses "in the arrogant style of the early
Stones"—Rolling Stones, living stones, whose underground life They
cannot see—somewhere out in the preterite "East End, or South of the
River," where the V-2 blitz was worst. Mythically and historically, the
Fool is a scapegoat archetype: behind his Tarot identity there lies the sacrificial year-god, and before it the institution of the medieval court fool,
all-licensed to mock but subject to beatings for doing so. The fool is
assimilable also to Dionysus in his aspect as chthonic year-god—son of
Zeus or of Hades, slaughtered, dismembered, and eaten by Titans, then
reassembled in Semele's or Persephone's womb for a glorious rebirth.
Thus, it is under chthonic-Dionysian auspices that the Fool of *Gravity's
Rainbow* can sponsor what Pynchon calls the preterite "gift" of invisibility.
Paul Huson writes that "Dionysus was the reborn younger image of his
father, in one branch of the myth ... held to be the subterranean god of
death, Hades himself.... one of Hades' chief attributes was the power of
invisibility ... [and] his son Dionysus retained this characteristic."[24]

Further, the talisman of invisibility called the Hand of Glory, "a candle in a dead man's hand" (750), was sometimes understood as the boon
of Dionysus—alternatively, of Hermes—to thieves who, like Säure Bummer, would burglarize houses. But at moments of danger Slothrop-as-
Fool needs only to stand immobile, "thinking *invisible, invisible*" (382)—
since by nature They, his enemies, already are, in Huson's words, "victims of the spell, [who] far from seeing through the practitioner, are said
simply to refuse to acknowledge his presence among them."[25] Of the
Tarot's Major Arcana, the Fool is the one that is numbered zero, or given
no number at all: the one with "no agreed assignment in the deck"
(724); his "invisibility" is the freedom of the irrational, the magical, of
absolutely uncoerced, open choice. The antiparanoid Slothrop, free
long since of the Pointsman Plot, lies spread-eagled at a mandalic
"crossroads" in the Harz, belonging now wholly to the universal flux
where "one road [is] as good as another" (556), no choice is determined,
but where, as in quantum physics, *something* yet is felt, mysteriously,
acausally, to structure chaos: "Traditionally [the Fool] represents ... the

24. Paul Huson, *The Devil's Picturebook* (New York: C. P. Putnam's Sons, 1971), p. 116.

25. Ibid.

somehow mysteriously structured chaos which seems to lie at the root of existence.... In most decks ... he is generally left unnumbered, or counted as zero. He is the cosmic cipher, the unmarshalable, archetypal square peg, the existential everyman, nonpartisan, nonaligned and 'wild,' as the poker term has it ... all over the place, at home everywhere and nowhere. The divine bum."[26]

The crossroads itself Pynchon associates with the Tarot Major Arcanum known as The Hanged Man, in whose symbolism Waite reads "that after the sacred Mystery of Death there is a glorious Mystery of Resurrection"[27] (and some such "resurrective" reading perhaps explains why Eliot's Madame Sosostris, in the context of the unredeemed Waste Land, complains, "I do not find / The Hanged Man"). *Gravity's Rainbow* dramatizes (625) the legend of the "common criminal" hanged at the fork of a crossroads, ejaculating in death, with the semen that drops to Earth bringing forth a mandrake: very equivocally, however, a resurrective movement, since the mandrake, when pulled out of the ground, can kill, but, when made into medicines by a magician, can heal. The both/and quality transfers itself also to the mandala-crossroads: a "cross in a circle" (625), cf. Blicero's rocket-launching platforms, signifying how differentiating "crosses, swastikas" may be drawn inside the Jungian mandala, archetype of Wholeness, to specialize "Zone-mandalas" (625) for 1945's fallen world. Differentiate a mandala with spokes, for example, and it becomes the Wheel, Major Tarot Arcanum No. 10: the Wheel of fate and of causal determinism to which Slothrop seems bound for a while, and whose "ratcheting" is the sound of manipulated and time-bound progresses still under the interdictions of plots:

> Is he off so quickly, like Katje on her wheel, off on a ratchet of rooms like this, to be in each one only long enough to gather wind or despair to move on to the next ...? (257)

> Before his throat can stir, he's away, on the Wheel, clutching in terror to the dwindling white point of himself. (383)

For Waite the Wheel denies "chance" and posits "fatality"—as in the

26. Ibid., p. 121. Also, W. T. Lhamon has plausibly connected the image of the Tarot Fool, with his connotations of non-alignment, to the second syllable of Slothrop's name: r.o.p., "run on paper," is "the term used when an editor has the right to place an ad wherever is convenient in a paper." Lhamon, "The Most Irresponsible Bastard," *New Republic* 168 (April 14, 1973): 624–31.

27. Waite, *Tarot*, p. 119.

Hindu expression of the same archetype as the Wheel of Karma, the ratcheting cosmic dance of cause-and-effect, as also the Prussian spa Bad Karma, where Greta Erdmann helplessly lives out her fate. Pynchon glances also at the amusement-park "Wheel of Fortune" at Brighton (275) and at the weather-stripped latticework of the ferris wheel at Zwölfkinder ("there only for the clear mission: to lift and to frighten"—422); Slothrop has his first paranoid intimations while standing by the Casino's roulette wheel. Windmill wheels, too, often evoke the fantasy of the ongoing control of the world by other orders; one windmill is even called "The Angel" (106). And, finally, "the crosses of ... turning windmills could be spoke-blurs of the terrible rider himself, Slothrop's Rider" (509), the hallucinatory sky-cyclist whom Slothrop "sees" in the course of his foolish visit to Peenemünde's ruins: "the Bicycle Rider in the Sky, the black and fatal Edwardian silhouette on the luminous breast of sky, of today's Rocket Noon, two circular explosions inside the rush hour, in the death-scene of the sky's light. How the rider twirls up there, terminal and serene. In the Tarot he is known as The Fool" (501).

This made-up "constellation" exists to constellate opposites: weirdly, serenely spoke-blurring mandala and cross, freedom and determinacy, Fool and Wheel. At the very end of the book, in William Slothrop's hymn, "The Riders sleep by ev'ry road"—but the image remains as terminally ambiguous as before, for those who would take it prophetically, since the hymn itself means to preserve an intimacy of relation between destruction and "true return" (130), apocalypse and rebirth. As the sense of Oneness and of doom's imminence rest inside each other, the Fool in his bliss may at any time step right over the edge of the cliff where some Tarot decks show him poised obliviously, his face turned beatifically to the mandalic sun in the sky.

It is likely that Pynchon has elaborated his rider from Rilke's Tenth Elegy, where "the new stars of Pain-land" (99) form figures named by the spirit-lament to the dead youth climbing the mountain:

> Look: the *Rider*, the *Staff*, and that fuller constellation they call *Fruit-Garland*. Then on toward the pole: *Cradle*; *Way*; the *Burning Book*; *Doll*; *Window*.[28]

These constellations of course do not really exist in tradition; but if astrology and art alike are projective tower-systems, Rilke can make

---

28. Rilke, Tenth Duino Elegy, lines   90-92.

them up, quite as for Slothrop and Säure, smoking dope under a tree in Berlin, "it is possible ... to make up your own constellations" (366). In the same way, the rocket world, as perceived by those (like Etzel Ölsch, below) who helped build it, can produce a rocket astrology featuring "a Brennschluss point for every firing site. They still hang up there, all of them, a constellation waiting to have a 13th sign of the Zodiac named for it.... but they lie so close to Earth that from many places they can't be seen at all, and from different places inside the zone where they can be seen, they fall into completely different patterns" (302).

These changeful "patterns" seem, somehow, skyward projections of history's manifold branchings from switchpoints in time; and in one passage Pynchon folds the railroad-switchpoint metaphor, in turn, onto an image of the Big-Bang melee of modern cosmology: "Separations are proceeding. Each alternative Zone speeds away from all the others, in fated acceleration, red-shifting, fleeing the Center" (519). But any disdain for mere astrology that any such relativities might be heard to imply is played off against a rhetoric of counter-signals: not only the narrator's apparently serious (or deadpan) astrological references ("by now—early Virgo—he has become one plucked albatross" [712]), but also, much more compellingly, the sudden mesmeric lyrics whose force is such that no reader can take them as wholly ironic or mocking: "The great cusp—green equinox and turning, dreaming fishes to young ram, watersleep to firewaking, bears down on us" (236).

And, centrally, there is Pynchon's clear sympathy for Leni Pökler's vague "astrological" faith in acausal cosmic relatedness, a faith that Franz can only take for a misguided causalism:

> [Franz] kept at her astrology without mercy, telling her what she was supposed to believe, then denying it. "Tides, radio interference, damned little else. There is no way for changes out there to produce changes here."
>
> "Not produce," she tried, "not cause. It all goes along together. Parallel, not series. Metaphor. Signs and symptoms." (159)

The impulse to a holistic belief, again, *precedes*, and in its essence is not to be confused with, the building of any Zodiacal towers: Pynchon's critics, like Jung's, confuse at their peril the possible signs of authorial faith in an ultimate territory for literal assent to a map.

In his specific astrologizing, Pynchon follows Jung in liking to play with Pisces, the twelfth and final Zodiacal House (its boundary with Aries the cusp of the spring equinox: "dreaming fishes to young ram").

244

For Jung in *Aion*, there is a meaningful but not causal conjunction between the fact of Christ's birth at the astral point where Earth's rotational axis precessed into Pisces—inaugurating the 2000-year Age of Pisces and of Christianity—and the fact that so much early Christian symbolism and iconography was fish-related. The historical Christ and remembered Christ-image functioned for Christians, Jung argues, as reifications of the archetype of the self in its common expression as Anthropos or God-Man. Yet, since Christian psychology (or, anyway, the part of it that may have reached pathology on St. John's Patmos) dissociated the archetype of inner wholeness into two "purified" halves, light and dark, early Christian tower architects identified the mutually perpendicular fishes of Pisces with, respectively, Christ, ruler of the first half of the age, and the apocalyptic Antichrist-to-come. To prophesy from the astrological image is to predict the dispensation of Antichrist during the period following the precession of Earth's axis from the first fish into the second; this occurred in the sixteenth century, a period that inaugurated the ages of Renaissance, Reformation, empirical science, total technology, and total war. In further prophetic vein, Jung observed that we stand now, in our time, at the end of the Piscean Age and on its cusp with the Aquarian. The Anthropos of the new age, a Water-Bearer of human form, will demand that man somehow reconcile his ego with the collective unconscious, the latter symbolized, as everywhere in Jung's work, by water: "The astrological image of the Aquarian period is an image of man … or of the great human personality which lives in every human being and in the collective psyche. He pours water from a jug into the mouth of a fish, of the constellation of the so-called 'Southern Fish,' which represents the unconscious. This could mean that the task of man in the Aquarian Age will be to become conscious of his large inner self … and to give the utmost care to the unconscious and to nature, instead of exploiting it."[29]

But what exactly does this disciple of Jung's intend by her offhand "this could mean …"? The enormous metaphysical problem conveniently blurred here is of course the One/Zero choice that Pynchon's work so compulsively worries: in seeing "parallels" between history as known to hindsight and Earth's progress through the Sign of the Fishes, are we playing games of connect-the-dots as arbitrary, in fact, as the

---

29. M.-L. von Franz, *C. G. Jung: His Myth in Our Time*, trans. William H. Kennedy (Boston: Little, Brown & Co., 1975), p. 136.

game of finding personal relevancies in horoscope columns, or is it really true that, as Leni and Jung believe, a system of transcendental meaning, interconnecting all cells of reality, here gives soft sign of itself? One of Pynchon's ways of underlining the question is to plot several reminders, with subtle glances into "Piscean depths" (579), of Earth's present passage across the astrological cusp. "Two goldfish are making a Pisces sign" inside a fishbowl (174); the Allied office of Psychological Intelligence Schemes for Expediting Surrender is explicitly acronymized PISCES, though we must do our own acronymizing when we see a periodical journal called "Proceedings of the International Society of Confessors to an Enthusiasm for Albatross Nosology" (712). And if the Pynchonian history of modern times finds its synecdoche in modern German history, as I have suggested, the Piscean resonance has it that rocketman Wernher von Braun was born at the spring equinox (361, 588); further, that at the same equinox he gives himself up to the Allies; even that "the spring equinox of 1871" saw "Bismarck's elevation ... to prince and imperial chancellor" (419), and the modern Reich's unification. These passages across secular history's singular points are connected *somehow,* we are invited to feel, with the astrological moment. The connection is surely not a mechanical-causal one, although to say this should not be to forget (for Pynchon reminds us often enough) that the signs and the sense of connection are *plotted,* first by the novelist and ultimately by the ancient Chaldean and Babylonian star-gazers who projected the Piscean House in the first place. But yet again, Jung would say, the very facts of the psychic projection and of the imaginative resonances of the archetypes imply that a whole, living inside and outside at once, does preexist, invisibly—in one of Pynchon's most urgently meant throwaway lines, "Just cause you can't see it doesn't mean it's not there!" (677).

Mercurius

In *Of a Fire on the Moon,* Norman Mailer remarks on the magnitude of the popular awe that the Space Race America of the 1960s directed to Wernher von Braun and his "creation," the Saturn V booster rocket used in the moon flights. Mailer finds this awe most ironic in view of the fact that the rocket was far less a technological marvel than the frail, tiny, ultra-electronicized landing module that brought men onto the lunar surface; therefore, he infers, "man worships his phallus in preference to a drop of his seed.... Electricity is an avatar of hate which gives pain to the senses.... Whereas thoughts of the sun and royal spectacle are in the mystery of a flame. So von Braun was the heat in rocketry, the animal in the program. By public estimate he had been a Nazi—that was glamour enough."[30]

The phallic, "Nazi" thrust is "glamour enough," certainly, for Pynchon's Thanatz, who recalls V-2, ascending, as "Cruel, hard, thrusting into the virgin-blue robes of the sky" (465)—charismatic, Thanatz goes on to imply, as Christ the redeemer, Christ the transporter of souls heavenward against every earthly objection: "I think of the A4 ... as a baby Jesus, with endless committees of Herods out to destroy it in infancy" (464).

The rocket's phallically charismatic aspect must of course be taken as only one way of framing a vast archetypal complex: V-2/Tower/Temple/ Redeemer/Body of God/*axis mundus*/phallus. At this point Freudianism would be likely to find that only the last of these represents the "true" psychic meaning, which all the others disguise. But Pynchon's allegiance here, as throughout his work, is to Jung, for whom no single symbolic frame for an archetypal image can be fundamental, since all equally are mere groping after an unconscious content that eludes definition in words. One way to approximate the rocket's root meaning in this connection is to speak of a unification of vertically "ascending" material and psychic energies within what Jung designates in *Mysterium Coniunctionis* as the Mercurius archetype: "the desperately evasive and universal Mercurius ... who is none other than the 'unus mundus,' the original, non-differentiated unity of the world or of Being.... While the concept of the *unus mundus* is a metaphysical speculation, the unconscious can be directly experienced via its manifestations."[31]

In myth, one "manifestation" of the kind was the image of the god Hermes, which probably evolved from the phallic stone markers, or herms, that the ancient "Pelasgian," i.e., pre-Indo-European, Greeks set up to mark boundaries of farmers' fields. As they grew into local earth-spirits protecting the plots and avenging their desecrations, the herms were assimilated to the vegetative death-and-rebirth myths, more specifically to the year-god in his chthonic phase. The herm mediated between the surface of Earth and its depths, guided the dead, and

30. Norman Mailer, *Of a Fire on the Moon* (New York: New American Library, Inc., 1971), pp. 64, 65.

31. C. G. Jung, *Mysterium Coniunc-* tionis, vol. 14, *The Collected Works of C. G. Jung*, 20 vols., trans. R. F. C. Hull (Princeton, N.J.: Bollingen Series XX, Princeton University Press, 1970), p. 462.

more generally, later, could magically cross any interface-boundaries between hostile orders—as the Homeric Hermes crosses the no-man's land between Troy and the Greek camp to bring King Priam into his enemy's tent. While in Greece this god came to sponsor all political skill, commerce, and crossroads, and became, further, a trickster spirit of thievery, canny diplomacy, and all forms of nimble deceit, his Egyptian manifestation, Hermes Trismegistus or Thoth, remained more purely a psychopomp who guided souls to the underworld—cf. Mr. Thoth in *Lot 49*, the old man eager for death, and, in *Gravity's Rainbow*, the ship *Anubis*, named for the Egyptian jackal god whose function also was to lead dead souls out of the world. Quite as Hermes/Mercurius bore life's reproductive and resurrective energy up from its underground sources, Pynchon's V-2 in one narratorial fantasy "Begins Infinitely Below The Earth And Goes On Infinitely Back Into The Earth it's only the *peak* that we are allowed to see" (726)—the image further suggesting, within the terms of the alchemical and Hermetic philosophy that Jung so extensively studied, the rising of the Life-principle, as by the agency of the alchemical "heat of transformation" in a fuming flask, along a vertical axis, to unite levels of being.

For Jung the archetypal Mercurius was, like most fundamental archetypes, essentially a both/and: "He is a hidden 'hell-fire' in the center of the earth, and at the same time 'the fire in which God burns himself in divine love.' Thus he is always *a paradox containing within himself the most incompatible opposites.*"[32] Thus when we blend within the archetype, as it is easy to do, Mercurius/Hermes and Christ in their symbolic functions as year- and mediator-gods, we can identify the benignly mediatory Christ as the one in whom William Slothrop believed, as opposed to the Puritans' "elect" Christ, an artificially dissociated and "purified" shard of the larger archetypal meaning. And Jung said of Mercurius: "He who ascends unites the powers of Above and Below and shows his full power when he returns again to earth."[33] If Mercurius also incorporates the Fool of the Tarot, who "stands at the brink of a new beginning and ushers in the next phase,"[34] we may see Slothrop (Fool) and Gottfried (mock-Christ) as complementary, equal-and-opposite

32. Von Franz, *Jung*, p. 208.

33. Jung, *Mysterium*, p. 227.

34. See Alma A. Paulsen, "The Spirit Mercury as Related to the Individuation Process," in *The Reality of the Psyche*, Proceedings of the Third International Congress for Analytical Psychology, ed. Joseph B. Wheelwright (New York: G. P. Putnam's Sons, 1968), pp. 74–85.

aspects of the archetype, Slothrop mediating with Earth on behalf of a human race that has lost touch with it; Gottfried ascending to the orders of angels that are the vital imaginations of man, and, in Jungian terms, projections of the self onto the cosmos. The Rocket–Mercurius, connecting Earth and Heaven, darkness and light, is humanity's messenger in search of grace, while it is at the same time also a tower of technology, system and language, elaborated by "coal-tar Kabbalists" (590) out of the "preterite dung" (166), that may bury us Babel-wise someday in falling rubble.

Mercurius also may be imagined as a force working for man's fuller civilizing, by bringing literacy, light, and reason up out of a primal darkness: Egyptian Hermes-thrice-greatest or Thoth was held to have invented writing and to have produced works on alchemy, magic, and divination. The archetype is thus further assimilable to another major figure from Greek myth, Orpheus, who functions importantly in Pynchon's novel; "song," which is the "magic cape," and that other major Pynchonian symbol of life's connectedness, flowing water, have at least distant, and sometimes very near, Orphic resonances in *Gravity's Rainbow*. As Slothrop is about to have his climactic rainbow vision, he comes down to a stream in the Harz, and the narrator whispers that "There are harpmen and dulcimer players in all the rivers, wherever water moves" (622). Some lines from Rilke's *Sonnets to Orpheus* invoking "Spirits of lost harpmen" are then inserted, and the lost Slothrop discovers his long-lost mouth harp in the magical stream: chthonic Orpheus has been kind. For the benign Orpheus of Rilke's *Sonnets* is celebrated as a divine instructor in civilized and ordered arts:

> But you, divine one, unto the last still singing, although attacked by
> the flouted Maenads' throng, beautiful god, above the shrieks rose
> ringing among the destroyers your ordered upbuilding song.[35]

Since the ancient Orphics believed, with most educated Hellenes, that the universe brims with indwelling life, that all divinities really were One, the Orphic message was benign in the sense that it urged, as Herbert Marcuse would have it, a kind of "reality principle" vastly different from the rival Promethean one of work, production, ego-aggrandizement, and suppression of Eros. Orphism was, Marcuse says, "the image of joy and fulfillment; the voice which does not command but sings; the gesture which offers and receives; the deed which is peace

35. Rainer Maria Rilke, *Sonnets to Orpheus*, trans. C. P. MacIntyre (Berkeley: University of California Press, 1971), Part I, Sonnet 26, p. 53.

and ends the labor of conquest.... This is perhaps the only context in which the word *order* loses its repressive connotation: here, it is the order of gratification which the free Eros creates ... a productivity which is sensuousness, play and song."[36]

Very well: but Jung's Mercurius is a union of opposites, and as "we know by now," nearly every important image/allusion in Pynchon is a both/and; indeed, in *Gravity's Rainbow* the word *order* never *does* quite lose "repressive connotation." The novel also takes Orpheus as a figure who, since he rises *out of* the Earth, in this sense rebukes earthly darkness and continuity, as in the myth of his trying to rescue his wife Eurydice from the underworld. The narrator rather sourly tags Slothrop with an "Eurydice obsession, this *bringing back out of*," when Slothrop tries to save Bianca from whatever lurks in the "fetid carbide" hold of the *Anubis* (472). In the ancient Orphics' considerable body of didactic poetry, immortality was promised to those who could slowly rid themselves of the body, in order that they might rise to union with Dionysus, the supreme Orphic god-figure. The Orphics, that is, despised the flesh; the body was an evil shard to be cast off as the soul grew upward, away from its earthly nature. This nature they called the Titanic, in reference to the myth, central in their cosmology, that the Titans had seduced infant Dionysus away from his play, then killed and eaten him; Zeus, having punished the Titans for this crime by smiting them with his thunderbolt, fashioned the visible world from their bodies, with the result that every man now has a spiritual, Dionysian spark hidden inside his gross "Titanic" flesh—the spark that the Orphics meant to set free. But *Gravity's Rainbow* consistently takes earthly "Titans" as more real than, antecedent to, any rarefied "spirit" that would escape them: "In harsh-edged echo, Titans stir far below. They are all the presences we are not supposed to be seeing—wind gods, hilltop gods, sunset gods—that we train ourselves away from to keep from looking further even though enough of us do, leave Their electric voices behind in the twilight at the edge of town and move into the constantly parted cloak of our nightwalk till Suddenly, Pan—leaping—its face too beautiful to bear" (720).

To the extent that doctrinal Orphism, like the Christianity that it influenced, spurned these Titans, it closed its senses to the mystic connectedness symbolized by the great All-God Pan of later Hellenic myth.

36. Herbert Marcuse, *Eros and Civilization: A Philosophical Inquiry Into Freud* (New York: Vintage Books, 1962), pp. 146, 147, 149, 150.

Pynchon thus can offer, besides his positive, redemptive Orpheus, a negative, betrayed, and betraying one, who patronizes the Word of Christianized culture and of the technologized arts. This is the spirit who presides, as the final rocket approaches, over the Orpheus movie theater in Los Angeles, whose night manager, Richard M.—Nixon—Zhlubb, has long before "come out against ... 'irresponsible use of the harmonica'" (754): of the original, magical, sensuous, Orphic [mouth]harp, now officially regarded as a subversive instrument solely, belonging, with the kazoo, exclusively to preterite countercultures. For the neo-Orphic "freaks" (755) who "come gibbering in at you ... playing harmonicas and even *kazoos*" (755–56), Zhlubb intends to find "a nice secure home ... down in Orange County. Right next to Disneyland" (756).

*   *   *

The Mercurius archetype, then, frames the rocket as ithyphallic tower, vertical channel, or *axis mundi* connecting primordial, subterranean energies with human systems of myth and belief "above." That these human systems tend typically to arrange themselves, at the base of the visible tower, around a sacred zone in which a static, timeless Great Time of the gods irrupts into mundane, linear, human time, Pynchon has learned chiefly from the mythographer Mircea Eliade, who discusses the worldwide occurrence of this Myth of the Center: the world-axis conceived as a sacred tower, hill, tree, or world-navel along which underworld, surface, and upperworld meet, and around which the visible human world coalesces.[37] An evolved culture's chief city or temple is felt to mark the point where the axis, tree, omphalos, etc., passes through the world; in Christianity's redaction, for instance, Golgotha was the site of Adam's creation and of his burial (with Christ's blood dripping off the Cross and onto Adam's skull in the ground), the site also onto which Celestial Jerusalem would descend. Pynchon gives us this Christian Cross/World Tree in the form of its final dialectic successor in the mushroom cloud at whose photo Slothrop stares: "The white image has the same coherence, the hey-lookit-me smugness, as

37. For the general theory see Mircea Eliade, *The Myth of the Eternal Return, or Cosmos and History,* trans. Willard B. Trask (Princeton, N.J.: Bollingen Series XLVI, Princeton University Press, 1954), pp. 1–49.

the Cross does. It is not only a sudden white genital onset in the sky—it is also, perhaps, a Tree" (694).

It is also, of course, the summarizing eschatological symbol for the entire course of Western tower-building—recalling not only the pre-Indo-European Great Mother Goddess but also the Christian and Germanic World Trees; the Kabbalistic Body of God with the Shekhinah at its base ("her maidenhead at the horizon"—with the further quibble that the Hiroshima attack broke the A-bomb's "virginity"); even the fact that, as Pynchon correctly reports, Fritz Lang invented the rocket countdown ("10–9–8 u.s.w." [753]) for the blastoff in *Die Frau im Mond*, unwittingly echoing the Kabbalistic counting of ten paths between the Sephiroth along the Body of God. And again, all these arcane framings and numerologies give sign of, though in their complexities they also conceal, the instinct for Oneness, the understanding of life's essential coherence in "parallel, not series": "although the Rocket countdown appears to be serial, it actually conceals the Tree of Life, which must be apprehended all at once, together, in parallel" (753).

The Myths of the Center assume, according to Eliade, that no act of man is original, but all are ritual, since all repeat the prototypical act of the god who once bent to touch mundane time; the purpose of any conscious ritual act is to revalorize this divine irruption—this "White Visitation"—that took place In The Beginning. And so, the narrator hints, just as Christ's crucifixion established a prototypical mythic time for the Piscean Age, Gottfried's Ascent in the 00000 has established or will establish a mythos for the Raketen-Stadt-Zeit: in that shadowy future time out of which the narrator seems to speak near the end, the Great Firing seems already to have been taken as defining a new zero-point with reference to which the systems men live by have been realigned. As "Kabbalist spokesman Steve Edelman" tells a "visitor" to the Raketen-Stadt-Zeit, the constellations themselves are now different:

> "The Tree itself is a unity, rooted exactly at the bodenplatte. It is the axis of a particular Earth, a new dispensation, brought into being by the Great Firing."
>
> "But with a new axis, a newly spinning Earth," it occurs to the visitor, "what happens to astrology?"
>
> "The signs change, idiot," snaps Edelman.... "Here—" hefting a fat Xeroxed sheaf, "the Ephemeris. Based on the new rotation."
>
> "You mean someone's actually found the Bodenplatte? The Pole?"

"The delta-t itself. It wasn't made public, naturally. The 'Kai-
sersbart Expedition' found it."

A pseudonym, evidently. Everyone knows the Kaiser has no
beard. (753–54)

The last line derives from an old German saw characterizing an irrele-
vancy—"Who cares about the color of the Kaiser's beard?"—and so
seems, like Edelman himself, a scrim concealing some private allusion
or joke: Pynchon likes rustling numerous veils in our faces at once. The
passage does confirm on its way, however, that all along Enzian has
meant mythically his apparent intention to make a self-sacrificial ascent
in the rocket, 00001, that his Schwarzkommandos have scavenged. The
act, he has hoped, might be "the only Event that could have brought
[the Schwarzkommando factions] together" (673), inside their own
mythic time. We have heard him dreaming vaguely of co-opting in this
way the White North's own symbol, the rocket, and using it to establish
a "black" mythos to keep the tribe going, living on underground. He
has called this a dream of "Return" to the Hereros' spiritual "Center,"
but it is the old wistfully anarchic wish to enter a historyless Garden,
before or outside of time: "What Enzian wants to create will have no
history. It will never need a design change. Time, as time is known to
other nations, will wither away inside this new one. The Erdschweinhöhle will not be bound, like the Rocket, to time. The people
will find the Center again" (319).

To imply again the real hopelessness of this hope we have echoes both
of outdated Marxist idealism ("wither away") and, in one of Enzian's
later speeches (525), of Martin Luther King's "I have a dream" oration.
To the fantastic, anarchic dream of Return the White North opposes the
hard reified reality of its linear one-way time—a predestinarian,
"Puritan" order of time whose mere *illusion* of free will is expressed
sometimes by the Borgesian image of a labyrinth of branchings from
points of binary decision: "And now [Pavel's] head in Christian's steel
notch at 300 yards. Suddenly, this awful branching: the two possibilities
already beginning to fly apart at the speed of thought—a new Zone in
any case, now, whether Christian fires or refrains—jump, choose" (524).
The name Christian, perhaps too obviously, is apt, since Judeo-Chris-
tianity replaced the hoary old models of the eternal recurrence of time
with its new model of a linear time punctuated by divine irruptions,
each bearing a *moral* point for the Chosen, implying all together a tele-

ological plot for history. The Schwarzkommandos' suicidal Empty Ones have opted, although they do not exactly know it, for such a teleological-paranoid dispensation of time, by virtue of having chosen Herero fragmentation, deliberately unto death. Believing that what they have chosen is "tribal" as against "Christian" death, they hide from themselves, by this superficial distinction, their legacy of corruption by the Rhenish Missionary Society's "Baby Jesus Con Game" (318).

The Judeo-Christian sense of linear time and of chosenness/election (the seventeenth-century Puritans were sometimes called "the second Hebrews") has considerable psychic connection, further, with the "German" elements of the novel. The Rhenish missionaries who brought Baby Jesus to Südwest apparently brought also, congruently, their heritage of Götterdämmerung mythos with which to influence the Hereros: "[The Empty Ones] calculate no cycles, no returns, they are in love with the glamour of a whole people's suicide—the pose, the stoicism, the bravery" (318). Since for Pynchon the love of death and of apocalypse as a corollary to the acceptance of linear time is a general property of the North, the novel can frame the mystique alike in Christian and Germanic-pagan mythologies. As early Christians expected, feared, and (presumably) secretly wanted the End, early Teutons perversely bestowed on their World Tree, the great ash Yggdrasil, an inherent death-fatedness symbolized by the gnawing of the serpent Nidhögg on one of the Tree's roots and the grazing of four stags on its tender buds. At the first approach of the enemies of the gods, as the Twilight battle impended, the light god Heimdall would blow on the golden horn that he kept concealed in Yggdrasil. His usual station was near the great rainbow bridge, Bifröst, that connected the dwelling places of men with Valhalla—this additional frame for Pynchon's Rainbow is one of the several more sinister images he borrows from the Teutonic apocalypse. The Northern Lights that scare Slothrop, and that Pynchon connects with the I. G.'s plastics, were for the ancient Germans the iridescences from the shields of Valkyries who visited Earth's battlefields to steal warriors' souls for the armies of Valhalla. In one degenerate myth, the thunder—"the madness of Donar" (455)—is caused by the riding of what Pynchon faithfully describes as the malignant " 'Wütende Heer,' that company of spirits who ride the heaths of the sky in furious hunt, with great Woutan at their head" (75)—after whom Myron Grunton of the White Visitation wants to name the Schwarzkommando. The novel's Teutonic miscellany also includes—besides Faust, Tannhäuser, and Hansel and Gretel—one Stefan Utgarthaloki, "ex-member of management at the Krupp works here in Cuxhaven" (709) and host of the party infiltrated by Mexico and Bodine. This is the enchanter-king Utgardaloki, who entertained (and, *contra* Pynchon, wholly confounded) the gods Thor and Loki when they visited him at his castle in disguise. Hank Faffner, "engineer-on-the-scene" in one brief narratorial fantasy (665), is the giant Fafnir, who, with his giant-colleague Fasolt, comes temporarily to possess the Nibelungs' hoard, and the magical Ring, in the myth dramatized in Wagner's *Rheingold*.

Joseph Slade has already pointed to Pynchon's chief allegorical uses of Wagner's *Ring*: "In [this] operatic cycle, the gods doom themselves by their own avarice; they steal the ring of the Nibelungs, the black pygmies who labor beneath the earth, hating the gods."[38] Within the terms of this myth, the white Teutonic gods, "They," must suffer their Götterdämmerung and extinction, finally, because they are guilty of seeking to transfigure Earth by forging from its treasure an "impersonation of life" (166) as technology, war, money, power-mystique. When Tchitcherine's father, watching ships take on coal in Südwest, senses "power flowing wrong" (351), he intuits the Wagnerian secret: in coal's "preterite dung" (166) sleeps nothing less than the Great World Serpent, carbon chemistry's organic Ring of Life. The mandalic form's transformation, in F. A. von Kekulé's dream, to a diagrammatic benzene molecule encoding secrets of plastics, *is* the whites' theft of that treasure that they can only interpret as Ring of Power. The theft then begins a general movement toward synthetic tower-artifices of "death-transfigured," as Walter Rathenau says: "Look at the smokestacks, how they proliferate, fanning the wastes of original waste over … masses of city" (167). In Wagner, the treasure in its original form is a lump of gold, innocuous so long as guarded by Rhinemaidens, that may be forged to a ring that can bring world domination to any man or god who, in stealing the gold, forswears love.

The Teutonic myth system thus can be seen to exemplify how myths may function as veils for impulses that frighten the conscious mind, as according to Denis de Rougemont, "a myth arises whenever it becomes dangerous or impossible to speak plainly about certain social or religious matters, or affective relations, and yet there is a desire to preserve these or else it is impossible to destroy them."[39] A myth of sexual

38. Joseph W. Slade, *Thomas Pynchon* (New York: Warner Paperback Library, 1974), pp. 188, 190.

39. Denis de Rougemont, *Love in the*

Western World, rev. ed., trans. Montgomery Belgion (New York: Fawcett Premier Book, 1958), p. 21.

love, for example that of Tristan and Iseult of which Rougemont writes extensively, "*is needed to express the dark and unmentionable fact that passion is linked with death,* and involves the destruction of any one yielding himself up to it with all his strength."[40]

The Tristan/Iseult myth, originally Celtic, acquired the permanent German accent ratified by Wagner's *Tristan* from Wagner's own chief source, the *Tristan* of Gottfried von Strassburg, namesake, as I think probable, of Pynchon's Gottfried. A passage in *V.* crystallizes for that novel the motif of love/death that Pynchon calls "the Tristan-and-Iseult theme, indeed, according to some, the single melody, banal and exasperating, of all Romanticism since the Middle Ages: "the act of love and the act of death are one" (*V.,* 385). That the "some" among Pynchon's sources probably includes Rougemont is apparent in the latter's *Love in the Western World,* which in general claims that "Tristan's inclination for a deliberate obstruction turns out to be a desire for death and an advance in the direction of Death ... a death that means transfiguration, and is in no way the result of some violent chance.... the aim is still to unite an external with an internal fate, which the lovers deliberately embrace."[41] As Rougemont's "transfiguration" telegraphs, Pynchon's Blicero devotes his chief imaginative allegiance to the Tristan myth, understood in this way: identifying perverse (here, homosexual) love with death (723), "embracing" the "flame" of the Reich (98) and (perhaps literally) of the rocket's exhaust (758), lifting "flame" and "transfiguration" unfairly from Rilkean contexts in order to imagine his culture's long foreplay with death at last consummated: "Death only rules here. It has never, in love, become *one with* ..." (723). He means his rocket as a perverse irruption through the repressively rational nature of *Their* rocket, the Apparat, a creation of science and technology—as Tristan "means" his mystique of love/death to smash through the prevailing conventions of high-medieval courtship and marriage. The rocket excites Blicero by bending back to destroy not only literally the technicians at the launch sites, but symbolically its own rationalized and rationalizing creators.

Rougemont emphasizes this process (and it is one that Goebbels well understood) whereby myths that seek to appeal to deep needs for charisma feed, perversely and secretly, on imageries of safe rationality—and this of necessity when the official rational imageries are the only

40. Ibid., pp. 21, 22.   41. Ibid., p. 47.

ones visible from inside the closed system: "The mental habitus which [technology] imposes upon us exaggerates the tyranny of schedules, of 'measurable yield,' of social discipline, and of rational behavior in general to such a degree that a revolution of the soul becomes inevitable, by way of compensation: will the invasion of our lives by technology provoke that 'outburst of eroticism' which would tend to neutralize its dehumanizing effects?"[42]

For the Freud of Marcuse's *Eros and Civilization,* history is an ongoing repression of Eros by the "reality principle"; the Pynchonian premise that modern history is a self-actualizing paranoid system develops in part out of the general Freudian premise that all religious and mythic systems, neurotic behaviors of individuals, and real historical movements are driven by this dynamic of "civilizing" repression. Pynchon seems to imply that when a perverse "erotic outburst" like Blicero's occurs, we may understand it in these terms, as an originally healthy erotic (or "Orphic") impulse wholly perverted, corrupted in passage up through civilized framings. Or, in cognate Eliadean terms, Blicero's Great Firing is an attempt to revalorize future time, calling down "Great Time" and, by the act, losing private identity—himself *becoming* the myth. Indeed Blicero as a character *is* in effect his own myth: he is never directly visible in the novel (and may already be dead when Slothrop enters the Zone) but exists solely inside other characters' memories of him; that is, he coincides exactly and solely with various myths of him inside the book, as he does, inside these, with the myth of Tristan. Like other of Pynchon's similarly apocryphal characters—Lady V., Pierce Inverarity, Laszlo Jamf, Wimpe—Blicero seems to occasion Rougemont's question, "Where do our myths come from? Are they our inventions, or are we theirs?"[43]

*   *   *

It is quite remarkable that, in a 1974 review of *Gravity's Rainbow,* Earl Rovit could have so misunderstood the novel and have so flatly panned it, since five years before the review's publication an essay of his in the *American Scholar* had defined an "apocalyptic imagination," declined

42. Denis de Rougemont, *The Myths of Love,* trans. Richard Howard (New York: Random House, 1963), p. 28.

43. Ibid., p. 15.

from Romanticism, as "our best model [in current fiction] for viewing
our contemporary human condition."[44] In literature's New Apocalypse, Rovit said, no gravitational center, no myth of communal commitment, can hold; gravity is transcended by the propensity of
apocalypse "to burst the circumference of a spherical form without
making a return—actual or symbolic—to some primal matrix, some
given and unalterable crucifixional center."[45]

The arch question of this arch-apocalypticism is identified as the
smart-mouthed "why not?"—the question, Rovit might have mentioned but did not, that *V.*'s Whole Sick Crewmembers keep continually
asking. *"Why not?"* implies, says Rovit,

> the Principle of Indeterminacy ... at the base of all ... reckoning. The
> naked form of the Apocalypse, the Word in metamorphosis, flesh
> becoming the Word and the Word spewing itself back into the world
> as macerated flesh.

> The Apocalypse is the cancerous dream that the alienated libido
> requires for its autoerotic consummation. It is the *Endlosung,* the
> extravagant solution of dissolution, whereby man shall be con-
> sumed with that which he was nourished by. The end of his exile, all
> the words torn syllable by syllable into flying fragments; the dis-
> memberment of all remembrance; Orpheus; boy-bomb.[46]

Depurple the prose as you read, and what you will still have must surely
be one of the clearest anticipations in modern critical writing of the prophetic imageries of a future novel. Now what has been often, as here,
loosely called the apocalypticism of so much post-1945 fiction, which is
for Saul Bellow's Herzog, and for Saul Bellow, essentially a long, naive,
self-indulgent whine, can indeed often appear as the mere indulgence
of un- or antihumanistic impulses. But some of the best among this
writing can as easily be taken as a new dialect of the ancient humanistic
voice that traditionally has warned *against* solipsistic tendencies, perverse death wish, and moral passivity. Why does Rovit, rhapsode of
apocalypticism, take Pynchon's novel when it arrives as "a gargantuan
bore ... a 760-page Rube Goldberg machine which depresses the
soul,"[47] unless, wrongly, he takes Pynchon's merciless exposé of the
psychology, history, and mythos of certain modern pathologies for,

44. Earl Rovit, "On the Contemporary
Apocalyptic Imagination," *American
Scholar* 37 (Summer 1968): 453–68; quote
from p. 463.

45. Ibid., pp. 464, 465.

46. Ibid., p. 462.

47. Earl Rovit, "Some Shapes in Recent
American Fiction," *Contemporary Literature*
15 (Summer 1974): 552, 553; quote from
p. 553.

instead, a perverse celebration of these (like, to all appearances, his own earlier celebration)? To defend, against Herzog and Rovit, this novel's claim to a moral and intellectual burden larger and saner than that, must be in part to demonstrate its concern for what may *in fact* exist beyond the self and all of the psychic techniques for self-projection to sky, angels, death mystique. In Pynchon's novel, I would argue, the One does appear, though in other psychic regions (for whose direction Pynchon's best code word is "Earth") than in that sky-dream of the All or the Nothing where shallower apocalypses can lose themselves, lose their Eros, their minds. In the rest of this chapter I move toward a definition of the One that, existing at least as a possibility in Pynchon's world, may save that world's sanity and, perhaps, any claims the novel may have to a "greatness" humanistically and humanely conceived.

Goddess and Serpent

Inside the mandalic (circular) shape of Blicero's rocket-launching platforms, already described, there appear differentiating lines, demon-like "sortings"—and beneath Nazi swastika and Christian cross there lurks their ancestor, the sun sign sorted by sun- and sky-worshiping Germanic tribes from a first, archetypal dimension of psychic experience, the mandalic shape of the One that obtained, presumably, before the earliest civilizations. Like slips of projection-test paper littered about a psychiatrist's clinic, these mandalas with designs inside are littered about Pynchon's novel: for example, the latrine graffito that Slothrop sees,

which is "the A4 rocket seen from below" (624), and the Schwarzkommando insignia

(361) that Enzian's men mysticize by identifying the rocket-firing switch positions with sites inside the Herero village, "itself ... a mandala"

(563).[48] When Sir Stephen Dodson-Truck finds Slothrop puzzled by a diagram of a rocket component, he breezily identifies in the image an ethnohistorical symbolism with Freudian overlays: "Oh … that coil symbol there happens to be very like the Old Norse rune for 'S' *sol,* which means 'sun' … the Goths … had used a circle with a dot in the center. This broken line evidently dates from a time of discontinuities, tribal fragmentation perhaps, alienation—whatever's analogous, in a social sense, to the development of an independent ego by the very young child, you see" (206).

Slothrop, who just now would rather be reading his Plasticman comic, "doesn't see, not exactly" (206), presumably because, like Carroll Eventyr in his inability to sense his psychic connection with the dead Peter Sachsa, "he doesn't *remember* … he's been brought up a Christian, a Western European, believing in the primacy of the 'conscious' self and its memories, regarding all the rest as abnormal or trivial" (153). It is at this point—among others—that Pynchon's mysticism and his historicism converge—with the scribbled mandalas of *Gravity's Rainbow* suggesting that you envision history as something like what you see when you look down a tubular kaleidoscope: angular colored shards, which are archetypal signs and culture's deployments of them, falling into new patterns with each twist of the outer, mandalic rim. The shards have fixed shapes, their mutual relations only changing, and so, it may be, archetypes as seen from outside recur as amusing clichés for the angels:

> After you get a little time in—whatever *that* means over here—one of these archetypes gets to look pretty much like any other, oh you hear some of these new hires, the seersucker crowd come in the first day, "Wow! Hey—that's the-th' *Tree o' Creation!* Huh? Ain't it? Jeepers!" But they calm down fast enough. (411)

The novel's conjuring trick is to rescue these shapes from cliché by always keeping them moving, since their historically effective life inheres in motion, in constant change of specific reference. One notably

48. Thomas H. Schaub notes a subtler, but very centrally placed manifestation of the differentiated-designs-inside-mandalic-circles image: Mexico's map of London shows V-2 strikes as *circles,* while Slothrop's map show his sexual conquests as *stars,* and, of course, the two maps coincide exactly, so that each site is a star inside a circle. Schaub doesn't mention the novel's other occur-rences of the image, however, and thus fails to mention that this one reverses the usual signs: star-inside-circle = love inside death, while elsewhere the outer mandala is a "life" sign, and the designs inside it signify a death-tending debasement, differentiation, of Oneness. See Schaub, *Pynchon: The Voice of Ambiguity* (Urbana: University of Illinois Press, 1981), p. 17.

busy shard is the sun-sign "S" of Dodson-Truck's "Old Norse rune," which recurs doubled (300 ff.) as the double-integral sign of the calculus, as the yew-tree rune standing for death, as the shape of the rocket tunnels at Nordhausen, and, single again, as the standard notational symbol for entropy in physics. Pynchon's narrator turns the book's kaleidoscopic rim, rescuing such shapes from symbolic inertness, as analogously, the author implies, the One dreams itself in slow turnings, governing all the patterned recurrences that let history know itself from inside.

With this metaphor for history Pynchon mixes the established railroad-switchpoint one: with the book's historicism suggesting that, in the West, five crucial point-transferences (or quantum-displacements of the turning rim) have marked changes profound enough to have made men "forget" an earlier dispensation. The most recent such "point," that of the 1945 Zone, is the one at which the novel's main action strategically places itself: the ephemeral openness here will soon vanish into the forms of the new cybernetic and atomic ages, succeeding the Age of Machines. At the next point back, in Descartes, Newton and Puritanism's seventeenth century, the new scientific order, ultimately to become the rational-bureaucratic, takes over from the medieval synthesis. At the point before that, synchronized to an astrological cusp, Christianity succeeds the pagan plurality. The fourth point back is that of the succession of Earth-worshiping, matriarchal peoples by the nomadic Sky-Father peoples whose descendants still rule Indo-Europe. Finally, half seriously, Pynchon even looks back as far as the Paleozoic coal swamps, proposed in Geli Tripping's mystical vision (as in some old, bad dinosaur movie) as "the world just before men," where the human species itself is about to "fall" from vegetative preconsciousness: "Canyons are opening up, at the bottoms are steaming fumaroles, steaming the tropical life there like greens in a pot, rank, dope-perfume, a hood of smell ... human consciousness, that poor cripple, that deformed and doomed thing, is about to be born" (720).

It is worth noting here that this whole model is quite likely indebted to Henry Adams's 1906 "Rule of Phase" explication of history, in which the durations of successive phases (analogized to changing phase-states of matter) follow a law of "inverse squares," each age lasting as long as its predecessor's duration's square root (so that Adams, like Pynchon, can finally get lost in vague extrapolations to geological time):

1917–1921: Ethereal Phase [age of Thought: thought was to
reach "the limit of its possibilities" 15 years after
Adams's essay]
1900–1917: Electric Phase
1600–1900: Mechanical Phase
90,000 B.C.–1600: Religious Phase
.... : Instinctive Phase[49]

Hovering over Geli's swamps there can again be made out, the narrator says, the Piscean "equinox ... green spring equal nights" (720), the same annunciatory sign that recurs, two turnings or switchpoints later, to mark the Christian advent, and again, still later, to mark the cusps of the secular history of modern Germany. The sign seems affixed to the mandalic outer rim of the shardlike world, to the great master gear of the One, of which the Zodiac is a tower-declension. This rim, further, appears most often in *Gravity's Rainbow* in its aspect as cosmic uroboros, the archetypal Great World Serpent holding its tail in its mouth, "the dreaming Serpent that surrounds the World" (412): one of Pynchon's two major mythological/psychic signs, the other being the Great Mother Goddess, that suggest ways of dimly discerning or working back to the "edge" of the One. Among the worldwide myths of the Serpent, Ayido Hwedo, the beneficent Rainbow Snake of modern West Africa, probably most closely resembles Pynchon's Rainbow Snake, "its coils in rainbow lashings in the sky" (721). But the archetype, with its root sense of unity and wholeness within an essentially static creational order, may be as old mythically as man's original wonder in contemplating what he feels as an insouled creation, before any gods interpolate themselves into what Henri Frankfort has called, after Martin Buber, man's sense of his I-Thou relatedness to the extrahuman.[50] In Jung's system the World Serpent, like other mandalic symbols, "express[es] the union of opposites—the union of the personal, temporal world of the ego with the non-personal, timeless world of the non-ego."[51]

Ancient European and Mediterranean peoples could link the Serpent with the great World Ocean that, as on Achilles' shield, surrounded all known lands—and Pynchon follows Jung's psychic

---

49. See Henry Adams, "The Rule of Phase Applied to History," in *The Degradation of the Democratic Dogma* (New York: Macmillan Co., 1919), pp. 267–311.

50. See Chapter 1 of Henri Frankfort, et al., *Before Philosophy: The Intellectual Adventure of Ancient Man* (Baltimore: Pelican Books, 1949).

51. Aniela Jaffe, in C. G. Jung et al., *Man and His Symbols* (New York: Dell Publishing Co., 1968), p. 267.

mythology in making flowing water itself a chief symbol for the Great Round or Underground that enfolds and precedes all consciously known realities. The Midgard Serpent of Teutonic myth lay submerged in the World Ocean and would join the other primeval monsters in defeating the gods of Valhalla; the Tarot Major Arcanum called the World was sometimes drawn (though not in Waite's deck) with a uroboros or a circular river around the margin. As in D. H. Lawrence's novel, the Aztecs' chthonic Plumed Serpent was a split-off complement to a holy Sky Bird—but the mystical Lawrence of *Apocalypse* imagines a cosmic "Dragon," far antecedent to any mythic differentiation, of starry primordial nights: "Don't let us forget that when the Dragon stirs green and flashing on a pure dark night of stars it is he who makes the wonder of the night, it is the full rich coiling of his folds which makes the heavens sumptuously serene, as he glides around and guards the immunity, the precious strength of the planets, and gives lustre and new strength to the fixed stars, and still more serene beauty to the moon."[52]

Further, in this late, strange book, Lawrence argues that just as, in John's vision, the Great Mother Goddess, who immemorially had lent "serene beauty" to her sky-aspect the moon, was cast out as the Whore of Babylon, so the Sky Snake was cast down as Lucifer to whisper evil to men thereafter from the black underworld. Earthly "depths" and their psychic correlatives, which potentially, in Jung, are our wellsprings of wisdom, were now to be feared and repressed: they had become the snake to corrupt what Laszlo Jamf calls "our ruinous garden" (413)— such being the neo-Christian beliefs that impel Them to act as They do in conditioning Slothrop and Tchitcherine to fear blackness. Apocalyptic consciousness turns archetypes against themselves, against the One out of which they arise; thus, although Pynchon's Great Rainbow Ser-. pent is clearly a symbol of the ever-recurrence of life in Earth's closed system, what They hear when the Serpent "whispers" in Kekule's dream is Satan's whisper to Eve that the system of life *"can be changed"* (413). The Serpent of cyclicality is betrayed "into a system whose only aim is to *violate* the Cycle ... No return, no salvation ... that's not what They, nor Their brilliant employee Kekule, have taken the Serpent to mean. No: what the Serpent means is—how's this—that the six carbon atoms of benzene are in fact curled around into a closed ring, *just like that snake with its tail in its mouth*, GET IT?" (413).

52. Lawrence, *Apocalypse*, pp. 145, 146.

If Pynchon can be said to take up the antirationalism of nineteenth-century vitalist thought, the line can be seen running directly back among scientists; with tangential connections to quantum physics, through Jung; and, among novelists, through the "prophetic" Lawrence, whose *Apocalypse* sets out to describe how "the cosmos became anathema to the Christians, though the early Catholic Church restored it somewhat after the crash of the Dark Ages. Then again the cosmos became anathema to the Protestants after the Reformation. They substituted the non-vital universe of forces and mechanistic order, everything else became abstraction, and the long, slow death of the human being set in."[53] And thus "we are unnaturally resisting our connection with the cosmos, with the world, with mankind, with the nation, with the family. All these connections are, in the Apocalypse, anathema, and they are anathema to us. *We cannot bear connection.* That is our malady."[54]

Lawrence's claim that medieval Catholicism somewhat "restored the cosmos" refers, of course, to the Virgin Mary cult that flourished in France during the thirteenth century—for Henry Adams the high point of European civilization—when the Virgin of Adams's *Education* and of his *Mont-Saint-Michel and Chartres* inspired the building of the great Gothic cathedrals and ruled the mysteries of heaven and earth, and of courtly love. In Pynchon's novels, in Adams, and in mythology, the Great Mother Goddess archetype has a more complex case history than does the Serpent—the Goddess being, of the two, the more highly visible and effective in history. If Jung is right, it is one individuational stage advanced from the uroboros, which in turn is an evolved specification of the mandala. As Erich Neumann explains the psychic process:

> The uroboros stands between the formless, purely effective phe-
> nomena of the "archetype *an sich*" and such already specified
> figures of the primordial archetype as the Archetypal Feminine or
> the Archetypal Masculine. But the transitions between the uroboros
> and the primordial archetype of the Feminine, and between the
> latter and the archetype of the Great Mother, are fluid. For the
> degree of mixture between the archeyptes and the difficulty of dis-
> tinguishing the still almost formless figures from one another
> increase as we penetrate more deeply into the collective uncon-

53. Ibid., p. 48.   54. Ibid., p. 198.

scious—that is to say, the older the symbol and the less developed the consciousness of the personality in whose psyche it appears.[55]

The "anima" archetype that Jung located in the unconscious of every male is a connective Eros, as opposed to the differentiating Logos, the "animus," which lurks in every female. Pynchon's fiction, here utilizing Jung and Adams at once, repeatedly emphasizes the fact that the Indo-European culture of dominant "aminus" has borne, indeed, its animus toward the Archetypal Feminine wherever she has attmpted to reassert her power. The early Puritans, notes Adams in *Mont-Saint-Michel and Chartres*, reacted furiously against all remainders of Virginolatry because the old cult of Mary had connoted a kind of benign cosmic lawlessness, a serenely arbitrary mercifulness toward preterite rabble, in whose minds the Virgin offered a gentle alternative to the strict justice and impersonal austerity of the Trinity. Adams's Virgin, knowing "that the universe was as unintelligible to her, on any theory of morals, as it was to her worshippers,"[56] remained fickly "inviolate and calm"—Pynchon's words to describe Lady V. as, in her Victoria Wren phase, she watches bloody political riots "as if she saw herself embodying a feminine principle, acting as complement to all this bursting, explosive male energy" (*V.*, 192). Against the rationalistic, Machiavellian "fox" of Signor Mantissa, V. incarnates Adams's Virgin who stood, self-absorbed, "above law; [taking] feminine pleasure in turning hell into an ornament"[57]—such an ornament, say, as Victoria's carved ivory comb with five crucified soldiers linking hands. The V-force again rears in *Gravity's Rainbow*, against Their bureaucratizing intentions, not only phallically, but simultaneously as Jung's "loving and terrible mother," a Rocket-Anima at once nurturant, succoring, stifling, and killing.

The novel's implied mythography of the Goddess seems to adopt the widely accepted premise that the Neolithic, possibly even the Paleolithic, period in Europe, the Near East, and India belonged largely to Her—with local goddesses of fertility slowly evolving, in the planting societies before the Indo-European migrations, into varying forms of a universal Earth Mother. This Mother, like her archetypal antecedent the

55. Erich Neumann, *The Great Mother: An Analysis of the Archetype*, 2d ed., trans. Ralph Manheim (Princeton, N.J.: Bollingen Series XLVII, Princeton University Press, 1963), p. 19.

56. Henry Adams, *Mont-Saint-Michele and Chartres* (Cambridge, Mass.: Riverside Press, 1933), p. 274.

57. Ibid., p. 274.

Great Serpent of the entropic round, spoke in all her forms of the mutability of life and death, of creation's indwelling divinity, of time's cyclical nature.[58] Thus the switchpoint at which the old matriarchal societies ruled by the Goddess were displaced by patriarchies brought with the Indo-European warrior-hunters, with their trinity of Sky-Gods, was the time of a separation into the foreground of a self-servingly "heroic," moralistic, "front-brain faith" (590) in male predation. Clearly, though, Pynchon wants readers to side with the Goddess: since the myth of Theseus slaying the Cretan Minotaur is very likely a memory-refraction of the Dorian or Mycenean Greeks' overpowering of the Minoan Earth-Mother culture (as Mary Renault assumes in her pleasant novel *The King Must Die*), it is appropriate that Theseus-in-the-labyrinth is Pointsman's favorite masturbatory fantasy, since it is also his masochistic metaphor for his own service to Them. Yet another most pertinent, and even slyer, reference to the displacement of Earth by Sky, female by male, occurs in *Gravity's Rainbow*'s "Evensong" passage about Christmas 1944 in England: The White Visitation's "longtime schiz ... believes that *he* is World War II," thus that he is "to die on V-E Day" (131), and the narrator comments, "If he's not in fact the War then he's its child-surrogate, living high for a certain term but come the ceremonial day, look out. The true king only dies a mock death. Remember. Any number of young men may be selected to die in his place while the real king, foxy old bastard, goes on" (131).

The decadent year-god rite to which the paranoid metaphor alludes is one that may have developed in Greece as religious allegiance and political power moved away from the priestesses of the Earth Mother. The ceremonial king, originally a powerless consort of the ruling priestess, one day deigned no longer to be sacrificed at the end of his ritual term, so that for his real death a mock death was substituted, the king yielding up his sovereignty for a day (or for some token period) to a surrogate boy-king who died at day's close. In the myth of Zeus's son Zagreus (Dionysus) being devoured by Titans, Robert Graves finds a memory of "the annual sacrifice of a boy which took place in ancient Crete: a surrogate for Minos the bull-king"[59]—cf. also Graves's glance at

58. This is the Goddess's "Tender Loving Care" as so designated in Günter Grass's farcical novel of mythic/sexual/culinary history, *The Flounder* (Der Butt)—the only other contemporary novel I know of in which the Goddess is given such a central role as in Pynchon.

59. Robert Graves, *The Greek Myths,* vol. 1 (Middlesex, Engl: Penguin Books, 1955), p. 119.

"Oenomaus [who] agreed to die a mock death on seven successive mid-winters, on each occasion appointing a surrogate [who] was killed in a chariot crash, and the King stepped out from his tomb where he had been lurking to resume his reign."[60] Male, Machiavellian mobilizations of Lion and Fox against the goddess Fortuna have gone on consistently, in Pynchon's view, from the times of Achaeans and Old Testament Hebrews down to the time of the plot, in *V.*, of the (lion) Gaucho and (fox) Signor Mantissa to kidnap the Venus of Botticelli, whom Mantissa claims to love.

Although the Lady of *V.*, descending from Henry Adams through Freud, is most visibly the goddess of history-as-neurosis, of Herbert Marcuse's and Norman O. Brown's neo-Freudian sexual politics, the V-2 Goddess of *Gravity's Rainbow*, while she includes this first Lady, discernibly reaches deeper, several historical switchpoints' worth earlier. She is essentially Jung's and Robert Graves's and mythology's mistress of vegetation, of the "green uprising" (720) that holds itself invisible until it can begin reinspiriting all men's cleared, rectilinear spaces, as in a family of reverent, whispered passages:

> They found the countryside, this year, at peace by a scant few days.
> Already vines are beginning to grow back over dragon's teeth,
> fallen Stukas, burned tanks. The sun warms the hillsides, the rivers
> fall bright as wine. (281)

> But trees, beech and pine, have begun to grow in again where
> spaces were cleared and leveled for housing or offices—up through
> the cracks in the pavement, everywhere life may gain purchase, up
> rushes green summer '45, and the forests are still growing dense on
> the upland. (502)

> The site is a charred patch becoming green with new weeds, inside
> a copse of beech and some alder. Camouflage metal stands silent
> across a ghostly crowd of late dandelions.... Forget-me-nots are
> growing violent blue violent yellow among the snarl of cables and
> hoses. Swallows have built a nest inside the control car. (560)

We may call by any of the Goddess' many names the influence that intervenes to make Slothrop "intensely alert to trees, finally ... understanding that each tree is a creature" (552); it is Her breath in the breeze that makes sentient pines whisper then to him their antimechanical counsel: "He shakes his head. 'There's insanity in my family [of loggers].' He looks up. The trees are still. They know he's there. They prob-

60. Ibid., vol. 2, p. 38.

ably also know what he's thinking. 'I'm sorry,' he tells them, 'what can I do?' A medium-sized pine nearby nods its top and suggests, 'Next time you come across a logging operation out here, find one of their tractors that isn't being guarded, and take its oil filter with you. That's what you can do'" (553).

And the Goddess is close also whenever her cult emissaries appear— sentient stones, snakes, and Pynchonian Holy Pigs, the pig having been, with the snake, her constant chthonic, "earthy," companion in myth. She may even be said to inspire the novel's very narrative energy, rather as Graves believes his White Goddess (though primarily in her malefic aspect as Pitiless Muse) to inspire all genuine poetic impulse: "The test of a poet's vision, one might say, is the accuracy of his portrayal of the White Goddess.... The reasons why the hairs stand on end, the eyes water, the throat is constricted, the skin crawls and a shiver runs down the spine when one writes or reads a true poem is that a true poem is necessarily an invocation of the White Goddess, or Muse, the Mother of All Living, the ancient power of fright and lust—the female spider or the queen-bee whose embrace is death."[61]

Of course, Pynchon's Goddess is primarily felt as benign, since she sponsors life's counterentropic "green uprising"; yet, were this uprising's image not also in part compounded of "fright," she could not also be assimilable to V-2. Her malign aspect creates the paranoid weather when Slothrop walks through ruined Berlin, where, all sheltering walls having been blown away, the green arrival of spring is understood only to promise a future death-whiteness: "Scarred trees are back in leaf, baby birds hatched and learning to fly, but winter's here behind the look of summer—Earth has turned over in its sleep, and the tropics are reversed" (373).

Greta Erdmann likewise feels threatened by the "green underbrush" that is reconquering ruins "out by one rocket site":

> Pieces of pavement were visible here and there among the green underbrush. It seemed that if they followed the road they would come to a town, a station or outpost ... it wasn't at all clear what they would find.... Gravel spilled salt-and-pepper downhill toward a river they heard but couldn't see ... Remains of houses could be glimpsed, back in the trees. There was now a retreat of the light, though it was still before noon, and the forest grew no thicker here. In the middle of the road, giant turds showed up, fresh, laid in

61. Robert Graves, *The White Goddess: A Historical Grammar of Poetic Myth* (New   York: Farrar, Straus & Giraux, 1966), p. 24.

twists like strands of rope—dark and knotted. What could have left them? ... Ahead of them, the path curved on, into trees. But something stood now between them and whatever lay around the curve: invisible, impalpable ... some *monitor*. Saying, "not one step farther. That's all. Not one. Go back now".... They were both terrified. (485)

The "fright" is to see the pavement but not to hear one's tread on it, to hear streams but not to be able to see them, to watch light retreat inexplicably, as if by unseen direction. This paranoiac nature excursion, like others in the novel, is sensitized to the shimmering, moted veils that one notes when passing "into the countryside, into the quilted dark fields and the wood, the beginning of the true forest, where a bit of the ordeal ahead starts to show, and our hearts to feel afraid" (239); anyone who has ventured into strange woods at night will have felt this fickle, unfriendly mood of the Goddess. And all of her cults, certainly including Pynchon's—every mythology of female Earth, Moon, and Night, more ancient than male Sun and Sky—contains inherently the maternal both/and. A final, non-European, example is offered by the rare glimpses we are afforded in *Gravity's Rainbow* of the Hereros' Südwest mythology, which was in general holistic. But now, to the elders' confused memories of the mythology of the One, the younger Hereros, raised in the Nazified North, oppose an identification of Moon with Wagnerian "destiny"; and the whole conflict is colored in turn, for both sides, not only by the rocket's mystique, but also perhaps by an original ambivalence about the Moon Mother herself: "There are those down in the Erdschweinhöhle, younger ones who've only known white autumn-prone Europe, who believe Moon is their destiny. But older ones can remember that Moon, like Ndjambi Karunga, is both the bringer of evil and its avenger" (322).

In fact, a going debate in *Gravity's Rainbow* concerns whether the moon, once reached, will prove to be kind and habitable, or only waste, dead rock. Blicero whispers of this to Gottfried at bedtime, as does Franz Pökler to Ilse, both children, of course, preferring the pleasant fantasy to their elders' rational knowledge. But the odd irony is that the elders' desire somehow to *get to* the moon by means of a rationalized technology expresses ultimately their own deep, preconscious intuition to the effect that planets, dead rock, creation in general, are somehow, after all, "alive." This is the faith or instinct or wish that lies at the core of Blicero's corrupted worship of Rilkean angels whose realm lies moonwards, and that likewise inspires Pökler's fantasies of space travel. Northern minds, no less than any Herero's or Kirghiz shaman's, participate at depth in the myth of stone-alive that is *Gravity's Rainbow*'s encoding of that "true" mysticism that can subvert all of northern culture's perverse rationalistic designs. The Earth Goddess is the last anthropomorphic image, the Great Serpent the last animal one, on the way of archetypal stations back down to the Jungian domain—not, here, the Masonic—of "living stones," where my final subsection begins.

The Dream of the One; Descent

Pynchon's geology is the least salient of his physical sciences in the novel, but there exist enough offhand allusions to certain recent developments in geological theory to make these seem, like the quantum mechanics in physics, pertinent and encouraging. Since the late 1950s, the Plate Tectonic theory of Earth's crustal movements has assembled much greatly persuasive evidence for its model whereby the rigid basaltic "plates" of the lower crust move like great conveyor belts over the surface, some of their edges being destroyed as they plunge, at plate boundaries, back into the mantle, while at other boundaries new crust is created from new basalt yielded by upwelling mantle material. The continents' light granitic plates ride passively on the lower plates' backs; thus the continents drift, and the map of the world changes, infinitesimally slowly. Or as Pynchon's narrator puts it, the Earth at depth is characterized by a "crust and mantle hum of mystery" whose rumor lies "beyond" our "poor hearing" (722). Pynchon having provided an old term for the single great southern hemispherical land mass before the jigsaw-split at the proto-Atlantic, Hereros and Argentines can dream of "Gondwanaland, before the continents drifted apart, when Argentina lay snuggled up to Südwest" (321); the proto-continent serves both groups, meretriciously or otherwise, as a symbol of the "pre-Christian Oneness" (321) that both want to recapture. Meretricious it may indeed be, as used against them, to con them: von Göll convinces the Argentines that his Martin Fierro movie can somehow effect a return to innocence, to brotherhood with the preterite Africans, as when—in fact, long before man existed—"the Mesozoic refugees took the ferry not to Montevideo, but to Lüderitzbucht" (388). Again, genuine and respectable science lends itself as easily to employment—fairly by Pynchon, spuriously by von Göll—in service of the Earth-alive myth as do diverse other systems, including of course philosophical/literary (Romantic) tradition. Thoreau at Walden, observing the "excrementitious" shapes that melting subsoil develops in spring, comparing these to the flowerings of organs out of animal germ cells, these further to the flowerings of words, etymologies, that would describe such growths, reached ultimately the assertion that "there is nothing inorganic.... The earth is not a mere fragment of dead history, stratum upon stratum like the leaves of a book, to be studied by geologists and antiquarians cheifly, but living poetry ... not a fossil earth, but a living earth; compared with whose great central life all animal and vegetable life is merely parasitic."[62]

Thoreau's vision rather resembles the one vouchsafed, late in *Gravity's Rainbow*, to the Massachusetts magnate Lyle Bland, who, after having an odd, inexplicable out-of-the-body experience, adopts a practicing mysticism whose professional-oriental cult-pushers ("Creeps ... with Strange Faraway Smiles" [589]) and rote yogic doctrines ("he knows that in theory he must not attach himself" [590]) Pynchon dismisses satirically. But Bland, it seems, *does* rise out of his body, and, looking back, is allowed to feel most powerfully that "Earth is a living critter, after all these years of thinking about a big dumb rock to find a body and a psyche ... he is in love with his sense of wonder, with having found it again, even this late, even knowing he must soon let it go ... to find that Gravity, taken so for granted, is really something eerie, Messianic, extrasensory, in Earth's mindbody" (590).

This passage begins as an answer to somebody's question, "why keep saying 'mind and body'? Why make that distinction?" (590). Bland, an arch-purveyor of the system evolved for three hundred years from Descartes, quite naturally always has said "mind and body"; what he comes to here is the refutation of the Cartesian dichotomization, to the instinct, I think, of Pynchon, as of the Romantics, as of the process philosophers, vitalists, pantheists, Taoists, etc., who are Pynchon's diverse marginal sources and fellow anti-Cartesian travelers, to the effect that "nothing is inorganic," that "Mother" Earth seems to have her own deliberate way of reunifying "wastes of dead species" (590). We are urged to think of Her as, metaphorically at the least, indeed a "living critter" that works not only by entropic death-tending but also by the constant counterentropic regeneration of forms. And gravity, here and ultimately in the novel, is not Pynchon's simple synonym for dark entropy, one-way death, as is too often claimed;[63] it is the Mother's will,

---

62. Henry David Thoreau, *Walden*, chap. 11.

63. Since this is far from the first of my passing swipes at "dark" critics who read Pynchon as a nihilist because, as I have put it earlier, they "take Pynchon's Entropy metaphor too literally and linearly," I will give one particularly good example here. Speer Morgan concludes a good essay (and at the last moment undercuts it, in my

the mindbody's breathing death-*and*-life spirit. "Eerie, extrasensory" gravity is at least as "occult" for Pynchon as it was for Newton, who could not explain it mechanically, and as it is still for modern physics, which cannot yet imagine how gravity might be unified with any of nature's other three fundamental forces (electromagnetism, "strong" nuclear force, "weak" force).[64] Contemporary physical theory at maximum depth may be said in this sense to give access to mysticism, or at least, in good faith, to the possibility of it: what the successors of Einstein in unified-field theory seek, since it has so far no name, conceptual frame, or master set of equations, we may as well call the One.

Regarding the place of science vis-à-vis mysticism in Pynchon's work, David Cowart has remarked that "science is for Pynchon both a destroyer and a creator of transcendental systems.... Pynchon offers imagination that somehow no longer seems fantastic, imagination endorsed as it were by the very science it once sought to transcend."[65] That empirical science is simply one among many systems for the projection of psychic contents—as, I hope, my previous section already has shown—is one of Pynchon's most characteristic subversive insights, as it was also a central insight of Jung's, best developed in his exhaustive studies of medieval alchemy. Jung saw the alchemists' mystical lapis, the "philosopher's stone," as their projection of the *unus mundus*, a symbol, like the more abstract mandala, of the self's wholeness and of its connection with the entire psychoid field. The lapis was compensatory to the more rarefied symbol of Christ the cosmic anthropos, in that the stone meant "the principle of matter [in which] the 'flesh' is glorified, but not by being transformed into spirit; instead the spirit appears to be

opinion, as a plausible reading of Pynchon) by remarking of the entropy metaphor that "One can only wonder if in some odd way Pynchon has not taken the concept of entropy too seriously, allowing an idea from physics, which has validity as a psychological delusion, to dominate his own view of human life. All life—all biological and historical events immediate enough to be of human concern—involves growth and self-regulation as well as decay and death, and in not recognizing that fact [!] Pynchon falls prey to a peculiar blindness, a heady eccentricity." See Speer Morgan, "*Gravity's Rainbow:* What's the Big Idea?," in *Critical Essays on Thomas Pynchon,* ed.

Richard Pearce (Boston: G. K. Hall & Co., 1981), pp. 82–98.

64. However, some very recent work has shown, to the satisfaction of most theoretical physicists, that electromagnetism and the weak force can be understood as different manifestations under different conditions of the same fundamental force; hope seems offered that eventually the strong force too, and even gravity, may be brought under a unified interpretation.

65. David Cowart, *Thomas Pynchon: The Art of Allusion* (Carbondale: Southern Illinois University Press, 1980), p. 117.

condensed or 'fixed' in matter. The stone is thus a symbol of the inner god in man and is not, like Christ, the 'son of man' but rather a 'son of the universe.' "[66]

Here then is another allusive bonding for the Pynchonian Living Stones, including the maternal Earth, as embodiments of the centripetal "aliveness" of material nature. To survey other such "open" allusive and metaphorical bondings is to show, thus, a number of cognate ways in which the motif points beyond itself, to transcendent realities that just *might* in some sense be real. Besides real geological science and Jungian alchemy, the Stones connect to the language of the Masonic Tower; to Whiteheadean pan-psychism; to the Orphic cult of the semi-divine musician who could inspirit and "move" stones; and to primeval cults of the Goddess. (Erich Neumann comments, "Numinous sites of the preorganic life, which were experienced in *particpation mystique* with the Great Mother, are mountain, cave, stone pillar, and rock ... as throne, seat, dwelling place, and incarnation of the Great Mother [who is] the mother of stones.")[67] But readers of course are not required to be literal-minded—as Pynchon's friend M. F. Beal, whom he cites (612), may be—about any specific, dogmatized forms of this mysticism; we may take exactly as seriously or unseriously as we want the sentient-rock worship of the Argentine anarchist Felipe, who believes "in a form of mineral consciousness not too much different from that of plants or animals, except for the time scale. Rock's time scale is a lot more stretched out. 'We're talking frames per century'" (612). Far from inhering in any ordered tower beliefs that require the assent of faith or the suspension of irony, the novel's real mysticism is a general, dispersed effect of a myriad of little dramatizations of the Jungian instinct that, in the world, the constant occurrence and frequent persuasiveness of given mysticisms, of thrusts to the One, itself implies the existence of something, by nature unknowable and indescribable, that is the transcendental matrix both of the physical world and of this generality of the psyche's expressions.

And further, Pynchon's many effects that insinuate a connected natural order whose central truth is "relation"—in Martin Buber's term—imply a *moral* vision of an ideal type of human relation resembling, and perhaps partly indebted to, Buber's "I-Thou" relation: it is the narrator's urgent demand that any "I" in receipt of grace view all other entities,

66. Von Franz, *Jung*, p. 231.   67. Neumann, *The Great Mother,* p. 260.

animal, vegetable, mineral, in nonutilitarian manner, as "Thou's." Slothrop talks to the trees and can receive answer from them because at this point he is starting to fade from Their world, which is Buber's It-world, that which compels the mutual use and manipulation of entities instead of leaving an openness in which pure mutual perceptions can take place. Slothrop, "intensely alert to trees, finally ... will spend time touching them, studying them, sitting very quietly near them and understanding that each tree is a creature" (552); try regarding the following passage from *I and Thou* as in some way a gloss for or source of this:

> I contemplate a tree.
>
> I can accept it as a picture: a rigid pillar in a flood of light, or splashes of green traversed by the gentleness of the blue silver ground.
>
> I can feel it as movement: the flowing veins around the sturdy, still living core, the sucking of the roots, the breathing of the leaves, the infinite commerce with earth and air—and the growing itself in its darkness.
>
> I can assign it to a species and observe it as an instance, with an eye to its construction and its way of life....
>
> I can dissolve it into a number, into a pure relation between numbers, and eternalize it.
>
> Throughout all of this the tree remains my object and has its place and its time span, its kind and condition.
>
> But it can also happen, if will and grace are joined, that as I contemplate the tree I am drawn into a relation, and the tree ceases to be an It. The power of exclusiveness has seized me....
>
> Whatever belongs to the tree is included: its form and its mechanics, its colors and its chemistry, its conversation with the elements and its conversation with the stars—all this in its entirety.
>
> The tree is no impression, no play of my imagination, no aspect of a mood; it confronts me bodily and has to deal with me as I must deal with it—only differently.
>
> One should not try to dilute the meaning of the relation: relation is reciprocity.
>
> Does the tree then have consciousness, similar to our own? I have no experience of that. But thinking that you have brought this off in your own case, must you again divide the indivisible? What I

encounter is neither the soul of a tree nor a dryad, but the tree itself.[68]

The tree is not soul or dryad; by stipulation its "conversations" with its surroundings are metaphorical, not literal. The "sentient" pines' talking back to Slothrop remains, after all, the comic-surreal play we naturally took it for at first reading. Pynchon, like Buber, claims "no experience" of any literal mystics' map; although intimations of panpsychism, of the Goddess-Lady of plants, etc., may frequently threaten to flicker out beyond their metaphorical functions, the function in question here is finally one that defines all selfless "relations," including human love, as just the fragile, impermanent thing that Buber says it is in *I and Thou*. Before the It-world (Theirs, Pointsman's) can reassert itself, Roger and Jessica know the I-Thou revelry in pure being, perception, touch: "How she loves the line of his neck all at once so—why there it is right *there*, the back of his bumpy head like a boy of ten's. She kisses him up and down the sour salt reach of his skin" (123–24). Pointsman, though, will "divide the indivisible," Jessica becoming Jeremy's and the British rocket's instrumentality, Roger returning to his "mother, the war" (39), the devouring, dividing Kali-mother whose rule continues, he knows, indefinitely past V-E Day: "There's *something* still on, don't call it a 'war' if it makes you nervous ... but Their enterprise goes on" (628).

The It-world, where love is ephemeral, is the "real world" of the vicious cliché, the "melancholy" one of Buber: "This ... is the sublime melancholy of our lot that every You must become an It in our world. However exclusively present it may have been in the direct relationship—as soon as the relationship has run its course or is permeated by *means*, the You becomes an object among objects."[69] That Buber's It-world seems largely to correspond to Pynchon's real-historical one may seem to suggest what we may call the "tragic" element in Pynchon's vision. However, as I have argued throughout this study, the really tragic fact in Pynchon is not the one generally delineated by over-dark critical readings: not that of man's helpless enslavement in apocalyptic systems, in decadence, in entropic determinism; not simply that, as Hendin puts it, "death wins" in the physical universe and the cultural one, however this may *be* a fact in the ultimate run for Pynchon.

68. Martin Buber, *I and Thou*, trans. Walter Kaufmann (New York: Charles Scribner's Sons, 1970), pp. 57–59.

69. Ibid., p. 68.

Throughout the novel the real pain's real correlative is not so much metaphysical and remote as ethical, existential, immediate: it is that life's contingent moments of openness, inside which moral imperatives can operate, in which an individual has really free choices, are so very fleeting and require so much sensitivity even to locate, moral courage to seize. It is that the paranoid option of acquiescence in a continual passivity is so attractive to most people that the systems that guarantee unfreedom, generate death, can be self-sustaining. And the best of Pynchon's analogies for this condition of tragically *unrealized* options for freedom is the one, already outlined, from quantum mechanics. Here, although waveform-shapes of probable human actions, as seen from above, i.e., in Their rationalistic and statistical terms, operate with the force of law, yet "below" them there exists the realm of particulate life, of life's felt particulars, in which each of us remains essentially undetermined. From Their perspective this lower world is the frightening one (witness Pointsman's terror) of chance, randomness; but as experienced from inside it is the living, sentient flux itself, at every point of whose infinite complex of points one may feel two options diverging like particles from a created pair, or like switchpointed thought. Either I may pursue "pure relation," relish the flux, and so in my tiny, invisible way subvert the patterns branching visibly over me, or else I may subsume myself in the patterns, which after all do offer me my security, and anyway, in the large view, never do stop prevailing. The chance of living smoothly, or even in paranoid immobility (572), the conditioned life—of obeying the deterministic equations—offers itself at each Δt moment to us. But, inconveniently for the morally lazy, there remains also the fact that between the moments we may "*choose* the master we wish to serve," in Jung's words; though every god be a psychic projection for whose creation we each necessarily bear some responsibility, still "we"—Jung means each one of us—"do not *create* 'God,' we *choose* him."[70]

*   *   *

As only Joseph Slade among published critics so far has mentioned,[71] the term from Jung that probably best connotes the nature of

70. C. G. Jung, "Psychology and Religion," in vol. 11 of *The Collected Works*; quote from p. 87.

71. See Slade, *Thomas Pynchon*, pp. 236, 237.

Pynchon's own mysticism of connectedness is *synchronicity*—Jung's word for the hypothesized principle of an acausal but meaningful ordering of events within a "psychic relativity of space and time."[72] Jung believed the world of experience to teem with "meaningful coincidences," usually unnoticed, between outer, objective events and inner psychic states of the observer, such coincidences being products neither of any magical causality (as in "sympathetic magic") nor of random chance, but, rather, sudden manifestations of a mysteriously "given," all-pervasive and timeless, transcausal orderedness in creation. Synchronicity works, Jung claimed, concurrently with, but, so to speak, across the grain of, causality: "Since [causality] is a merely statistical truth and not absolute, it is a sort of working hypothesis of how events evolve one out of another, whereas synchronicity takes the coincidences of events in space and time as meaning something more than chance, namely, a peculiar interdependence of objective events among themselves as well as with the subjective (psychic) states."[73]

Among Jung's examples of synchronistic events were a rare golden beetle's flying through his open window as he was trying to help a patient interpret an archetypally significant dream about a golden scarab; his "chance" encounters with fish, and with fish imagery in works of art, throughout a day when he had been starting to write of the fish symbol in ancient myth; parapsychological cases such as the settlings of flocks of birds on a house just before the unforeseen deaths of family members. These visible "constellations" of upwelling archetypal contents externalize the "acausal orderedness" that prevails even among things that lack any causal relationship to each other. They are to be regarded (here Jung's language is reminiscent of Bergson's) as "creative acts"—as manifestations of, paradoxically, a "continuous creation of a pattern that exists from all eternity."[74] Jung's concept of synchronicity may be the best available paraphrase of the sense of Leni Pökler's key speech, often quoted already: "Not produce ... not cause. It all goes along together. Parallel, not series. Metaphor. Signs and symptoms"

---

72. C. G. Jung, "On Synchronicity," in vol. 8 of *The Collected Works*; quote from p. 524.

73. C. G. Jung, "Foreword to the *I Ching*," in vol. 11 of *The Collected Works*; quote from p. 592.

74. C. G. Jung, "Synchronicity: An Acausal Connecting Principle," in vol. 8 of *The Collected Works*; quote from p. 518.

(159).[75] Jung in this light may sanction Leni's mystical optimism, perhaps even too her political activism in service of idealized Communism. The fact that we may, if we choose, notice synchronistic events and act on their implications argues our essential freedom to choose to know truths "below" the life of cause-and-effect: each event is a potential window out of the It-world or paranoid grid. Most people most of the time will miss the signs—though a few at the White Visitation do vaguely try on the appropriate "Jungian frame of mind" (276) when they learn that real black rocket troops existed in Germany even as Operation Black Wing's putative fantasy was being filmed.

Synchronicity, further, would seem to offer the "true" explanation for the phenomenon from which Pynchon's main plot proceeds—Slothrop's sexual precognition of rocket hits. We may nicely explain the Slothrop Effect, wisely not "excluding middles" between "stone determinacy" and pure chance, Pointsman and Antipointsman, by saying that the effect shows precisely "an interdependence of objective events among themselves as well as with subjective states of the observer." The relevant psychic state here is Slothrop's long-standing—conditioned—sexual fetish for Imipolex, or, behind this, his culture's general equation of love/sex with death. There is also the purported time coincidence ("at the instant it happened") between the Hiroshima explosion and Slothrop's seeing the newspaper wirephoto of it: strictly, "at the instant" is of course impossible, but it perhaps alludes to Jung's assumption that space and time are relative to psychic states, and that time therefore might, as in dreams, "disappear" in psychic solution. In some synchronistic events (like that of the golden scarab), time and space seem to behave normally, but we may imagine the rocket-hardon and Hiroshima phenomena as blends of two kinds of synchronistic cases as Jung described them: "The coincidence of a psychic state with a corresponding (more or less simultaneous) external event taking place outside the observer's field or perception ... and only verifiable afterwards, [and] the coincidence of a psychic state with a corresponding,

75. Leni's "not series" may allude to an alternative theoretical structure for explaining "synchronistic" events—one proposed by Paul Kämmerer and explicitly rejected by Jung in his main synchronicity paper. Kämmerer thought that these events are linked, not by a general property of the transcendental reality, as in Jung, but by a more immediate "law of series," Kämmerer's definition of which Jung found incoherent and self-contradictory. Slade mentions Kämmerer's theory in *Thomas Pynchon*; see also the discussion of it in Arthur Koestler's *The Roots of Coincidence*.

not yet existent future event that is distant in time and can likewise only be verified afterward."[76]

Among the older intuitional systems acknowledged by Jung as forerunners of synchronicity,[77] the one that he seems to have found most beautiful, and the most suggestive in this light of the "atemporal" nature of psychoid time, is Chinese Taoism, especially as expressed in the *I Ching* (mentioned by *Gravity's Rainbow*, 746, in a terrible joke's context). Jung first used the word *synchronicity* in print in his foreword to Richard Wilhelm's German translation of the ancient oracular book. Jung used the book for divinatory purposes in his personal life, since it seemed to him to work reliably by tapping the real synchronistic connectedness given, for Chinese thought, within Tao, the transcendent yet immanent, fluid ground of being. The applicant to the *I Ching* states his question, then throws dice or draws yarrow stalks in a sequence that yields a diagrammatic hexagram that, with the book's accompanying text, draws a portrait of that given moment of time in all its completeness. In this way the *I Ching* gives its "intelligent answer" to the applicant's question, in terms of the state of the present and probable state of the future if he should act wisely. Because the answer depends on how one "reads himself into" the language, the rationalistic objection, as Jung acknowledged, is obvious: "Any person of clever or ver-

---

76. Jung, "On Synchronicity," p. 526.

77. When Jung, in his main synchronicity paper, does an erudite job of citing numerous forerunners of his developed idea, he is of course trying to show synchronicity as a finally crystallized form of a long though fitful tradition of holistic thought of the kind.

Joining a diffuse group of ancient philosophers—Heraclitus, Hippocrates, Plotinus—in the idea that, as Hippocrates wrote, "There is one common flow, one common breathing, all things are in sympathy," were, first, the medieval alchemists and astrologers; then later Kepler, Gauss, and Schopenhauer (whose "On the Apparent Design in the Fate of the Individual" Jung calls the "godfather" of synchronicity). In Jung's own time there were, beside the quantum mechanics in all its holistic implications, J. B. Rhine's experiments which, Jung was satisfied, verified and empiricized various ESP phenomena

(Pynchon gives Zener cards, such as Rhine used in his ESP experiments at Duke University, to the psychics at the White Visitation, *GR*, 78). In the *Monadolgy* of Leibniz Jung found a very direct antecedent of synchronicity; Ira Progoff, in *Jung, Synchronicity and Human Destiny: Noncausal Dimensions of Human Experience* (New York: Dell Publishing Company, 1973), explains the connection by taking Leibniz's "preestablished harmony," stripped of its deistic-teleological implications, as an intuitive statement of the "holding together of the pattern of things [such that] the individual and separate entities [i.e., windowless monads] must be maintained in correspondence to each other as part of the harmonious pattern of the cosmos." Finally, Jung ran his own experimental statistical study of astrological data as applied to the fortunes of married couples and came up satisfied that here, too, synchronistic connectedness manifested itself.

satile mind can ... show how I have projected my subjective contents into the symbolism of the hexagrams. Such a critique, though catastrophic from the standpoint of Western rationality, does no harm to the function of the *I Ching*. On the contrary, the Chinese sage would smilingly tell me, 'Don't you see how useful the *I Ching* is in making you project your hitherto unrealized thoughts into its abstruse symbolism?' "[78] The sage means that the texture (the Tao, if we like) of creation is not specified by mind alone, matter alone, or by how one of these acts causally on the other; it is not dualistic, but One.

The manner in which Eastern thought, as Jung suggests, imputes active and positive moral effects to such realizations is echoed in *Gravity's Rainbow* by Pynchon's imputation of "kindness"—his crowing moral tag—to those characters who, like Kevin Spectro, do not "differentiate ... between Inside and Outside" (141). Such people share with the Taoists a sense of reality not as a Manichaean, paranoid, or apocalyptic struggle between warring absolute principles, light and dark, but as a graceful dance of appearances, of interweaving manifestations of Yin and Yang. And Spectro, of course, is killed: Pynchon would emphasize that even illusory wars of illusory principles can reify real wars, real death-systems. In this, his vision of history, a "Western" one after all, is unlike that serene vision of the Taoists to the effect that since separateness is illusory, "There is ... no *serious* conflict, no ultimate threat ... no possibility of final annihilation," in Alan Watts's words.[79] The East's assurance of ultimate harmony within the world-destroying and -creating dance of Shiva is, for Pynchon, no satisfactory comfort against the screamings across history's skies. But meanwhile, Pynchon's ethical system, like that of Taoism, saliently urges humor, kindness, and (a key word in both systems) "grace," as ways of drawing down, as Taoism puts it, the smooth flowing of the transcendent Tao to a felt immanence in human life. Ideally, for both systems, that life is sensitive, graceful, kind to the weak, self-reliant, good-humored: at once supple and strong as flowing water, a favorite symbol in Taoism as in *Gravity's Rainbow* of effortless integration with the ground force of creation.

And characters, like Spectro, who have the right intuitions about such things are never preachy about them, never smug true believers.

---

78. Jung, "Foreword to the *I Ching*, p. 607.

79. Alan W. Watts, *The Two Hands of*

God: The Myths of Polarity (New York: George Braziller, 1963), p. 61.

They have, usually to their detriments in the It-world, no more interest in articulating or systematizing these knowledges than did the Lao-Tse of legend, who, having reluctantly yielded to the request that he write something down before disappearing—it was, legend says, the *Tao Te Ching*—rode tranquilly off on a water buffalo into the mountains, into "invisibility," never to be heard from again. It is rather easier to discern the intellectual sketch of Pynchon's mysticism than to get its tone right: I suspect it will feel attractive only to those who, like Pynchon, are temperamentally unsuited to *live* mysticisms in, say, the self-conscious ways now fashionable with the shallow wherever East has been hyped onto West—hence Pynchon's mockery's distant sound in the joke about the "*I Ching* devotees" (746). We should not, the novels imply, hang our sense of the One up high on a Cross or Tower; better, as McClintic Sphere's slogan in *V.* has it, to "love with your mouth shut ... keep cool but care" (*V.*, 342–43). Or, to cite one of the recurrent antitheses of *Gravity's Rainbow*, "linear" Western religiosity is to the spherical—ideally shaped, maximally graceful—as Beethoven's music is to Rossini's. Here Pynchon is unequivocally on the side of Rossini-lover Säure Bummer's smiling "grace," as opposed to Gustav Schlabone's Beethovian solemnity:

> "You're caught in tonality," screams Gustav. "Trapped. Tonality is a game. All of them are. You're too old. You'll never move beyond the game, to the Row. The Row is enlightenment."
>
> "The Row is a game too." Säure sits grinning.... "*Sound* is a game, if you're capable of moving that far, you adenoidal closet-visionary. That's why I listen to Spohr, Rossini, Spontini, I'm choosing *my* game, one full of light and kindness. You're stuck with that stratosphere stuff and rationalize its dullness away by calling it 'enlightenment.' You don't know what enlightenment is, Kerl, you're blinder than I am." (621–22)

Säure's instinct that *everything* is a game, his ideals of grace and "light and kindness" within the game, echo the serene sensibility of the knowers of *Tao*. But a Western world ever ready to love grandiose Germanic parabolas consumes itself, reflexively answering even the most disingenuous Beethovanism in a way suggested by the probable outcome—repression—of Gustav's encounter with Allied military police:

> Gustav ... raves ... to a blinking American lieutenant-colonel, "A parabola! A trap! You were never immune over there from the simple-minded German symphonic arc, tonic to dominant, back again to tonic. Grandeur! Gesellschaft!"

"Teutonic?" sez the colonel. "Dominant? The war's over, fella. What kind of talk is that?" (443)

Jung pronounced the atmosphere of the *I Ching* "dreamlike," and Pynchon, with Jung, finds reality itself, one of whose mirrors may be the *I Ching*, dreamlike. As is hardly surprising for a novel that so habitually implicates matter in manner, a cognate dreamlikeness appears in virtually all of *Gravity's Rainbow*'s attributes of style and form and appears the more so the more closely one looks. There is, first, Pynchon's program, which will strike readers initially as more or less perverse, of flouting every old-fashioned convention of scene exposition, development, and narrative causality in his way of organizing his players: the characters who get big play at first, then disappear for hundreds of pages, only to leer out later in random frames; scenes beginning *in medias res* and then fading before they are "resolved"; conflicts finessed apparently by some weird "magic." The eerie non sequiturs of the dream life are imitated also by profound tonal shifts between frames, within them, or within the narrator's passages of pure rhetoric—for example, while Marvy's Mothers pursue Slothrop in the Mittelwerke. Though the tone up to now has been purely comic (indeed, comicbook-parodic), somebody shoots off a flare, and a "center" that this dream has been "skirting," and that now reveals itself as an archetypal content, wells up: "the Icy Noctiluca breaks ... Whiteness without heat, and blind inertia: Slothrop feels a terrible *familiarity* here, a center he has been skirting ... faces and facts that have crowded his indenture to the Rocket, camouflage and distraction fall away for the white instant" (311–12). The frontlit slapstick yields to the dream-terror that lies embedded for Slothrop in the experience—in all his experience.

Pointsman's dream of the apocalyptic Hound, Minotaur, or Final Beast whose Face Slowly Turns Your Way is the first occurrence (but for a prelude on the previous page) of another of *Gravity's Rainbow*'s obsessive dream motifs:

It might be a vast lorry-park just at dawn ... the hooded olive trucks standing each with a secret, each waiting ... at last sifting among them, [Pointsman] finds it, the identifying code beyond voicing, climbs up into the back, under the canvas, waits in the dust and brown light, until through the cloudy oblong of the cab window a face, a face *he knows* begins to turn. (142)

until at last they are on some hillside at the end of a long afternoon of dispatches from Armageddon, among scarlet banks of bougainvillea, golden pathways where dust is rising, pillars of smoke far

away over the spidery city they've crossed, voices in the air telling
of South America burned to cinders, the sky over New York glowing purple with the new all-sovereign death ray, and here at last is
where the gray dog can turn and the amber eyes gaze into Ned
Pointsman's own. (143)

The pilot is turning to Rózsavölgyi, who is still strapped in safety
harness behind him. The face is covered with helmet, goggles that
reflect too much light, oxygen mask—a face of metal, leather, isin-
glass. But now the pilot is raising the goggles, slowly, and whose
eyes are those, so familiar, smiling hello, I know you, don't you
know me? Don't you *really* know me? (635)

This satanic, psychotically paranoid image sometimes visits too as
"the terrible Face That Is No Face, gone too abstract, unreachable: the
notch of eye socket, but never the labile eye, only the anonymous curve
of cheek, convexity of mouth, a noseless mask of the Other Order of
Being" (222). This, Slothrop's impression of Katje's face averted against
his pillow at the Casino, anticipates the description, much later, of that
end of the Island of Usedom where Peenemünde was built—"On the
maps, it's a skull or corroded face in profile … a small marshy lake for
the eye-socket, nose-and-mouth cavity cutting in at the entrance to the
Peene" (501). The rocket-connection, of course, is appropriate for Katje,
since They have engineered her birth-out-of-the-sea to accumulate
associations of Botticellian Venus, of V-ness, of the Terrible Mother
whose ultimate icon is the V-2. So, again, while she undresses for
Slothrop at the Casino: "The moonlight only whitens her back, and
there is still a dark side, her ventral side, her face, that he can no longer
see, a terrible beast-like change coming over muzzle and lower jaw,
black pupils growing to cover the entire eye space till whites are gone
and there's only the red animal reflection when the light comes to strike"
(196).

Slothrop, becoming sexually aroused as he watches (as if for V-2's own
"light coming to strike") is here synchronized with his chief pursuer
and controller, Pointsman, for whom the Minotaur at the labyrinth's
heart = orgasm = destruction; Slothrop and Pointsman, We and They,
both indeed seem to be preconsciously, oneirically, "in love, in sexual
love, with [their], and [the] race's, death" (738). The obsession is finally
communal; the dream-face, visiting everywhere, belonging to no separate self alone, blurs the boundaries of selves such that, in the end,
"we," all starers, can share the vision, seeing it up on the screen at the
book/movie/dream's apocalyptic conclusion, as the final rocket
approaches: "And in the darkening and awful expanse of screen some-

thing has kept on, a film we have not learned to see ... it is now a closeup of a face, a face we all know" (760).

For we are all One in dreams; all archetypes finally belong, as Jung knew, to a collective unconscious. The best way to understand the much-complained-of cartoonlikeness, insubstantiality, blurriness of Pynchon's characters is indeed to read them as psychic terms whose nature it is to waver, shimmer, threaten to interpenetrate, dreams within dreams. Pökler and Blicero, although like Slothrop and Points-man "opposites," We and They, are in effect merged, folded in and defined by the same fantasy, when they both whisper to their young bedpartners, Ilse and Gottfried, the half-waking living-stone dream of a habitable moon (410, 723); they are "one" in the same sense in which Ilse and Gottfried themselves (with Bianca) are said to be "the same child." The memory of the infant Slothrop's experience with Jamf's Imipolex, in order really to function as what it pretends to be, namely a point of departure for a conventional plot, would seem required to belong uniquely to Slothrop. In fact, however, whenever Slothrop's drugged or dreaming mind begins to approach it, the memory seems to float off as if to recrystallize elsewhere, in some other mind, and to take the discrete Slothropian self or "identity" along with it. It comes to the spiritualist Peter Sachsa, in bed with Leni Pökler and, in turn, "acting out Franz Pökler's fantasy for him, here crouched on her back, very small, being *taken:* taken forward into an aether-wind whose smell ... no *not that smell* last encountered just before his birth ... the void long before he ought to be remembering" (219). And, far more importantly, it visits the "Schwarzgerät" child Gottfried (Slothrop was Jamf's "Schwarzknabe") as, encased in the plastic, he prepares for Ascent: "The soft smell of Imipolex, wrapping him absolutely, is a smell he knows ... it was in the room when he fell asleep so long ago, so deep in sweet paralyzed childhood" (754).

In fact, in the cases of Pynchon's child characters these fluid interiden-tities can be shown more directly than in the adults' cases, since apparently Pynchon, like many of the early Romantics, regards children as closer to the psychoid ground of reality out of which adults' egos have long since illusorily differentiated themselves. For Pynchon, as for Wordsworth in the Immortality Ode, childhood is a sleep and a dream-vision, a holist knowledge: Tchitcherine's Kirghiz shaman sings mysti-cally that his Light "must change us to children.... Now I sense all Earth like a baby" (358). The synchronicities of movie and rocket history that unite Ilse, Bianca, and Gottfried, "the same child," are surely "signs and symptoms" (159) of this ultimate psychoid ground and may be caught manifesting themselves coyly, *I-Ching*-wise, in history's affairs.

*   *   *

And so at last, in "this old theater" on the novel's concluding page, we take our seats for "Descent"—surely one of the most majestic, exalted, and horrifying conclusions that any big novel, "prophetic" or otherwise, has ever had. One secret of its power is in its effect of exploding completely at last the frame of the narrator's dream, of Pynchon's fictional world, such that all reader/starers see that we have all along, in our lives, been dreaming communally the same forms that the narrator and his creator have here been dreaming, presumably, "for" us. David Cowart has said of the final rocket that strikes the theater that it has "escaped from the movie in which it was fired."[80] That is to say, Blicero's 00000, during its impossible flight over the Pole's singularity, has become a warhead that reaches a theater in Californian America (Richard M. Nixon/Zhlubb, night manager) and can strike also the America that *we* have dreamed and in which we dream. Now, literally "Everybody" awaits the light whose coming the Kirghiz shaman had foretold, the light that "must change us all to children":

DESCENT

The rhythmic clapping resonates inside these walls, which are hard and glossy as coal: Come-*on*! *Start-the-show*! Come-*on*! *Start-the-show*! The screen is a dim page spread before us, white and silent. The film has broken, or a projector bulb has burned out. It was difficult for us, old fans who've always been at the movies (haven't we?) to tell which before the darkness swept in. The last image was too immediate for any eye to register. It may have been a human figure, dreaming of an early evening in each great capital luminous enough to tell him he will never die, coming outside to wish on the first star. But it was *not a star*, it was falling, a bright angel of death. And in the darkening and awful expanse of screen something has kept on, a film we have not learned to see ... it is now a closeup of a face, a face we all know—

And it is just here, just at this dark and silent frame, that the pointed tip of the Rocket, falling nearly a mile per second, abso-

80. Cowart, *Thomas Pynchon*, p. 57.

lutely and forever without sound, reaches its last unmeasurable gap above the roof of this old theater, the last delta-t.

There is time, if you need the comfort, to touch the person next to you, or to reach between your own cold legs ... or, if song must find you, here's one They never taught anyone to sing, a hymn by William Slothrop, centuries forgotten and out of print, sung to a simple and pleasant air of the period. Follow the bouncing ball:

> There is a Hand to turn the time,
> Though thy Glass today be run,
> Till the Light that hath brought the Towers low
> Find the last poor Pret'rite one ...
> Till the Riders sleep by ev'ry road,
> All through our crippl'd Zone,
> With a face on ev'ry mountainside,
> And a Soul in ev'ry stone ...

Now Everybody— (760)

Perhaps, it might occur to us, this old theater was all along the destination of Their forced evacuation of Us, on the book's first page: "A screaming comes across the sky.... the Evacuation proceeds, but it's all theater" (3). Cowart has noticed that the crowds queuing up for the show, five pages before the end, had come to see a "Bengt Ekerot/Maria Casares film festival" (755), and that these movie players are noted chiefly for their portrayals of Death.[81] On one level, then, the theater seems to have been designed by Them as death's antechamber for Us— and there is ambiguous comfort indeed, perhaps mockery, perhaps mostly just mourning, in the narrator's urging that "There is time, if you need the comfort, to touch the person next to you, or to reach between your own cold legs." (Reaching for the rocket-dowser between his legs never helped Slothrop much: whenever, in great cities, he wished on the first star, wished essentially for love, he found only his conditioned love for death, for the rocket that *was not* a star—as his "last image" here has been resurrected from Earth to remind us.) The theater clearly is meant, as well, to suggest the cave of Plato's allegory,[82] where bound solipsists mistake the flickering shadows on walls for final realities, while the true light waits outside. Beyond the "last delta-t," our imminent waking, like that of Plato's suddenly unbound men, like that of

81. See Cowart, *Thomas Pynchon*, pp. 93 ff.—and, further, some notice of how "Descent" adapts the "Shadow" image in T. S. Eliot's "The Hollow Men." See Eliot, *Selected Poems* (New York: Harcourt, Brace & World, 1936), pp. 75–81.

82. As Douglas Fowler has remarked in his *Reader's Guide*, p. 267.

Gottfried before ascent, into "what was always real" (754), may indeed bear some revelation, perhaps one to be found someday out among the commuter-line stars that the rocket, as Pökler had hoped, will take us to. But the light, of course, may also be what it more simply appears to be—thermonuclear mass death—and we be "changed to children" in the bitter if labored sense of being melded or exploded back to the ground of being, below all separation, where no individual consciousness is.

Yet, by definition—"Now Everybody"—it is also clear that They are inside the theater with Us, awaiting what We await; We and They after all are only interdependent illusions, ontological phantoms, in the face of whatever the light will bring, and the theater is as much "Our" creation as "Theirs." The reader's real difficulty here will be in deciding what to make, not so much of the worldly theater, but of the light outside—the mystic revelation or apocalyptic bull's-eye that seems to irrupt into the blank white space on the page after words run out. The Kirghiz light had seemed benign, redemptive of life; but its prophecy, not surprisingly, is now seen to have contained a both/and whose mystery, effectively, is that of *Gravity's Rainbow's* ultimate "message," mood, or meaning. Even to this last whiteness the novel persists in sending mixed signals to mixed readerships: William Vesterman, for example, finds only apocalypse, and "Pynchon's horror," in the hymn of William Slothrop that prepares us for the light,[83] while Lance Ozier sees the light as containing, like others of Pynchon's mystical "singularities," "a sustained affirmation of possibility" that picks up Rilke's Tenth Elegy's song of "jubilation and praise to affirmative angels."[84] And William's hymn itself partakes of the same mystery; it may bring hope to the preterite, and that either by William's intention or despite it, or it may confirm doom, and this in almost any conceivable sense—depending on how the hymn, and William's odd presence here, are read.

Here again is the hymn:

> There is a Hand to turn to time,
> Though thy Glass today be run,
> Till the Light that hath brought the Towers low
> Find the last poor Pret'rite one ...
> Till the Riders sleep by ev'ry road,

83. See William Vesterman, "Pynchon's Poetry," *Twentieth Century Literature* 21 (1975): 211–20.

84. See Lance Ozier, "The Calculus of Transformation: More Mathematical Imagery in *Gravity's Rainbow*," *Twentieth Century Literature* 21 (1975): 193–210.

All through our crippl'd Zone,
With a face on ev'ry mountainside,
And a Soul in ev'ry stone ...

Despite its obviously crucial placement, most critics so far have avoided examining this hymn very closely. One exception is Versterman, who, in his excellent paper, "Pynchon's Poetry," describes the prosody, syntax, and tone of the poem in much detail. Having convincingly shown how the songs and poems in Pynchon's novels have consistently worked to imply the complexity of Pynchon's feelings for his own materials (through parody of his serious ideas allowing readers to pick their own risky ways among both/and's), Vesterman claims that in William Slothrop's hymn Pynchon at last "surrenders" this customary manner of ironic distancing and thus announces the end of his whole artistic "show": "taking himself with complete seriousness," "crying in his chains," the author simply grieves for the world that he has in some sense given up on; he will write no more novels. Such a conclusion, Vesterman thinks, may be drawn from the deliberate introduction of metric irregularities into the hymn's iambic pentameter, from its syntactical ambiguities, and from its general tone of horror. In fact, though, and with a few specialized exceptions (like the "maniacally regular" pentameters of *Lot 49's The Courier's Tragedy,* mentioned by Vesterman), Pynchon's metrics have never been very regular, and, further, tonal self-interferences in the poems have usually followed metrical and syntactical ones—this hymn being no exception. If the hymn, as I think, maintains the possibility of "dual solutions," in Nabokov's phrase in quite another connection, it is because the whole novel does so, and because all three novels have done so. We are given no reason to expect or hope that the One/Zero problem, hope and despair held equally in suspension, will suddenly be resolved on this last page of the canon, despair alone prevailing. The mystery, the dual solution, persists up to and even beyond the last rocket's strike: beyond the equivocal, perhaps not quite final, zero.

Vesterman ignores the fact of the hymn's attribution to William Slothrop, but the fact must be important, since William is recalled, most surprisingly, after two hundred pages of total absence, to mediate the lines. That William, a rebel against the society of self-designated elect into which he had been born, had loved and wanted to succor the preterite, may at least explain why the hymn has been "centuries forgotten and out of print," why They never taught anyone to sing it. We might expect the hymn, if not necessarily to permit hope, at least to be meant in kindness. We might further expect its imagery to hint at William's experience of Puritanism—as, in fact, it does in the image in its first two lines: the Puritan ministers often clocked their sermons by turning small hourglasses on their pulpits beside them.[85] William, quite in preterite character, has subverted the Puritan image to make it suggest not one-way time, but an Eastern and cyclical metaphysic of time, what Pynchon has consistently called "Return." Judeo-Christian eschatology's "great white hand reaching out of the cloud" to signal the End has become a shadowy "Hand" turning intervals in an ongoing, cyclical, perhaps endless process (endless as a bad sermon, if vastly more complex). Taken this way, the image suggests that the preterite, though they will die in a moment, might hope for at least a communal sort of rebirth—might return, as do other buried species, as pure life-force, when their organic and psychic materials have been recycled against the entropic current. The implication is strengthened by Pynchon's description of the walls of the theater as "glossy and black as coal." It is possible also that William for his own, conscious part may mean to hint at the communal Resurrection, beyond the Last Days, of Christian millennarian doctrine. But on Pynchon's higher, concurrent frequency, Vesterman may be correct to allow the hymn to remind him obscurely of Emerson's "Brahma," a poem about the transcendental, Brahmanic identity of earthly opposites. The hymn's first line can even be heard as echoing the last line of Emerson's opening stanza:

> If the red slayer thinks he slays,
> Of if the slain think he is slain,
> They know not well the subtle ways
> I keep, and pass, and turn again.

But these hints (if hints they are) of "Return" open out almost immediately, by way of the looseness of syntax in lines 3 and 4, to hints of return's opposite, which is one-way death: Yang inside Yin. For Vesterman the first striking ambiguity in the syntax is in the connection of the "one" at the end of line 4: "Will the light 'find' (subjunctive?) the last individual of the preterite class, or will it find that class united as one?" But even if we must choose between whether "the Light that hath brought the Towers low" will seek out its last poor victim in hiding or

---

85. Marcus Smith and Khachig Tölölyan have pointed out that the imagery of the hymn is full of refracted versions of typical jeremiad figures—part of their argument that *Gravity's Rainbow* as a whole is consciously a modern redaction of the classic Puritan jeremiad. See Smith and Tölölyan, "The New Jeremiad: *Gravity's Rainbow*," in Pearce, ed., *Critical Essays on Thomas Pynchon*, pp. 169–86.

will find all its victims bravely united as one, the choice either way will not, I think, much affect our sense of the hymn's meaning and tenor. It is an earlier, much trickier ambiguity that really does put our reading of the hymn at a crossroads: the problem of finding the larger connection of the subordinate clause that depends from "Till," beginning line 3. Does this clause bind itself to the main one in line 1—in which case the time will be turned only *until* the light comes to end the cycle forever—or does "Till," instead, develop out of line 2's subordinate clause, in which case what has run out is only *today's* glass, and we are consoled with the thought that other times will exist to be turned? The uncertainty is that of the One/Zero problem itself and persists through the rest of the poem, since the second "till," beginning line 5 and drawing the last four lines after it, is parallel to the first.

William, or Pynchon, speaks oracularly thus in order not to dogmatize about whether what lies "beyond the Zero" is simply void, with maximum entropic equilibrium and no chance of renewal, or whether time after all is an endless cycle of Rilkean "little deaths" followed by returns. But if, as I think, the book as a whole urges on us a sort of Pascal-gambling faith in return, then the urging, which all along has inhered in the novel's very superabundance of energy and of imagistic detail, inheres here likewise in the very presence of the hymn's final four lines, which repeat in the strongest terms the established codes for the mysterious life that pervades Earth's closed system—the life persisting independently of human time, human history, and individual deaths. The novel asks that we see the source of its own energy, of its counterentropic impulse to creation, elaboration, and celebration of life, in its emotional—not intellectual—faith in a metaorganic connectedness among Earth's extrahuman things. "The Vision of Dame Kind" is W. H. Auden's name for this species of impersonal, areligious, asexual mysticism, his description of which fits Pynchon's mystique of connectedness well:

> The objects of this vision may be inorganic—mountains, rivers,
> seas—or organic—trees, flowers, beasts—but they are all non-
> human, though human artifacts like buildings may be included....
> The basic experience is an overwhelming conviction that the objects
> confronting [one] have a numinous significance and importance,
> that the existence of everything [one] is aware of is holy. And the
> basic emotion is one of innocent joy, though this joy can include,
> of course, a reverent dread.... So long as the vision lasts the
> self is "noughted," for its attention is completely absorbed in

what it contemplates; it makes no judgments and
desires nothing.[86]

To name the One with which Pynchon's characters sometimes feel themselves to be in contact—egos transparent, invisible, "noughted," as
when Slothrop faces his Rainbow—we may choose from the novel's collection of terms, all by definition inadequate: pan-psychic sentience,
living stones, negentropy, I-Thou relation, Earth Goddess, psychoid
field, synchronistic connectedness, Tao. But throughout this fictional
world, beyond all the name-frames, a Great Life (final inadequate
name) is felt to be watching silently, watching inside itself, whether or
not history's fool-made riders sleep.

Of course Pynchon knows that such a mysticism, even should we
adopt it, may be cold comfort enough for the preterites (including preterite readers) who must operate in life's practical, political, moral and
mortal dimensions, where each man must necessarily feel the doom
that is closing in on "his own ass, his precious, condemned, personal
ass" (544). In *Gravity's Rainbow's* nearly obsessive imagery—particularly
in its last reel—of asses, assholes, and the black, already anonymous,
half-decomposed stuff that emerges from them, we find the symbol that
most closely integrates Pynchon's moral and practical concerns with his
more distant, more fundamental "Dame Kind" mysticism. "Shit 'n
Shinola" (687–88) asserts, for example, that They are afraid of the tough
persistence, the recyclability, of the life-stuff: They wish to equate shit
falsely with *final* death, with unreal systems of value (shit = negritude
= Schwarzkommando "blackness"), and with counterprocreative sexual perversion (Blicero's and Gottfried's anal sodomy). They would send
life out of sight "forever," down the hard, plastic or porcelain, politely
white maw of the illusion of one-way time—the irony of course being
that white, not black, is the effective color of death in *Gravity's Rainbow:*
"Shit, now, is the color white folks are afraid of. Shit is the presence of
death ... the stiff and rotting corpse itself inside the whiteman's warm
and private own *asshole,* which is getting pretty intimate. That's what
that white toilet's for. You see many brown toilets? Nope, toilet's the
color of gravestones, classical columns of mausoleums, that white porcelain's the very emblem of Odorless and Official Death" (688).

The moral business of individual lives, before individual deaths can
merge them into life's underground generality, is, then, to "touch," to

86. W. H. Auden, "Four Kinds of Mystical Experience," in *Understanding Mysticism*, ed. Richard Woods (New York: Doubleday & Co., 1980), pp. 379–99; quote from p. 384.

see in each others' beings the transcendent unity of particular lives with the general life. It is for particular lives to "see" each other, approximately in the "transparent" manner of Buber's I-Thou relation—a manner that is paradoxically at once concrete and intimate to the highest degree, and beatifically impersonal. Life's business is also to see, coolly, straight through, "not through to but through *through*" (688), the presumptively opaque illusions that They propagate; it is consciously to fight Them exactly because They themselves are illusions, projected aspects of Us. And meanwhile you *might* believe, if only half believing, in a Great Life, respiring in myriad rainbow-falls of our own and future lives. You may, "if you need the comfort," feel this life enclosing beautifully, though it does not intervene in or try to cancel, the horrible turnings of tower-systems back on themselves to visit Rilkean "little deaths" on everyone. The concluding "Now Everybody—" may be in part derisive, is surely horror-stricken—but beyond the Zero into which it points, Pynchon will certainly write more novels.

Bibliography

This listing is, of course, only a partial one. It includes a selection of critical essays on Pynchon's work; a few very general reference works; some generally helpful essay anthologies on various subjects of interest to Pynchon; and, separately, some specifically apposite pieces from those anthologies. Except for Rilke's works, no poetry or fiction is listed. Asterisks indicate materials that Pynchon himself very probably or certainly used as direct sources for his novels.

*   *   *

Abrams, M. H. *Natural Supernaturalism: Tradition and Revolution in Romantic Literature*. New York: W. W. Norton & Co., Inc., 1973.

Adams, Henry. *The Education of Henry Adams*. New York: Modern Library, 1931.*

———. *Mont-Saint Michel and Chartres*. Cambridge, Mass.: Riverside Press, 1933.*

———. "The Rule of Phase Applied to History." In *The Degradation of the Democratic Dogma*, by Henry Adams. New York: Macmillan Co., 1919.*

Allen, Bruce. Review of *Gravity's Rainbow*. *Library Journal* 98 (1973): 766.

Angus, Samuel. *The Religious Quests of the Graeco-Roman World*. New York: Biblo and Tannen, 1967.

Auden, W. H. "Four Kinds of Mystical Experience." In *Understanding Mysticism*, edited by Richard Woods. New York: Doubleday & Co., Inc., 1980.

Auerbach, Erich. *Mimesis*. Princeton, N.J.: Princeton University Press, 1968.

Barth, John. "The Literature of Exhaustion." In *On Contemporary Literature*, edited by Richard Kostelanetz. New York: Avon Books, 1969.

———. "The Literature of Replenishment." *Atlantic* 245: pp. 65–71.

Barzun, Jacques. *Classic, Romantic and Modern*. 2d ed. Toronto: Little, Brown & Co., 1961.

Beer, John J. "Coal Tar Dye Manufacture and the Origins of the Modern Industrial Reasearch Laboratory." In *The Development of Western Technology Since 1500*, edited by Thomas Parke Hughes. New York: Macmillan Co., 1964.

Bell, Pearl K. "Pynchon's Road of Excess." *New Leader* 56 (April 2, 1973): 16, 17.

Bercovitch, Sacvan, ed. *The American Puritan Imagination*. Cambridge, Eng.: At the University Press, 1974.

Bergonzi, Bernard. *The Situation of the Novel.* Middlesex, Eng.: Penguin Books, Ltd., 1972.

Bergson, Henri. *Creative Evolution.* Translated by Arthur Mitchell. New York: Henry Holt & Co., 1911.*

Booth, Wayne C. *The Rhetoric of Fiction.* Chicago: University of Chicago Press, 1961.

Borkin, Joseph. *The Crime and Punishment of I. G. Farben.* New York: Free Press, 1978.

Bossenbrook, William J. *The German Mind.* Detroit: Wayne State University Press, 1961.

Bradbury, Malcolm, ed. *The Novel Today: Contemporary Writers on Modern Fiction.* Manchester, Eng.: Manchester University Press, 1977.

Brillouin, Leon. *Science and Information Theory.* 2d ed. New York: Academic Press Inc., 1962.

Brown, Norman O. "Apocalypse." *Harper's Magazine* 222 (May 1961): 46–49.

———. *Life Against Death.* Middletown, Ct.: Wesleyan University Press, 1959.*

Buber, Martin. *I and Thou.* Translated by Walter Kaufmann. New York: Charles Scribner's Sons, 1970.*

Burtt, E. A. *The Metaphysical Foundations of Modern Science.* New York: Doubleday Anchor Books, 1954.

Byington, Ezra Hoyt. *The Puritan in England and New England.* Boston: Roberts Brothers, 1896.

Campbell, Joseph. *The Masks of God: Occidental Mythology.* New York: Viking Press, 1964.

———. *The Masks of God: Primitive Mythology.* New York: Viking Compass Book, 1970.

Clerc, Charles, ed. *Approaches to "Gravity's Rainbow."* Columbus: Ohio State University Press, 1983.

Cohn, Norman. *The Pursuit of the Millennium.* London: Secker & Warburg, 1957.

Collier, Basil. *The Battle of the V-Weapons.* New York: Viking Press, 1965.*

Cooper, Peter L. *Signs and Symptoms: Thomas Pynchon and the Contemporary World.* Berkeley: University of California Press, 1983.

Cowart, David. "Pynchon's *The Crying of Lot 49* and the Paintings of Remedios Varo." *Critique* 18 (1977): 19–27.

———. *Thomas Pynchon: The Art of Allusion.* Carbondale: Southern Illinois University Press, 1980.

Crowther, Bosley. *The Great Films: Fifty Golden Years of Motion Pictures.* New York: G. P. Putnam's Sons, 1967.

Dampier, Sir William Cecil. *A History of Science.* 4th ed. Cambridge: At the University Press, 1961.

De Feo, Ronald. "Fiction Chronicle." *Hudson Review* 26 (Winter 1973/1974): 773–75.

Dornberger, Walter. *V-2.* New York: Viking Press, 1954.*

DuBois, Josiah E. *Generals in Gray Suits.* London: Bodley Head, 1953.*

Ehrenberg, W. "Maxwell's Demon." *Scientific American* 217 (1967): 103–12.

Eisner, Lotte H. *Fritz Lang.* New York: Oxford University Press, 1977.

Eliade, Mircea. *The Myth of the Eternal Return, or Cosmos and History.* Translated by Willard Trask. Princeton, N.J.: Bollingen Series XLVI, Princeton University Press, 1954.*

————. *Myths, Dreams and Mysteries.* Translated by Philip Mairet. London: Fontana Library of Theology and Philosophy, 1968.

d'Espagnat, Bernard. "The Quantum Theory and Reality." *Scientific American* 241 (1979): 128–40.

Fahy, Joseph. "Thomas Pynchon's *V.* and Mythology." *Critique* 18 (1977): pp. 5–18.

Fiedler, Leslie. "The Middle Against Both Ends." In *Mass Culture*, edited by Bernard Rosenberg and David Manning White. Toronto: Free Press, 1957.

Forster, E. M. *Aspects of the Novel.* New York: Harcourt, Brace & World, 1927.

Fowler, Douglas. *A Reader's Guide to "Gravity's Rainbow."* Ann Arbor, Mich.: Ardis, 1980.

Frankfort, H., Frankfort, H. A., Wilson, John A. Wilson, and Jacobsen, Thorkild. *Before Philosophy: The Intellectual Adventure of Ancient Man.* Baltimore: Pelican Books, 1949.

Franz, Marie-Louise von. *C. G. Jung: His Myth in Our Time.* Translated by William H. Kennedy. Boston: Little, Brown & Co., 1975.

————. "Time and Synchronicity in Analytic Psychology." In *The Voices of Time*, edited by J. T. Fraser. New York: George Braziller Inc., 1966.

Fraser, J. T., ed. *The Voices of Time.* New York: George Braziller Inc., 1966.

Frazer, Sir James. *The Golden Bough.* abridg. ed. New York: Macmillan Co., Inc., 1922.

Freud, Sigmund. "Psychoanalytic Notes Upon an Autobiographical Account of a Case of Paranoia (Dementia Paranoides)." In Freud, *Three Case Histories.* New York: Collier Books, 1963.*

————. *Totem and Taboo.* Translated by James Strachey. New York: W. W. Norton & Co., 1950.*

Friedman, Alan J., and Puetz, Manfred. "Science as Metaphor: Thomas Pynchon and *Gravity's Rainbow.*" *Contemporary Literature* 15 (1974): 345–59.

Fussell, Paul. *The Great War and Modern Memory.* New York: Oxford University Press, 1975.

Gamow, George. *Biography of Physics.* New York: Harper & Bros., 1961.

Gardner, John. *On Moral Fiction.* New York: Basic Books, Inc., 1978.

Gay, Peter. *Weimar Culture.* New York: Harper & Row, Publishers, 1968.

Graves, Robert. *The Greek Myths.* 2 vols. Middlesex, Eng.: Penguin Books, 1955.

————. *The White Goddess: A Historical Grammar of Poetic Myth.* New York: Creative Age Press, 1948.*

Green, Mason A. *Springfield, 1636–1886: History of Town and City.* Springfield, Mass.: C. A. Nicholas & Co., 1888.

Guardini, Romano. *Rilke's Duino Elegies: An Interpretation.* London: Darwen Finlayson, 1961.

Guillemin, Victor. *The Story of Quantum Mechanics.* New York: Charles Scribner's Sons, 1968.

Guthrie, W. K. C. *Orpheus and Greek Religion: A Study of the Orphic Movement.* New York: W. W. Norton & Co., Inc., 1967.

Heisenberg, Werner. *Across the Frontiers.* Translated by Peter Heath. New York: Harper & Row, 1974.

————. "The Uncertainty Principle." In *The World of Mathematics*, edited by James R. Newman. 2 vols. New York: Simon & Schuster, 1956.

Heller, Erich. *The Disinherited Mind: Essays in Modern German Literature and Thought.* New York: Farrar, Straus & Cudahy, 1957.

Hendin, Josephine. *Vulnerable People: A View of American Fiction Since 1945.* New York: Oxford University Press, 1979.

Hipkiss, Robert A. *The American Absurd: Pynchon, Vonnegut and Barth.* Port Washington, N.Y.: National University Publications Associated Faculty Press, 1984.

Hite, Molly. *Ideas of Order in the Novels of Thomas Pynchon.* Columbus: Ohio State University Press, 1983.

Hofstadter, Richard. *The Paranoid Style in American Politics.* New York: Alfred A. Knopf, 1965.

Huson, Paul. *The Devil's Picturebook.* New York: G. P. Putnam's Sons, 1971.

Huzel, Dieter K. *Pennemünde to Canaveral.* Englewood Cliffs, N.J.: Prentice-Hall Inc., 1962.

Hyman, Stanley Edgar. "The Goddess and the Schemihl." In *On Contemporary Literature,* edited by Richard Kostelanetz. New York: Avon Books, 1969.

James, William. *Essays in Radical Empiricism and A Pluralistic Universe.* New York/Toronto: Longmans, Green & Co., 1943.*

———. *The Varieties of Religious Experience.* New York: Modern Library, 1936.*

Jauch, J. M. *Are Quanta Real? A Galilean Dialogue.* Bloomington: Indiana University Press, 1973.

Jensen, Paul M. *The Cinema of Fritz Lang.* New York: A. S. Barnes & Co., 1969.

Jung, C. G. *The Collected Works of C. G. Jung.* 2d ed. 20 vols. Translated by R. F. C. Hull. Princeton, N.J.: Bollingen Series XX, Princeton University Press, 1970.*

———. et al. *Man and His Symbols.* New York: Dell Publishing Co., 1968.

Kazin, Alfred. *Bright Book of Life: American Novelists and Storytellers from Hemingway to Mailer.* Boston: Atlantic Monthly Press, 1971.

Kenner, Hugh. *The Pound Era.* Berkeley: University of California Press, 1971.

Kermode, Frank. *The Sense of an Ending: Studies in the Theory of Fiction.* New York: Oxford University Press, 1968.

Klee, Ernst, and Mark, Otto. *The Birth of the Missile.* Translated by T. Schoeters. London: George G. Harrap & Co. Ltd., 1965.*

Kline, Morris. *Mathematical Thought from Ancient to Modern Times.* New York: Oxford University Press, 1972.

Koestler, Arthur. *The Roots of Coincidence.* New York: Random House, 1972.

Kolodny, Annette, and Peters, Daniel James. "Pynchon's *The Crying of Lot 49:* The Novel as Subversive Experience." *Modern Fiction Studies* 19 (1973): 79–87.

Kostelanetz, Richard, ed. *On Contemporary Literature.* New York: Avon Books, 1969.

Kracauer, Siegfried. *From Caligari to Hitler: A Psychological History of the German Film.* Princeton, N.J.: Princeton University Press, 1947.*

Krafft, John M. "'And How Far-Fallen': Puritan Themes in *Gravity's Rainbow.*" *Critique* 18 (1977): 55–73.

Kreiling, Frederick C. "Leibniz." *Scientific American* 218 (1968): 94–100.

Kubat, Libor, and Zeman, Jiri, eds. *Entropy and Information in Science and Philosophy.* Prague: Academia/Elsevier Scientific Publishing Co., 1975.

Laing, R. D. *The Politics of Experience.* New York: Pantheon Books, 1967.

Laqueur, Walter. *Weimar: A Cultural History.* New York: G. P. Putnam's Sons, 1974.

Lawrence, D. H. *Apocalypse.* New York: Viking Press, 1966.

Lehmann-Haupt, Christopher. Review of *Gravity's Rainbow. New York Times,* March 9, 1973, p. 35.

Levine, George. "V-2." *Partisan Review* 40 (1973): 517–29.

Levine, George, and Leverenz, David, eds. *Mindful Pleasures: Essays on Thomas Pynchon.* Boston: Little, Brown & Co., 1976.

Levinson, Olga. *The Ageless Land.* Capetown: Tafelberg-Uitgewers, 1961.

Le Vot, Andre. "The Rocket and the Pig: Thomas Pynchon and Science Fiction." *Caliban* 12, Annales de l'Universitè de Toulouse, Nouvelle Serie 11 (1975): 111–18.

Lewis, R. W. B. *Trials of the Word.* New Haven: Yale University Press, 1965.

Lhamon, W. T., Jr. "The Most Irresponsible Bastard." *New Republic* 168 (March 3, 1973): 624–31.

———. "Pentecost, Promiscuity, and Pynchon's *V.:* From the Scaffold to the Impulsive." *Twentieth Century Literature* 21 (1975): 177–92.

Locke, Richard. Review of *Gravity's Rainbow. New York Times Book Review,* March 11, 1973, pp. 1, 2, 12, 14.

Mackey, Douglas A. *The Rainbow Quest of Thomas Pynchon.* San Bernardino, Calif.: The Borgo Press, 1980.

Mailer, Norman. *Of a Fire on the Moon.* New York: Signet Books, 1969.

———. *The White Negro.* San Francisco: City Lights, 1959.

Marcuse, Herbert. *Eros and Civilization: A Philosophical Inquiry Into Freud.* New York: Vintage Books, 1962.*

———. *One-Dimensional Man.* Boston: Beacon Press, 1964.

Martin, James Stewart. *All Honorable Men.* Boston: Little, Brown & Co., 1950.*

McConnell, Frank D. *Four Postwar American Novelists.* Chicago: University of Chicago Press, 1977.

McGovern, James. *Crossbow and Overcast.* London: Hutchinson & Co. Ltd., 1965.

McLuhan, Marshall. *Understanding Media.* New York: McGraw-Hill Co., 1964.*

Mendelson, Edward, ed. *Pynchon: A Collection of Critical Essays.* Englewood Cliffs, N.J.: Prentice-Hall Inc., 1978.

———. "Pynchon's Gravity." *Yale Review* 62 (1973): 624–31.

Mills, C. Wright. *The Power Elite.* New York: Oxford University Press, 1968.

Mosse, George L. *The Crisis of German Ideology: Intellectual Origins of the Third Reich.* New York: Grosset & Dunlap, 1964.

Murray, Gilbert. *Five Stages of Greek Religion.* 3d ed. Garden City, N.Y.: Doubleday & Co., Inc., 1955.

Nagel, Ernest, and Newman, James. "Gödel's Proof." In *The World of Mathematics,* edited by James R. Newman. 4 vols. New York: Simon & Schuster, 1956.

Neumann, Erich. *The Great Mother: An Analysis of the Archetype.* Translated by Ralph Manheim. Princeton, N.J.: Bollingen Series XLVII, Princeton University Press, 1963.

Newman, James R., ed. *The World of Mathematics.* 4 vols. New York: Simon & Schuster, 1956.

Olson, Richard, ed. *Science as Metaphor.* Belmont, Calif.: Wadsworth Publishing Co., 1971.

Ordway, Frederick I, III, and Sharpe, Mitchell R. *The Rocket Team.* New York: Thomas Y. Crowell, 1979.

Ozier, Lance. "Antipointsman/Antimexico: Some Mathematical Imagery in *Gravity's Rainbow.*" *Critique* 16 (1974): 73–89.

———. "The Calculus of Transformation: More Mathematical Imagery in *Gravity's Rainbow.*" *Twentieth Century Literature* 21 (1975): 193–210.

Pachter, Henry. *Modern Germany: A Social, Cultural, and Political History.* Boulder, Col.: Westview Press, 1978.

Pauli, Wolfgang. "The Influence of Archetypal Ideas on the Scientific Theories of Kepler." In C. G. Jung and Wolfgang Pauli, *The Interpretation of Nature and the Psyche.* New York: Bollingen Series LI, Pantheon Books, 1955.*

Pavlov, I. P. *Conditioned Reflexes.* Translated and edited by G. V. Anrep. New York: Oxford University Press, 1927.*

———. "Feelings of Possession (Les Sentiments D'Emprise) and the Ultraparadoxical Phase" and "Attempt at a Physiological Interpretation of Compulsive Neurosis and Paranoia." In Pavlov, *Psychopathology and Psychiatry: Selected Works.* Moscow: Foreign Languages Publishing House, 195-?*

Pearce, Richard, ed. *Critical Essays on Thomas Pynchon.* Boston: G. K. Hall & Co., 1981.

Peckham, Morse. *The Triumph of Romanticism: Collected Essays.* Columbia: University of South Carolina Press, 1970.

Plater, William M. *The Grim Phoenix: Reconstructing Thomas Pynchon.* Bloomington: Indiana University Press, 1978.

Poirier, Richard. "The Importance of Thomas Pynchon." *Twentieth Century Literature* 21 (1975): 151–62.

———. *The Performing Self.* New York: Oxford University Press, 1971.

———. "Rocket Power." *Saturday Review: The Arts* 1 (1973): 59–64.

Progoff, Ira. *Jung, Synchronicity, and Human Destiny: Noncausal Dimensions of Human Experience.* New York: Dell Publishing Co., Inc., 1973.

Reich, Charles A. *The Greening of America.* New York: Random House, 1970.

Rilke, Rainer Maria. *The Duino Elegies.* Translated by Stephen Garmey and Jay Wilson. New York: Harper & Row, 1972.*

———. *Letters to a Young Poet.* Translated by M. D. Herter. New York: W. W. Norton & Co., 1954.

———. *Sonnets to Orpheus.* Translated by C. F. MacIntyre. Berkeley: University of California Press, 1971.*

Robertson, J. G. *A History of German Literature.* 4th ed. London: Wm. Blackwood & Sons Ltd., 1962.

Rose, William, and Craig, Houston J. *Rainer Maria Rilke: Aspects of His Mind and Poetry.* New York: Haskell House Publishers, Ltd., 1973.

Rosenberg, Bernard, and White, David Manning, eds. *Mass Culture.* Toronto: Free Press, 1957.

Ross, Mitchell S. "Prince of the Paperback Literati." *New York Times Magazine,* February 12, 1978.

Rougemont, Denis S. *Love in the Western World.* Rev. ed. Translated by Montgomery Belgion. New York: Pantheon Books, 1956.*

———. *The Myths of Love*. Translated by Richard Howard. London: Faber and Faber, 1963.*
Rovit, Earl. "On the Contemporary Apocalyptic Imagination." *American Scholar* 37 (1968): 453–68.
———. "Some Shapes in Recent American Fiction." *Contemporary Literature* 15 (1974): 552, 553.
Russell, Bertrand. *A History of Western Philosophy*. New York: Simon & Schuster, 1945.
Sadhu, Mouni. *The Tarot*. London: George Allen & Unwin Ltd., 1962.
Sale, Roger. "American Fiction in 1973." *Massachusetts Review* 14 (1973): 841–46.
Salmon, Wesley C. "Determinism and Indeterminism in Modern Science." In *Reason and Responsibility*, 3d ed., edited by Joel Feinberg. Encino, Calif.: Dickinson Publishing Co., 1975.
Sanders, Scott. "Pynchon's Paranoid History." *Twentieth Century Literature* 21 (1975): 177–92.
Santayana, George. *The German Mind: A Philosophical Diagnosis*. New York: Thomas Y. Crowell Co., 1968.
Sasuly, Richard. *IG Farben*. New York: Boni & Gaer, 1947.
Schaub, Thomas H. *Pynchon: The Voice of Ambiguity*. Urbana: University of Illinois Press, 1981.
Schaya, Leo. *The Universal Meaning of the Kabbalah*. Baltimore: Penguin Books, 1973.
Schrödinger, Erwin. "Causality and Wave Mechanics." In *The World of Mathematics*, edited by James R. Newman. 4 vols. New York: Simon & Schuster, 1956.
Schulz, Max. *Black Humor Fiction of the Sixties*. Athens: Ohio University Press, 1973.
Sheppard, R. Z. Review of *Gravity's Rainbow*. *Time*, March 5, 1973.
Siegel, Jules. "Who is Thomas Pynchon … and Why did he Take Off With My Wife?" *Playboy* 24 (1977): 97, 122, 169, 170, 172–74.
Siegel, Mark Richard. "Creative Paranoia: Understanding the System of *Gravity's Rainbow*." *Critique* 18 (1977): 39–54.
———. *Pynchon: Creative Paranoia in "Gravity's Rainbow."* Port Washington, N.Y.: Kennikat Press, 1978.
Sissman, L. E. "Hieronymus and Robert Bosch: The Art of Thomas Pynchon." *New Yorker* 49 (May 19, 1973): 138–40.
Sklar, Robert. "The New Novel, USA: Thomas Pynchon." *Nation* 205 (1967): 277–80.
Slade, Joseph W. "Escaping Rationalization: Options for the Self in *Gravity's Rainbow*." *Critique* 18 (1977): 19–27.
———. *Thomas Pynchon*. New York: Warner Paperback Library, 1974.
Snow, C. P. *The Two Cultures: And a Second Look*. Cambridge, Eng.: At the University Press, 1965.
Solberg, Sara M. "On Comparing Apples and Oranges: James Joyce and Thomas Pynchon." *Comparative Literature Studies* 16 (1979): 33–40.
Stammer, Otto, ed. *Max Weber and Sociology Today*. New York: Harper & Row, 1971.

Stark, John O. *Pynchon's Fictions: Thomas Pynchon and the Literature of Information.* Athens: Ohio University Press, 1980.

Stern, Fritz. *The Politics of Cultural Despair: A Study in the Rise of the Germanic Ideology.* New York: Doubleday & Co., 1965.

Tanner, Tony. *City of Words: American Fiction 1950–1970.* New York: Harper & Row, 1971.

Thompson, Don, and Lupoff, Dick, eds. *The Comic-Book Book.* New Rochelle, N.Y.: Arlington House, 1973.

de Tocqueville, Alexis. *Democracy in America.* Edited Richard D. Heffner. New York: New American Library, 1956.

Vesterman, William. "Pynchon's Poetry." *Twentieth Century Literature* 21 (1975): 211–20.

Vidal, Gore. "American Plastic: The Matter of Fiction." In Vidal, *Matters of Fact and of Fiction: Essays 1973–1976.* New York: Random House, 1977.

Waite, A. E. *A New Encyclopedia of Freemasonry.* 2 vols. Walnut Creek, Calif.: Weathervane Books, 1970.*

———. *The Pictorial Key to the Tarot.* New York: Samuel Weiser, Inc., 1973.*

Wasson, Richard. "Notes on a New Sensibility." *Partisan Review* 36 (1969): 460–77.

Watts, Alan W. *The Two Hands of God: The Myths of Polarity.* New York: George Braziller, 1963.

Weber, Max. *From Max Weber: Essays in Sociology.* Edited by H. H. Gerth and C. Wright Mills. New York: Oxford University Press, 1958.*

———. *The Protestant Ethic and the Spirit of Capitalism.* Translated by Talcott Parsons. New York: Charles Scribner's Sons, 1958.*

Weisenburger, Steven. "The End of History? Thomas Pynchon and the Uses of the Past." *Twentieth Century Literature* 25 (1979): 54–72.

Weston, Jesse. *From Ritual to Romance.* Garden City, N.Y.: Doubleday & Co., 1957.

Wheelwright, Joseph B., ed. *The Reality of the Psyche.* Proceedings of the Third International Congress for Analytical Psychology. New York: G. P. Putnam's Sons, 1968.

Whitehead, A. N. *Alfred North Whitehead: An Anthology.* Edited by F. S. C. Northrop and Mason W. Gross. New York: Macmillan Co., 1953.

———. *Science and the Modern World.* New York: Macmillan Co., 1925.*

Wiener, Norbert. *Cybernetics.* Cambridge, Mass.: MIT Press, 1948.*

———. *The Human Use of Human Beings.* Boston: Houghton Mifflin Co., 1950.*

Winner, Thomas G. *The Oral Art and Literature of the Kazakhs of Russian Central Asia.* Durham, N.C.: Duke University Press, 1958.*

———. "Problems of Alphabetic Reform Among the Turkic Peoples of Soviet Central Asia, 1920–1941." *Slavonic and East European Review* 31 (1952): 133–48.*

Winston, Matthew. "The Quest for Pynchon." *Twentieth Century Literature* 22 (1975): 278–87.

Wood, Michael. "Rocketing to the Apocalypse." *New York Review of Books,* March 1973, pp. 22, 23.

Young, James D. "Enigma Variations of Thomas Pynchon." *Critique* 10 (1967): 69–77.

Ziff, Larzer. *Puritanism in America: New Culture in a New World.* New York: Viking Press, 1973.

Zimmerman, E. J. "Time and Quantum Theory." In *The Voices of Time,* edited by J. T. Fraser. New York: George Braziller, 1966.

Index

Absurd, the, 3, 47
Adams, Henry, 160, 161, 163, 166, 167, 222, 261, 262, 264, 265
Ajtys, 98, 100
Alpdrücken (film), 87, 212
Amp, Lucifer, 83
Angels: as paranoid projections, 14, 249; as astral pointsmen, 93, 204; and "White Visitations," 58, 59, 164; and secular power, 71, 72; Rilkean, 14, 42, 43, 72, 212, 269; Kabbalistic, 222; Lübeck Angel, 93; mentioned, 70, 74, 213, 243, 260
Anubis(ship), 39, 89, 134, 164, 248
Apocalypse: and paranoia, 52, 59, 236, 237; and "White Visitations," 128, 164, 287; and "made" history, 200, 237; in contemporary literature, 257-59; and Christianity, 2, 237, 263; and Teutonic myth, 254; and Hiroshima, 11, 252; and Minotaur, 282-84; and last page of *GR,* 69, 128, 243, 287-91
Argentina, Argentines, 51, 98, 270
Ascent: mythology of, 50n, 104, 106, 252; and Bergson, 194; and Romanticism, 201; of Rocket 00000, 76, 105-7, 194, 252, 284; of Rocket 00001, 104
Astrology, 16, 28, 226, 243-46
Automata, 159, 165, 166, 169, 172, 178

Bad Karma (spa), 89, 243
Baku Conference, 99, 100
Barth, John, 12, 14-17, 20
Beaver, Jeremy, 81, 105, 110, 275
Beethoven, Ludwig von, 112, 281
Bellow, Saul, 15, 258
Bergson, Henri, 28, 188, 192-94, 199, 277
Bianca, 38, 39, 87, 105, 250, 284
Blackness: as organic unity, 23, 89, 102, 263, 291; as mud, 88, 89, 90; as excrement, 90, 91, 291; as coal, 98, 102, 166, 255, 289; and King Kong, 38n, 55, 102; and Hereros, 166; and Slothrop, 198, 238, 263; and Enzian, 97, 101; and Tchitcherine, 97, 98, 101
Bland, Lyle, 65, 72, 73, 160, 235, 236, 271

Blicero (Weissmann): in *V.,* 94; and "German mind," 74, 208; and Tristan myth, 256, 257; and Rilke, 74, 205, 207, 212, 213, 256, 269; feeling for V-2, 74, 76, 77, 165, 256; and plastics, 74; source of name, 74; as Witch, 48, 74, 75; and Freudian paranoia, 75, 76; as charismatic, 76, 256; homosexuality of, 76, 256, 291; final whereabouts, 77; and Enzian, 31, 61, 74, 102, 104; and Gottfried, 107, 218, 269, 284; and Pökler, 95, 190, 191, 211, 284; mentioned, 39, 83, 84, 89, 92, 158, 232, 242, 285
Bloat, Teddy, 81, 92
Blobadjian, Igor, 100
Bodine, Seaman: "Pig" of *V.,* 112-14; name change in *GR,* 114; and drugs, 113; and invisibility, 114; mentioned, 18, 34, 123, 134, 201, 255
Bohr, Niels, 9, 185
Borges, Jorge Luis, 13, 21, 22, 84
Borgesius, Katje: "framing" of, 84, 85, 103; in limbo frame, 85, 86; at Casino, 83, 283; as V-ness, 84, 91, 283; in Counterforce, 83, 84, 110; with Pudding, 90, 91; mentioned, 31, 37, 48, 74, 77, 105, 131, 160, 165
"Both/and"-ness: as stylistic effect, 6, 128, 129; and *GR's* metaphysics, 10, 129, 287, 288; and sadomasochism, 85, 86; and history, 139, 158; and quantum physics, 181, 185; and McLuhan, 168; and the Rainbow, 10, 11, 190, 204, 205, 213, 215; and Rilke, 205; and the "star," 217, 218; and mandala crossroads, 242, 243; and Mercurius, 248, 249; and Orpheus, 250, 251; and Great Mother Goddess, 268, 269
Bounce, Hilary, 81
Boyle, Robert, 153
Braun, Wehrner von, 40, 92, 196, 246, 247
Buber, Martin, 262, 273-75, 292
Bummer, Säure, 48, 55, 61, 112, 170, 241, 244, 281
Bureaucracy: nature of, 90, 91, 125, 126;

Index

power slots in, 72; and charisma, 123, 124; and paper, 125, 126; and Puritans, 131; and I. G. Farben, 139, 140
Burroughs, William, 13, 14
Byron the Bulb, 47, 145–47

Calculus: Newton & Leibniz develop, 188, 195, 196, 212; and Bergson, 192–94; delta-t in, 40, 188, 189, 190; and "singularities," 212; mentioned, 33, 40, 49, 153, 191, 192, 213, 217, 261
Casino Hermann Goering, 57, 83, 184, 215, 216, 218, 283
Charisma: in Weber, 119–24; pure, 121, 122; co-option of, 123, 124; and Christ, 119, 247; and V-2, 120, 125, 247; and Dillinger, 113; and Nazism, 124, 207, 211, 247; and paganism, 131, 207; and Freemasonry, 235; and Byron the Bulb, 146
Cherrycoke, Ronald, 92, 93
Chess metaphors, 88, 95
Chiclitz, "Bloody," 35, 36, 81, 82
Christ: birth of, 109, 217, 245; as charismatic, 119, 247; and Mercurius, 106, 248; as year god, 106, 248; and astrology, 245; mentioned, 65, 103, 104, 272
Christian, 103, 104, 253
Christianity: and repressiveness, 131, 263; and paranoia, 237, 245; and Grail legend, 240; and astrology, 245; and Orphism, 250; and Myth of the Center, 251; and Hereros, 253, 254; and linear time, 253, 254, 289; mentioned, 109, 217, 233, 261, 262
Chu Piang, 97
Clausius, Rudolf, 158, 162
Closed systems: novels as, 7; in *Lot 49*, 118; V-2 as, 166, 173, 174; and Mass Society, 118; and bureaucracy, 126; and Puritanism, 127; in "Entropy," 163; as cultural metaphor, 173–75; and Gödel's Theorem, 118, 185; and Richard M. Zhlubb, 68, 69; mentioned, 8, 168, 203, 290
Cold War, 171, 172
Colonel's haircut, 146–48, 170
Comic books, comicbook heroes: and framing, 28, 34, 73, 121; and the Raketenstadt, 44; "comicbook colors," 54, 58
Complementarity Principle, 9, 185
Conrad, Joseph, 22, 23
Counterculture, 17–19, 55
Counterforce, 83, 110, 111, 112, 123
Crutchfield/Crouchfield, 67
Crying of Lot 49, The: closed systems in,

118, 128, 163, 164; epistemological choices in, 47; the Word in, 128; "magic" in, 221, 222, 228; *The Courier's Tragedy*, 156, 157, 288; mentioned, 78, 110, 177, 199, 232, 248
Crystal Palace, 161
Cybernetics, 158, 159, 168–75, 191, 225, 232

Day at the Races, A (film), 35, 36
Delta-t. *See* Calculus
Descartes, Rene & Cartesianism, 24, 152, 154, 156, 159, 186, 187, 261, 271
Differentiation: in calculus, 33, 188; as multiple senses of words, 55; and bureaucracy, 125; and color and Whiteness, 188; and mandalas, 242, 259, 260n
Dillinger, John, 33, 59, 113, 210, 235
Dionysus, 241, 250, 266
Dishonored (film), 84
Dodson-Truck, Nora, 92, 227
Dodson-Truck, Sir Stephen, 83, 260, 261
Dora concentration camp, 75, 96
Dostoevsky, Fyodor, 26, 224, 226
Dreams: *GR* as Dream, 12, 13, 282, 285; movies as, 35; and characters' interidentities, 283, 284; and Dostoevsky, 26; Slothrop's, 35; Prentice's, 71; Pökler's, 96; Pointsman's, 282; F. A. von Kekule's, 66, 140, 204, 255, 263
Drugs: and *GR*, 17, 28, 113, 235; as creating connections, 55; and I. G. Farben, 82, 97, 219, 220; and Säure Bummer, 112; and Seaman Bodine, 113
Dulles, Allen, 117, 143
Dzaqyp Qulan, 98, 100

Earthliness: celebrated in *GR*'s rhetoric, 60–62, 201, 259; and concrete life, 214, 215; Earth-alive mysticism, 270, 271; and pre–Indo-Europeans, 261; exploitation of by whites, 166; and Christianity, 263; and Orpheus, 250; and Kabbalah, 238; Pökler "marries," 97. *See also* Blackness
Edelman, Steve, 67, 252, 253
Einstein, Albert, 156, 180, 196, 272
Election, the Elect: and Puritanism, 51, 52, 126–28, 134n, 248, 254; as power elites, 71, 117, 121, 223; and preterite parables, 146; in William Slothrop's heresy, 136
Eliade, Mircea: theory of movies, 32, 33, 39; and Great Time, 32, 251, 257; and Ascent, 50n, 104, 106; Myth of the Center, 104n, 251–53

Index

Permissions

Excerpts from *I and Thou* by Martin Buber, translated by Walter Kaufmann, copyright © 1970 by Charles Scribner's Sons. Excerpts from *The Protestant Ethic and the Spirit of Capitalism* by Max Weber, translated by Talcott Parsons, copyright © 1958 by Charles Scribner's Sons reprinted by permission of Charles Scribner's Sons.

Excerpts from *From Max Weber: Essays in Sociology* by H. H. Gerth and C. Wright Mills, editors and translators, reprinted by permission of Oxford University Press.

Excerpts from *Understanding Media* by Marshall McLuhan reprinted by permission of McGraw-Hill Book Company.

Excerpts from *The Crying of Lot 49* by Thomas Pynchon reprinted by permission of Harper & Row Publishers, Inc. Excerpts from *Gravity's Rainbow* by Thomas Pynchon, copyright © 1973 by Thomas Pynchon, reprinted by permission of Viking Penguin, Inc. Excerpts from *Slow Learner: Early Stories* by Thomas Pynchon, copyright © 1984 by Thomas Pynchon, reprinted by permission of Little, Brown and Company. Excerpts from *V.* by Thomas Pynchon reprinted by permission of Harper & Row Publishers, Inc.

Excerpts from *Duino Elegies* by R. M. Rilke, translated by Stephen Garmey and Jay Wilson, reprinted by permission of Harper & Row Publishers, Inc.

Excerpts from *The I Ching or Book of Changes*, translated by Richard Wilhelm, rendered into English by Cary F. Baynes, Bollingen Series XIX, copyright © 1950, 1967, renewed 1977 by Princeton University Press; reprinted by permission of Princeton University Press. Excerpts from "On Synchronicity" and "Synchronicity: An Acausal Connecting Principle" in *The Collected Works of C. G. Jung*, translated by R. F. C. Hull, Bollingen Series XX, Vol. 8: *The Structure and Dynamics of the Psyche*, copyright © 1960, 1969 by Princeton University Press; *The Collected Works of C. G. Jung*, translated by R. F. C. Hull, Bollingen Series XX, Vol. 11: *Psychology and Religion: West and East*, copyright © 1958, 1969 by Princeton University Press; Vol. 14: *Mysterium Coniunctionis*, copyright © 1965, 1970 by Princeton University Press.